Sylvia

Pg 24 s
on suffering

Sermon
Bishop Bud
June 7
2003

Check out
Lawrence of Rome
St. Barnabas

THE
FATHERS
OF THE
CHURCH

THE
FATHERS
OF THE
CHURCH

COMBINED EDITION OF

The Fathers of the Greek Church

AND

The Fathers of the Latin Church

HANS VON CAMPENHAUSEN

Hendrickson Publishers, Inc.
P. O. Box 3473
Peabody, Massachusetts 01961–3473

First published in two volumes:

The Fathers of the Greek Church. From the German *Griechische Kirchenväter*
© 1955 W. Kohlhammer, GMBH, Stuttgart. English translation © 1959 Pantheon Books, Inc., New York; English translation, revised by L. A. Garrard
© 1963 A. & C. Black Ltd. English translation rights assigned 1975
W. Kohlhammer.

The Fathers of the Latin Church. From the German *Lateinische Kirchenväter*
© 1960 W. Kohlhammer, GMBH, Stuttgart. English translation by Manfred
Hoffmann © 1960 A. & C. Black Ltd. English translation rights assigned 1998
W. Kohlhammer.

Hendrickson Publishers' combined edition of *The Fathers of the Greek Church*
and *The Fathers of the Latin Church* is published by special arrangement with
W. Kohlhammer, GMBH, Heßbrühlstraße 69, 70565 Stuttgart, Germany.

ISBN 1–56563–095–5

Printed in the United States of America

Second Printing — September 2000

CONTENTS

THE FATHERS OF THE GREEK CHURCH
THE FATHERS OF THE LATIN CHURCH

This combined edition reprints the texts of the two original volumes exactly as they originally appeared. Thus the bibliography and index to The Fathers of the Greek Church *appear in the middle of this volume, followed immediately by* The Fathers of the Latin Church, *with its original pagination.*

THE FATHERS OF
THE GREEK CHURCH

BY

HANS VON CAMPENHAUSEN

PROFESSOR OF ECCLESIASTICAL HISTORY
IN THE UNIVERSITY OF HEIDELBERG

Dedicated to

HERMANN DÖRRIES

as one of the fruits of
twenty-five years' friendship

IN PLACE OF A PREFACE

'FRANKLY I do not consider it very difficult, especially in our days, to write a learned book, or what is accounted such, namely a book with learned quotations, notes, explanations and appendages of that sort. It is much harder, in my opinion, to write a book which dispenses with all the apparatus of learning but *presupposes* solid and well-grounded study. I consider this not only much harder, but rarer; for it involves a certain power of renunciation, a willingness to bring oneself to forgo the applause of the many, who judge learning by the outward apparatus. But the rarer it is, in my opinion, the more fruitful and rewarding; indeed I consider it the noblest type of authorship. . . . We have enough and to spare of light-weight, entertaining goods on the one hand and ponderous works serviceable to comparatively few readers on the other; and the cream of the educated Christian public goes empty away.

I have now indicated the ideal that I kept before me in writing this book. No one can be more conscious than I am how far I have fallen short of it. But I have made the effort; and I hope that this will be recognized by the discerning and fair-minded critic.'

FRIEDRICH BÖHRINGER

Die Kirche Christi und ihre Zeugen,
oder die Kirchengeschichte in Biographien,
I, 2 (1842), p. viii f.

CONTENTS

PATRISTICS AND THE FATHERS OF THE CHURCH

THE 'Fathers of the Church' is the term used to describe the orthodox writers of the early Church. Anyone undertaking to write about them does not find himself on new ground but on a very old, oft-ploughed field, and one which has been the subject of fierce controversy. A few indications as to the concept and origins of what is known as 'patristics' or 'patrology' may therefore be appropriate.

The normal task of patrology is the investigation, evaluation, and expounding of the literary and theological achievements of the Church Fathers. It is a kind of literary history of the Church, proceeding alongside and supplementing the history of doctrine and dogma, and forming at the same time an appendix to the literary history of classical antiquity. Patristics did not originate, however, in philology or in the general history of the Church. If it did it would be impossible to fathom the curious limitation of the field imposed by the denominational and theological standpoint of the authors. In fact the term 'Fathers of the Church' itself stems from the sphere of dogma and originated in the needs of Catholic apologetics. Patristics originated in the urge to assemble witnesses to the 'authentic' orthodox tradition, that it might add its weight of authority to valid or disputed doctrines. To this end efforts were made as early as the fourth century to establish the views of authoritative theologians who were expressly described as 'Fathers of the Church'. Their authority was accepted as valid in the present and was added to the earlier and more evident authority of the Bible.

This dogmatic interest in ecclesiastical 'tradition' still plays a considerable part in the Catholic Church today. That is the reason why the title 'Father of the Church' is withheld from some teachers, such as Origen, who were fully recognized in their own time. The authority of others, such as Clement of Alexandria, is regarded as uncertain and others, like the Alexandrian patriarch Cyril, are singled out for a position of special distinction as *doctores ecclesiae*. These later classifications constitute a parallel to the corresponding consideration of the canon of Scripture and early Christian literature. In the latter case a series of documents was judged to be 'apostolic' and combined in the New Testament into a dogmatic, authoritative 'canonic' collection, while other writings, possibly just as ancient and originally just as highly regarded, were considered 'apocryphal' or even rejected outright. No attention will be paid to such distinctions in the present work, the intentions of which are wholly historical. Even though they may be ecclesiastically significant and, in the case of the New Testament, entirely justified, it is nevertheless clear that they are irrelevant to the purposes of a purely historical exposition of the Fathers.

On the other hand, an approach limited to the aspects of literary history is certainly not the only acceptable method and is quite inadequate by itself. It has to be remembered that the men with whom we are concerned did not wish in any sense to be thought of merely as writers. They considered themselves the exponents of divine truth, which it was their duty to preserve in the local churches and preach to the world at large. They expressly rejected literary and academic ambitions—such at least were not their main interests in life. They thought of themselves as the authorized teachers of the Church, as Christian philosophers, as trained, enlightened interpreters of the Bible, which contains God's saving revelation. It is in this light that we have to understand and study them. Otherwise, the main purpose of their work and activity will be distorted. This also applies to the historical judgment of their achievement. There can be no doubt that the combination of the Christian and classical inheritance which is the foundation of Western civilization was first created and established by the Fathers of the Church. They meditated on the problem contained in this double legacy and attempted to find a fundamental theological solution. They were not, however, concerned with the much-discussed problem of the adaptation and preservation of the classical tradition: they were concerned with the absolute truth which they found in the Bible and in the tradition of the Church.

The studies which follow are intended to depict the Church Fathers in the light in which they regarded themselves. They are not intended to be read as a summary of the literary history of the early Church or as a short history of Christian dogma. We shall be concerned rather with the personalities, with their intellectual aims, within the context of their own world and age, and with the ecclesiastical function which they fulfilled with their teaching and instruction. The present book is confined to the Church Fathers who wrote in Greek. The Christian literature available to us begins in the Greek world, and Greek theology occupies the leading place in the first four centuries of the Church's history. It develops quite independently, and the self-contained picture which emerges should not be confused by introducing other phenomena, whether Western or Eastern, merely because they were contemporaneous.

It is no accident that the first personality of stature who must be set at the beginning of the series appeared at a time when the idea of the New Testament canon was gradually attaining decisive importance. The Fathers no longer considered themselves direct witnesses of the Christian revelation as did the generation of apostolic and subapostolic times. In all their work they presupposed the witness of that earlier age. They did not write gospels, apocalypses, and apostolic letters but interpretations and treatises, polemical and apologetic tracts of a devotional, systematic, and, occasionally, historical nature, keeping to their own background of knowledge and method. They wanted to serve the Church with their special gifts and abilities, but as entirely free men.

It is more difficult to determine the end of the patristic age than to decide on its beginning. I have decided to place its ending at the point where the work of the Fathers themselves had already established a tradition with a validity of its own, which was restricting the freedom of Biblical and systematic research. This constraining influence led to a change in the method and status of theology. From the fifth century, theology became 'scholastic' in the sense that the authority of the old Church Fathers overshadowed more and more the influence and responsibility of the contemporary teacher.

It goes without saying that the twelve men whom we are to discuss constitute only a small selection of the innumerable host of Greek Fathers; their number could easily be multiplied. But I hope that none of the most significant personalities is missing and that the most essential points in the development of ideas will be represented.

CHAPTER I

JUSTIN

THE early Church did not engage in theology. It lived on its traditions and the revelations of its leaders and prophets. Their prophecies, instructions, and epistles were imparted to some extent anonymously, with the authority of the Holy Spirit, but later on pseudonymously as well, in the name of the original apostolic witnesses. Theological teachers relying on their own intellectual work, who presuppose a background of scholarly training and strive to defend, establish, and develop Christian truth, appeared only in the course of the second century. This development is inseparable from the influence of the Greek mind, the Greek conception of reason, and the whole tradition of Hellenistic culture. The Greek influence was not merely external, although certain contacts were unavoidable since the Church had become detached from its native soil, spread to the Roman Empire, and become part of its world-wide civilization. As the parallels offered by Judaism and Islam indicate, the acceptance of the Greek legacy was spiritually inescapable and a vital factor in the creation of what we now call theology. The first theologian in this sense was Justin—'the philosopher', as he was called in his own time, or 'Justin the Martyr', because he set the seal on his life as a Christian philosopher with a martyr's death.

It may well be asked whether Justin was really the first to strive to interpret Christianity from the Greek point of view. The history of ideas is in constant flux, and every turning-point, every end and beginning posited by the historians, is a purely symbolic simplification. In fact attempts had occasionally been made before Justin to present the Christian gospel in the forms of a rationalistic 'philosophical' culture, in order to make it available to a wider public. But apart from the earliest attempts recorded in the Acts of the Apostles as recorded by St. Luke, these earlier efforts were so bungling, derivative, and primitive that they can safely be disregarded. Such efforts did not acquire any theological weight and standing until the appearance of Justin, and to that extent he was a pioneer and an innovator though he never made any such claims for himself. It is wrong to place him alongside the other apologists of the latter half of the second century as if he were merely part of a larger group and typical of a general intellectual current. The later champions of Christianity such as Tatian and Athenagoras nearly all learned from him, and he stands head and shoulders above the earlier ones like Aristides and the little-known Quadratus. This was not merely the result of his richer and deeper education; above all, it stemmed from a new and different attitude to education and culture. Justin did not wish only to appear to the heathen in the guise of a philosopher; he wanted really to *be* a philosopher, and what he had to tell them interested him not simply as a Christian apologist but because he has convinced himself first. His Christian philosophy went beyond copying of Jewish and sceptical attacks on idolatry for apologetic purposes; it resulted from his own intellectual development and independent commitment. This is what makes his work so interesting, however many of the details are derivative and in spite of the modesty and incompleteness of his theology as a whole.

According to his own statement, 'Justin the son of Priscus and grandson of Bakcheius' was born in Flavia Neapolis (near Sichem, in Palestine) (*Apol.* I, 1). He once described the Samaritans as his fellow-countrymen, but that does not mean that we must think of him as an 'Oriental'. The old city had been razed to the ground by Vespasian in the Jewish war and had then been rebuilt as a Greco-Roman colony. In any case, Justin was originally a pagan. He seems to have been a typical representative of the urban upper-middle class of the time—

loyal, detached from ancient traditions, and cosmopolitan in outlook, intellectually active and interested, honest of mind and economically independent. Justin did not have to earn his own living; he devoted himself to his intellectual interests and became a 'philosopher'. As such he met the Christians and became one of them. 'This is the only really reliable and useful philosophy that I have found.' His conversion probably took place in Ephesus, where he placed his *Dialogue with the Jew Trypho*. Later on we find him in Rome. It was there that in his fifties he published, among other things, an *Apology* addressed to the heathen, and it was there that he was executed as a martyr about ten years later.

At the beginning of the *Dialogue* Justin gave an elaborate account of the course of his development. He found the superiority of Christianity to reside pre-eminently in the clear knowledge of the true, divine Being, which is possible only if virtue and justice are practised simultaneously. In the *Apology* Justin laid particular emphasis on the Christian love for one's enemies, on Christian patience, chastity and truthfulness, and, above all, fortitude in death. These qualities should, he believed, suffice to dispel the usual calumnies about the Christian way of life, in which he himself had once believed.

Justin's Christianity is marked by an urge to give practical expression to his faith and by the absolute certainty of his ultimate convictions. Christians possess the truth on which to base their lives; this is proved by the high moral standard of their conduct. The sources from which they derive their knowledge of God are, furthermore, undoubtedly reliable. To that extent their teaching fulfils the real mission of philosophy, which, according to Justin, is above all to explore the Divine.

Even more revealing is the criticism which he directs against the pagan schools of philosophy. In his search for the truth Justin desires to explore in all directions, to become acquainted with the whole 'many-headed' monster (*Dial.* 2, 2) of philosophy. He finds the teaching of the Stoics a barren field because they do not go into the real problem of God. The peripatetic philosopher disappointed him even more because after a few days he brought up the question of payment, which is so unworthy of a philosopher. The Pythagorean deterred the seeker after knowledge no less, for he presupposed a mass of musical, astronomical, and geometrical information which Justin neither possessed nor had the time to acquire. In his opinion philosophy should not be a specialized branch of learning, and so in the end he kept to Plato and called himself a Platonist. Nevertheless, he simplified the Platonic philosophy to suit the requirements of the new theology: the main—dualistically tinged—ideas of Platonism which were important for Justin were the pure truth of Being, which is accessible to the pure thinking of Reason; God who is One, beyond the created world, and one with the Good and Beautiful. The average pagan philosopher of the time probably possessed no deeper understanding of what Plato really taught. It is clear that Justin not only read Plato but had, in his own way, a lively understanding of him. In his writings he referred to and imitated him repeatedly. For Justin, as for so many who came after him, Plato became the intellectual bridge leading to the better, 'more ancient philosophers' (Dial. 7, 1) whom Plato himself was supposed to have known and used, i.e., the prophets of the Old Testament, and hence Christ himself. Justin henceforth took his intellectual position with them, and Plato became a forerunner and an ally rather than a leader.

Justin's intention, therefore, was not to carry out a kind of philosophical penetration of the Christian message and blend Plato with Christianity. For Justin Christianity was philosophical truth itself; Plato was, in his estimation, already very largely in agreement with the truth of Christianity. God had acted at all times and among all peoples. He had at all times revealed to them, through Christ and outside the confines of the Jewish people, fragments and crumbs of his truth. But in Jesus Christ his eternal reason had appeared in definitive form. Therefore it was possible to say that 'all men who have lived in accordance with reason' had been Christians, including, for example,

Socrates and Heraclitus among the Greeks, and Abraham, Elijah, and many others among the 'barbarians' (*Apol.* I, 46). With one bold stroke the whole history of the human spirit is summed up in Christ and brought to its consummation. Jesus Christ was the Son of God. For this basic Christian dogma Justin gave to the pagans something like a rational philosophical justification, which was intended to dispel the suspicions of polytheism. Christ was the Logos, i.e. divine reason itself, which God the Father suffered to go forth from himself without diminution of his own being. Through him, too, the creation of the world was accomplished. And as the 'Word' of God, the Logos was able in the end even to assume human flesh in order to teach men the perfect truth and wisdom. The surest proof of the truth of these statements lies in the miraculous fulfilment of all the prophecies which occurred when Jesus Christ appeared. In conjunction with the miracles which he wrought and still works today and with the sublimity of the Christian gospel itself, no further doubt about his divine origin is possible. Christ is the new lawgiver who overcomes all demonic resistance and brings unlimited salvation to the world before its approaching end. His suffering and death must not be allowed to confuse our minds, any more than the present persecution which Christians are undergoing, and which is the fate of true philosophers in every age.

It is surprising how Justin takes it for granted that the faith he is defending is a reasonable and all-enlightening knowledge, and how little he is offended by the doctrines that fly in the face of classical philosophy and which had provoked scorn and criticism at all times. The crucifixion of the Son of God, the miraculous effects of his Last Supper, the Resurrection of the flesh, and even the ancient hope of the millennium with the New Jerusalem as its centre—which was already being called in question in the Church itself—all these are accepted by Justin as irrefutable certainties based on the testimony of the Bible, and they clearly offer him no serious problems. It is obvious how firmly and naturally he is rooted in the Faith and the ideas of the Church despite all his philosophical training. It is clear that he regards the validity of the Bible as absolute. Probably this would be still more evident if all his strictly ecclesiastical works, i.e. those expressly written for Christian readers, had not been lost. They were not adequate for a later age and were bound to appear perhaps even dangerous.

Nevertheless Justin knows himself to be a philosopher, and, expressly as a Christian, he now began to teach and be active. He moved into premises of his own in Rome 'above the Bath of Timothy', and he gathered disciples, including some who later became well known as Christian teachers and writers. As an authentic teacher of wisdom, he naturally refused payment for his lessons. He imparted without question the 'precepts of wisdom' to anyone who wished to come to him (*Act. Just.* 3) and continued to wear the philosopher's cloak with pride. Of course from the effects of his teaching he might also be described as a missionary of the Church. But he appeared in public in his own name and no longer worked, like the early Christian teachers, within the religious community, but within the new sociological framework of a private philosophical 'school'. He and his pupils were drawn into the usual competitive struggle of the philosophical schools and cliques, the only difference being that these bickerings now acquired an added intensity and danger because of the religious conflict that raged behind them. Justin himself reports (*Apol.* II, 8 [3]) how he personally challenged the Cynic philosopher Crescens, who had attacked the Christians, and records that he proved the Cynic's complete ignorance, though naturally without avail. The malignant braggart continued to calumniate the Christians and to talk about things he did not understand or did not want to understand; according to Justin he therefore did not deserve the name of philosopher at all. In his *Dialogue* he presents his own conception of a serious philosophical discussion on questions of faith. The Christian and the Jew who here stand opposed both make an effort to conduct the debate in dignified tones and achieve an objectivity and impartiality conducive to rational argument. Each allows the other to have his say, and they both forgo cheap polemical victories. Their sole concern is to arrive at the truth, and this truth must be brought to light in a dispassionate, so to speak scientific, discussion. This is the new 'philosophical' attitude which is also reflected in the pleasant urbanity of the discussion —a quality also derived from Plato. This kind of discussion was beyond the scope of the earlier spokesmen of the Church.

But as we study the contents of the discussion, the connection with the earlier Christian tradition is everywhere apparent, and the philosophical elaboration of the introduction seems an almost accidental and unnecessary disguise. Justin himself in one place says that he is bound to forgo the elaborate rules of methodical and rhetorical exposition. In place of a systematic treatment of the Christian ethic he simply presents, in the arrangement of a catechism, the commandments of the Lord; instead of an exposition of what the Church is, he describes what goes on within it, and what its services are like. Even in purely theological contexts he sometimes contents himself with the traditional formulations—for instance, the Trinitarian Credo. Justin regards his main task as the interpretation of the Scriptures, above all, of the Old Testament. Like the first Christian teachers, he proclaims that he has received the 'gift of grace' for this task from God himself. But he lays particular stress on the importance of his clear and rational method. The merely mechanical repetition of sayings learned by heart is liable to provoke contradiction and contempt. And in yet another respect Justin progresses beyond his predecessors: he wishes to develop scriptural proof to the utmost limit. The *Dialogue* thus becomes a comprehensive compendium of all the Old Testament proof-texts confirming faith in Christ. In this respect it has rarely been surpassed. Needless to say, in this work Justin relies in the first place on the allegorical and typological methods already used in Judaism, combined with a truly rabbinical thoroughness in the assembling of apparently related clues and hidden affinities. The 'tree of life' in Paradise, the rods of green poplar with which Jacob colours the lambs, the anointed stone 'pillar' of Bethel and all the 'anointed' in general, the staffs of Aaron and Moses and all the other staffs and trees of the Old Testament, including the 'tree planted by the rivers of water' and the 'rod and staff' of which the Psalmist sings—for Justin these are all clear hints and prefigurations, 'types' of the Cross of Christ and prophecies of Christ himself. However tiring and complicated such expositions may appear to us today, written in a laborious and by no means agreeable style, it cannot be said that Justin lost sight of the broader considerations: he rose above his material. And his concluding exposition of Christendom as the new people of God, of its holiness and spirituality and the marvellous universality of its fellowship which embraces the whole world, is particularly impressive. This interpretation of the Church is another token of the enlightened and cosmopolitan approach on the basis of which Justin the philosopher welcomes Christianity as the new world religion and the unique truth, which must be proclaimed to his own age.

So much is everywhere apparent: Justin addresses himself to all men, no matter whether he is speaking in particular to Jews, heretics, or pagans, and the reason for this is not merely a delight in discussion nor an interest in general intellectual advancement and edification, but it is done to force men to a clear-cut decision. Truth no longer stands in cool neutrality above the contending parties: it has become concrete in Christ and it lives within a particular fellowship, in a particular doctrine, in a particular Word. The fact that in this form it has become accessible not only to the educated, to philosophers as hitherto understood, but to every man, seems to be a new proof of its perfection. That is why it is supremely important to stand up for it publicly against all prejudices and calumnies, fearlessly, as befits a philosopher, and if need be at the risk of life itself. To be a philosopher means to have a mission and to devote one's life to it.

Justin's *Apology*, which was written in Rome before the *Dialogue*, is the most impressive evidence of this intention. It takes the form of a formal complaint addressed to the Emperor, Antoninus Pius, and his fellow regents, the Senate, and the whole Roman people. It is an injustice, he declares, that Christians are regarded as a criminal sect and constantly persecuted. Their alleged misdeeds should first be proved; they themselves would then be the last to defend the guilty. In fact they are the most just, most loyal and pious subjects that the Empire has; they are the real and natural allies of the government in its struggle for the peace of the world. An enlightened government would not want to reproach them for refusing to share the corrupt prejudices of superstition. Behind the persecutions for which the heathen mob is responsible there lurk in reality only hostile demons which are afraid of losing their hold over man. Justin was here adopting a popular notion which was already playing a part in philosophical circles, and he merely gives it a new polemical twist. 'Reason directs those who are truly pious and philosophical to honour and love what is true, declining to follow traditional opinions, if these be worthless' (*Apol.* I, 2, 1). Justin thus seeks to appeal to the emperors as philosophers and to remind them of their oft-repeated claims to represent enlightened and up-to-date methods of government. But this *captatio* has nothing in common with mere flattery. 'Do you then, since you are called pious and philosophers, guardians of justice and lovers of learning, give good heed . . . if ye are indeed such, it will be manifested. For we have come not to flatter you by this writing nor to please you by our address, but to beg that you pass judgment after an accurate and searching investigation, not flattered by prejudice or by a desire to please superstitious men, nor induced by irrational impulse or evil rumours which have long been prevalent, to give a decision which will prove to be against yourselves. As for us, you can kill but not hurt us' (*Apol.* I, 2, 2).

The importance of Justin's *Apology* lies in the novel combination of the moral and theological with the legalistic and political elements. It is true that Justin did not fathom or refused to see the ultimate presupposition of the persecutions of the

Christians: the fundamental connection between State and religion which the Roman Empire was bound to take for granted and demand, like every other political organization of antiquity. The rhetoric of his quasi-legal arguments therefore sometimes appears rather artificial and far-fetched. But on the whole his arguments and also his practical references to Christians as taxpayers, to the futility of persecution and the moral painfulness of such proceedings are quite shrewd. It is rather touching to note how eagerly he assumes that everyone is interested in his concerns and presumes, for example, that the emperors have already heard of him and his disputes with Crescens. But instead of smiling at such naïvetés and counting up the blunders which occasionally slip into his long polemical discussions of pagan philosophy and mythology, one ought rather to admire his honesty, the candour and unparalleled audacity with which a man here champions the cause of a community the hopelessness of whose situation must have been perfectly obvious to him. It is not surprising that he finally had to pay with his life.

The account of Justin's end has come down to us. Under the city prefect Rusticus (A.D. 163–67) he was arrested along with six other Christians. He was described as 'reasonable and well informed', and at the trial he was their spokesman. Like his companions, he categorically refused to obey the judge's orders and deny his Saviour, Jesus Christ; after careful examination he had recognized the truth of Christ's teaching and intended to stand by it 'even if it does not suit the people who are slaves of delusion' (*Act. Just.* 2, 3). He professed his firm belief in the Resurrection and the Last Judgment, and, with the others, he received his sentence unafraid: 'Because they will not sacrifice to the gods and refuse to obey the Emperor's commands, they are to be scourged in accordance with the law and led away to be beheaded (*Act. Just.* 5, 8).

Justin stands before us as a simple, straightforward, not over-complicated character. He openly states what he believes and what he intends and does not doubt that it is the truth, that the teachings of Christ which he brings mean salvation for the whole world. Neither his relationship to philosophy nor his position in the Church represented a problem for him. It was only later that men slowly came to realize the difficulties which his position entailed. But the life of this 'philosopher and martyr' (Tertullian, *Adv. Val.* 5) was an exemplar. Nearly all the Greek Fathers of the Church were, consciously or unconsciously, his imitators.

CHAPTER II

IRENAEUS

IRENAEUS was a generation younger than Justin and theologically influenced by him. In spite of this, he represents in some ways an earlier type of Christian teaching and ecclesiastical teacher. Irenaeus did not come to the Church from outside with particular problems and expectations: he grew up in the early Church, he knew its traditions and lived for its service. He had no wish to be a philosopher but rather a disciple of the earlier Fathers, an inspired guardian of the authentic apostolic tradition. It is true that the only writings of his that have come down to us were intended for readers within the Church. The situation here is the reverse from that of Justin, who is known to us only as an apologist. Probably Irenaeus too would have given closer study to the problems and tastes of the pagans when he set out deliberately to speak to them. But it is evident that this task was secondary to his activity and writing for the Church. The only apologetic treatise which Irenaeus addressed to the Greeks was, according to Eusebius, 'striking' but also 'very short' (*Hist. Eccl.* V, 26). Apologetics was not the main centre of his interest. That is also obvious from his style of presentation, from the whole tenor of his thought in the writings that have survived. Irenaeus has the manner of an experienced preacher, not that of a philosopher or a missionary wooing his hearers. His style is leisurely, fatherly, edifying, sometimes coarse and jarring. As a writer he is a failure when he attempts to be scholarly or witty, but he succeeds by the warmth, urgency, and earnestness of his basic religious beliefs, which he develops with a convinced and convincing enthusiasm. Irenaeus thus became the prototype of the conscientious pastor and the tireless champion of the Church's teaching. The centuries that followed looked back on him with grateful admiration as the great witness to apostolic truth in a difficult and dangerous period.

Irenaeus came from the old Greek coastal district of Asia Minor. As a boy in Smyrna he had, as he delighted to point out, listened to the sermons of the great bishop and martyr Polycarp, who was regarded as a disciple of the apostles themselves. Here he came to know the genuine, unadulterated gospel, to which he remained faithful throughout his life. When he grew up he became a presbyter in the Church at Lyons. In the year 177 their aged bishop fell victim to persecution at the hands of the mob, and Irenaeus, still comparatively young, was appointed his successor. As such he was at the same time Bishop of Vienne and other small parishes or groups of parishes throughout southern Gaul which were connected with the main centre. Greek, which was Irenaeus's mother tongue, was still spoken here by a considerable part of the population and was understood without any difficulty in all the towns and cities. In the second century Greek was still a sort of ecclesiastical language for Western Christians in general. No one was offended because a citizen of faraway Asia was made a bishop in Gaul. The cosmopolitan character of the Roman Empire and its Hellenistic civilization also helped to carry the Church forward. But it was not tied to one language and culture. In Africa the first Latin sermons were being delivered at this period, and Irenaeus himself, for the sake of his Celtic listeners, sometimes used their own language. In its missionary zeal the Christian Church was even more ecumenical and less prejudiced than the rest of Greco-Roman society, which ignored the 'barbarian'.

The influence which Irenaeus exerted was not limited to Gaul. Just as he himself adhered to the unity of the one Church and proclaimed and extolled it as a divine miracle, his voice was soon heard and heeded throughout almost the whole of Christendom. While he was still a presbyter he was sent with a warm recommendation to Rome by the captive leaders of the

Church at Lyons to deliver a letter which appealed for an understanding of the 'new prophecy' of Montanism. This was a revival movement originating in Asia Minor which was upsetting the whole Church. But Irenaeus was sympathetic toward it. Its old-world belief in the miraculous power of the 'spirit' and its somewhat reactionary moral severity touched a homely and familiar note in his heart, and he did not want to see these pious stirrings of the Church and its 'prophets' liquidated without any understanding by official ecclesiastical action. Later on Irenaeus wrote letters in his own name which went to Rome and Alexandria. It was his concern to make peace and mediate between contending parties. When Victor of Rome allowed himself to be persuaded to break off ecclesiastical relations with the Churches in Asia Minor because of long-standing differences about the Easter festival, Irenaeus wrote him a forceful letter in which he condemned this dictatorial action 'in a befitting manner' (Eus., *H.E.* V, 24, 11).

Differences on practical matters in the Church can be tolerated without harm being caused; indeed, to a certain extent they merely underline the continuing unity which is created by the Faith. The all-important thing is this ancient Faith itself, the truth of the gospel transmitted by the apostles; but it is nevertheless important to be on guard when new doctrines appear, which attempt to steal or falsify the original treasure. Irenaeus personally called to account men whose theology seemed questionable to him; he urged that they should no longer be tolerated as members of the clergy, and to the deacon who represented him in Vienne he conveyed dogmatic instructions as to how heretics were to be instructed. Fighting against false doctrines was part of true preaching and an urgent problem to which Irenaeus strove to devote himself throughout his life. His writings were also dedicated primarily to that end.

His chief work, the five volumes of the *Refutation and Overthrow of Gnosis, Falsely So-Called*, was devoted exclusively to the struggle against heresy, and it still remains today the most important source of information about the theological and sectarian history of the second century. Irenaeus must not therefore be regarded as a narrow-minded and pugnacious fighting-cock to whom dogmatic quarrels were a necessity for their own sake. Owing to its rapid expansion in a foreign and pagan world, the Church at this period had in fact reached a serious crisis which threatened to change the religious substance of the Faith and destroy its historical foundations. Only a vigorous counter-attack could succeed in warding off this danger. Irenaeus stands, with Justin and various other theologians of his generation, on one and the same front in this respect. The enemies they had to fight were to some extent still inside the Church, but most of them were already outside, split up into innumerable groups and schools and occasionally united in clear-cut, self-contained societies of which the followers of Marcion represented the strongest and most important. The only thing they seemed to have in common was that they were altering and attacking what Irenaeus considered the original apostolic teaching. But in fact, despite all the individual differences, they formed a coherent religious movement at one in its ultimate impulses and intentions, which pervaded the whole world of late antiquity. We now describe it as 'Gnosticism' because its representatives often claimed for themselves a higher, but in Irenaeus's view 'falsely so-called', religious gnosis, or knowledge of spiritual mysteries.

The Gnostics turned Christianity into a dualistic escapist religion of redemption and abandoned not only the Old Testament but also the early Christian understanding of the Faith and the plan of salvation as a lower stage on the road to perfection. Christ was no longer regarded as a real historical man of flesh and blood, who brings to fulfilment the promises of Israel, but as a semi-mythical heavenly Being of cosmic dimensions. His decisive achievement was the transmission of the revealing knowledge by which the human soul is torn from the world of the senses and recalled to its true, eternal home, to which it must turn again by means of the new knowledge of the spirit, directly, or with the help of particular sacramental and ascetic practices. It will thus return to the spiritually divine Being to which Christ bore witness. It will then have no more to do with this world; the Creator God, with his angels, demons, and laws, is the really hostile power from which escape must be sought.

Irenaeus did not succeed in fathoming and fighting the bewildering mass of Gnostic ideas, myths, and speculations in the simplified form in which we have sketched them here. He took the trouble to explore the teaching and origins of each individual sect, which only increased the impression of confusion and intricate fantasy. Irenaeus tried to set out his *Refutation* as systematically and in as much detail as possible. But he himself lacked the clarity, unprejudiced objectivity, and organizing expository power which were needed for the task. Thus the work became the typical example of an unorganized and tiresome attack on heretics which, lacking intellectual superiority, seizes upon every argument which will disparage, cast suspicion on, and caricature the enemy. Their ludicrous pretensions, the contradictions and absurdities of their arbitrary theories, the constant quarrels between their various groups and parties, and, not least, the immoral lives and unprincipled attitude of their leaders are repeatedly exposed. As soon, however, as Irenaeus turns to a positive exposition of the Church's faith, the level of the writing rises and it is clear that he has a true feeling for the fundamental issues in the conflict. He is concerned to repel the blasphemous Gnostic attitude to Creation and to disprove the claim that there is a Jewish creator-God standing over against Christ. In opposition to this the important thing is to grasp the connection of Creation and Redemption, the inner unity of the threefold working of Father, Son, and Holy Ghost in its true meaning.

In the beginning God created and adorned the world with his two hands, the Son and the Spirit, and made man in his own image for this world. True, man and the whole Creation have fallen, but God has not left them fallen. In three stages he has raised man up again: in the Old Covenant the prophets bore witness to him as the Lord, and he has now bestowed on us power to become the children of God through his Son. And at some time to come he will reveal himself as Father in his kingdom. He remains for ever essentially unfathomable, but in love he has come near to us and given us of his spirit. 'It is God's glory that man should live; but it is man's life that he sees God' (*Haer.* IV, 20, 7). This is the key to the meaning of the history of the world, and Redemption does not cancel out, but leads transcendently beyond, Creation. Irenaeus is not urging a cheap belief in progress. Everything in his thought is concerned with the new relationship of sonship which Christ has established. But it is one and the same God who in his triune power fulfils all things and leads the world and mankind to eternal perfection, according to his mysterious decree.

It is not easy to be certain how far such statements are the product of Irenaeus's own thinking. He himself, as we have already seen, set no store on appearing original; on the contrary, he refers throughout his work to the witness of the 'ancients', which he only seeks to preserve and transmit. The best of what he had to give did not grow in his own field. Since this has become apparent, Irenaeus has lost a good deal of his former reputation as a great theologian. All the same, he made the fruits of his reading very much his own and was quite capable of expressing them in his own way. Irenaeus seems most independent where he is no longer fighting heretics on purely dogmatic grounds but attacking them with historical arguments. He treats them as 'innovators' and does not weary of stressing the absurdity and rootlessness of their Christianity, contrasting it with the original and authentic witness of the apostolic faith. The true Church can tolerate no arbitrary alterations to the possession that it has received from the beginning. Needless to say, Irenaeus does not ask whether his own Church, in spite of its historical securities, indeed perhaps because of its absolute commitment to Scripture and the testimonies of the past, may not also have been undergoing a transformation. He contents himself with a reference to the ancient documents as evidence of the authentic message of the Church. If we study the apocalyptic writings of the Gnostics, with their myths and their various apocryphal traditions, we shall be quite justified in concluding that Irenaeus was perfectly right to reject them.

He was the first consciously literary theologian of the Christian Church. He was the first to set the canon of the four Gospels, with a series of further apostolic writings, though not quite the present selection, alongside the Old Testament. Like it, they are quoted as 'scripture'; the two-volume Christian Bible was coming to birth. But the important thing is the basic attitude which Irenaeus adopts toward the Christian Bible, his declared intention of refusing to go beyond that which was revealed in the beginning, and the conviction that the final and irrevocable *depositum* of apostolic teaching is once and for all sufficient for salvation. The texts are unshakable, and Irenaeus wants to defend even his own writings against all attempts to improve on them. The tradition of the Church is no longer an independent factor alongside the Scriptures: it merely confirms the witness of the Bible. When the Gnostics refer to their allegedly secret special traditions it must be stated that they are upstarts and that only the elders of the Church, its bishops and teachers, have maintained direct continuity with the apostles. They must therefore be in possession of the authentic and original tradition. The example of the Roman list of bishops that had recently been established and which Irenaeus records (*Haer.* III, 3, 3) shows this continuity with apostolic beginnings in exemplary fashion, and the splendid unanimity of all orthodox congregations confirms once again where the truth is really to be found.

With this emphasis on catholicity and the succession of the bishops, which the Roman example illustrates so clearly and instructively ('above all others'), Irenaeus introduced ideas which proved especially valuable to the clerical thought of a later ecclesiasticism. He himself only used them as weapons in the fight against the claims of the Gnostics, and apart from this polemical intention he took no further interest in them. For him the Church as a whole is founded directly on the old apostolic word of truth, and, through the Holy Spirit, who gives her his wonderful gifts, she is everywhere united in the spirit. This is particularly evident from a later pamphlet, which has survived only in an Armenian translation, which assembles the main tenets of Christian teaching in an edifying way 'as evidence of the apostolic message'. There is here no longer any mention at all of 'canonical' or official considerations. The Christian message is presented in the simple form of a Bible story, beginning with the Creation and the Fall and leading, by way of the sacred history of Israel, to Jesus Christ, who has redeemed man by his suffering, death and resurrection, and renewal of life. This decisive event needs no other support than that of scriptural proof from the Old Testament, which Irenaeus, like Justin, expounds again to its fullest extent. Then the apostles spread the gospel throughout the world and established the Church; she is a new paradise planted in this world. She is impregnated by the Holy Spirit in all her branches, and he makes plain the path of worship and righteousness. The power of idols and idolatry has now been broken and a new life of perfect holiness has begun. Judaism also now belongs definitely to the past. 'For we possess the Lord of the law, the Son of God, and through faith in him we learn to love God with our whole heart and our neighbour as ourselves. But love for God has no part in sin and love of neighbour works no evil on our fellow men' (*Epid.* 95). The holy Church is protected in its simplicity from all human temptations. Its members know that an ignorant man of God is always better than an impudent Sophist.

Justin had put forward the 'philosophical' claim that Christianity could be shown to be truth in an absolute sense even to the rational critical judgment. Irenaeus reminds us that Christianity can nevertheless never be a mere philosophy, that it rests rather on revelation and sacred traditions, that it acts in the Holy Spirit and is transmitted only by the Catholic Church and its apostolic word. With this testimony he is still a fundamentally significant figure, and he continues to influence the Western world especially, even today. His writings were translated into Latin at an early period, then into Syrian and Armenian. His orthodox testimony to tradition was thoroughly approved also by the Greek Fathers of the Church, but although he was a Greek himself his writings fell remarkably quickly into the background and were almost completely forgotten by his fellow-countrymen. His simple, clumsy, and naïve style seemed too old-fashioned and too primitive. The Greek theologians, in seeking a fuller understanding of Christianity and the Church, at once found themselves confronted by new and difficult questions which it was impossible to answer along the traditional lines of communal devotion. They are more 'philosophical' than Irenaeus, and they search for new ways of understanding the old truth and making it intelligible to their contemporaries, in a spirit of astonishing independence.

CHAPTER III

CLEMENT OF ALEXANDRIA

Like Justin, Clement of Alexandria came to Christianity by way of philosophy. But the word has a much deeper and richer content for him than for Justin, who in his zealous endeavour to educate and convert always tried to take the shortest road and whose philosophical equipment contained nothing out of the way. No Father of the Church has been judged in so many different ways as Clement. For all his charm and the flexibility of his nature, he had at bottom a complicated or at any rate a many-sided nature containing many strata; he never kept to the beaten track, deliberately avoided established formulas and slogans, and never came to an end with his questioning, research, and thinking. He was a master of discussion, one might almost say a typical man of letters and a bohemian. But he too, in becoming a Christian, has taken a clear, decisive step which gives an ultimate and immovable goal to all his interests and intellectual efforts. Clement too is a servant, and regards it as the purpose of his life to lead men to Christ—a mission which he maintained in a strangely flexible, undogmatically personal way. Clement was not a public teacher of the Church and, despite his extensive knowledge, not really a scholar. He was a man of conversation, a man of spiritual experience, and a cultured pastor of souls. As such he acquired insights, posed questions, and pondered possibilities and problems which we meet almost nowhere else. Some teachers in the Gnostic conventicles may have resembled him, and later on he was read and esteemed in particular by a number of eminent monks. But they were usually bordering on the heretical themselves or had already crossed its frontiers unintentionally. In

Clement's own century he was apparently tolerated without difficulty.

We know little about the outward course of his life. He is said to have been born in Athens, but possibly this information is only symbolically correct. Like Justin, he was a traveller and even after he became a Christian he journeyed through all the Greek-speaking provinces of the Empire, from Asia Minor and Syria to lower Italy and Egypt, striving everywhere to further his education. It is characteristic that later on he thought of these journeys as a search for a real 'teacher'. Only the sixth master that he found really satisfied him: Pantaenus, who, in his judgment, surpassed all others in his interpretation of the Bible but who scorned to leave any of his lectures in writing. Like the 'ancients', the teachers of the early Christian period, Pantaenus taught only by word of mouth; it is impossible therefore for us to judge of his quality. *Circa* A.D. 180 Clement met him in Alexandria and there he settled, working as a teacher, like Justin in Rome. Naturally, he was in touch with the Christian congregation, but there is no reason to suppose that he gave lessons on behalf of the Church, as the appointed leader of its catechetical instruction, as tradition relates. His was an independent 'school' with pupils freely enrolled from every camp. Pagans, Jews, and 'philosophers' of all kinds probably came together with educated Christians and Christians with a thirst for education, some of them originally heretics, and all were taught and helped and no doubt many of them were ultimately won for the Church.

Clement thought of himself as an orthodox, Catholic Christian, and rightly so inasmuch as he adopted the most important outcome of the struggle against the Gnostics, the Bible of the Church. He accepted the Old Testament and its belief in Creation, and he strove to base his teaching on the Scriptures. As a theologian Clement, too, was therefore above all an exegete: he regarded the interpretation of the Bible as his real task and vocation. At the same time, however, he took into account all the other theories and 'philosophies' around him and tried to draw them into fruitful conversation. He fought against the false doctrines of the Gnostics and other heretics, but he also studied them and tried to learn from them. His arguments were aimed at instructing and understanding rather than straightforward 'anathema'. He also lived in a common intellectual world with the pagan philosophers in so far as they were not Epicureans who denied the existence of divine Providence. Once again, Plato stood in the forefront and was regarded as coming nearest to the truth of Christianity.

The metropolis of Alexandria, with its motley, richly animated life, was an ideal spot for the activities of a man like Clement. I am not thinking merely of the academic and, in the strict sense, philosophical culture of the place. The mixture and interchange of cultures, schools, and traditions had been going on here for a long time and had embraced every sort of religion and outlook. Above all it was a place where the theosophical tendencies of late antiquity were able to spread rapidly, here in the vicinity of the ancient Egyptian world of magic.

All this had in the past facilitated the penetration of Judaism, as it was now doing for Christianity, among intellectual circles. It is impossible to understand Clement unless he is seen against this wider background. He was ardently interested in all the ancient revelations, secret traditions, and mysteries, even when he condemned their content, and he thought of Christianity not only as a 'philosophy' but also as a mysterious reality and power which changes and exalts the whole man.

Unlike some of the Gnostic teachers, however, Clement did not become lost in this magical dream world, for he sought for the shudder of the mysterious not for the mere sake of the shudder and the frenzy. He sought in all places rather for the truth, the serious, whole truth which can establish and bind together human life, the truth which signifies for him the knowledge of God, moral decision, and reason, all in one. It was this that he perceived in Plato and apprehended at its most perfect in the earthly 'appearance' of the divine Logos, Christ. Since the coming of Christ all true spiritual life and experience could be but a development of this one clear and inexhaustible, mysterious and yet revealed and recognized, living truth of God.

Clement's literary legacy underwent the same fate as that of all the Fathers of this early period: most of it disappeared. A good deal has survived, however, and enough to enable us to follow this man's curiously versatile mind in the most varied fields. The *Protrepticus* is a Christian missionary tract composed entirely in the style of the ancient philosophical 'admonitions'. Its intention is the same as that of the usual Christian 'apologies' of the second century, but it reached quite a different level and has nothing of the usual swaggering banality of these tracts. According to Eduard Norden (*Die antike Kunstprosa*, 1898[1], 549), even the preface, with its short, rhythmic, ornamental sentences, is one of the most polished products of sophistical prose. With great vigour of spirit it challenges the reader to listen henceforward to the new song whose singer and subject is the new Orpheus, the Logos proceeding from Zion, rather than to the mythical songs in praise of the ancient gods. There follows the traditional attack on the folly and immorality of the pagan myths, mysteries, sacrifices, and images. The relative truth contained in the message of the philosophers is acknowledged. But full, unclouded knowledge is to be found only in the prophets and above all in the Logos, which leads to all truth.

The continuation of this admonition is to be found in the comprehensive *Paedogogus*, or 'Educator'. The purpose of this treatise is to deal with questions of moral and social interest for Christian beginners in an easy, unpedantic manner. The discussion turns above all on practical questions of life and behaviour of great interest to the student of the history of manners: customs of eating and drinking; the life and organization of the home; festivals and amusements; sleep and recreation; make-up and adornment; intercourse in society and between the sexes: all these topics are discussed. A whole chapter is devoted to footwear, another of considerable length exclusively

to perfumes, ointments, and garlands. It is clear that Clement
took his material very largely from the literature on etiquette
that was available to him; nor are his comments on the virtuous
and the natural always original. Nevertheless, it is evident that
Clement is pursuing a definite line through all the uninhibited
chatter and examination of every possible consideration, that
he has a goal in view which lies beyond all these apparently
trivial discussions.

Christianity must not be thought of as a merely external
commandment or requirement which has to be fulfilled according to the letter of the law. It is rather a matter of the heart,
of the whole man, and a Christian ethic is an ethic of intention,
in its commitment as in its freedom. Clement therefore has no
sympathy with radical ascetic ideals. Paul himself reminded us
that the Kingdom of God does not consist in eating and drinking (Rom. xiv. 17) nor, therefore, in the abstention from meat
and drink, but in righteousness and peace and joy in the Holy
Spirit. One can be rich and poor at one and the same time, have
possessions and not have them, use the world and not use the
world (I Cor. vii. 31). 'Just as humility consists not in the mortification of the body but in meekness, so too abstinence is a
virtue of the soul, which has its being not in the visible but in
the hidden places' (*Strom.* III, 48, 3). All external things as such
are neutral, *adiaphora* in the Stoic sense, and the Christian
is entirely 'free' in regard to them. But this freedom is not
synonymous with caprice and licentiousness. All excess is unworthy of a man, and therefore of a Christian. Clement can
explain the fact that Jesus' feet were anointed with precious
ointment (Luke vii. 37 f.) only by pointing out that the woman
who anointed them was unconverted. He uses an allegory to
interpret the incident: the extravagant ointment typifies the
divine teaching which was to be carried out into the world by
the feet of Jesus, i.e. by his apostles. In general, moderation,
self-control, unobtrusiveness, usefulness, and common sense are
to be commended as Christian virtues, the practice of which is
always seemly and therefore to that extent in accordance with

the requirements of philosophy. However, the ultimate power which governs Christian freedom is not mere reason but the love that loves God and therefore neighbour also and gives him willingly all that he needs. This love, which had already been enjoined on man in the Old Testament, is in accord with justice and common sense, the basic concepts of the social philosophy of the ancients.

It is understandable that Clement has always been a favourite of all humanists. He wishes to keep faith with the classical, Hellenistic ideals, and the fact that he always tries to give sound philosophical and rational as well as Scriptural reasons for what he has to say should not be dismissed as mere conformism. For him there is no irreconcilable antithesis between the two. The classical philosophers and the 'barbaric' prophets of the Old Testament seem to stand almost completely in line with one another as pioneers of the truth which was revealed in Christ. No people was ever utterly forsaken by Providence, and ultimately 'the one true God is the sole author of all beauty, whether it is Hellenic or whether it is ours' (Strom. I, 28). The fact that many 'weeds' are to be found in the philosophers, unlike the Bible, and that 'not all nuts are edible' (Strom. I, 7, 3) does not affect this fundamental insight. Clement refuses to be in the least intimidated by the anxious spirits who mistrust science and scholarship and are afraid of Greek philosophy 'like children who are frightened by the black man' (Strom. VI, 80, 5). If we add that he rejects the demands of asceticism with absolute determination and affirms the noble enjoyment of earthly goods as natural and according to the will of God ('Why should I not enjoy them? For whom have they been created if not for us?' [Paed. II, 119, 2]), he seems to be almost the prototype of a liberal theologian, with his worldly piety. But in fact Clement was no more a liberal than he was a pietist. He strove deliberately to reach out beyond both these basic attitudes, extolling Christianity as a religion on its own, which towers above paganism and Judaism alike. Christianity is newness of life from a new Being which is perfect above all former ways of life, beyond all mere rationalism and legalistic morality. It is a new enthusiasm of fellowship with God in faith, hope, and love, and it is therefore the crowning of all human culture and religion: it is perfection of life in God.

To know Clement thoroughly it is necessary to turn to his *Stromateis* ('Patchwork', 'Carpetbags'), which is a wide-ranging work really leading nowhere in particular, the strangeness of which only increases as one gets to know it better. Even the external form of the work, in which no clear plan can be detected, seems rather puzzling. The title sets it among similarly assorted productions of the classical writers known as 'tapestries', 'embroideries', 'meadows', or 'helicons'. They are miscellanies, preliminary studies and drafts, which were developed into a kind of art form in Greece. In the last, the eighth miscellany (Carpetbag), the material is not arranged at all: it consists entirely of preliminary drafts and excerpts which Clement intended to make use of later on. It may be asked, however, how far the *Stromateis* was intended for a wider public at all. Perhaps it represents the teaching material of the Clementine school, and as such it may be able to give us an idea of his methods of instruction, rather in the manner of lecture notes. All the same, the literary intentions of the work seem to go beyond that. The content of these 'Carpetbags' is extremely varied but always related to certain fundamental and central questions. Clement deals, for example, with the significance of classical philosophy, and he discusses faith and knowledge, the love of God and problems of marriage and virginity. Longer sections deal with the purpose and meaning of true martyrdom, the Christian testimony of word and blood. Clement discusses particular doctrines of the heretics; he refers to the tradition of his own teachers and the 'elders' and Fathers of the Church. Finally, he turns with especial love and sympathy to the picture of the perfect 'gnostic', the Christian who is completely at one with God in knowledge and love. The word 'gnostic' is therefore by no means limited in this context to the heretics, as it often is in modern usage. On the contrary, Clement's whole conception of Christianity is consummated in the ideal of the 'knowing' Christian.

It is well-nigh impossible to discern a continuous line of thought running through the 'Carpetbags'. But the greatest difficulty arises from the constant change not only of subject but also of point of view, style, and intellectual level. The point of reference is again and again the Bible, echoes of which even unintentionally pervade the whole of the discourse. But poets and philosophers are also quoted in great abundance, and Clement follows them very closely over long stretches. He deals with objections and differences of opinion; he seems to oscillate backwards and forwards, in a perpetual conversation, to ask questions, listen, discuss, and then continue on his own, after making a few reservations. He is not afraid of forming judgments and taking up his own position; but these are often merely provisional; he seems never quite to exhaust the subject, and he often refers the reader to expositions which are to come later. One has the impression that what he has in mind is an ultimate whole towards which he is steering, but which eludes him again and again, which he finds it impossible to grasp. The ambiguity and confusion of the exposition, which impel the reader to further thought and questioning, are, however, quite intentional. Clement is indeed not a strictly systematic thinker, but it would be doing him an injustice to interpret his commitment to this odd style as a shamefaced confession of his own helplessness or even as a careful evasion of the criticism which might be provoked by this free and literary discussion of sacred matters.

Clement stated at the beginning of the work, and many times quite clearly elsewhere, why he had to make a principle of irregularity and so often changed his standards and points of view. The method follows from the nature of the cause it is intended to serve. Christianity cannot simply be taught, at any rate it cannot be communicated by writing and made available to everyone once and for all. Its reality is mysterious and is fully revealed only to those who are ripe for it and sufficiently blessed by God. Faith must be appropriated by each new person and is not spread but only desecrated by overhasty publication. The 'Carpetbags' therefore constitute a deliberate thicket, a 'spiritual park' where fruitful and unfruitful trees are planted higgledy-piggledy, so that the merely inquisitive and the hypocrite cannot steal the fruit but those who are inwardly prepared will immediately find and enjoy them. Clement is content if he has written for one reader who really understands him, but this reader will understand him not merely by reading him but on the basis of his own living experience and an inner affinity which discovers that to which it is akin.

As we can see, there is more to Clement than the usual mystery-mongering of arcane disciplines and queer disguises. He is concerned, albeit in the fashionable outer garb of such ideas, with 'truth as an encounter' and an experience, with the difficulties and possibilities of an individual and existential communication and appropriation of the truth. This was a problem with which Plato had already wrestled, when he deliberately renounced the direct, dogmatic communication of his teaching by writing. Clement is therefore quite justified in referring to him.

Real life-establishing knowledge has to be acquired personally; it can be taught, shown, and witnessed only personally, by word of mouth, in direct responsible encounter. The ultimate knowledge cannot be acquired from books, and it should not be revealed in books. One does not put a knife into the hand of a child. That is why the teacher's personality is so extraordinarily important and so absolutely indispensable for a living Christianity. Clement urgently exhorts everyone to choose such a spiritual guide and friend as will tell him the truth quite openly, and who is not afraid, if the need arises, to buckle to in earnest, as a means of helping and healing. In the sphere of higher religious knowledge the figure of the teacher attains even more far-reaching importance. He is not merely the vigilant teacher, the Socratic helper and partner on the way to an independent appropriation and appreciation of the truth;

as the man who has been caught and consecrated by God, he is the proper mediator of the truth, the first to make it really alive and visible to the beginner. By gradually introducing him to the new world of Christian prayer, vision, and love he transforms the seeker and the simple believer and so for the first time turns him into an understanding, ardent, and radiant 'knower' of his Lord. Measured against these ultimate realities and experiences, all merely theoretical knowledge can be no more than a preparation, a kind of pre-knowledge and pre-understanding, like such aids to philosophy as geometry and other *propaideumata*. Even a Christian book, indeed the very Bible itself, in which all wisdom is contained, cannot simply as a book replace the teacher. The fire of the spirit can be kindled only by a living fire.

Perfection is attained at the highest level of knowledge. The perfect gnostic no longer needs the human teacher, since he has become directly linked with God through the Logos and thereby become the friend and intimate of God. He has been raised far above the cares and passions of this world; they no longer reach him, although outwardly he continues to live freely and without constraint in the world. He is no longer lured or frightened by visible things. Through the inner attachment of his will to God he has entered the choir of eternally adoring angels. He may travel and associate with other people, rest, read, engage in business—but basically his whole life is an uninterrupted prayer, a continuous intercourse with God, a constant feast. God always hears this striving toward him, though it may not be expressed in words. The true gnostic, however, no longer lives for himself in this state of blessed perfection. In his love for God, the love of God lives in him; he becomes the living, active image of Christ and descends with joy to his fellow-men who are all—like him—called to the Highest and are to enter the kingdom of divine knowledge through him.

In this praise of the perfect gnostic Clement is describing himself, the ideal which he tried to realize with his pupils who saw in him their teacher, pastor, and pattern. Clement hardly ever mentions the wider fellowship of the Church and its organization. When he does speak of clerics and their tasks, as the Old Testament texts necessarily invited him to do, they automatically become types and allegories of the degrees of spiritual perfection by which he is exclusively preoccupied. Fundamentally, the officials of the Church do not interest him. The gnostic and the gnostic teacher are the really priestly characters, and the spiritual legacy on which they feed cannot be transmitted through official channels. This relative disregard for the clerical and ecclesiastical must not be interpreted, however, in the sense of a rejection or an expression of secret hostility. On one occasion Clement himself says that the genuine gnostic should not shun the public worship of the Church, even if he no longer needs it himself. We even have a lengthy sermon which Clement himself preached. To be sure, it is not clear whether this was a sermon actually delivered in church or a kind of 'Bible lesson' or religious lecture meant only for a limited circle of his own pupils. Here at any rate we can see how well Clement understood how to develop a train of thought with perfect simplicity and clarity when necessary and bring it to its conclusion without any ostentatious frills and with real feeling. But the academic level of the sermon and the problem it deals with seem aimed at particularly high levels of Christian society. Clement shows in connection with the pericope of the 'rich young man' that it could not have been Jesus' intention to exclude the rich from the Kingdom of God altogether. Here again, the issue is fundamentally inward and spiritual—namely, the loosening of the heart from the bonds of earthly greed. Once this has been achieved, riches, rightly used, are a good thing and can even become a means of eternal salvation. No one should despair of achieving this end. The sermon concludes on a lively and moving note, with the story of the 'young man who was saved' (which Herder turned into a German poem). The old story of the apostle John, who wins back for the Church an unfaithful disciple who has become the leader of a band of robbers, illustrates the boundlessness of the divine forgiveness, the rescue of the apparently lost by the force of repentance and the marvellous power of the transforming Christian gospel.

Toward the end of his life we lose track of Clement again. He did not stay to the end in Alexandria, where he had lived for so long. In the year 202 or 203 he left it for good, it appears, to escape from the hardships imposed by measures instituted against the Christians and their missionary propaganda, which were intensified under Septimius Severus. About the year 211 we hear from Cappadocia that in that place Clement had 'strengthened the local church and extended its knowledge' and had travelled from there to Syrian Antioch bearing a message from the Church (Eus. *H.E.* VI, 11, 5 f.). He must have died soon after this, since about the year 215-16 the former Cappadocian Bishop Alexander already included 'holy Clement', his excellent 'master and brother', with Pantaenus, among the 'fathers who have gone before us' (Eus. *H.E.* VI, 14, 8 f.).

The later Church scorned to include Clement among its recognized saints. Too little was known of him, and some of his teaching seemed suspicious. He was judged far too much from the standpoint of a different age. He deserved to be remembered more favourably by posterity. But the lack of enthusiasm is understandable when one remembers that of all the Fathers of the Church, Clement was without any doubt the 'most unecclesiastical' of all, in other words, the one who was most indifferent to the organized Church. And yet, even as early as his time, the question of the Church—its law, its functions, and the orthodoxy of its preaching—was becoming more and more important everywhere. Henceforward, it was no longer possible to treat these matters, as he had done, as of more or less secondary importance, or simply leave them alone. Living Christianity now came to be understood in terms of the Church and not as a matter of purely personal training and knowledge, the teaching of extravagant personal spiritual perfection.

CHAPTER IV

ORIGEN

COMPARED with the achievement of Origen, the work of the earlier Fathers of the Church seems a mere prelude. According to their personal background and character they single out from the profusion of early Christian traditions the things that appeal to them most, and these they commend to the pagan world with missionary zeal, orienting themselves to the requirements and expectations of the educated and extolling Christianity as the fulfilment of all wisdom and religion. They think of themselves as preachers of the truth that has been revealed, and the Bible, freely interpreted, is their one firm support. But they nowhere establish a systematic body of theological thought, and with the exception of Clement their use of philosophy and learning is somewhat amateurish and determined by their own particular apologetic and polemical interests. They did not realize the problematical nature of their position in the Church.

The most important of these men was Hippolytus of Rome, who worked for part of the same period as Origen (until the year 235). Hippolytus was a pupil of Irenaeus and probably, like him, a native of the East. He became a Roman presbyter and bishop at Rome, and as such he felt a proud sense of responsibility for the representation and defence of the old Catholic tradition which derived from the apostles. Hippolytus was also a 'philosopher' and a profound scholar who wrote, besides his sermons, the first continuous commentaries on the Bible and also a chronicle and calendrical tables. His followers put up a statue in his memory which shows him teaching on his bishop's throne, with a catalogue of his works on the sides.

But respectable though Hippolytus's philological studies and dogmatic zeal may have been, all in all he was far too rudimentary and superficial to be able to create the comprehensive intellectual and ecclesiastical self-confidence which the Christians needed in the new century. Origen was the first to bring this about.

Apart from the pagan Plotinus, he was the most comprehensive mind of his time and he appeared at a historical turning point when the Church was abandoning the narrowness of a conventicle-like existence forever and the points were being set for the future. By moulding the outlook, ideals, and Churchmanship of his contemporaries he determined the direction of Greek theology for more than a century, influencing its destiny and contributing to some extent to its ultimate catastrophic downfall.

We are much better informed about the life and work of Origen than about his predecessors. Eusebius devoted practically the whole of the sixth book of his *Church History* to him and was able to draw on Origen's own library in Caesarea, which contained his entire literary estate and also the letters that are now missing. Of his writings, which are said to have numbered thousands, a considerable quantity has survived, although many of them are now extant only in translations and anthologies in which the most audacious and therefore the most offensive of his ideas have been omitted or 'improved'. We must confine ourselves here to the most important of his ideas.

Origen was probably the first Christian writer of whom we know for certain that he came from a Christian home and was given a Christian education. Like Irenaeus, Origen did not come to the Church from outside, he did not seek for bridges and approaches to open it up and make it intelligible to the world: the Christian faith was for him a given fact, the centre of truth from which he looked at everything. His intellectual development proceeded without fanaticism and without compromise, without a break, smoothly, and without pause. One has the impression that this man—whose life, as Eusebius says,

is 'noteworthy from his swaddling clothes onwards' (*H.E.* VI,
2, 2)—never lost a moment's time and never suffered any
spiritual checks. The intellectual tendency also came from his
parents. His father, Leonides, had been a teacher in Alexandria
and would certainly have taught his own son not only the
'encyclical' subjects—mathematics, grammar, rhetoric—but
also the beginnings of Christian knowledge. In the year 202 he
fell victim to a persecution of the Christians. Origen, who was
about seventeen or eighteen at the time, had encouraged his
father in a letter not to weaken or give in for the sake of his
wife and children. According to a legend, he himself escaped
martyrdom only because his mother hid his clothes and so prevented him from going outside. Such were the auspices under
which he entered into adult life. He had nothing of the carefree,
sometimes almost playful enjoyment of culture so typical of
Clement, who was escaping from persecution at this same time.
Behind the gigantic work of scholarship which he was to
achieve there was from the very beginning an austere and
ascetic earnestness and the iron resolution of a man who never
lost sight of the possibility of martyrdom. It may be that in his
youth his enthusiastic radicalism bordered on the heretical.
Basing his action on a word of Jesus (Matt. xix. 12), Origen
took the step, of which he himself later disapproved, of castrat-
ing himself 'for the sake of the Kingdom of God'. From the
beginning, however, he was a member of the orthodox Church.
He joined it in Alexandria and remained loyal to it later on,
even on the long journeys which, like Justin and Clement, he
made to Asia Minor, Greece, and Rome.

To begin with, Origen also became a teacher, concentrating
even more than his father had done on Christian instruction.
There was a lack of Christian teachers and teachers of Christianity, since persecution had affected them more than anyone
else. Origen was not deterred, and Demetrius, the vigorous
Bishop of Alexandria, recognized his quality and secured him,
in spite of his youth, for the regular instruction of catechumens.
Under his direction this semi-official school acquired a rapidly

growing importance and, so to speak, academic status. It was also attended by heretics and pagans, needless to say, free of charge. Origen lived on the proceeds of the sale of his father's library of pagan authors, drawing a modest annuity just sufficient for the life of an ascetic who was constantly working and denied himself all unnecessary pleasures. Origen did not, however, keep to this path for ever. Although he won the admiration of his friends, he was not content with the training he had had and decided to become a student again and study the encyclical sciences, and, above all, philosophy.

This could be done only at the feet of pagan teachers, and Plotinus's master, Ammonius Saccas, appears to have been Origen's teacher too for about five years. In his school Origen met the future Alexandrian Bishop Heraklas, whom he secured as a colleague in his own school. Later on, he left the teaching in the lower part of the school entirely to him and devoted himself to the higher philosophical, theological, and Biblical teaching of his more advanced pupils. After the break with Demetrius, Heraklas succeeded Origen as director of the school.

The importance of these years of philosophical study for Origen can hardly be overestimated. Origen was the first Christian to join the intellectual élite of his age, drawing attention to the teaching of Christianity in a way that forced even his enemies to take notice. No less a man than Porphyry, the biographer of Plotinus, testifies to this with mingled admiration and exasperation. Origen, he thinks (Eus. *H.E.* VI, 19, 7 f.), professed the teaching of the barbarians and lived as a Christian contrary to the laws; but nevertheless in his view of God and the world he was Hellenistically-minded. 'He was quite familiar with the writings of Numenius, Cronius, Apollophanes, Longinus, Moderatus, Nicomachus, and the celebrated Pythagoreans.' Only, 'unfortunately', in the opinion of the pagan Hellenes, he 'introduced Platonic ideas into foreign myths'; in other words, he interpreted them as affirmations of the Jewish-Christian Bible.

Naturally, Origen himself would never have agreed with

this description. He studied the pagan philosophers in order to be able to refute them, and he was firmly convinced that he had himself earlier and more completely drawn from the Christian revelation whatever elements united him with them. He cannot, however, have thought the methodical study of philosophy useless, since he also made it a compulsory subject for his students. It may therefore be asked whether his opponents' pungent judgment of him was not in fact justified. Origen offers the first great example of a theology which, while its intentions are exclusively Christian, nevertheless unconsciously runs the danger of falling into line with the enemies which it takes so seriously—at the time with Neoplatonism which was just arising, as with many later thinkers like Kant, Hegel, or Heidegger. It is impossible to give a straightforward yes or no to the question whether a theology of this kind is Christian or not. Even in Origen the blending of the elements is far too organic and complicated to make a simple answer feasible. In contrast to modern philosophical developments, the Middle Platonic philosophy of that period had not yet been influenced and conditioned by Christianity; but it was sustained to an increasing degree by the same Gnostic atmosphere that permeated and directed the Christian thinking of late antiquity. Theological and anthropological problems such as theodicy, moral development, the doctrine of immortality, the demand for withdrawal from the material world, the problem of the meaning of the material world's decay and its possible return to the original Divine unity, the investigation of the concept of Being itself with these considerations predominating—all these were topics and problems which forced themselves to the front and were interpreted as the basic problems of Platonic philosophy, just as they were, in Origen's view, the basic problems of Christianity itself.

On the whole, historically considered, Origen was in advance of the philosophical developments of his time, in the questions he asks and the answers he gives. His point of departure was different in so far as he was already able to proceed from the

reality of an all-sufficient divine revelation based on the testimony of the Bible. Jewish theosophists and 'philosophers' such
as Philo of Alexandria, Christian Gnostics and theologians such
as Clement, had preceded him, and even the pagan philosophers
had long been interested in the sacred wisdom of ancient myths
and mysteries and had made a start with an allegorical-philo-
sophical interpretation of the Homeric epics in particular. If one
looks, for example, at the doctrine of angels and demons in
which Origen was vitally interested and which the Neoplaton-
ists were in the habit of treating as an important part of their
theology and interpretation of the world, it is quite impossible
to separate its origins and paths of development and influence
with any certainty. The new element which Origen gave to the
Church was primarily the great systematic summary. He was
responsible for the change from an occasional and superficial
interest in philosophy to a methodical study of intellectual
problems, from the aphorism of educated discussion to the responsible construction of a well-established theological system.
There is not a sentence in Origen which was written per-
functorily, not an idea that cannot be taken seriously and followed up further. Just as he led his own students in a careful
educational plan through the study of logic and ontological
'physics', of geometry and astronomy to ethics and thence to
theology proper and the study of the Bible, the holy essence of
the spiritual universe, so in his system of thought every single
idea is set and examined within a broad context of knowledge.

None of the later Greek Fathers achieved this integration to
the same degree. Origen is the only one to present the whole of
Christianity in the form of a workable philosophical system.
In the first Alexandrian period of his life, when he was about
forty years old, he wrote his most characteristic work: *Peri
archon* (Latin: *De principiis*), a Christian work on dogma 'about
original things' (or 'about the main doctrines'). Admittedly,
the boldness of this essay inevitably brings to light the problematical nature of Origen's whole theology. The Christian gospel
can be brought into the framework of an objectified doctrine

of God and the world only with the help of a radical reinterpretation of its content. The tradition of the Church, with its mythology and scheme of redemption, is blended with the abstract categories and value-concepts of philosophy into a strange mixture—a kind of cosmically theosophical history of the spirit and revelation which is developed along speculative lines on the basis of certain Biblical postulates.

The work has not come down to us entirely in its original form. At the outset Origen asserts that he does not intend to deviate by a hair's-breadth from the teaching of the Church; what in fact he offers, however, is more like a Gnostic myth of the fall and rise and passing of the world, the only difference being that the myth is very largely transposed into philosophical concepts and interpreted more or less 'symbolically'—a kind of demythologizing which brings the whole thing very close to the later neoplatonic system of Plotinus. To begin with, the doctrine of God is considered—God, who is the absolute, immutable spiritual substance, the original unity, who must also be thought of as the original living Being and eternal Creator. From him the Logos arises eternally as his image. Through the Spirit the divine nature is extended to the Trinity, and finally, through the Logos, God creates the unbounded world of spirits, who surround him, loving and beloved. As personal beings they are free; they can therefore also abuse their freedom and commit the sin of departing from God. By their doing so, the world comes into being, advancing into ever wider circles in a process of 'cooling off', of becoming estranged from God amidst ever-increasing darkness until the stage of corporeality is reached in which the fallen spirits—human souls are also pre-existent—are enclosed as a punishment and a purifying prison. But fallen Creation is always sustained and guided by the providence of God who ceaselessly strives for the recovery of the apparently lost. The sending of the Logos, Christ, who is united with a pure human soul, is a decisive event in this process. At the end of the process, because evil is not a positive power and can have no lasting reality, even the blackest devils of hell are completely restored to God. Like all sin, punishment, and pain, evil is only a dark transition leading, by God's guiding care, to the best in the end. Freedom and with it the possibility of recovery can never be lost.

Origen does not acknowledge the existence of 'absolute evil' or the possibility of eternal separation and damnation. The heretical nature of this idealistic conception is increased by the fact that for him the final restoration of the Kingdom of God can hardly consistently form a final and absolute end. It follows from the nature of spiritual freedom and from the character of divine education (which leads but never forces) that new darknesses and new eras of redemption may be unleashed in the infinite distances of time. But Origen did not stress this idea. To him time itself is not an ultimate, seen from God's point of view. The true life lies beyond time, in eternity. In our earthly state, however, we are not in a position adequately to grasp this eternal being. When Origen does actually overstep the limits of the Christian revelation he is quite well aware that all his speculations are indubitably marked by an element of metaphor, imagery, and poetry. But he does not doubt that in this way he approaches more closely to the truth contained in the Bible than he would if he simply kept to the literal 'disguised' assertions of its anthropomorphism, as the simple unphilosophical mass of the faithful are in the habit of doing.

The anthropology and ethics suited to this metaphysic display the same idealistic and ascetic characteristics. By the knowledge of its origin and vocation which Christ has brought, every single soul is summoned to loose itself from the fetters of this visible world and to begin the return journey and ascent to God in new holiness. Origen does not keep to cool description and contemplation. He thinks of himself as a missionary and pastor of his students and tries to train them to become men of prayer, martyrs and saints. Everyone must, as a spiritual warrior, join the ranks of the Christians, the spirits and angels on God's side, and take up arms against the vices and demons of the world. There are various forms of service and help; but the decisive force leading to salvation and victory remains gnosis, the full knowledge of divine truth. It is only truly to be found in Christ, the teacher and pattern of all Christians. He meets the soul, as the soul requires; he makes plentifully available in the Church spiritual helpers and means of grace. But the soul must make its own decision, and in the final resort it is by the innate capacity for spiritual freedom that the truth is known and redemption obtained.

This conception of freedom and guidance not only confirms the immortal spiritual dignity of man; it also serves to justify the ways of God and the apparently imperfect divine government of the world. The idea of theodicy occupies a good deal of space in Origen's work and establishes a clear relationship between his theology and the contemporary systems of Middle Platonism. There is no room left for the genuinely Christian conception of judgment, sin and forgiveness, or even redemption in the strict sense of the word. Origen does not realize how the Biblical concepts are transformed under his hands, believing that he is only trying to understand them more deeply. It almost seems as though the Christian character of his outlook is shown only in the greater warmth with which he professes his belief, and the personal devotion and cordiality with which he strives to win new believers. Origen describes the process of redemption less anthropologically than the philosophers, that is to say, not simply as a myth of the Fall and the possible return of the soul to its home, but theologically, as the expression of a divine purpose of love and guidance. In the end, however, these are mere nuances and slight differences in emphasis within the same basic view of life. The only decisively Christian factor is that Origen—contrary to the formal logic of his system—never fails to relate all knowledge and sanctification to the person and pattern of Christ and that the Bible remains the all-important document, guarantee, and support of his faith. In this he follows the line of the earlier Christian 'teachers', and no philosophical scorn for the barbarism of his 'myths' ever disturbs him.

The last section of his main work introduces an explicit justification for this procedure: a detailed theory of the Scriptures and the principles by which they should be 'spiritually' interpreted.

Like all the early Fathers, Origen must be judged primarily as a Bible theologian inasmuch as the great bulk of his literary work, which reflects his method of instruction, consists of Biblical exegesis. It is true that, besides the *Peri archon*, it is possible to name a few further theological monographs of smaller compass: on the Resurrection, on prayer, on martyrdom, and also a work, which has unfortunately disappeared, with a title we have already met—*Carpetbags*—which is said to have contained a sort of Harmony of Biblical and philosophical doctrines. But apart from the fact that these writings also consist very largely of exegesis, they almost vanish beside the mass of extended Biblical commentaries, shorter 'scholia', for the most part explaining individual points, and the homilies, or sermons, which deal sometimes with whole books of the Bible, consecutively. About a third of these works have survived but nothing at all of the 'scholia' commentaries in connection with them. As a Biblical scholar Origen did not confine himself, however, to exegesis. With his usual care he sought to set everything on a broad and firm foundation, and so as a first step he made for his own use a comprehensive edition of the text of the Old Testament the so-called *Hexapla*, or sixfold edition. Alongside the unvocalized Hebrew text it gave first of all a Greek transliteration, to preserve the original sounds, and there followed in further columns the various Greek translations—above all, the venerable Jewish Alexandrian translation of the Septuagint (LXX), the deficiencies and additions of which were specially indicated by the usual signs. As a rule the edition offered four translations, making altogether six narrow columns, which it was possible to compare at a glance. But in certain cases Origen added a fifth, sixth, or seventh translation. Of one such text he remarks incidentally that it was found in a pitcher near Jericho. The modern sensational discoveries in the caves by the Dead Sea therefore had their predecessor in the third century.

The so-called *Tetrapla* (an extract from the *Hexapla*) was produced for a wider circle of readers. This contained only the four Greek translations, without the Hebrew text. The original of the *Hexapla* itself was probably never reproduced. But one hundred and fifty years later Jerome was still able to use it in the Catholic library in Caesarea, and he was especially struck by the corrections which Origen had made in his own hand.

In his exegetical work Origen was therefore able to refer from time to time to this solid manuscript foundation. His exegesis was intended to be a strictly scientific achievement, especially in the great *Commentaries*. In the matter of sheer detail they are not inferior to any modern commentary. The interpretation of the Gospel According to St. John (as far as Chapter xiii, verse 33) covers no less than thirty-two 'volumes'. The explanation of the first six words, 'In the beginning was the Word', required a whole volume. Origen attached not the slightest importance to literary decoration or rhetorical effects. He was not artistic by nature, and he despised 'the teachers who never want to do anything but compile well-sounding statements and resounding sentences' (*Hom. Ezech.* 3, 3). He is concerned exclusively with the matter in hand. He puts the questions and gives his answers quietly and in a clear and orderly manner. He deals in detail with differing views and shuns no delays or detours where they seem necessary for a proper understanding. Now and then he discusses problems of textual criticism and historical background. Generally speaking, however, this occurs but rarely and is quite secondary. The real interest is of a purely theological-systematic nature.

The Bible is the authoritative document behind all Origen's teaching and research: the inexhaustible source of all metaphysics and ethics, all theology, philosophy, and scientific knowledge. Origen is convinced that in its present form the Bible, as the book of the Church, represents a wonderful and many-sided whole which God has created by direct inspiration. He interprets the inspiration behind the Bible not as 'testimony' that is, the deposit of a sacred history or a profession of belief on the part of its human authors, but as the timeless essence of the divine revelation itself, 'a sea of mysteries'. The individual narratives and words are explained to the last detail and made to express new and sometimes extremely surprising mysteries. We have already met this method of interpretation in the work of Justin and Clement; the method as such was no novelty in the Church. But because of the reflective thoroughness with which Origen handles it, it now assumes an all-embracing theological significance. To our way of thinking it thereby becomes quite fantastic, but it is of the essence of allegory that the more uncompromisingly and consistently it is applied the more it seems to be justified and confirmed. Its results can no more be contradicted than the presuppositions on which it is based can be checked by the actual text.

Origen was therefore in no doubt that his procedure was methodical, perfectly scientific, and appropriate. As we have said, he was able to refer to the theories of Hellenistic philology, and for him the allegorical method is justified above all because it is sometimes used even in the Bible. With its spiritual relativity and gradations, it fits in marvellously with his whole outlook. It should therefore not surprise us that he was quite convinced of the validity of his insights.

For every text in the Bible Origen distinguishes between a physical (or material), a psychic, and a spiritual meaning. This corresponds roughly, though not entirely, with the later distinction between historical, moral, and theological meaning. Normally, however, the two higher levels coincide and the first, the physical or historical interpretation, is sometimes left out altogether. In Origen's view there are texts which it would be quite absurd and immoral to interpret literally. They are intended, through the offence they give, to point to the real, deeper meaning which lies below the surface of the text. 'What reasonable person will believe for example that the first, second, and third day, evening and morning, came into being without the sun, moon, and stars, and the first day even without the sky?' Or 'Who would not be led to regard unchastity as nothing, when he reads how Judah lay down with a harlot or the patriarchs had several wives simultaneously?' (*De Princ.* IV, 16) —unless all these things are only taken figuratively, as it is proper that they should be, and affirmed in their true spiritual sense. Otherwise a Christian would have to blush for the divine law of the Old Testament in view of the 'much finer and more sensible laws of the Romans or Athenians' for instance (*Hom. Lev.* 5, 1). Such considerations make it clear that the moralizing, rationalistic, and unhistorical conception of the Bible forces Origen to accept allegory as a way out. It was impossible to defend the Old Testament against the pagans and above all against the criticisms of the Gnostic and Marcionite heretics in any other way. It must also be admitted that in spite of the essential wrongness of the method, the allegorical interpretation does not necessarily always miss the point at issue in the Bible. In the course of the Church's history it has often been the means of arriving at the true meaning of the text, albeit in a round-about way. This is, however, seldom the case in Origen. It is deeply moving to note with what energy and earnestness this great and devout scholar dedicates the work of a lifetime to fathoming the truth of this one ardently loved book, firmly convinced that he is on the way to penetrating ever more deeply into its content, while in fact he remains the prisoner of the assumptions of his Platonizing and Gnosticizing outlook, incapable even of seeing what separates him from the Old and New Testaments.

None of those who fell under his spell fared any differently, and their numbers grew rapidly. Origen was by nature no solitary scholar, but primarily a teacher who devoted himself, like Clement, but with far greater thoroughness, to the oral instruction and tuition of his pupils. We still have the vale-dictory address of one of them, Gregory Thaumaturgus ('wonder-worker'), who later became an equally famous bishop and missionary in Asia Minor. In this address he expressed his enthusiastic thanks to his beloved teacher. For him Origen was the only man he knows who 'understands the divine utterances purely and clearly and knows how to interpret them to others' (Greg. Thaumat. XV, 175). Under the guidance of this teacher, he says, nothing had remained 'hidden and inaccessible'. Origen knew the right answer to every question and set every fact in its right place. Through a well-to-do patron called Ambrosius, whom he had himself converted previously from heresy to the Catholic truth, abundant resources for scholarly work and publication had been made available to him. 'Seven stenographers who relieved one another at definite intervals, and just as many book scribes and female calligraphers' (Eus. H.E. VI, 23, 2), were always available and saw to it that as far as possible not a word of his was lost.

The almost incredible productivity of this man, who, according to his own testimony, had never known a moment's rest throughout his life and acquired the somewhat ambiguous nickname of the 'worker with brazen bowels' (Chalkenteros), can only be explained if we bear all this secretarial help in mind. Nearly all his writings bear the marks of unpolished oral delivery. But they were read throughout the Greek-speaking Church, far beyond the confines of Alexandria and his own school.

Meanwhile Origen had become a world celebrity. The pagan Governor of Arabia appealed to his Egyptian colleague and also wrote to Bishop Demetrius a courteous letter asking for Origen to be allowed to give a few lectures in his presence. On the orders of the Empress Julia Mammaea he was escorted to her court at Antioch because she wished to receive 'a sample of his universally admired insight into divine things' (Eus. H.E. VI, 21, 3). There also existed letters from a later period which Origen had sent to the Emperor Philip the Arab and his wife, who were favourably disposed toward the Christians. Within the Church itself Origen was naturally regarded even more as an authority. He received invitations from all quarters, and he was

called in to help especially when it was a case of refuting a
learned heretic or clarifying difficult theological problems.
Origen not only knew how to impress his opponents by his
learning and sagacity but also how to convince them inwardly
and win them for the Catholic Church. The recently discovered
proceedings of one such disputation which the whole congregation attended give a vivid picture of his bearing as modest as
it was distinguished, and his thoroughly objective method of
attack.

At first sight it seems astonishing that this man became involved more and more in ecclesiastic differences and difficulties
in his immediate homeland, which were ultimately to lead to
open conflict. The 'case of Origen' is the first celebrated example of rivalry and conflict between the free, unofficial power
of an independent 'teacher' and the authority of his ecclesiastical superiors. It is no longer possible to unravel all the details
of the dispute. Besides personal disagreements, doubt regarding
his orthodoxy may have played a part from the outset. The
decisive factor, however, was probably the question of the legal
position of the school of Origen in relation to the doctrinal
authority of the 'apostolic' bishop. Demetrius was a determined
hierarch who was already making a successful effort to gain
recognition for his authority throughout Egypt. He wanted to
bring the 'catechetical school' also under his immediate supervision; but here he met with opposition. One recalls the carefree nonchalance with which, a generation earlier, Clement of
Alexandria had fashioned his theological teaching. It had not
occurred to him to refer to clerical authority, nor was there any
need for him to do so in view of his completely independent
position. Origen was more ecclesiastically-minded from the
very outset. He wanted to serve the whole Church as a teacher
and at the same time be a loyal member of his own Alexandrian
Church. He too regarded himself, however, as free to teach
what he thought fit, and not subject to any human judgment,
willing though he was to face any criticism and questions. God
himself had blessed him, like an early Christian prophet, with

the gift of wisdom and a knowledge of the Scriptures which, by their very nature, were reserved to the few. It is true that Origen had no desire to upset the Christian faith of the simple Church member and warmly acknowledged the value of simple faith. But the higher knowledge still had rights of its own and ought not to be measured by the normal standards of the average Christian. Origen was striving to combine and hold in balance the different degrees of spiritual maturity and illumination, but this only draws attention to the mental reservations and superiority of the 'Gnostics'; the difference cannot be overlooked and the suspicions of the 'simple' were aroused. This was the situation that faced the bishop. Origen tried to overcome the threatening breach by purely spiritual means, pointing to the substantial orthodoxy of his 'higher' theology and his willingness to share in the life and worship of the Church. But Demetrius required formal integration and submission legally and in practice: the God-ordained, monarchic episcopacy was to be the living guarantee of orthodox truth and the clear and sole expression of Church unity.

In Origen's view the simplest solution of the tense situation would have been to ordain him to the priesthood and combine his official and unofficial authority in a kind of personal unity. It seems that he made efforts to this end, but in vain. Demetrius wanted submission to himself, and in view of the almost episcopal standing of the Alexandrian presbyters the independence of the head of the school would only have been increased if he had also been ordained. Outside Egypt no one understood the way ecclesiastic politics was run in Egypt. In Jerusalem, whose bishop had been friendly with Clement of Alexandria, in Caesarea, where a pupil of Origen's was at the head of the Church, he was allowed to preach in church without any question. The violent protests which Demetrius made against this 'unheard-of' innovation were rejected. But when some years later Origen was staying in Palestine again, on his way to Greece on Church business, it was suddenly decided to ordain him to the priesthood. Origen made no objection, clearly

hoping that he would now be free from further restrictions on
his activities. But the opposite happened. The move made his
position in Alexandria quite untenable. On his return home he
was given such an unfriendly reception that he was forced to
the decision to abandon altogether his field of activity at home
and move to Caesarea, where he was received with open arms.
At a synod of priests held in Alexandria, Demetrius had him
formally banished, and in the year 231–32 a second synod deposed him from the priesthood because it had been conferred
on him without reference to the proper authority and was in
any case illegal since he was a eunuch.

This apparently fortuitous, arbitrarily provoked conflict
points to a deeper antithesis of which the immediate participants were probably not completely aware at the time. It is
clear that for all his love of peace and personal humility, Origen
could not concede to the office of bishop the importance which
was claimed for it, and that for reasons of theological and religious principle. In his opinion, the thing that matters in the
long run, the living knowledge of the truth, cannot be transmitted and controlled by officials. All the rights which the
bishop is accorded and possesses, the sacraments which he ad-
ministers, the power of excommunication and absolution which
he exerts, remain purely external so long as they are not impregnated with real spiritual power. This cannot be effected by
the office as such but only by the Holy Spirit, by the right
attitude of love and the knowledge which God gives and which
the spiritual teacher above all communicates. Origen's views
are not in the least revolutionary. He knows and gladly emphasizes that Christendom must, like every 'people', have its
rulers and that order in the Church is absolutely necessary. For
this reason alone office-bearers deserve obedience and respect,
and Origen desires with his whole heart that they should all be
enlightened to the greatest possible extent with spiritual gifts
and be real teachers and patterns to their flocks. But he also
knows and sees just as clearly that that is all too often just what
they fail to be, and the spiritual man is in principle free and

independent of their authority. With one half of his nature Origen is a conservative, ecclesiastical pietist; but with the other half he remains a liberal idealist who at heart lives more in the invisible than in the visible Church. He was the first for whom this momentous distinction came to assume fundamental theological importance.

He bore with calm dignity 'all the winds of malice' (*Comm. Joh.* VI, prol. 9) which Demetrius now let loose against his former protégé. By concentrating on his theological work he tried to overcome his bitterness, and he consoled himself with the remembrance of the Biblical saying that no one should trust in man. His enemies were, he thought, more to be pitied than hated. One should pray for them, not curse them, since we have been created to bless. Outwardly Demetrius was unable to do him any further harm. He tried in vain to stir up his episcopal colleagues outside Egypt against Origen. The school was re-established in Caesarea. Origen also laboured eagerly as a preacher to the congregation. His pupils and episcopal friends loved and revered him as a saint. It was in Caesarea that Origen finally secured the supreme glory known to the Church: suffering unto death for the truth of his Faith and his Lord.

The major part of Origen's life fell in a period of 'peace', a period of calm, sometimes even friendly understanding between the State and the Church. As a good Platonist Origen showed much appreciation for the rights of rulers and the responsibility which every citizen is called to bear for the welfare of the State. But a cheap syncretism and political compromise were equally alien to his mind. Christians were different from all the other peoples contained in the Roman Empire inasmuch as they were the holy people of God, who do not interfere in the affairs of the world and can never be made subservient to its aims. Christians fulfil their external duties and also pray for the Emperor and his army, but they must refuse to bear arms themselves since they are a priestly race, recognizing only the warfare of the spirit. In his old age Origen wrote an elaborate *Apology* in which he tried to refute the criticisms

which the pagan philosopher Celsus had made of Christians two
generations ago. Once again his two sides come out: the close
affinity of outlook with his philosophical opponent and his
proud sense of superiority as a Christian. Soon afterwards, with
the accession of the new Emperor Decius in the year 249, a
political change occurred and the first systematic persecution of
the Christians to cover the whole Empire was launched.

It was no longer feasible to destroy the Church by direct
physical extermination of its individual members. It was a
matter of forcing them to surrender by terrorism and well-
conceived measures of coercion, and the first and most important step was the subjugation or removal of their leaders.
Origen, who was now an old man of nearly seventy, was
arrested, cast into prison, and cruelly tortured. It was clearly
not intended to kill him, but he was put to the rack and his feet
stretched for days on end 'as far as the fourth hole'. He was
threatened with death by burning, but for all this nothing was
achieved. Origen had to be released, but he was physically
broken. Nevertheless he wrote a few more short treatises
'which were of great use to those in need of consolation' (Eus.
H.E. VI, 39, 5). He died at the latest in the year 254.

To the very end the picture presented by the life and character of this strange man was remarkably clear and consistent.
Austere and yet kind, wholly pure and honest, entirely dedicated to intellectual work and ascetic piety, he was a scholar
and above all a systematic thinker, capable of taking on any
opponent. He was in no sense a problematical character nor in
the final analysis an original one. He combined the unphilosophical tradition of the Church with the Gnostic-Neoplatonic
tendencies of the century on a higher intellectual plane and thus
created a theological structure of admirable grandeur and completeness. But he had no feeling for the deeper, essential problems of a truly Christian theology. For that very reason his
solutions met with an easy and apparently uncontroversial success. They were the solutions of a theorist of genius who constructed reality from the idea, without being moved at a deeper

level by doubt and suffering. Such people do not find it difficult to obtain pupils and successors. It was only among the succeeding generations of his followers that the progress of historical development brought to light slowly but surely the spiritual inadequacies of the theology of Origen. The new generation confronted this development all the more helplessly because it was unable to refer to its revered master for guidance for its troubles and problems, while it knew at the same time that it was his inferior in systematic power and discipline of thought, in universality and thoroughness of philosophical culture, and in purity of intention and conviction.

CHAPTER V

EUSEBIUS OF CAESAREA

HALF a century after the death of Origen his theology had spread throughout the Eastern Church. It was regarded as the only really scientific theology in harmony with higher and, in particular, philosophical culture. The literary champions of Christianity, the intellectually active, working Christians at the schools and training centres, the bishops of the larger sees, adhered to it and strove to teach and act in its spirit. Imperceptibly the tradition began to change, to become mingled with other traditions, and to adapt itself to new situations in the Church and the world of ideas. As these changes took place, intellectual divisions arose and inner weaknesses became apparent, which were the less easily overcome because it was no longer possible consistently to maintain Origen's philosophical assumptions. Aristotelian concepts and ideas were altering the Platonic foundations of the system, ecclesiastical interests and consideration for the literal truth of the Bible were demanding their rights, and new problems were coming to the fore.

Origen had been a systematic thinker, and as such he had shaped his exegesis and his theology and ontology into a single, unifying pattern. The new generation of theologians tried to use new methods. The change-over from philosophy to philology, to the critically exact examination of the biblical foundations, is discernible in the personality and work of Pamphilus. Pamphilus was a wealthy lawyer from Berytus, in Phoenicia, who decided, under the influence of Pierius, the director of the catechetical school in Alexandria, to abandon his public career and devote his whole life to the service of the Church. As presbyter of the church in Caesarea he became the librarian in charge of Origen's literary estate, which he began to sort and sift. Above all, he endeavoured to produce a reliable text of the Bible on the basis of the *Hexapla* and Origen's commentaries on the Old and New Testaments. In this task he required assistants and collaborators, and the young Eusebius became the most useful and industrious member of his team. He helped Eusebius to achieve economic and intellectual independence, and Eusebius, who owed everything to him for his start, expressed his attachment by combining, in the manner of a liberated slave, his master's name with his own. Thus, he entered literature and the history of the Church as 'Eusebius Pamphili'. There is still extant a manuscript of the Bible with a note recording their joint work of revision. Eusebius took over from his master a profound veneration for Origen and occupied himself with his literary remains in order still further to enhance the reputation of the incomparable teacher. He tried to produce a complete corpus of Origen's correspondence which was intended to prevent its dispersion and the disintegration of the tradition. During the last great persecution Pamphilus was cast into prison, and in the face of death he decided to write another *Apology* for the great teacher which was intended to protect him from the criticisms levelled at Origen by his fellow-prisoners and various recent theologians. This was Pamphilus's only independent piece of writing and at the same time the first production of his pupil Eusebius, who assisted him and had to finish it independently. Pamphilus died a martyr; Eusebius, who was still unknown at the time, escaped with his life. His fame as a scholar was soon to outshine that of his master.

First of all, Eusebius continued his academic studies indefatigably in spite of the storms of continuing persecution, and he collected like an archivist all the information about martyrdoms and other events in the Church that he could lay his hands on. He then came forward with writings of his own. Apart from purely philosophical, historical, and exegetical researches, they consist mainly of a number of comprehensive tracts directed against the pagan and Jewish opponents of Christianity.

Eusebius was a believing Christian and felt most deeply an obligation to help the cause of the Faith and the Church with his learning and gifts. From the year 313 the Church had again acquired the freedom to develop without hindrance and appeared to be moving into a new and finer future.

If one compares the early theological works of this period with the works of the earlier apologists like Justin, the difference in the situation and the personal quality of Eusebius at once become apparent. Christendom was no longer the poor little band of 'barbaric' sectaries which had to struggle laboriously for its right to exist and enjoy a modicum of intellectual respect in a rich, self-assured world. It had long since spread through the entire civilized world; cities and countrysides were influenced by its churches, and in all professions and not least the intellectual the activity of Christians had grown to immense proportions. Whereas pagan society had become impoverished and morally degenerate at the time of the civil wars and universal decline, thanks to its firm coherence, discipline, and the unbroken courage of its Faith the Church had maintained itself and continued to grow uninterruptedly. Thus it now appeared in a different light. For Eusebius the apologetic evidence for the truth of Christianity no longer depended on certain miraculous details and correspondences which relate the prophecies of the Old Testament to Christ. The victory of the true monotheistic knowledge of God, the new life of virtue which had come to life in the Church, the expansion and visible triumph of the Church 'among all peoples'—all these things speak for themselves. It is merely a matter of demonstrating that this whole astonishing development lay in God's plan from the beginning and could only have been brought to the brink of fulfilment by the wonderful aid of God himself. Paganism, with its polytheism and blood sacrifices, its demonic superstition and the everlastingly fruitless conflict of its philosophies, now seems like an outdated form of religion which must and will disappear. It can no longer hold its own in the forum of enlightened reason and a higher morality.

The change in the situation also brought a shift of emphasis in the meaning of the Christian hope. It was no longer centred exclusively in the world to come: it began to be realized in the present world. Christianity was the decisive power behind the moral progress of the world, the crowning consummation of the history of thought and religion, and its prophecies and commandments had become the bases of a programme of human renewal. Monotheism and the new idealistic morality, which constituted the heart of the gospel of Jesus for Eusebius, were unable to rule the world from the beginning. First of all, the nomadic stage of civilization had to be overcome; cities had to be built, laws made, arts and skills developed, and 'life, which was still to some extent animal and unworthy', had to be tamed and moulded by the beginnings of philosophy and civilization (*H.E.* I, 2, 17-19). When the Roman Empire brought peace to the world and overcame the multiplicity of governments, the hour for the international and peaceable Christian race had come, according to the will of God (*Praep. Ev.* I, 4). To begin with, they remained with their claims half in the background, in order not to provoke the Roman rulers and disturb the peace of the Empire; now, however, in the age of fulfilment Christians had become the open and natural allies of the secular power. This is an idea that had long been latent in the conception of Christianity as the consummation of ancient philosophy and culture. The beginnings of Eusebius's conception are to be found in Origen, especially where he contends with the pagan enemies of the Church. But fundamentally his frame of mind was far too otherworldly and dualistic seriously to pursue such ideas.

Origen was not interested in world history and politics. The victory of the Church was for him perhaps an idea which might be considered theoretically but it was not yet a goal to which all one's energies could or should be bent. Eusebius's attitude was quite different. It is true that for him too God himself was a completely transcendent reality, and he regarded pure, ascetic withdrawal from the world and the worship of the divine

Being as the supreme goal of Christian piety. The celibate priests of the Church, its holy, spiritual top layer of leaders, must satisfy in a representative capacity this demand. But with this representative service, the claims of the world-renouncing ideal have been essentially met. It is beyond the scope of a 'universal, human way of life' and must therefore remain the exception to the rule. The majority of Christians have their tasks within this world, yet in spite of that they have their full share of salvation and the saving teaching of the Church (*Demonstr. Ev.* I, 8, 29 f.). God has protected his Church in the world from all the demonic onslaughts of its enemies 'plainly from on high' and has led it to victory and success as a light to lighten the nations.

Such are the ideas that made Eusebius a Church historian. Early Church history grew out of apologetics just as modern history grew out of the Enlightenment. That is the reason for the inner weakness of Eusebius's position. His works on Church history and contemporary history favour a moralizing, black-and-white technique because their intentions are apologetic; he has a fondness for the rhetorical and the edifying and strives all the time to impress and convince the reader. He is lacking in strict theological criteria. Of course it is God who achieves the Church's successes, and they are all miraculous; its defeats are the work of the demonic powers and the human villains who are their accomplices. But they can also be imposed by God to test or punish the Church. They are in no case the last word; even within the Church the apostolic truth will always win in the long run against all heretical innovations. The old mythological framework, which reckoned the history of the world according to Daniel's 'weeks of years' and ended with the return of Christ at a date which can be calculated, was abandoned by Eusebius once and for all; the optimistic scheme of a progressive, God-guided education of the human race is the basis of his whole view of the world and the plan of salvation. Beyond that he was not interested in the fundamental problems of a theology of history, and for that reason his critical sense and his interest in the materials of history were able to develop without restraint.

In this respect his work was exemplary for its period and deserves all praise. Eusebius was really a scholar, and the conscientiousness and precision of his philological, archaeological, and historical researches are apparent wherever we are able to test them. But for him we should know about as much of the first centuries of the Church's history as we should know of early Christianity if Luke had not written the Acts of the Apostles. In contrast to the latter work, Eusebius's *History of the Church* is, admittedly, by no means a work of art. The multifarious material is laid out in columns rather than worked up into a definite shape. For pages on end quotations are allowed to break into the exposition and the overwhelmingly vigorous style pours over us in a torrent of solemn-sounding, hardly intelligible words and phrases. Yet in his own time Eusebius was esteemed as an orator. His reputation as a scholar may have influenced this judgment of him.

Even before he began his *History of the Church* Eusebius had worked out his 'chronological tables' on the model of the earlier Christian chroniclers, though more thoroughly and in greater detail. After a long and learned introduction about the different chronological systems he presents synchronistic tables of the history of the world. The juxtaposition of Biblical and secular dates was intended to prove that Christianity, far from being a recent religion, was, with its Old Testament witnesses, the oldest and most venerable religion in the world. Christ brought in its final period, which was now unfolding itself in the history of the Church. From this point on, the material in the column devoted to the plan of salvation becomes larger and larger, almost crowding out the secular records. The *History of the Church* is to some extent an independent version of this part of the chronicle, issued as a new book. The rather external manner in which it sets information about famous bishops, theologians, heries, persecutions, the destinies of the Jewish people, and other matters side by side still shows the influence of the earlier

method. Nevertheless, Eusebius rightly stressed the novelty of
his undertaking and the special difficulties presented by a first
attempt of this kind. He regarded himself as treading a completely new path 'without finding the slightest trace of men
who have trod it before me, only occasional minute records in
which one man in one way, another in another left behind a
fragmentary account of his own time' (*H.E.* I, 1, 3). These earlier
records must give him his direction, like beacons or distant calls
in the dark. As we have said, Eusebius was fond of quoting such
records verbatim, especially when they seemed to have chronological value, and in this way numerous fragments of a literature
have been preserved which would otherwise have been completely lost. Seen as a whole, Eusebius did his work so thoroughly
that it remained authoritative for a long time. The Church historians of the following century merely continued or simply
translated this basic work.

Eusebius's exposition begins with Jesus Christ, whose nature
and activities 'present themselves to a conscientious investigator
so sublimely and so powerfully that they can no longer be
human' (*H.E.* I, 1, 7). He then leads up in seven books to his
own immediate period, and he deals with this in the last three
books. Even today it is possible to see that Eusebius did not
write these parts all at once but continually worked at them and
improved them, as further developments took place and new
information reached him.

His judgment on the rulers varies according to the measure
of their success and their changing attitude to Christianity. The
author's personal bias and propagandist intentions now become
very pronounced and cast a dubious light on his often mutually
contradictory reports. In the final edition the work achieved its
manifest consummation; history itself supplied the historian of
the Church Triumphant with the appropriate conclusion. The
victory of the Emperor Constantine, friend of Christians and
beloved of God, and the beginning of his sole reign in East and
West alike (324), brought the previous development to its goal
and a new epoch opened. For Eusebius too a new era began in

his own life. Up till then Eusebius had not been a public man or a Church politician. He was a scholar with heart and soul and as a theologian a champion of the truth and the rights of the Christian Church. Like Origen, he held the position of a presbyter in Caesarea, and in 313–14 this accomplished and cultured priest was made bishop of that city. As a cleric he no doubt fulfilled his duties according to rule; but fundamentally he remained the man he really was, devoted above all to his scholarly labours. He was not a teacher like Origen; he was primarily a research worker, a historian, a philologist, and an apologist. He also preached much less often than Origen, in spite of the acknowledged and representative position he had gained in the Church. This was not due to indifference toward the duties of his office and spiritual calling. We have seen that he put his whole work, including his strictly academic studies, at the service of the Church, and he now thought he discerned entirely new opportunities for service. With the victory of Constantine the Church emerged from the period of preparation into the age of fulfilment. 'These things were foretold by Isaiah and laid down in Holy Scripture from time immemorial; the infallibility of these oracles now had to be proved by deeds' (*H.E.* X, 4, 53). The political victor becomes the bringer of salvation to the world.

Eusebius had stressed the providentially intimate relationship between the Empire and the Church on an earlier occasion; he now included the institution of emperorship and the person of the Emperor in this relationship. The Emperor sent by God, the redeemer who appears after the long torment of dissension and persecution, is God's chosen herald for the whole world. His earthly dominion is the image of the rule of God and the rule of Christ which the Bible foretold. The final order of things had now been achieved. 'God himself, the Great King, stretched forth his right hand from above and made him to this day victor over all his haters and enemies' (*Laus Const.* 8). This Emperor, beloved of God, is a philosopher and a pattern of all piety, the essence of all kingly virtues, dignity, beauty, and strength, culture, inborn reason, and divine wisdom. Eusebius claims that he had realized this many years ago when he saw the then quite unknown prince for the first time.

Eusebius has often been criticized for the extravagance of such utterances and the insincerity of his 'Byzantinism'. But it is easy to forget the degree to which such expressions had come to be taken for granted in the Orientalized court style of the time. Moreover, Constantine knew how to handle people. He obviously attached importance to the support of the distinguished scholar and his propaganda for the Church, and met him with due deference and the most flattering regard. Eusebius was a man of lowly origin, by no means at home in the great world of politics, and it is not surprising that he allowed himself to be hoodwinked. The important thing, however, was his realization of the basic agreement which bound him to the Emperor with a kind of theological inevitability. This rationalistic philosopher and apostle of the new Christian order was inevitably a 'Byzantine Christian'. His whole theology was aimed at fulfilment in a moral civilization united to a world church. Unknown to himself, it became the up-to-date Christian version of the old pagan ideology of Empire and Emperor. Eusebius would have had to surrender his own self if he had not at this moment followed the Emperor as the 'chosen instrument' of God for whom he had hoped and in whose mission and destiny he believed. For him a final 'victory' for the Church could be conceived only in alliance with the Empire and only under the auspices of the permanent unity of a Christian order and a holy, world-wide peace which it was the task of the Emperor to create and preserve.

This was Eusebius's Christianity, and it led to his ruin as an ecclesiastical politician. The Arian controversy was dividing the Greek Church at the very moment of Constantine's victory. Fundamentally, it had nothing at all to do with politics, but it could not have come at a more awkward moment. It was essentially a struggle for the bases of the Christian belief in salvation, which had its origin and foundation in the divine and

human person of Christ. Eusebius was by no means the convinced 'Arian' which he has been alleged to be by historians of
heresy. Christ was for him more than a mere creature and more
than a superior demigod. Arius, whom Eusebius had taken in
as a refugee, had cleverly, but rather deceitfully, misled him to
begin with as to the radicalism of his Christology. Eusebius was
persuaded to see in the exile an innocent victim of persecution
who had, like Origen, come to Caesarea because the power-
loving Alexandrian patriarch refused to permit the development of a scientific theology. Old errors about the complete
identity of the Father with the Son, which had long since been
refuted by Origen, appeared to be coming up again in the
camp of the enemies of Arius. For Eusebius their massive confessions of faith meant the end of an up-to-date, philosophically
grounded and scientifically defensible theology. He therefore
became a convinced supporter of Arius. But fundamentally
he was not interested in the 'mystery of human redemption'
as such; he was fighting rather for the intellectual and moral
aspirations which the Church's monotheistic preaching now
had to uphold in the new world order. Against this background,
the Christological disputes seemed like mere quibbles, or at any
rate they were not entitled to a place in the foreground of
ecclesiastical politics as his opponents desired. With genuine
horror Eusebius noted how in the historical hour of liberation
and God-given victory theological quarrelsomeness and intolerance threatened to shatter the relationship of the Empire
and the Church and the united Christian front was breaking up
'so that the holy mysteries of the divine teachings suffer shame-
ful derision in the very midst of the theatres of unbelievers'
(*Vit. Const.* II, 61). On this point there was a genuine unanimity
between himself and Constantine. They both had the same goal
in view: to overcome this unpleasant situation as quickly as
possible, cost what it might. Only Eusebius was also a theologian and bishop of his Church. By half unconsciously making
tactical and political ends the criterion of his decisions he involved himself in contradictions which landed him in personal

humiliation and forced him, despite his honest intentions, to take steps which irreparably compromised his reputation. At the Council of Nicaea (325) Constantine was compelled to yield to the opponents of Arius. Even Eusebius must now have come to realize how dubious the Arian teaching was. Nevertheless, he strove to remain loyal to his protégé. In the end, however, he had to drop him in order to save himself from excommunication and deposal. The mediating confession of faith which he submitted to the Council was publicly praised by Constantine but modified so extensively by all kind of anti-Arian additions that Eusebius himself could no longer have honestly accepted it. He was nevertheless forced to sign it, and the tortuous letter in which he justified his action to his own church proves, with its untenable reinterpretations and evasions, that he knew perfectly well what he had done. Nor was this the end of his dishonesty. In favour with the Emperor once again and deemed worthy of intimate intercourse with him, he used his influence to get the decision that had been taken reversed by indirect ways in striking a personal blow at the supporters of the Nicene Creed and giving his enthusiastic assent to their dismissal and banishment by political means.

We do not need to study the events in detail. Needless to say, the theological treatises which Eusebius wrote still reached a high intellectual level even though they were inspired by personal annoyance. He also continued his scholarly researches, and he was regarded as the leading spokesman of the Church, an outstanding champion of the imperial policy for Church and State in the new era. His supreme triumph was when Constantine had him appointed bishop of the bitterly contested see of Antioch. Eusebius modestly declined the appointment on the ground that his acceptance would infringe certain ecclesiastical statutes. Perhaps he sensed his own limitations. Anyway, he preferred to stay with his incomparable library in Caesarea, amidst his familiar surroundings. He died there peacefully a few years after Constantine (339–40).

In the end Eusebius was able to believe that he had attained the goal of his life's work. State and Church had come together; the 'peace' of a unity based on political foundations seemed to be firmly established; a middle-of-the-road theology, such as appealed to him, dominated the field. And yet this impression was based on an illusion. In the very next generation the opposition to the régime in power, which had been officially reduced to silence, was to emerge again with renewed passion and compel a basic revision of all the decisions which Eusebius and his friends had secured on tactical and political rather than dogmatic and ecclesiastical grounds. Later on, the Church decided more or less firmly that Eusebius could not be regarded as orthodox and saw in him a 'double-faced' man (Socr. *H.E.* I, 23) even though it could not dispense with his historical and philological works 'for the sake of the factual information which is useful for instruction' (*Decr. Gelas.* 5, 22). In this it has been less than just to his qualities as a man. His destiny reveals more than the personal failure of an otherwise respectable scholar who was not equal to the difficulties of imperial and ecclesiastical politics which confronted him. It reveals more the bankruptcy of a theological trend which was unable, for political reasons, to free itself from the power and opportunities of the moment and could not take itself or its faith in Christ really seriously. The crisis of Origenism thus became evident and made a new understanding of the Church's teaching urgently necessary. This was bound to have an effect on the position of responsible theologians and teachers.

CHAPTER VI

ATHANASIUS

ATHANASIUS belongs to a much younger generation than Eusebius. He was born *circa* 295, and his memories did not go back earlier than the last persecutions. These he did experience, however, and the hardness of his character, his mania for absolute, cut and dried decisions, may have been increased by these early experiences. As a young man, however, Athanasius grew up within the order of the Imperial Church: this was an accepted institution to which he held fast throughout his life. But with him a new era begins in theology too. Athanasius was the first Greek Father of the Church who was not at home in the academic atmosphere of Christian philosophy. He was a 'Churchman' who was also well-versed in theological matters, but he was trained in the administration of the Alexandrian hierarchy. His spiritual home was the divine service and the administrative desk in the ecclesiastical office, not the school platform. At the beginning of the third century no bishop possessed such a large, well-organized, and efficient administrative machine as the Patriarch of Alexandria. From the time of Bishop Demetrius, who died in 232, ecclesiastically Alexandria dominated the whole of Egypt and also the adjacent areas of Libya and the Pentapolis. He had appointed the first bishops in his province, and they remained dependent on him and he had taken up the cudgels with heretics and other recalcitrant elements. We have already encountered Demetrius as the opponent of Origen. But theology had not died out in Alexandria since his banishment. Bishop Dionysius 'the Great' (who died in 265) had been a pupil of Origen and was also well known as a theologian. But just as the catechetical school had lost its old independence, so theology now had to take into account the practical demands of Church life and Church politics. One senses this in the very beginnings of the Arian controversy. For the new Bishop Alexander the main thing was to force the refractory presbyter Arius to submit to the official discipline of his spiritual superior. Furthermore, the earlier Egyptian schism caused by the breakaway of the supporters of Melitius, whom Arius had joined for a time, became mixed up with the theological controversy. From the very outset the dogmatic problem became in Egypt a problem of episcopal authority and the 'church law'.

Athanasius became familiar with this whole world of ecclesiastical politics and administrative problems perhaps while he was still half a boy. He was reader, then deacon and as such the special confidant and theological adviser of his bishop, whom he was allowed to accompany to the Council of Nicaea. When Alexander died in 328, he is said to have wanted Athanasius to succeed him. His rapid election was not carried through without opposition. Perhaps people were afraid of the ruthless energy of this unusually young but no longer unknown candidate. His opposition to the Arians was certain. He also sought to take immediate and brutally decisive action against the Melitians, with whom negotiations were still in progress, with the result that their resistance flared up again. But Athanasius would undoubtedly have coped with these domestic problems. The important thing was that the Arian controversy had long since extended beyond the vicinity of Egypt itself and had penetrated the whole of the East. By taking up the attack again with renewed vigour Athanasius once again called into question the almost complete victory of the opposition party. From now on the struggle was never to let him go nor he to let it go. For forty-five years he continued to wage it with unvarying tenacity, agility, and energy, showing versatility in his methods and formulations, unshaken and relentless on the essential issues, reassured by no partial success, and discouraged by no failures. When Athanasius died, he stood on the brink of victory. The whole subsequent development of the Greek-Byzantine Imperial Church was based on the struggle and success of this one man.

The decision of Nicaea was no accident; but the way it was brought about was essentially the result of tactical measures and pressure on the part of the Emperor. What Constantine was worried about above all was the pacification and firm unification of the Imperial Church he had founded. The condemnation of Arius and the Nicene Creed were both intended to serve this end. When complete success was not achieved the Emperor was, as we have seen, persuaded by his advisers to extend the limits of comprehension in the universal Church somewhat further, and he subsequently revoked the decision that had been made. Finally Arius was taken into favour. The formal order to recognize this decision in Alexandria and to admit the condemned heretic to his old sphere of activity for the sake of 'harmony' arrived there just as Alexander was dying. He died before he could answer the Emperor's communication. It fell to his successor to make the decision.

Athanasius was not in doubt for a moment about what should be done. To restore Arius would be out of the question. Whatever explanation he might have given, such a step would be taken by the public only as implying a withdrawal and as a theological and political defeat of the Alexandrian bishop from which his opponents alone would have benefited. Athanasius took the position that the admission of people 'who had invented a heresy in opposition to the truth and had been anathematized by a general synod' was fundamentally impossible (*Apol.* II, 59, 5). To expect Arius seriously to change his mind was also out of the question, and Athanasius was therefore able to consider himself in the right not only on tactical grounds. Unlike Alexander, he had realized the scope and significance of the theological conflict from the outset. The Arian doctrine of 'createdness', that is, the no longer essentially divine nature of the Redeemer, was for him not the questionable or perverse solution of a theological problem but the end of the Christian

Faith itself, the betrayal of everything the Church had been concerned with from the very beginning. Athanasius did not regard the wider theological and political ideals to which Eusebius had so ably devoted himself in the struggle for his rationalist and relativist Christology of any importance. The Church is not concerned with any secular programme, but with man's eternal salvation. The world of the created and man's much-praised reason had obviously not been able to save him from corruption. It needed the coming of Christ 'the Logos, who was the Logos through himself' (*Contra Gentes* 40); he had to take our flesh and thus unite our nature with God and God's eternal life. The Incarnation was the decisive event in the process of salvation. God himself acted by pulling down the barrier to his fallen creature and bringing to light life and immortality, with the knowledge of his true nature. A demi-god would have been of no use to man. The moral aspect of the process of Redemption, the idea of the knowledge of sin, of atonement, and the forgiveness of sins, are of only secondary interest to Athanasius. Salvation from death and the life-giving fellowship with God are central. With genuine religious fervour he acclaims the miracle of Christ's coming. This is a theology that has little in common with Origen in any shape or form. Athanasius naturally knew 'the supremely learned and diligent Origen' and occasionally tried to defend him from an allegedly improper 'Arian' interpretation (*De Decr.* 27, 1; *Ad Serap.* 4, 9); but on the whole he mentions him very seldom. He reminds us most of all of the emotional faith of the aged Irenaeus.

According to Athanasius, the whole Church can live only on the one truth of the true God and Saviour Jesus Christ, which is proclaimed in the preaching of the Church and represented miraculously and effectively in its sacraments. Whoever does not believe and feel this truth, whoever is satisfied with general theories of virtue and pale speculations about the spirit, the world, and a creaturely Logos-Christ, is an 'Arian', though he deny it a thousand times over. There is something almost mono-

maniacal about the monotonous regularity with which Athanasius rams home the same basic ideas and harks back incessantly
to the same complaints and accusations. But it would be wrong
to suspect stupidity or theological incompetence behind this
highly effective method. Athanasius knew how to organize his
material clearly and shrewdly; in the development of his ideas
he shows a striking dialectical skill and art, and his Biblical
exegesis, which has to carry the dogmatic proof, is often discerning and profound, for all its violence. It is obvious that he
had been a good student in his youth and is a well-trained
theologian. But it is difficult to feel that theological work as
such gave him any pleasure, let alone that he had any desire to
make use of it for the purpose of educating others or set himself
up as a 'teacher'. For him theology was simply a weapon.
Athanasius's writings were devoted almost entirely to controversy. There is an occasional note of mistrust in Hellenistic
culture; at any rate, he completely ignores its treasures. As a
person he naturally thought of himself as a Greek. But it is
hardly an accident that he was, as we know, the first theologian
of any standing to preach in Coptic. There was something un-
Greek about his nature, which is harsh and rigid, without a
touch of intellectual grace or charm. His portrait, if we possessed one, would probably recall the ancient Pharaohs and
their officials more than a Greek philosopher.

Even before Constantine was able to return to the case of
Arius, further complaints had been lodged against Athanasius
by the Melitians. He was alleged to have bribed an imperial
messenger, to have overturned an altar, smashed a sacred chalice,
and even murdered a Melitian bishop in the course of his violent
proceedings against the sectaries. As far as the last of these
charges is concerned, Athanasius was able to vindicate himself.
His secret service succeeded in tracing the alleged victim, who
was hiding in a monastery in Upper Egypt and, when the
wanted man escaped in time, he was later discovered in Tyre
and identified by the bishop of that place. Complaints about
acts of violence and illegal encroachments on the rights of others

accompanied the patriarch throughout his life. It is no longer possible to assess their credibility in every case. Athanasius rejected every complaint in the most violent terms. He knew how to hold his ground amid the press of intrigues and dishonest polemics and was a master at impressing the masses. His pamphlets reveal the intelligence and clarity of an outstanding personality, but at the same time they employ every possible means of defamation and constantly caricature his opponents in the most lurid colours. Blood was shed repeatedly in the Alexandrian struggles, and in his later years Athanasius came more than once near to committing high treason. But it was impossible to humble him, and he continued to believe in and assert his rights.

For a time it seemed as if Athanasius might win over the Emperor to his point of view. It is true that his enemies at court were at the helm of affairs and they had already been in touch with the Melitians in Egypt. But Athanasius refused to appear before their seat of judgment. When he finally had to present himself before a Council in Tyre he talked his way out by protesting uninterruptedly, and before sentence could be passed he had secretly escaped by sea. He turned up again in Constantinople, forcing himself on the Emperor and demanding an audience. In a letter the Emperor himself described how Athanasius had taken him completely by surprise. Even he clearly found it difficult to stand up face to face against this bishop's leonine fury. New discussions with his opponents were begun, but when they explained to the Emperor that Athanasius, whose predecessors had already played a great part in the Egyptian corn trade, was now about to cut off all supplies to the capital city, the Emperor's patience was exhausted. According to Athanasius's own account, Constantine became extremely angry and banished him to Trier without any further discussion. It was the first of five exiles which Athanasius underwent and which kept him away from his see for seventeen years altogether.

We cannot follow his story in any further detail, through all the ups and downs of political and ecclesiastical developments. Two circumstances above all made it possible for him to assert himself in the end. The first was the support that he found in the Latin world. The traditional good relationships between the sees of Alexandria and Rome were revived by his sojourn in the West. The whole of the West became consciously Athanasian. The difficult philosophical speculation which formed the background to the Arian controversy met with no understanding in the West, which took it for granted that there must be a close connection between the Father and the Son. There was in fact a widespread inclination to identify in practice the two persons of the Godhead—the greatest theological crime imaginable for a Greek theologian trained in the school of Origen!

In order that this Western sympathy might become effective a further purely political factor had to come into operation. Constantine had divided the Empire among his sons, and this had led to a loss of unity in the State's ecclesiastical politics. Each separate ruler now favoured the tendency prevailing in his own part of the Empire and strove to promote it to the best of his ability in the neighbouring zone as well. Thus the weaker son, Constantius, who ruled in the East, was twice forced by his brother to readmit Athanasius. The first time this happened was immediately after the death of Constantine in 337. Instead of going straight to Alexandria, Athanasius travelled for months on end through the provinces of Syria and Asia Minor in order to reinstate his party in the East and to strengthen its unity. When he was recalled after a further period of several years in exile in the West, in similar circumstances, he managed to exploit his victory even more intensely. The Emperor who had banished him was forced to invite Athanasius no less than three times before he would appear before him again in Antioch. He then travelled on by way of Jerusalem, where a synod was in session, entering his episcopal city in triumph.

When Constantius became sole ruler in 353 and was able to take action against Athanasius, the situation again seemed desperate. The issue was decided by a letter which Athanasius maintained was a forgery from which it appeared that he had been conspiring in the intervening period with a Western usurper. This time even the Western synods were compelled to drop Athanasius, and in spite of the furious opposition of the people of Alexandria an attempt was made to remove him by military force. Athanasius had, however, escaped in good time; he stayed in the city in successful concealment and organized the continuous resistance of his followers. Even when a successor had been appointed the riots went on and the struggle continued.

Looking at the tempestuous outward course of these events, one is tempted to interpret them as struggles for political power in the Church. This is precisely what Athanasius's opponents always maintained. They carefully avoided stressing the theological background of their opposition, and treated Athanasius simply as an obstinate trouble-maker, an intolerant, power-seeking hierarch but for whose wilfulness and violence the Church would have been living undisturbed and at peace.

This method of making purely political and criminal accusations was the surest way of reducing the theological opposition to silence when you had the power of the State on your side. In contrast to these not entirely honest tactics, Athanasius immediately lifted every controversy onto the theological plane. In a tone of supreme indignation he mercilessly declared that anyone who opposed him was a notorious heretic, a 'mad Arian', a blasphemer of Christ goaded by the meanest motives, and an enemy of the true Church. He admitted no doubts about the validity of his own position. The absolute self-confidence of his attack and defence gave his pamphlets the stormy atmosphere and booming echo which he needed for success. Athanasius was a very deliberate and determined propagandist for his cause. It must not, however, be inferred that the theological principles he claimed to be defending were mere pretexts and without any true significance for him. Athanasius believed in what he asserted. But he lacked all sense of the distance between the religious concerns which he represented and the ecclesiastical position that he wanted to hold. He did not really think of the Church as a sacramental institution but in terms of the sacred dogma which sustains it.

To all intents and purposes, however, belief, creed, and the Church—or rather, the ecclesiastical party which supported him —were all one to him. There was no such thing as a creed without followers, and their political exigencies were hallowed by the cause which was the object of the whole struggle. This is what gave rise to the unscrupulousness and self-righteousness and also the passion and reckless courage with which Athanasius fought his life's struggle, sacrificed his security and peace, his reputation and, when the need arose, even his friends. Thus he became the living symbol of orthodoxy and the unconquerable Church. He was the centre from which friend and foe alike had to take their bearings—a better and clearer one than the tangled formulas and decisions of Councils which accompanied the struggle round his personality.

In the main principles of his theology Athanasius remained constant. But the methods with which he carried on his struggle and the way in which he established and confirmed his theological position were subject to development. In his early period he had ingenuously appealed to the Emperor and striven to win his agreement. The personality of the holy Emperor-Liberator impelled him to certain indispensable considerations, though as we have seen his submissiveness to the Emperor had its limits in an emergency. His attitude to Constantius, who had none of his father's superior qualities, was quite different from the very outset. Athanasius was in almost continuous conflict with him, and more and more dropped all consideration for this 'patron of godlessness and Emperor of heresy' (*Hist. Ar.* 45, 4). The fact that the Arians had dared to trouble the Emperor at all with ecclesiastical affairs, that they submitted their synodal decisions to him for his confirmation and mobilized soldiers to enforce them, was now declared to be a 'scandalous crime' contrary to all canonic tradition: 'What has the Emperor to do with the Church?' (*Hist. Ar.* 52, 3). For the first time, the idea of 'Church freedom' was advocated, by Athanasius and his friends, against a Christian ruler. Even when one sees through the tactical motives that lay behind it, this is still a significant fact. From the standpoint of a Eusebian theology such a procedure would never have been possible.

Athanasius also developed in his method of dogmatic controversy. In the early years he hardly made any use of the Nicene Creed. The proofs of the absolute deity of Christ were purely objective and Biblical, and anyone who curtailed them was, as we have seen, at once denounced as an 'Arian', even after Arius himself had long since disappeared from the scene and died or, as Athanasius avers, 'split into pieces in the public lavatory' (De Morte Ar. 3, 3). He only gradually came to see the possibilities which the concept of Homoousios ('of one substance') used in the Nicene Creed contained for his own theological position, whereas it could never be accepted by his Arian and Eusebian opponents. He proceeded regularly to refer to this sacred Council and its Creed as the one sure shield of orthodoxy. He made recognition of its authority the indispensable condition for genuine pacification. Athanasius thus created the conception of the first 'ecumenical' synod. The Nicene, or later the expanded Niceno-Constantinopolitan Creed, has been regarded ever since as the sole or at least the only permanently authoritative and valid Creed of the Christian Faith. Its very exclusiveness and rigidity provided a welcome opportunity for deriding as transparently godless manœuvres the new formulas which were constantly being used by the opponents of Athanasius in their efforts to accommodate themselves to changing circumstances in ecclesiastical politics. According to Athanasius, the truth has long since been discovered and a genuinely serious theology can consist only in the interpretation of what the Church has already established once and for all.

In his own thinking, however, Athanasius remained thoroughly flexible. His obstinacy was not intended to promote the formulas as such, but the cause of his party and of the one unchanging truth concealed in the Nicene symbol. Towards the end of his life he gave an impressive proof of this. At bottom he was interested in only one thing: the complete and absolute divinity and unity with God of the Logos Christ who became man. Because of this he had for a long time left in peace those friends who did not make a clear distinction of any kind between the two divine persons. At first he ignored as a dubious or unnecessary speculation the idea of three interrelated Hypostases within the one divine Being. But theology could not remain static, and once again it was developments in the world of ecclesiastical politics that opened Athanasius's eyes and took him a further step forward.

In the last years of his rule Constantius came nearer and nearer to a radically Arian position, and the policy of 'unification' which he was following no longer affected only Athanasius and the strict upholders of the Nicene Creed. Many members of the former party of the centre and the younger generation of theologians felt no less affronted and attempted to get in touch with like-minded theologians of the 'right' wing in order to obtain their support in the fight against the unscrupulously opportunistic policy of the ruling Churchmen. They might have been able to accept the Nicene Creed but they were afraid of the idea of the complete identity of the divine persons which it seemed to encourage. Thus Athanasius decided to take a firm stand against this interpretation and to acknowledge the feasibility of the three Hypostases, provided that the inseparable unity of the one divine Being was clearly preserved. The decisive offer of peace was made in the year 362 at a synod in Alexandria, the background of which was the change in the Church's situation under the new pagan Emperor Julian. Julian had allowed all the exiles to return and appeared determined to leave the Church entirely to itself and its own bickerings. The policy of coercion pursued hitherto had collapsed, and the way was open for a regrouping and a fresh agreement among the parties. The work of reconciliation was not achieved so quickly as Athanasius had probably hoped; but a beginning was made and the final assembly of the right-wing group which came about years later originated in the policy initiated in the year 362.

To begin with, it was a matter of surviving a new wave of repression on the part of the State. In his attempt to revive the old pagan worship Julian had met the universal resistance of the Church, and Athanasius was the last man to make any sort of concessions to the romantic on the imperial throne. He was soon compelled to vacate his see again. But this kind of thing had apparently ceased to make much impression on him. It is said that he comforted the broken-hearted crowd that pressed around him as he said farewell, with the words that became famous: 'Do not be led astray, brethren; it is but a little cloud and it will quickly pass' (Ruf. *H.E.* I, 34: *Nolite, o filii, conturbari, quia nubicula est et cito pertransibit*). He proved to be right. Once again Athanasius was forced into exile under Julian's 'Arian' successor. Then peace gradually descended on his life. The government had probably reached the conclusion that the simplest thing would be to leave Athanasius in peace in Egypt, in spite of his refractoriness, rather than to inflame the people, who were devoted to him, by repeated intervention. When he died in the year 373 victory had not yet been achieved throughout the Empire, but a few years later the new Emperor Theodosius from the West brought the whole development to a close by declaring that all his subjects were to regard the Nicene Creed as a binding authority. What the strongest political and theological personality in the Church of the fourth century had striven for had become established.

Even to his own contemporaries Athanasius seemed an almost mythical figure; even pagans credited him with supernatural knowledge. In later ages he was regarded as the incomparable 'pillar of the Church', through whom God had protected and preserved the true Faith in a most difficult period (Greg. Naz. *Or.* 21, 26). 'If you find something of the writings of St. Athanasius,' an abbot of the sixth century wrote, 'and you have no paper handy, write it on your clothes' (Joh. Mosch. *Prat. Spir.* 40). His works—the authentic as well as the innumerable unauthentic ones which were put out under the protection of his name—enjoyed a circulation in accordance with his high reputation. From a historical point of view, however, his importance lies not so much in his writings themselves as in the things he defended and sustained by his actions in a life full of tension and disturbance. In an unusually critical moment in the Church's history, when all the old ideas and organizations were being transformed and rebuilt in the new Church of Constantine, he maintained the essential character and spiritual independence of Christianity in his struggles with the emperors and all the authoritative representatives of the theological world. As a result of his labours, belief in Christ remained, in the strictest sense, belief in God and was kept distinct from all pagan, philosophical, and idealistic theories. But for him, as Harnack has said (*Lehrbuch d. Dogmengeschichte* II [1909⁴], 224), the Church would probably have fallen completely into the hands of the philosophers (of the Eusebian type); its creed would have run wild or become an imperial regulation governing the worship of the 'radiant Godhead'. Athanasius saved the Church from becoming entangled in the idea of cultural progress and from the snares of political power. Through him it again became an institute of salvation, that is, a Church in the strict sense of the word, with the preaching of Christ as its essential purpose. It is no accident that the Church came to be regarded as an autonomous body in the legal sense, the independence of which must be preserved in all circumstances.

We have already pointed out that this also involved a new departure within the Church itself. Athanasius was the first Greek Father who did not regard himself as a 'Christian philosopher' but who, even as a theologian, remained the bishop. As such he sought to bridge the gap between theology and the mass of Church members and their devotion. Unlike Clement and Origen, he did not regard spiritual 'perfection' as the affair of a select circle of highly educated Gnostics and intellectuals. He addressed himself to the organized celibates within the Church, he ventured to preach in Coptic, and if he was forced on the one hand to carry the watchwords of the theological conflict to the masses he took their crude ideas of holiness and their belief in miracles as his point of departure. He succeeded in getting in touch with the religious revival movement which erupted from the very depths of the Egyptian people, and so he managed to steer it into the paths of the development and devotion of the Universal Church. That was certainly not the least of his historical services. Athanasius discovered monasticism and gave it the form in which from now on it permeated the Greek Church in its multifarious developments and ramifications and also determined the clerical way of life and the fundamental religious conceptions of the theologians.

The beginnings of Egyptian monasticism are older than Athanasius; they go back to the second half of the third century. The monastic movement was the result of the wholesale conversion of the flat lands, which had hardly been touched by Greek civilization, and of their primitive fellaheen population. These people seized on the old ascetic commandments of the Church with a new enthusiasm and tried to carry them out unconditionally in the deep solitude of the desert rather than inside the local churches. In this respect 'Father' Anthony was only one of many similar contemporary figures. It was Athanasius, who knew him personally, who made him the 'inventor' and prototype of eremitic monasticism. The book in which he described his life introduced the Church to a new phenomenon and stimulated universal imitation and emulation. Even in the story of the conversion of Augustine the *Vita Antonii* plays a part, and innumerable Greek lives of the saints were planned on the pattern which it had established. In his account of Anthony's life Athanasius kept to the facts, but he described monasticism in the way in which he wanted to see and promote it. The little book was not written without apologetic and propagandistic intentions. Without detriment to his simple and original nature, Anthony was presented as the incarnation of the philosophical virtues which are truly to be found only in Christians and can be acquired only through the power and grace of Christ. At the same time he attacked the pagan sages and Arian heretics and showed a profound and sincere regard for all the representatives of the spiritual estate. The saint sets the pattern for the Church by experiencing and effecting the greatest things in his ascetic zeal: he receives illuminations and becomes the instrument of supernatural powers. The ascetic ideal was presented to educated and uneducated alike as a new and alluring way of life, and yet it remained clearly established on Christ and the orthodox teaching of the Church. In this sense Athanasius strove to combine monasticism with Nicene orthodoxy and blended them in the depth of popular feeling and the consciousness of the Church.

The theologians who succeeded Athanasius continued to be Origenists, philosophers, and Greeks. But they did not dissolve the solid unity into which he had fused the claims of dogma, asceticism, and the Church. In the fourth century that unity became universally predominant. Athanasius himself had been above all a dogmatist and a hierarch and as such an ecclesiastical politician. But with him and his generation a new era began in the life of the Greek Church in the inner realm of theology and spiritual life as well.

CHAPTER VII

BASIL THE GREAT

ABOUT the time that Athanasius was made a bishop, possibly ten years before the death of Eusebius of Caesarea, Basil was born. The Church in which Basil grew up was recognized and assisted by the State, and all the political, social, and intellectual currents of the 'world' were coming to be accepted in it. The Church had become an outstanding factor in public life. Its bishops often found themselves in glittering positions and enjoyed public esteem and wealth and extensive spheres of influence. There was a strong tendency to a more cultural and opportunistic type of Christianity, though this was sadly or mockingly criticized by keen-sighted observers both inside and outside the Church. The question as to the religious foundations of the Church which had been raised by the Arian controversy had still not been decided. Many Churchmen were trying to avoid making a decision, by abandoning themselves to general activities with a devotional trimming. On the other hand, the message of Christ was threatening to become the subject of all kinds of theological conflict. The imperial government was endeavouring to limit the boundless tension and controversy and to hold the Church together by occasional decrees, synodal resolutions, and coercive measures. No one's conscience was quite reconciled to all this, but most of the bishops sought somehow to come to terms with the elastic formulas which were being offered or silently to slip out of the predicament. They made a habit of ignoring protests and more or less openly let theology go to the devil. In a period of outwardly brilliant material and cultural progress the Church was threatened with decline and the loss of its conscience. In the process of attempting to master the situation the possibility of responsible action in the future was being slowly but surely blocked.

This is the background against which the personality and work of Basil 'the Great' have to be seen. Basil was essentially an ascetic and a theologian. As such he opened up a path for his endangered contemporaries; but he was in strong and conscious opposition to the great mass of his episcopal colleagues. As a 'young Nicaean', Basil was a follower of the aged Athanasius; he continued his life's struggle in another geographical sphere and in a different theological spirit. But although he personally was spared from exile and serious injury, he found it much more difficult to assert himself, since Cappadocia was nothing like so self-contained an ecclesiastical province as Egypt. Basil had also to contend with greater spiritual problems because he was a far more sensitive nature and a more richly endowed character who felt the ambiguities of the enervating struggle more deeply and suffered more keenly than the inflexible old Patriarch of Alexandria.

As a man and a theologian Basil was not rooted in the clerical world, and his character was not moulded to begin with by the struggles of ecclesiastical politics. Pride and independence were native to him from the very outset. As a Christian he deliberately repressed these qualities, but his self-assurance was based on the memories of a great family and an ancient countryside which was just exposing itself to the Christian life on the broadest front.

According to an often quoted remark of Mommsen's, the formerly Hittite and then Persian province of Cappadocia was 'hardly more Greek at the beginning of the imperial age than Brandenburg and Pomerania were French under Frederick the Great' (*Röm. Gesch.* V, ch. 8). Christianity had been disseminated here by Gregory Thaumaturgus, the disciple of Origen, and may in turn have spread the influence of Hellenism. Both forces, Hellenism and Christianity, were a jointly accepted tradition in Basil's family. His grandparents were Christians and had had to escape for a time during the last persecution under Maximinus. An uncle, then two brothers, were, like Basil himself, made bishops, and his sister Macrina dedicated herself entirely to the ascetic life. Higher education in the Hellenist spirit was as much taken for granted in this family as Christian, that is, Nicene-Christian, education. His father did not want Basil to receive a 'one-eyed' education (Greg. Naz. *Or.* 43, 12) but to enjoy a full classical and philosophical training. In view of the princely wealth of the family, derived from estates which were spread over three provinces, there were no financial obstacles.

Basil began his studies in Cappadocian Caesarea when he was about fifteen years old, and he continued them in Constantinople. He spent the decisive terms in Athens from 351 onwards. Gregory of Nazianzus, with whom he entered upon a lifelong friendship at this period, later recorded how he had saved his friend from the exploitation to which freshmen were usually subjected, and he asserted that in their ardent passion for study they had spent their whole time in the lecture room or in church.

We may take into account, besides the desire for sanctification which Gregory emphasizes, his social position and an early sense of intellectual superiority. At any rate in these years Basil acquired a comprehensive education. His writings show that he retained a lifelong intimacy with Plato, Homer, and the historians and rhetors, and they certainly influenced his style. He felt no embarrassment in his contacts with pagans. He knew the famous orator Libanius personally, and had some correspondence with him. Basil never became an enthusiast for culture like Gregory, however, and as a monk and bishop he later looked back somewhat critically on the 'idle rapture' of the period in Athens (Greg. Naz. *Or.* 43, 11). Basil did not ignore the moral dangers of classical literature, but the advice that he gave to his nephew on what books he should study shows that he was not prepared on that account to renounce the treasures of classical learning. The important thing was to choose one's reading with care. He denied that the pagan writers had anything more than a purely propaedeutic significance (that is, serving as an introduction to higher study), but their usefulness was not limited to the merely formal and aesthetic aspects; they were welcome aids in the moral education of the Christian too.

It seems that Basil himself wavered between the possibilities of the career of a rhetor and his Christian ideals. He returned home 'a ship heavily laden with culture' (Greg. Naz. *Or.* 43, 21). He was sought after on every side, and every public career stood open to him. But he broke resolutely away. He did not want to serve the 'world', and he became baptized in order to begin a purely ascetic life according to the Lord's commandment. It is not quite clear how he came to make this decision. The family tradition, his sister's zealous persuasion, the impression made on him by a journey through the hermitages of Egypt, all these things probably played a part. Basil had also probably received a decisive stimulus from an earlier ascetic movement in his homeland, and especially from a man whom he greatly admired at the time and came to despise later on: Eustathius of Sebaste, in Lesser Armenia. This pioneer of the monastic ideal had also attracted many followers in Cappadocia, so that he was regarded with suspicion by some of the bishops who were but little inclined to intense asceticism. Basil, however, became his disciple. Much of what he taught about the monastic life and the art of spiritual guidance probably derived from Eustathius. The two men separated later on for dogmatic reasons. Eustathius opposed the Nicene Creed and was thereupon decried as an 'Arian'; and at this juncture the Creed was more important for Basil than the old friendship and fellowship in the service of ascetic ideals. He did not want a Christianity that ignored dogma.

To be understood, Basil must nevertheless be studied primarily as a monk. He was an ascetic, body and soul; strict asceticism was the element in which he lived and moved and had his spiritual being. He was an ascetic to the extent to which it is possible to be one without conflicting with the Church and its Christian doctrine. He respected these limits throughout his life, however, and in Cappadocia this was not unimportant. Basil never turned the monastic life against the Church, never believed it was impossible for married Christians to be saved, as the followers of Eustathius came to do. For him even the strictest asceticism was not dualistically motivated in a Marcionite or Manichaean sense. Basil remained in this a 'Greek'. Doubtless, his thinking was based on the antithesis between flesh and spirit, earth and heaven, time and eternity, and the eschatological point of view always played a very vital part in his theological thinking; but the physical and temporal world was, in his view, not evil in itself, but merely a constant incitement to evil. Only that life is completely meaningful that is based on the spirit, on God and his blessed eternity. But by striving after this goal and subjecting himself to hard training and self-discipline the monk does not destroy his true human self. On the contrary, his true self is liberated, furnished with wings, and raised up beyond the constricting barriers, that it may give itself wholly to God, see God, and become one with God.

This conception derives from Neoplatonic metaphysics and the ideas of Basil's beloved master, Origen. But Basil lays greater emphasis than all his predecessors, with the possible exception of Clement, on the point that the real power of this liberated life is not merely knowledge but love, love not only in the 'theological' sense of love for God but also love for one's neighbour. For Basil the monastic life is therefore fundamentally a life in community where all can serve one another and each can be helped and developed by the other, thus becoming the true life in which all human potentialities are sublimated, the Christian life par excellence.

What happened in fact is that Basil retired to the estates which his family owned on the river Iris and where his mother and sister had already been living for a long time in pious seclusion. He gathered together like-minded companions who submitted to his leadership and established further monasteries to which he offered spiritual instruction and advice. The dis-

cipline was strict, obedience absolute, humility in all things the
spiritual goal. In addition to spiritual contemplation the monks
did simple manual labour. A return to the world was impossible. But the spirit and atmosphere of these communities were
not intended to be ridden with rules and regulations: the
brethren lived in freedom of the spirit. Prayer is the sustaining
power of monastic life; the fixed hours of praise and prayer
give it a rhythmic pattern. The greatest importance was attached to the interchange of the brothers. In their meetings they
were able to air their various desires, problems, and questions
quite freely. They were able to have their own spiritual counsellors and later on themselves became the spiritual counsellors
of other monks. The regular practice of monastic confession
derives above all from Basil. This life did not exclude delight
in intellectual work and theological knowledge. For most of
the brothers, however, the central activity was the study of the
Bible and especially of the writings of Paul and the Synoptic
Gospels. It was, however, at this time that Basil compiled the
Anthology from Origen's writings in co-operation with his
friend Gregory.

As a monk Basil was wholly himself. The powers with which
he was able to overcome the ever-present temptations, to know
God's truth and enjoy every 'divine beauty', increased in the
beloved peace and quiet of the cloister. The famous letter (*Ep.
14, ad Greg.*) in which he tried to entice Gregory, who was still
living at a distance, to join him is a surprising document in this
respect. The description of his hermitage, which offers him a
splendid view high up in the valley near a waterfall, and has
given him peace at last in the midst of the unsullied freshness
of nature, is the first deeply-felt description of a landscape
known to the Western world—an ancient idyll which has
something of a foreboding mystery that places it outside all
traditional categories.

Anyone who is able to enjoy solitude to that extent cannot
expect it to last for ever. Basil was far too much a man of action,
or at least of actively moral responsibility, to be able to stay

undisturbed for ever in this beloved way of life. Theological cares and obligations drew him irresistibly back into the public life of the Church. At this period the Emperor's anti-Nicene policy had just reached its most relentless stage. In the year 360 Basil accompanied Eustathius to Constantinople for negotiations on dogmatic matters. The Nicene party was not quite so weak as it seemed, but it lacked the courage to declare itself openly. Two years later Basil received the penitent confession of his own bishop, who had betrayed the Nicene Creed but called Basil to his deathbed.

The new Bishop Eusebius of Caesarea (in Cappadocia, not Palestine, where the famous Eusebius had been bishop) succeeded in drawing Basil into the full-time service of the Church. In the year 364 he was ordained presbyter. The proud country nobleman was probably not a comfortable subordinate; perhaps his ascetic zeal also made him distrusted. Tensions soon arose between the presbyter and his bishop, with the result that Basil, who had no desire for quarrels within the Church, suddenly decided to return to his hermitage.

This interruption did not, however, last for long. Eusebius himself sought for a reconciliation, and Basil did not hesitate to come to terms with him. The Church needed his work. He now rapidly grew into the role of a coadjutor of his bishop, and as such it was his task to administer a large diocese. He did not evade the irritating details and guerilla warfare of everyday life in the Church. As usual, everywhere there was a lack of really useful clergy, conscientious preachers, and selfless rulers. Out of sheer laziness the Church had often appointed quite unsuitable men to positions of responsibility. Offices had been bought and cases of bribery had occurred; there were married clergy who refused to give up their wives, and besides all the dogmatic conflicts there were the usual party bickerings, slander, and gossip. Basil took strong action where it was a question of re-inforcing hitherto neglected ecclesiastical regulations. But he always tried to give intelligible reasons for his measures. He discussed them with his bishops, and whenever complaints were made he was always willing to take the blame himself. A generous nature, with an innate dignity, he had no difficulty in achieving a true balance between the demands his office made on him and the personal humility he had to maintain as a Christian and a monk. Basil became the first great representative of the monastic ideal of the priest and bishop, to whom the age that followed referred back again and again.

He soon became popular with the people of Caesarea. He created, no doubt very largely from his own resources, a whole complex of charitable welfare institutions. There arose a whole 'new city' (Greg. Naz. Or. 43, 63) of neighbourly love and social care grouped around the church and monastery, consisting of hostels, almshouses, and hospitals for infectious diseases, and the bishop himself took up residence there. The foundation was imitated and much admired, and also criticized. It was regarded as a threat to the independence of the State administration, an objection which Basil himself refused to accept. The early Christian activity in works of love was acquiring new 'medieval' dimensions in the imperial Church; the spirit that inspired these works of charity was more monastic than political and hierarchic. It was not intended that the laity should sink back into passivity. Basil's sermons were full of practical exhortations and examples, stimulating to acts of Christian love and the practice of virtue. Especially during the great famine of the year 368 he proved his mettle in impressive sermons against the profiteers and the indifferent rich. He himself organized free meals for the people which were also available to immigrant foreigners, pagans, and even the infidel children of Israel.

It would be wrong, however, to judge Basil primarily as an ecclesiastical man of action and an administrator. In the midst of his affairs and above all in his preaching he was always at the same time the pastor and the theologian. Basil is regarded as the initiator of the formal sermon in Greek. He deliberately moulded the religious address according to the rules of rhetoric, thus establishing a precedent. This carefully cultivated oratorical splendour, with its artificial and flowery display, is something quite strange to us today in religious diction; what is far more fascinating in Basil is the vigorous down-to-earthness, the precision and simplicity of his basic ideas, which nevertheless distinguish his sermons. Nearly all of them are based on Biblical texts. The moral sermon predominates, but even the theological sermons are not purely theoretical and 'dogmatic' in the bad sense of the word. They reflect the actual dogmatic conflicts of the contemporary Church in which Basil had to take a stand and in which he soon gained a position of authority.

In the year 370 he was made Archbishop of Caesarea, and from that time on the whole responsibility and worry of the confused situation in the Church rested above all on him. At this juncture there was no such thing as a united Nicene front. Basil himself used the simile of two fighting fleets which have been whirled together by the tempest so that it is impossible to distinguish friend from foe. It was only through his influence that Cappadocia slowly became something like a bulwark of the orthodox Church, though the conflict still raged all around it. The government's ecclesiastical policy was still heading in another direction and everywhere put obstacles in the way of Basil whose instructions were to co-operate with the political authorities. The division of the province of Cappadocia, which was intended to lessen the ecclesiastical influence of Caesarea, must also be mentioned here. Basil refused to be intimidated. He travelled in person from place to place, trying to tie the threads more closely together, establishing new dioceses, and conducting an indefatigable correspondence in all directions. The tension reached its climax when the Emperor Valens made a personal visit to Caesarea. It was expected that Basil would either surrender or go into exile. He did neither. It seems that the calm determination with which he stood up to the autocrat persuaded the Emperor to move cautiously and avoid a conflict. Nicene orthodoxy was gaining ground all the time in Cappadocia.

The successes which Basil achieved are to be reckoned the

more highly inasmuch as to begin with his position was anything but secure. Unlike Athanasius, he did not possess a band
of blindly devoted followers ready to go with him through
thick and thin. Perhaps he would not have wanted that kind of
support. His successes were primarily the fruit of the genuine
ecclesiastical and theological work which he carried out with
his friends, building on the foundation of the earlier Nicene-
Origenistic tradition of the country. Basil realized that the conflict with the Arians was due to an elemental conflict of belief.
Christ cannot be a creature if he is to make available the salvation of the Creator. He was really God's Son before all time
and God by nature, who came down to our poor humanity to
redeem lost mankind from the power of death and the devil
and to restore the freedom on which the new Christian life,
transfigured by grace, is based. Basil was a fully convinced
Trinitarian theologian and saw in the doctrine of the Trinity the
very essence of the Christian religion. He began therefore with
a systematic clarification of the relationships which exist within
the Godhead. Going beyond Athanasius, he underlined the
Trinity of the 'Hypostases', the segregating peculiarities of
which do not destroy the unity and completeness of the divine
Life. He also meditated on their mutual relationship. Such reflections never became an end in themselves; they were not
driven to death. There must always be a meaning which can at
least be conjectured behind dogmatic statements, and above all
they must be based on the Scriptures. In spite of the pressure
of his friends and enemies, Basil refused to make more precise
assertions about the person of the Holy Spirit which would
have been mere words. It is true that for him, as for Origen,
the Holy Spirit unquestionably has its place alongside the
Father and the Son. In the scale of being, that there can be
nothing between the uncreated Godhead and the creature is a
foregone conclusion, to which he repeatedly drew attention.
Nevertheless he avoided as far as possible roundly describing
the Spirit as 'God', and he was quite silent about the Spirit's
peculiar position within the Trinity. On the contrary, he

'confesses without fear' that the best thing and also the least 'dangerous' is frankly to admit one's ignorance (*Contra Sab. et Ar.* 24, 6).

We come across such admonitions in Basil again and again. There is not the least naïveté in this deliberate confinement to the 'simplicity of sound belief'. Basil realizes that the mania for controversy has brought the Church to the edge of the abyss and dissolution. He wants to avoid adding any new fuel to the fire of boundless dispute; he wants rather to set bounds to all the scholastic logic-chopping and lead the faithful to spiritual composure and adoring praise of the mystery of God. This was in his view the real purpose of all theology. Where the Bible is silent, theologians should be silent too and not upset people with their splitting of hairs. Man knows God by keeping his commandments, by knowing the Good Shepherd who gave his life for the sheep, and 'not by asking questions about supramundane things, and not by pondering over the things one cannot see' (*Hom. in Mam. Mart.* 4). These are unmistakably monastic motifs, pointed by the bitter experiences of a long ecclesiastical struggle. Only Basil had no wish to escape altogether from theology and end up with a mere *praxis pietatis*. He wanted to establish the foundations for the fruitful kind of theology which would draw together all true and serious theologians.

To this extent his reserve on matters of dogma also had a significance for church politics. This is especially clear in relation to the doctrine of the Spirit. Basil made the greatest efforts to win over the so-called Pneumatomachians, who appealed to Nicaea and refused to accept the divinity of the Holy Spirit, which had not been expressly formulated there. He also tried to enter into discussion with representatives of the so-called Centre Party and with many doctrinal individualists. His efforts were not without success, but it is not surprising that the liberality of an attitude with both theological and ecclesiastical significance did not make things any easier for a Churchman who had to maintain his position in the midst of party warfare. Basil's lack of principle, or his spiritual pride, was commented on in all kinds of quarters, though he attempted to refute the criticism again and again by always offering to enter conversations and discussions. A highly important factor was that Athanasius gave Basil his utmost support. In spite of certain theological differences, he had discerned the outstanding significance of this comrade in arms and acknowledged it throughout his life.

Basil realized from the outset that the Church's dogmatic problems could not be solved on a particularistic basis. It is true that it would have been comparatively easy for him to keep to his own Cappadocian circle, where his authority was unquestioned anyway. But he would have regarded that as a betrayal of the common cause of all Christians. Basil required an 'ecumenical' outlook of all bishops. Contrary to appearances, there is a unity, a single voice of the true believers throughout the world. The important thing is to be seriously concerned about 'the brotherhood which exists everywhere' (*Ep. 133 ad Petr. Alex.*), which puts its members in touch with one another and thereby makes the unity visible and effective. This was the end served by Basil's gigantic and ever-increasing correspondence. 'Ask the Pisidians, Lycaonians, and Isaurians, the inhabitants of both parts of Phrygia, the Armenians, in so far as they are your neighbours, the Macedonians, Greeks, Illyrians, Gauls, Spaniards, the whole of Italy, the Sicilians, Africans, the sound centre part of Egypt and what is left of [orthodox] Syria, who all send letters to me and also receive replies from me': this is what Basil once wrote to Pontus (*Ep. 204, 7 ad Neocaes.*).

Apart from the old bulwarks of orthodoxy, Rome and Alexandria, a new centre arose in which, as was soon to appear, an independent line was to be followed. All Basil's endeavours were based on the assumption that the important thing was to apply the weight of the Nicene West to a corresponding reformation of the Eastern Church, though preserving the latter's character and theological comprehensiveness as far as possible. He overcame the innate pride of the Greek and turned to his

Western colleagues for help, imploring their 'sympathy'. He turned above all to the most important of them, Bishop Damasus of Rome.

There were special difficulties to be overcome in Antioch, and it was here that Basil hoped the Pope would intervene in the first instance. The great majority of the orthodox Antiochenes acknowledged Bishop Meletius as their bishop. After some initial doubts he had come out clearly on the side of the Nicene Creed. Unfortunately, however, a small band of irreconcilable old campaigners had championed a stricter adherent of the Nicene Creed. The opposition between old and young Nicaeans which Athanasius had overcome had broken out in the capital of Syrian Christianity again. It became more intense and threatened to wreck the whole work of unification. Basil at once supported Meletius. He knew very well that the West, which found it almost impossible to grasp the finer distinctions which caused these dogmatic conflicts, inclined to the opposition party and would have preferred to speak quite plainly of the one divine Hypostasis. But he took the view that now that theological peace between the two orthodox camps had been declared it was possible to reckon on Rome's understanding and to win Damasus's support for the one feasible method of reaching a settlement. He was mistaken. Damasus, who has been called the 'first Pope' and who almost had the outward airs of a prince, was only moderately interested in theological problems; to him church unification meant, in a sentence, favouring partisans of Rome and securing subjection to Papal authority. The negotiations were therefore inconclusive, to begin with. Basil gave vent to his feeling about this way of caring for the churches in these bitter words: 'I am reminded of the words of Diomedes (Il. IX, 698 f.): It is futile to implore, for the man is presumptuous' (Ep. 215 ad Euseb. Sam.). In other respects too Basil was driven to the brink of bitterness and contempt in his struggle with the hydra of the party spirit. But he did not slacken his efforts, and gradually he gained ground.

Basil himself was not to attain the goal of his endeavours. He wore himself out before his time. Ill and suffering from a liver complaint, like so many ascetics, he died at the age of about fifty in the year 379. Two years later there took place in Constantinople, under the chairmanship of Meletius, the so-called second Ecumenical Council, which the Emperor Theodosius the Great used in order to reorganize the Eastern Church on the lines laid down by the Nicene Creed. Athanasius and Basil had already laid the ecclesiastical and theological foundations. Theodosius, the Westerner, had also, in the beginning, based his policy on the Rome-Alexandria 'axis' but quickly changed his mind. As Basil had wished, he now opened the gates of the revived Imperial Church to everyone who accepted the Nicene Creed, and he ignored the protests of the steadfast old Nicaeans of East and West. But this was a settlement brought about for purely practical reasons. At the critical moment ecclesiastical politics proved far stronger than theology. If Basil had still been alive things would probably have taken a different and happier course. The age of the epigoni was dawning.

Basil's true greatness becomes apparent only when he is studied in the context of the conflicts of his age and his role is properly understood. As an ecclesiastical politician Basil did not display the rocklike strength of Athanasius; as a theologian he did not possess the harmony and universality of his younger brother, Gregory of Nyssa; as a monk he did not possess the subtle refinement of some of the later mystics. But these things must not be interpreted as signs of natural incapacity or a weakness in his character. On the contrary, it was his very devotion to the needs of the hour, the necessity of adapting himself to the difficulties of his situation, which compelled him constantly to vary his tactics and made it impossible for him to develop his rich talents in peace or follow the bent of his spirit as he wished. He found his work as an ecclesiastical politician so difficult because he was not only wiser and more far-seeing but also more profound and more honest than most of his colleagues.

It is thanks to him in the first place that the State Church of the Nicenes, which had been built so quickly, not only celebrated easy victories but retained a real theological life and intellectual freedom. Whereas others never progressed beyond the theology of their school, never saw beyond their party interests and purely material considerations, Basil had always kept in view the whole life of the Church. He suffered from the narrow-mindedness and lack of spiritual insight of his fellow-bishops far more than those who were too other-worldly, too sensitive, or too complacent to enter the fray themselves. And Basil discerned, beyond the worries and problems of the moment, profound changes which had to be accepted. He realized it was impossible to put the clock back.

From the historical point of view this is perhaps the most interesting aspect of his character. Basil sensed the gulf that had arisen between the intentions and desires of the present and the original spirit of Christianity. Again and again he contrasts the sins of the present with the Church as once it had been. The longing for an ideal original Christianity corresponded in his theology to the longing for eternal perfection. That is why Basil became a monk. The monastic community revived for him, within a strictly limited sphere, the life of the early Church, and his intention was that the monastic life should influence the whole Church in this direction. The idea was that in monastic life the spiritual gifts, the primal love, the devoted intensity of mutual relationships, should flourish once again. This was the purpose behind the so-called 'Rule' which he formulated. Monastic asceticism was regarded as the way to the radicalism and sanctity of the early Church. And Basil also hoped that this would lead to a revival of theology. The endless dogmatic arguments and disputes were no longer concerned, in his view, with the substance and basic problems of the Christian Faith. What was needed was an attempt to return to the beginnings again, to the eternal validities, to overcome the dissension and the errors of the heretics from within. The emphatic Biblicism to which Basil withdrew again and again was rooted in this conviction. It was a confession of faith in the old ecclesiastical tradition.

Both factors, the Bible and tradition, had already played an important part in the Church in the second century. They were closely related in Origen. But whereas he saw the task as one of advancing ever further away from tradition, Basil turned back rather to Irenaeus. Basil stood for confinement rather than further expansion. It was only the heretics' mania for innovation that made it necessary to evolve more and more complicated formulas. In their vain jealousy the professional theologians set their 'traps' not for the sake of truth but for the mere sake of argument (*De Spir. S.* 1). 'We refuse to accept a new faith, prescribed to us by others; but we are not bold enough to transmit the products of our own thinking and to turn the word of religion into human words. As we have been taught by the holy Fathers so we proclaim it to those who inquire of us' (*Ep. 140, 2 ad Eccl. Ant.*). Dogma and tradition again assume a decidedly defensive purpose, as a shield and safeguard. Indefatigably Basil advises all Christians to keep to the Nicene Creed and not be lured away from it by any subtle, captious questions.

Karl Holl speaks in this connection of a perceptible 'aging of Hellenism'. The expression does not seem quite appropriate. It was not Hellenism that had grown old and tired, at least not in the person of Basil the Great, but the burden of the ecclesiastical situation and the advances in theology had begun to weigh heavily on the freedom of research and were forcing theologians to consolidate and contain their energies rather than make fresh advances. What now seemed pre-eminently necessary was the stabilizing and stability of dogma, a clear commitment to the Bible and authoritative traditions. It is clear that this old necessity meant something different in the fourth century from what it did in the age of Justin or Clement, of Origen or even Eusebius of Caesarea. To that extent there is a sense in which it is true to say that the Greek Church had aged, because its theological traditions had aged and one does feel that an epoch in the Church's history was coming to an end. Basil felt the gravity of the situation, but amidst the almost desperate dangers of the time he thought above all of the need to concentrate all available forces against the heretics and to restore peace in the Church, that it might lead a truly spiritual life again. He was not concerned with the fate of theology in the future because he was truly absorbed in its present life and felt a strong sense of responsibility to give it all he could of his own spiritual vitality.

In the year 368 Basil wrote an obituary notice on Bishop Musonius of Neo-Caesarea which paints in noble diction and with rhetorical verve the picture of a leading bishop whom he came nearest to resembling himself. 'Is there', he asks (*Ep. 28, 1 ad Eccl. Neocaes.*), 'in the life of this man any feature which ought to be forgotten or silently concealed? I cannot mention everything at once and yet I am afraid of not doing justice to the truth by rendering a piecemeal account. A man has gone from us who surpassed all his contemporaries in human capacity; he was the support of his homeland, the adornment of his churches, a pillar and bulwark of the truth, a firm support of the Christian Faith, a loyal helper of his friends, an unconquerable might of resistance to his enemies, a keeper of the statutes of the Fathers, and an enemy of all innovation. He embodied in his own person the ancient pattern of the Church; he moulded the life of the Church set under him according to the original holy prototype. Those who were privileged to live with him might think they had lived with the men who illuminated the world like stars two hundred and more years ago.'

CHAPTER VIII

GREGORY OF NAZIANZUS

It is traditional to combine in the trinity of the 'great Cappadocians' Basil and his slightly older friend Gregory of Nazianzus and his younger brother Gregory of Nyssa. But Basil was the outstanding figure, the leader and guide of his friends and collaborators. Gregory of Nazianzus became his follower and sought his help; he also regarded him as his teacher theologically. With deep intensity, he took up the new ascetic piety for which Basil enlisted supporters, and was equally anxious to see it influential in the Church. Gregory was not, however, a dominating personality and was constantly being thwarted by the hard and common realities which he ignored in his thinking. He was a rhetorician, a man of letters and something of a poet, a soft lyrical nature who was always dependent on the company and response of other people, one of those personalities that cannot live without sympathy and admiration. This was what impelled him into the public life of the Church, which constituted for him, by his upbringing and conviction, the whole of his world. But the stormy times did not allow him to develop his talents in peace and constantly involved him, a man who was strong only in his words, in tasks to which he was not equal and which he had to give up. Disappointment and defeat, retreat and flight from the obligations he had undertaken, were always the end; to make up for all his troubles and pains he sings the praises of the solitary life, of the life of 'philosophical' monastic contemplation, of richness and silence in God, with all the greater enthusiasm. The fact that Gregory's nervous, oratorical nature made it impossible for him ever to be really silent made the situation all the more painful; all his personal bitterness, vanity, and bad temper found expression in a never-ending run of skilfully turned effusions and reflections.

There was nothing heroic about Gregory. To be just to him one must study him as he was in his private life. There one perceives, in spite of everything, a purity of intention, a delicacy of moral feeling and, with all his introspectiveness, a genuine sensitivity which remained capable of compassion and deep religious devotion to the end. Gregory's nature was extroverted and declamatory, but he was not shallow and he knew as well as Basil, and perhaps even better, the meaning of the spiritual life.

He was at home in the same intellectual and social milieu as Basil and many of his friends. He came from the same rich nobility of Cappadocia which gave to the country its bishops and to this ancient people a sudden and surprising impetus by bringing them into touch with the Christian Faith and Greek culture. Gregory also grew up in a Christian tradition. His father, Gregory, had originally been a Hypsistarian, an adherent of a hybrid Jewish-pagan sect which believed in the imageless worship of the 'supreme' God; but his mother was a zealous Christian and had secured her husband's conversion. He had then been made bishop of the country town of Nazianzus. Gregory was born not far from there, on one of his parents' country estates at Arianzus, in 329–30. He was the ardently longed-for late offspring of a marriage which had long been childless and was, as he himself records, 'given up' and dedicated 'to the Lord' (Or. I, 77) by his mother from the very beginning. The intensive religious education which he received fell on fertile soil. Gregory never seriously pursued 'worldly' ideals. He wanted to live wholly for the Saviour who had redeemed him, and he found the word of God 'sweeter than honey'. But 'the world' in which he developed was no longer a pagan world. With a voracious appetite the gifted youth devoured all the cultural good things that were offered to him in the schools of Caesarea in Palestine, in Alexandria, and above all in Athens. In Athens he lived in a close and 'holy' fellowship

with Basil, who arrived there somewhat later. At that time
Gregory still thought of himself as the older and superior of the
two. He took his younger fellow-countryman under his wing,
introduced him to academic life, and tried to protect him from
the temptations of his environment. Inwardly, however, he
gave himself up to the intellectual delights of study with much
greater abandon than his quiet young friend. For Gregory intellectual culture, poetry, conversation, and art were life itself,
provided that the poisonous saps of paganism were drawn off
from the moral and aesthetic contents of classical literature and
that one was prepared to offer to Christ all the light and help
one gained from it. 'The wisdom of the Holy Spirit that comes
from above and derives from God, must rightly be the mistress
of all the lower kinds of culture' (*Carm. II, 2, 8 ad Seleucum*,
245 ff. This poem attributed to Gregory was probably written
by his younger cousin Amphilochius of Iconium; but it breathes
his spirit).

The term 'lower' culture used in this poem was meant entirely in the traditional sense of the word. Gregory took over
the cultural ideals of late antiquity, with its formalized rhetorical techniques and innumerable moral and philosophical plati-
tudes. But he also appropriated the classical texts, above all the
poetry of Homer and the tragedians, with lively enthusiasm and
with the assurance of the born orator, for whom it is a pleasure
to revive the old forms and apply them in a hundred different
ways. Gregory's knowledge of literature was unusually wide
and rich. He also had a philosophical training, but this did not
make him an independent thinker and scholar. He became a
rhetor. His numerous religious speeches and addresses were not
sermons on Biblical texts but oratorical masterpieces consisting
of official lectures, encomiums, memorial and funeral addresses
and addresses delivered on all kinds of ecclesiastical and personal
occasions. He can clearly be shown to have taken into account
the oratorical rules in the way he constructed his speeches and
developed his subject. He used in abundance the methods of
the contemporary 'Asian' style, comparisons and antitheses,

consonance and parallel rhythms, in mostly short sentences, displaying all the skill of the oratorical virtuoso. It is difficult for us to enjoy these much-admired addresses today. But they are thoroughly characteristic of Gregory's style. They surprise us by their constant and almost childlike self-centredness. Alongside the uninhibited description of the author's own character, opinions, and feelings, there is much self-praise but also self-accusation and extensive moralistic and psychological reflection. Nevertheless, they were intended to be spiritual and devotional works: they constantly introduce references to Biblical examples, words, and images, and everything is set in the light of eternity. They often close with a prayerful adoration of the Holy Trinity.

Needless to say, Gregory too attacked the Arian heresy in his addresses. He declared that the doctrine of God—that is, the orthodox confession of the Trinity—was the heart of the Christian Faith and of all true religion. In smooth, beautifully balanced formulas he unhesitatingly professed his faith in the essential unity of the three divine Hypostases. 'The Godhead is worshipped in the Trinity and the Trinity is gathered into a unity. It is worshipped as a whole and has royal power, sharing a single throne and a single glory, supramundane, supratemporal, uncreated, invisible, untouchable and incomprehensible, known only to itself as far as its inner structure is concerned, but worthy of our reverence and worship' (*Or.* VI, 22). 'To curtail the Trinity even a little is equivalent to destroying it completely, as though one were to make an assault on the doctrine of God altogether and with uncovered head' (*Or.* VI, 11). Gregory lays far more stress on the divine status of the Holy Spirit than did Basil, who hesitated to commit himself. For Gregory, with his Origenist training, the world of the spiritual and the spirit is the fundamental realm of religion. The Holy Spirit of God must liberate our spirit from its earthly fetters, and the ultimate goal of the Christian life is some day to become wholly divine.

No one was attacked and condemned by Gregory with such

anger and personal bitterness as the Emperor Julian the Apostate. Out of hatred for him, Gregory described his enemy, the 'Arian' Emperor Constantius, almost as a paragon of piety and virtue. Julian had issued the order which forbade Christians to be taught the classics. He was the worst kind of tyrant because he wanted 'to obstruct our education'; he was a hateful pioneer of folly because he hoped to triumph with unequal weapons in the struggle for the truth (Or. IV, 6). Gregory's personal interests were touched here. For him what he called 'Attic' education was a vital necessity and a vital element, and the more he failed to achieve a balance between the Attic and the Christian ideals at a deeper level, the more violently he protested when the classical values were turned against the Christian Faith. In his view the victory and the superiority of the Church would best be shown in its complete adoption of the traditions of classical culture. If Gregory sometimes acts as though he did not really care much for pagan wisdom, all that this indicates is a very slight sense of uncertainty. Such remarks need not be taken more seriously than the equally common and typically rhetorical assertion that his sole desire is to speak plainly and to the point, leaving on one side all the superficial brilliance of artificial eloquence. In fact he still regarded rhetoric as a 'weapon of virtue' in the hands of an honest man (Or. IV, 30).

Soon after Basil had left Athens, to devote himself again for a short time to the life of the world, Gregory decided to devote himself entirely to the 'theoretical' devotion and 'philosophy' of the monks: he made up his mind to go into quiet retreat. The exact dates are uncertain. This decision, he later remarked, might seem difficult to appreciate, but anyone who had ever been seized by the same longing would understand. It now seemed to him an incomparably wonderful thing 'to hold converse only with one's own self and with God' and to 'live one's life beyond the confines of the things one can see'. He wanted always to preserve 'these divine inspirations, unsullied by the impressions and the deceits of the world, and to be, and constantly to become afresh, a truly unblemished mirror of God and the divine realities'. He wanted 'to add light to his light and receive brightness to replace the twilight, enjoying already by hope the blessings of the world to come; to have intercourse with the angels and, whilst sojourning on the earth, yet be taken away from it and be raised up to heaven by the Spirit' (Or. II, 7). It appears, however, that Gregory was not able to carry out his intentions. His parents wanted to have him with them in Nazianzus, and he was unable to leave them. He was baptized and in the end, at the request of the Church, consecrated presbyter by his own father. He must of course have given his consent in some way or other; all his complaints about having been forced into it and about his father's 'tyranny' cannot alter that (*Carm. I, 1, 11 de vita sua 345*). But he had hardly been ordained when he left the Church in protest, and retired to the Iris with Basil, to recuperate in solitude and to be inspired by his friend with new confidence and courage. He then returned and explained the reasons for his behaviour in no less than three pompous addresses. He had now, he declared, overcome his 'cowardice and weakness' (*Or.* I, 2). Fundamentally, they had only been the result of an overestimation of the spiritual office from which the pious were often the first to shrink back (*Or.* II). Now he had returned, but the congregation which had torn him away from his beloved solitude had not, unfortunately, responded to his sacrificial love with the love that was due in return and had thereby hurt him deeply (*Or.* III, 1-5). It is almost impossible to discover from these oratorical tirades and inflated private feelings what he really meant and what was behind the flow of words.

It was not long before the dogmatic conflicts began to beat upon Nazianzus. Gregory's own father had allowed himself to be misled into denying the Nicene Creed by signing the 'peace' formula which was laid before him. This led to disturbances in the Church in which monks took a leading part. But Gregory succeeded in inducing his father to make a new, orthodox declaration and to restore good relations. He also celebrated this event with a great speech. On the whole, Gregory had no liking for dogmatic quarrels, especially when they infected people outside the circle of expert theologians. He strove rather to appease than to incite the Church. He realized that there are limits to the desire for peace in Church affairs, but he did not believe in taking action out of mere distrust. 'Patience is better than rashness' (*Or*. VI, 20), and one must bear in mind those members of the Church whose faith is still not robust. The Church must express its orthodoxy 'not so much in words as in deeds' (*Or*. III, 7). Gregory's efforts for peace were purposeful and by no means fickle and unprincipled. But they do sometimes seem rather sentimental and personal. Even in church he was always speaking about his own feelings, his love for the Church and the worship of the common Father. This was connected with his deep need for friendship. He loved his younger brother Caesarius tenderly, and there was something ecstatic about his relationship with Basil. 'If I have gained anything from my life, it is my friendship and association with you!' (*Ep. 58, 1 ad Basil*). He was all the more deeply hurt by any difference of opinion with his friends or by any injustice, real or imagined, that was done to him.

Basil responded sincerely to Gregory's friendship but did not become infatuated. After he became Bishop of Caesarea ecclesiastical politics kept him very busy, and it is not surprising that he now tried to draw his friend Gregory into closer political association with him. Through the partition of the ecclesiastical province of Cappadocia, his power had been grievously weakened. He tried to fortify the fluctuating position of the Nicaeans by establishing new bishoprics. So Gregory should be made a bishop: the small, disputed frontier village of Sasima, in the neighbourhood of Nazianzus, should be kept loyal through him. This was a mistake. Basil should have taken into account his friend's character and limitations instead of making straight for the goal with his usual determined energy. At first, however, Gregory submitted and allowed himself to be consecrated (372). He began to resist violently only when the moment came to enter seriously upon the duties of his office. In the end he escaped to the mountains resentful, unhappy and depressed. He never took up his duties in Sasima, and years later his anger would break out when he came to speak of this episode. What presumption it was, he declared, to transplant him, Gregory, for purely political ends, to such a God-forsaken post town where no green leaf and no free man could thrive!

> *The spiritual welfare of the faithful formed the pretext;*
> *but lust for power was the real reason—*
> *not to mention interest and tax money,*
> *for which the world tears itself to pieces.*
>
> (*Carm. II, 1, 11, de vita sua 460 ff.*)

It is not an attractive spectacle, this attempt on Gregory's part to conceal his own failure by making the most unworthy charges against the dead friend whom he had always praised so highly. But it was his misfortune that he could never refuse the ecclesiastical tasks which were offered him, partly from a sense of duty and partly from vanity and weakness. If he had been more independent and less considerate he would have saved himself considerable embarrassment and many a painful exposure of his impotence.

This time too the pause for breath did not last long. For the second time Gregory was unable to withstand his father's fervent entreaties. He went back to Nazianzus to work as a kind of coadjutor until his father died, almost a hundred years old, in the year 374. Gregory refused to become his successor, and when his mother died too in the following year there was nothing to keep him in the desolate town so he retired to Seleucia in Isauria, where he pursued his intellectual and theological interests for a few years in the manner of an ascetic, conducting an extensive correspondence with his fellow Nicaeans throughout the world. They turned to him and he had to advise them. After the death of Basil, Gregory had become the leading authority for many of the young Nicaeans. But even now he was not happy. Although not yet fifty years old, he was lonely and exhausted. There is something moving about his hypochondriac complaints: 'You ask how I am,' he writes to a rhetor friend. 'Well, I am very bad. Basil I have no longer, Caesarius I have no longer; my spiritual and my physical brothers are both dead. "My father and mother have left me," I can say with David. Physically I am ill, age is descending on my head. Cares are choking me; affairs oppress me; there is no reliance on friends and the Church is without shepherds. The good is vanishing; evil shows itself in all its nakedness. We are travelling in the dark; there is no lighthouse and Christ is asleep. What can one do? I know only one salvation from these troubles, and that is death. But even the world to come seems terrible to judge by the present world' (*Ep. 80 ad Eudoxium*: this is the complete text of this beautifully written little letter).

In fact the great change for which Basil had striven all his life was now imminent, and it was to give Gregory another chance to act. It was to take him for the first time beyond the sphere of Asia Minor and put him for a brief while in the very centre of events in the Church.

The disaster of the Battle of the Visigoths at Adrianople (378), in which the Emperor Valens had lost his life, had had an important effect on the organization of the Church. Theodosius the Great, an orthodox Spaniard, had succeeded to the imperial throne, and the reformation of the Church in accordance with Nicene theology was now only a matter of time. The Emperor was still residing in the Latin West, but Gregory was already receiving from various quarters an invitation to accept the small Nicene church at Constantinople, which was without a pastor, so as to fill the vacuum in the capital city, which had been occupied by an Arian for the past forty years. To his followers, Gregory seemed the best, most representative man available for the post, and he accepted the appointment, under protest and from 'compulsion' as usual, but, all the same, he accepted it. This time a refusal would in fact have been justified on tactical grounds, in view of the risks involved in the obscure political situation then prevailing in the Church. One has the impression that Gregory had correctly appreciated the significance of the moment, for this time he really did apply his whole strength to the difficult task, and tackled it not without courage and skill. The next two years are the highlight of his life.

When this outwardly unimposing man appeared in Constantinople, the Nicaeans did not even have a church at their disposal. Gregory had to begin by holding services in a modest chapel, under threats of tumults and disturbances which for a time seriously endangered him. But he refused to be intimidated, and the great theological lectures which he began to deliver immediately provided just what was expected of him. They offered a brilliant and well-considered exposition of Nicene theology, lucid arguments with no descent to pettiness, and a firm exhortation to his tiny flock to set a worthy example in the practical life of the Church, which would stimulate all lovers of peace to join them. Gregory was clearly determined to maintain as far as possible a position above party struggle without surrendering his own dogmatic convictions and thus prepare in an effective way for his own appointment and the future reorganization of affairs.

His limited knowledge of human nature and lack of experience of ecclesiastical politics were already demonstrated in an incident which might have had serious consequences. One of the people who joined his church and tried to become particularly attached to Gregory was a certain 'philosopher' called Maximus, from Egypt, a Christian rhetor like Gregory himself. Gregory later derided him as a Cynic and an untruthful windbag who had been, with his golden dyed hair, an utterly trivial, idle fop and a shameless hypocrite. But to begin with he had apparently given him a warm welcome as a kindred spirit and, as was his habit, had immediately made a public speech about him. In fact the man was a rival in disguise who, as Gregory had been by the Nicaeans, had been marked out by the jealous patriarch of Alexandria as the future bishop and ordered to go to Constantinople. A premature attempt to have him consecrated brought the plot to light, and Maximus was forced to disappear. When Theodosius appeared in Constanti-

nople for the Christmas festival in the year 380 he found that
Gregory was the sole Nicene candidate. The Arian bishop, who
had ruled the city hitherto, was now summarily sent into exile
and Gregory was welcomed as his presumptive successor.
Under strong military escort he took possession of the Church
of the Apostles, at the side of the Emperor. But he did not yield
to the pressure to have him installed as bishop right away because he wanted stronger ecclesiastical backing. This was to
be provided by the Synod that met in the spring of the year
381.

The so-called second Ecumenical Council was attended, to
begin with, almost entirely by the young Nicene partisans of
Asia Minor and Syria. Everything therefore promised well.
Meletius of Antioch, who presided, had Gregory elected immediately. He was consecrated and enthroned and formally
installed as bishop of the capital. For the first time in his life he
appears not to have put up any serious resistance and showed
himself ready to accept the lustrous and responsible post. But
the opposition of the various groups and factions soon began
to make itself felt again. Shortly after Gregory's election,
Meletius died unexpectedly, and the old, unhappy dispute
about the occupation of the See of Antioch came once more
on the agenda (cf. p. 97). Gregory now hit upon the unfortunate idea that the whole Antiochene Church should be
handed over to the former old Nicene candidate Paulinus. This
was in accordance with an earlier agreement and was now put
forward as a token of true justice and reconciliation, but politically it was impossible to put into practice. Gregory failed to
overcome the opposition of his own friends. In vain he used the
old method which he had applied after the Maximus affair, of
threatening to resign and take flight. He was compelled to
admit defeat. His position became really desperate when the
'Western' bishops, that is, first and foremost, the Egyptians,
appeared at the Council and set about him from the opposite
side. Gregory was unable to hold out any longer. He declared
that although he was innocent he wanted, like Jonah, to plunge

into the sea for the good of all, and he then announced his resignation, which was accepted. It was a bitter decision. His farewell address was dignified and saved his face, but it is not surprising to anyone who knows Gregory that on later occasions, especially in his great autobiographical poem, he gave vent to his profound annoyance and ill feeling and pulled to pieces the uneducated, narrow-minded bishops, the quarrelsome Council, and councils in general.

Once again, therefore, the old orator failed in an attempt to occupy an ecclesiastical post—this time even more painfully than usual, because he had really done his best and not reckoned on such an ending. To the outside world he repeatedly declared that he was only too glad to be away from the turmoil of the day-to-day struggle and be able to return to philosophical peace and quiet. But it took time for the wound to heal and before he could really enjoy his newly-won freedom. First he went back to Nazianzus, which was still without a bishop, and he took on the work there until he was able, after some difficulties, to appoint someone else as bishop. The new Christological heresy of the Apollinarians gave him much trouble at this period. In the end he retired to his father's estate at Arianzus, where for about seven years he really was able to live a life of leisure. He must have died in the year 389–90.

Gregory did not change in these last years of his life. He complained a great deal, criticized profusely, spoke and wrote incessantly about himself, his moods, and his sufferings. But the complete freedom with which he was now able to express himself made him seem more amiable, more natural, and also more serious than in his earlier years. Always a keen letter-writer, he now devoted himself to this most personal form of literature with special affection. As far as we know, he was the first Greek author to collect and publish his own letters. He also took up a new hobby: writing poetry in all possible classical meters. He wrote epigrams, surveys of past events, theological treatises, and, above all, 'about himself'. Much of his writing is simply prose turned into verse, like, for example, a poem on the differences between the family trees of Jesus as given by Matthew and Luke respectively. Other poems are more elegant and more personal, but even at their best his efforts do not amount to anything more than successful humanistic verse. Gregory's extensive classical education made it easy for him to find apt phrases, images, and similes for every mood and every thought. His writings are full of allusions and literary references. He believed that verse forced a writer to practise self-discipline. He wanted to prove that the new Christian culture was no longer inferior to paganism in this field. He apparently hoped for an even more immediate effect of his poems on the Apollinarians, who also, like the Arians, used verse in their propaganda. Above all he enjoyed the new opportunities his freedom gave him for literary activity and expression, now that his days as an orator were over.

> As an old man it has done me good
> to write verse and to sing to myself
> no lament, but a song of farewell
> like the old swan that whispers consolation
> to itself with its tired wings.
>
> (Carm. II, 1, 39, in suos versus 55 ff.)

Gregory expresses himself with the greatest simplicity, warmth, and directness whenever he speaks about those dear to him, his dead relatives and friends, and when he testifies to his faith in Redemption. We have already noted that as a Trinitarian theologian Gregory was not really creative, but merely completed and continued to defend in polished terms the position held by Basil. Much more important and revealing are his late anti-Apollinarian statements on the work and person of Christ. Apollinaris curtailed the human nature of Christ in order to strengthen his relation with the Godhead. Gregory was concerned to stress the complete humanity of the Saviour, alongside his complete divinity. Just as Christ's human nature and, particularly, his human spirit, the reality of which was denied by the Apollinarians, are raised wholly into the divine,

so our spirit is to be transfigured and deified through its association with Christ. Gregory is, however, not satisfied with this
spiritualistic conception of Redemption. Christ, the God-man
and the Lord, is indispensable to him above all because his holy,
unfathomable suffering and death have provided the atonement
by which the power of the devil and of sin, the whole burden
of our human failings, is truly overcome. It is as though in his
individualistic weakness and the disunity of his existence this
most delicate of the Church Fathers felt an irresistible need to
fix the final assurance of his salvation beyond all the 'vain'
human possibilities of religion, which otherwise meant so much
to him. In this respect Gregory perhaps went deeper than all
the Greek theologians before and after him. The nickname of
'the theologian' which was given him for his 'theological
addresses' in Constantinople was not wholly unjustified in a
deeper sense, though he owed his extraordinary reputation in
the succeeding age primarily to the formal qualities of his
writings, which were often used as models of style. It was the
orator, the 'Christian Demosthenes', as the Byzantines called
him, who had the strongest influence on posterity, not the
'theologian'. The real theologian, in the scholarly, 'philosophical' sense, was rather his namesake and occasional confidant, Basil's younger brother, Gregory of Nyssa.

CHAPTER IX

GREGORY OF NYSSA

GREGORY OF NAZIANZUS had regarded himself as dedicated to God from his youth onwards, but he had nevertheless remained, even as a Churchman and bishop, the rhetorician. Gregory of Nyssa came from the same intellectual and social world, and his friends probably took it for granted that he would devote himself to spiritual affairs and the clerical profession. By nature, however, he was not cut out to be a bishop. He was a thinker and a philosopher; he had a sharp, observant eye and an unusual talent for systematic thinking, but he was not a man for Church life and life in community. The energy which Basil used up in the outward service of the Church was, in Gregory, concentrated on intellectual pursuits, and he was not without ambition in this sphere of activity. That this man nevertheless became first a rhetor and then a bishop is typical of the age in which he lived. Culture was based on the rhetorical tradition, and the Church attracted to itself everything which helped in the development of the spiritual life. Gregory's life appears to differ according to whether it is examined from the outside or from the inside, and this gives him a difficult, problematical quality.

Although Gregory is usually described as timid and shy, he was perhaps originally not so unlike his brother Basil. Both felt the same need for independence, both had a conscious pride which was sometimes expressed rather contemptuously, and both were determined to develop their intellectual and spiritual personalities. Basil, however, voluntarily sacrificed these things, whereas Gregory had to struggle for the rights of his personality, had to fight for his position and way of life. He was burdened with the fate of the younger brother; he was the camp follower of a great generation, and he never acquired the certainty of a wholehearted surrender which gave such harmony to the character of Basil. Despite his outstanding cleverness, he long remained in the second rank, and in consequence there is a veiled, remote, and sometimes ambiguous quality about even his originality and his theology.

Admittedly, he too became very famous in the end, and occasional references which he made to it show that his fame gave him pleasure. As the brother of Basil the Great he was regarded as, with Gregory of Nazianzus, the man best qualified to preserve Basil's legacy, and on all dogmatic questions he was considered a leading authority. But, apart from his closest relatives, he had hardly any friends. His interesting correspondence is silent on this score. As a scholar and monk he lived his own life. He made supreme demands on himself, and his greatest achievements were in the fields of theology and philosophy. Basil had interpreted in his own way, given a Biblical depth to and tested in a new way the monasticism which Athanasius had won for the Greek world. Gregory followed him, but he gave to the ideal which he had taken over a different expression in the combination of reflection and meditation, and in the development of the basic ideas. He evolved and put his own stamp on a new theory of monastic, mystical piety which continued to live on.

For long stretches of time the outward course of his life is shrouded in darkness. He began to write only in his maturity, and it is impossible to reconstruct his previous development with any certainty. He must have been born *circa* 335. It seems that less money was spent on his education than on that of his elder brother Basil. We hear nothing about attendance at foreign universities, and Gregory himself confessed that he had nothing 'brilliant' to record about studying with famous teachers (*Ep. 13, 4 ad Liban.*). Again and again he pointed out that one man alone, Basil, had been his own 'teacher and father', and he praised him rapturously. For Gregory, Basil was 'the wonder of the whole world' and the prototype of the true philosopher (*Or. in XL Mart.*, Migne *Gr. 46, 776 A*); he sets him alongside the saints and declares that his writings are inspired. He was 'truly created according to the will of God and fashioned in his soul in the image of the Creator' (*De Hom. Opif.*, Migne *Gr. 44, 125 B*). His readers would perceive his dependence on Basil even where he does not refer to his teacher by name (*De Virg., Praef.*, Migne *Gr. 46, 320*). Gregory was indeed a pupil of Basil, but this rather deliberately fulsome praise does not mean at all that he stood still and had nothing independent to offer himself. The unconcerned way in which he 'makes the hard, refractory bread of Scripture' digestible by means of a free allegorical interpretation (*Hom. in Cant.* 7, Migne *Gr. 44, 925 B*) breathes a different spirit. Gregory must have read an unusual amount on his own, above all, Plato, Plotinus, and other Platonizing philosophers, and also Philo and, among Christian authors, Origen especially. He admired the pagan rhetor Libanius as the supreme living representative of classical Greek culture. Gregory was possibly the most versatile theologian of the century. His writings even contain discussions about natural science and medicine which reveal understanding as well as knowledge. In all this he was akin to Basil but undoubtedly superior even to him in the exhaustiveness and completeness of his knowledge.

In his youth Gregory had occasionally served as a lector. But he did not feel committed to this work. From sheer 'ambition', as Gregory of Nazianzus furiously declared in a letter, he allowed himself to be persuaded to exchange the Scriptures for the 'bitter and unpalatable books' of the world, to 'let himself be called more a rhetorician than a Christian' (*Greg. Naz. ep. 11 ad Greg.*). And he took a further step. He married Theosebia, a woman of high intellectual standing and greatly beloved. In his first treatise, *On Virginity*, he lamented that he could speak of this ideal only as a witness of the bliss that others experience, since he had himself once 'set his foot in worldly life' (*De Virg.* 3, Migne *Gr. 46, 325*). Such complaints should not be taken too seriously. Neither rhetoric nor the marriage, which he later conducted on a purely 'spiritual' level, obstructed his religious development. Gregory kept in touch with the monastic centre which his family maintained on the Iris, and he appears to have stayed there from time to time. His eldest sister, Macrina, the head of a nunnery there, was especially close to him. He called her his 'teacher' and devoted a little book to a moving account of her life and, in particular, of her death, at which he was present. Later on he composed a Dialogue, on the model of Plato's *Phaedo*, consisting of a conversation 'on the soul and the resurrection' which he claims to have had with his sister at this last meeting on earth.

At that time Gregory had long since given up his free life as a rhetorician and philosophizing theologian and had become bishop of the little town of Nyssa (in 371). From a life of personal culture, study, and contemplation he too had in the end been called to the service of the Church, by a way which he himself once described as the best and the most useful approach to ecclesiastical office. It appears that here too Basil had exerted his influence. As in the case of Gregory of Nazianzus, the place which was to be upheld by the appointment of Basil's brother was relatively modest in itself but politically important. Gregory of Nyssa also had to be 'compelled' forcibly to accept the post (*Basil Ep. 225 ad Demosth.*). He resigned himself to the new role, however, and soon began to take a more zealous part in ecclesiastical politics than was agreeable to Basil. The particulars are not quite clear. It is possible that Gregory maintained contact with the old Nicaeans with whom Basil had broken off relations, without admitting the deviation quite candidly. We have an unusually violent letter in which Basil even accuses Gregory of having forged certain letters and thereby brought about an extremely embarrassing situation. He said he would henceforth refuse to allow Gregory to take part in ecclesiastical negotiations; it had been proved that his words did not correspond to the facts. He flatly refused when it was suggested to him that Gregory should be sent to Rome as a legate; his brother was, he declared, quite inexperienced in

ecclesiastical affairs and ill suited for such missions on account
of his straightforward nature. Yet Gregory was equally under
the pressure of the anti-Nicene régime and was affected even
more directly than Basil himself, whom the State did not dare
to touch. Accused of financial irregularities, he was deposed and
an Arianizing bishop was put in his place. All the protests which
Basil made to the governor were in vain: Nyssa was lost and
Gregory was suspended and had to go abroad. He was able to
return only after the great change that occurred in the year 378,
when he was given a great ovation by his congregation. He
took part in the Council of Constantinople in 381. By this time
the brother of the great Basil, who was now no longer among
the living, had become well known to a much wider public.
By a decree issued by Theodosius the Great, he was appointed
central bishop of the whole diocese of Pontus, which means
that, in spite of the unimportance of his ecclesiastical position,
he was made confidential adviser to the government and he had
the last word in the matter of removing Arians and appointing
new Nicene bishops. Even before this we find Gregory attend-
ing foreign synods. He travelled by the State post to Arabia and
visited Jerusalem; he conducted the election of the Bishop of
Ibora in Armenia Minor and only just escaped being elected
Bishop of Sebaste himself. In the story of her life he made
Macrina say that his fame now outshone that of his ancestors,
his name was mentioned in cities, churches, and among the
nations, and 'churches call and send for him, that he may stand
by them in their struggle to create order' (*Vita Macr.*, Migne
Gr. 46, 981 B).

Nevertheless, Gregory remained a difficult colleague to work
with, and with his critical comments was far from universally
popular. He summed up his impressions of the Holy Land in a
letter which represents an outright attack on conditions in that
country. 'I know perfectly well what people will say in reply'
(*Ep. 2, 11 ad Censit.*), but it is a fact that disorder, depravity, and
immorality nowhere thrive so greatly as in the great centres of
pilgrimage. Genuine piety is now more at home among the

Cappadocians. People should be dissuaded from going on pilgrimages—on grounds of principle. The truly holy, philosophical life seeks for quietness and solitude; God does not limit his presence to holy places. If the spirit blows where it listeth, we shall share in his gifts by faith—'according to the proportion of faith' (Rom. xii. 6) and not 'according to the proportion of our physical stay in Jerusalem'. Gregory did not succeed in establishing a tolerable relationship with his own metropolitan. The latter's jealousy for his more famous subordinate, who was also the brother of his predecessor, may have had something to do with this failure.

In later years Gregory was twice again invited to Constantinople. He was asked to deliver funeral orations for members of the imperial family. In the year 394 he took part in a synod for the last time. He must have died soon afterwards. The fragmentary information which we have about him hardly suffices to build up a complete picture of his life, though it does suggest the unusual aspects of his character. To get to know Gregory properly, one has to concentrate on his theology and his writings.

It would be quite wrong to regard Gregory, with his self-willed and critical manner, as a sceptic or even a deliberately unecclesiastical theologian. Theologically he stands on the foundation of Mother Church, and his political activity suffices to show how unhesitatingly he recognizes and defends its public and sacred rights. The days of Clement of Alexandria were long past; there was no longer any theology which could develop in a purely academic atmosphere. The worship of the Church occupies a large space in his writings and sermons; he emphasizes the importance of the rule of law and the redeeming action of the sacraments, especially Baptism. He was the first Christian theologian clearly to define the concept of the priest, emphasizing the sacramental transforming power of his consecration and his distinguishing role of liturgist. To that extent he was a direct forerunner of the Areopagite, who, a century later, was to develop his momentous doctrine of the heavenly and ecclesiastical 'hierarchies'. But the Church's doctrine and 'philosophy' are the all-important thing, and Basil's reserved way of keeping within the bounds of the Bible on these matters was fundamentally alien to Gregory. In his methodical approach, he goes back rather to Origen. He regards the preaching of the Church merely as a starting-point for more advanced ideas, and the intellectual consistency and logical foundations of the coherent system are more important than proving its bases in the Scriptures. The teaching of the Church was now much more strongly articulated and established than hitherto, and Gregory was careful to respect it and avoid all open resistance. Basically, however, he revived the old Gnostic scheme of theology as an interpretation and development of a huge temporal and supratemporal drama in which, once removed by the Fall from its original unity and God-relatedness, the spiritual being is returning by broad, laborious ways to its origin. The fantastic elements now recede into the background and the philosophical interpretation of the mythology is more rigorously carried through. The mythological elements are now interpreted from a more strictly philosophical standpoint. In this respect Gregory is still nearer to Plotinus than to Origen. On the other hand, however, speculation is never regarded as an end in itself; like ethics and natural philosophy and the whole of secular culture, it has 'only to adorn the divine temple of mysterious revelation' (De Vita Moysis, Migne Gr. 44, 360 C). Christ stands at its centre, and the real issue is the redemption of man, that is, the elevation, purification, and return of the individual soul to its Creator and Lord. Gregory seeks for a living relationship with God, not a neutral order of graduated being. He does not believe that there is any permanence in human nature; it can be understood and truly realized only on the basis of its divine destiny. Theology ends in the worshipping, loving union with God who is incomprehensible and unfathomable. Everything that takes place between created and uncreated being is conceived in terms of grace, and is fulfilled in the realm of freedom and sanctification. Here is the dividing line between Christianity and Neoplatonic pantheism. Gregory is fond of speaking of the deification of man, but he means the likeness unto God which man is called to attain, as an animated mirror cleansed from all the mire and rust of an earthly being, as the true image of God. For all eternity the one goal of man and blessedness itself is to be illumined and sustained by God. And it is the magnanimity of God, not our work, which alone permits and makes possible this homecoming and fulfilment.

In the years when he held a leading position in ecclesiastical politics, Gregory also occupied himself with the current controversies regarding the Trinity and the nature of Christ. In a number of treatises directed against the Arian Eunomius, he defended the orthodox doctrines of the Church with acumen, shrewdness, and accuracy. Gregory was more interested than Basil in the inner unity and permanent co-operation of the three divine Hypostases. He strove to relate the Spirit not only to the Father but also to the Son and he already broached the later problems of Western 'realism', that is, the problem of the real content of general concepts in their relation to concrete individuation. He also came to grips with Apollinarianism. Unlike Gregory of Nazianzus, he advocated a Christology which comes near to the later 'Antiochene' conception, in so far as a sharp distinction is made between the divine and the human nature in the person of the Saviour. In the 'Great Catechism' he dealt with the doctrine of the Trinity and the doctrines of the Incarnation and the Redemption, ending with Baptism, Communion, Faith, and Rebirth. The work was conceived as an aid to apologetic preaching; but in spite of its somewhat popular form it was the first major attempt since Origen to expound the whole teaching of Christianity as a unity. What moves Gregory most deeply, however, are not the topics of traditional theology, but the problems of man. The realization of salvation, the elevation and transformation of the individual, the relation to the life of the body and the survival of the soul after death—these are problems to which he returns again and again, however circuitously. They bridge the gap between his Platonic-Origenistic view of the world and the possibilities of personal moral development and education. In this connection the practical experiences of the philosopher-monk were useful and he probably drew also on more obscure sources, hidden in his own interior life. Gregory was a good and therefore, in the final analysis, a very discreet psychologist.

His early treatise On Virginity is already of interest from this point of view. Gregory, the Churchman and a married man, refuses to condemn marriage and its joys summarily, and he knows how to describe them vividly. However, only the life of chastity can really do justice to man's ultimate destiny, life in the freedom and power of the absolute holiness which embraces the soul as well as the body. All-destroying death lurks behind all the joys of the earth and the senses. Abiding life is to be found only in the spirit, which rises above the world. This raises at once the difficult problem of the meaning of the life of the body. It cannot simply be evil, but it is indissolubly bound up with sin. Gregory believes that it was created for us by God for the sake of later sin. But what happens when the soul leaves the body? What is its manner of existence between its individual death and the final, general resurrection? How is it possible for the body to receive back from the world the various elements belonging to it? What becomes of the organs of nourishment and reproduction which the sexless soul no longer needs? For a long time Gregory strives with acute, almost scientifically precise reflections to keep away from Origen's dangerous spiritualism. He partly revives the earlier criticisms directed against Origen. In the end, however, he accepts the pure spirituality of the heavenly body. After long detours he returns to an only slightly modified form of Origenism.

The soul, and the soul alone, is created in the image of God and for eternal communion with him. What this means is described by Gregory in glowing colours far surpassing the corresponding descriptions in Philo and Origen. Gregory was the founder of a new mystic and ecstatic piety. The progressive asceticism which he required of his monks is no mere exercise on the way to a future goal but leads to a loving encounter and union between Christ and his Church, between the soul and its God in the present. According to Gregory's allegorical interpretation, all of the Scriptures are concerned with these spiritual experiences. Whether it is a matter of Old or New Testament texts, of the 'Life of Moses' or the example of the Apostle Paul, he finds the same ideals, of purification, miraculous sanctification, and blessed communion with God. In particular, the Song of Solomon is made to bear fruit in mystical piety. The purified soul, full of the intoxication of sanctified sobriety, feels in the bright darkness of the divine night the approach and the beauty of its bridegroom, although, or rather because, he is always in part invisible, intangible and inexhaustible. 'Blessedness, says the Lord (Matt. v. 8), does not consist in knowing about God, but having God in oneself' (Or. de Beat. 6, Migne Gr. 44, 1269 C). To have God within, the soul must, like Christ, have already died to the world. 'If it does not die, it remains entirely dead; only through dying, and putting off everything mortal, can it attain to life' (Hom. in Cant. 12, Migne Gr. 44, 1020 B). The soul is always journeying on a yearning yet blissful 'journey to God, which can never end' (Hom. in Cant. 12, Migne Gr. 44, 1025 D), in a most wonderful unity of peace and movement. The waters of the liberated soul rush on to God like a fountain; 'it has the depth of the fountain, but the constant movement of the river' (Hom. in Cant. 11, Migne Gr. 44, 977 C). It is itself filled by God as by a stream; it is kindled by the light like a torch and borne aloft by the spirit as by a carriage. Whoever has experienced this will transmit what he has learned, as the prophets and apostles have done. The Church extends increasingly and the great upward movement of spirits is irresistible. Belief in the restoration of all to God is to be found in the end in Gregory as in Origen. For him too this is no cold metaphysical proposition. It is a confession of belief in the living experience of the Spirit who is God himself and therefore the ultimate royal power and victorious reality over and above all things.

Gregory was never condemned by name for this heresy. But the condemnations of the fifth and sixth centuries naturally had him in mind. Gregory defended his theses more boldly than the other Origenists of his age. At the same time, however, he stressed their hypothetical character, and he probably considered that the doctrine of the last things did not pertain to the dogmatic centre of theology but to questions the discussion of which should remain open and on which, as his friend Gregory of Nazianzus said, even an error is quite 'undangerous' (Greg. Naz. *Or.* 27, 10). This distinction is very characteristic. On the one side there is the doctrine of God as a universally binding, rigidly fixed dogma and, on the other, free mystic speculation fed from other sources which nevertheless touches on the most burning problems of personal life and faith. The intention seems to have been to remove or relax the tension between the individual and the Church as an all-sustaining whole. Basil had already been guided by such considerations in his ecclesiastical politics. The dogmatic tradition was becoming a power with which the theologian had to reckon. It was at this period that the first theological 'Florilegia' came into being, that is, collections of quotations from the older, recognized teachers of the Church for practical use in controversies about the valid truth. Gregory not only accepts with a new kind of emphasis everything the Scriptures say but also the guiding 'explanations of the Fathers' (*Contra Eunom.* III, 10, 9). 'It is enough for the proof of our doctrine that the tradition has come down to us from the Fathers, like an inheritance which was handed down from the apostles by the saints who came after' (*Contra Eunom.* III, 2, 98). Gregory appeals in the same vein to his older brother Basil the Great, but he does not go the whole way with him. He deviates into his own realms of thought and spiritual life, where he feels unconstrained and free.

CHAPTER X

SYNESIUS OF CYRENE

STRICTLY speaking, the man to whom this chapter is devoted was not one of the recognized Fathers of the Church. He was a marginal figure and an outsider, although his writings were eagerly read and used and even commented on in the Byzantine Middle Ages. It is true that Synesius was a philosopher, which at this period meant also a theologian, but he was a pagan rhetorician and aesthete, not a Christian. Nevertheless he was made a Christian bishop toward the end of his life. That this was possible is very revealing. The course of Synesius's life and development confirms in a surprising way what has already emerged in the last few chapters concerning the comprehensive character of the Christian Church, attracting and uniting all the intellectual forces of the time. It shows how broad had become the stream which bore its life and teaching. There was a close affinity between the last of the pagan philosophers and the Fathers of the Church. There was on both sides the same element of spiritual inwardness and devout speculation, the same striving after moral purity and sanctification, the same reverence for the treasures of revelation, culture, and knowledge which the ancient traditions held for those who were prepared to learn. There was ultimately, however, only one organization in which these ideals could be put into practice and find a socially responsible expression: the great Catholic Christian Church. In the end, even the recalcitrant and even the pagans found their way to its portals.

In this respect Synesius may be compared with the great Cappadocians. His homeland, Cyrenaica, was originally a 'barbaric' region which had been opened up to Hellenistic culture and Roman order at an earlier date and even more thoroughly

than Cappadocia. Here too there was a rich, land-owning
nobility, and Synesius was a member of one of the oldest
families in the area, which traced its descent back to a companion of Herakles. Like the Cappadocians, he combined
Hellenistic cosmopolitanism and the imperial outlook with a
vigorous and assured patriotism which was rural and provincial
rather than urban and bourgeois in character. He too had a
deep sense of family. He cultivated friendships and spent much
of his time in social intercourse. To all who came to him he
gave his generous help. For him, too, Platonism—in his case,
pagan Platonism—implied a philosophical obligation which
was also, in the full sense of the word, religious. He strove to
spend his whole life as it were under the eyes of the one omni-
potent God and never tired of praising and adoring his glory.
His piety was lacking, however, in the monastic and ascetic
features which gave to the faith of his Christian contemporaries
a far more impassioned but also a more violent and tortured
quality. Synesius gives an impression of wholeness, harmony,
and purity. In his writings, too, he is quite open and natural and
unaffected. His writings are, he says, his children which he has
begotten partly with philosophy, partly with the poetry that
is worshipped in the same temple, and partly with the rhetoric
of the times. 'But one can see that they are all children of the
one father who has sometimes given himself up to the most
serious effort and at others to cheerful pleasure' (*Ep. 1, 1 ad
Nicand.*). In the philosophical style of his late period Synesius
is fond of reflecting on his ideals and way of life, but he is not
so obtrusively vain as many other pagan sophists, and a man like
Gregory of Nazianzus among the Fathers of the Church. He
is concerned to defend his cheerful versatility against the attacks
of cantankerous critics, and appeals on this score to Dio
Chrysostom, of Prusa, the philosophical world citizen of the
first century A.D., his ideal example. Why should he too not be
allowed to alternate freely between theory and practice, between philosophical and artistic pursuits, and nevertheless be a
complete philosopher?

The culture and reading of this unpedantic man are amazing. He has the whole of Greek literature at his command—philosophers, poets, orators—and in his fervent admiration for the 'classical' tradition he reminds one of the early humanists. He writes a faultless, carefully polished Attic, though he writes his hymns, appropriately, in the Doric dialect. He seems to be able to turn his hand to anything; he will quote and imitate and then write quite freely in his own style. He wrote tracts and reports, speeches, poems, occasional pieces, letters, and diaries. But the impression he leaves is that not of the trained writer but rather of the superior aristocrat and master of the art of life who has everything well under control. He does not evade the political obligations of his social position. 'Books and the chase are my life—when I am not on a mission' (*De Insomn.* 18). He loved his quiet country estate of Anchemachos as Basil had loved his monastic homestead on the Iris. But his studies did not exclude military and equestrian exercises, for which he had a 'wild passion' from his young days (*Ep. 105 ad Fratrem* [Hercher p. 706]). The philosophy of such a man is bound to be an eclectic construction, but it should not be condemned as mere dilettantism, for it permeated his whole life and was based on the foundation of a serious education.

Synesius studied in Alexandria, the great cultural metropolis. He had the good fortune to be introduced to the world of the mind not merely by the purely academic route: in Hypatia, the greatly admired Neoplatonist who taught philosophy, he found a teacher who charmed and inspired him and became a lifelong friend. At the same time he entered a circle of like-minded young people and later found a wife in a distinguished Christian family living in the city. One is reminded of the intellectual friendship which Basil and Gregory of Nazianzus—no less hungry for culture, and enthusiasts for Platonism—began in Athens. Synesius later visited Athens but it disappointed him, in comparison with Alexandria. In his opinion, only the famous name and the 'husk' of its former life remained. Philosophy had long since vanished from it and 'changed its quarters'. 'In our time the soil of Egypt is developing the seeds which Hypatia sowed there' (*Ep. 136* [*135*] *ad Fratrem* [Hercher p. 722]).

Unfortunately, the information we have about the teaching of this unusual woman is only indirect and incomplete. She was an austere scholar yet impressed everyone, even the populace of Alexandria, as a personality. Synesius was introduced to the foundations of ancient culture and all his life retained a keen interest in astronomy in particular. But everything was ultimately fused in a great Neoplatonic system in which the ideas of Porphyry were revived. The ultimate 'mysteries' of this school hardly became public knowledge because it was decidedly pagan and did not dare come into conflict with the laws of the Christian State.

The study of nature and its mysterious forces led to a higher knowledge of the intellectual and spiritual world, which led back by degrees to the divine One who is reflected in the whole cosmos but can be worshipped worthily only in a state of vision and adoration which transcends the whole visible world. What this conception meant to Synesius is seen perhaps most vividly in a little treatise which continues to arouse interest even today: the treatise on dreams which the author claimed to have written in the early hours of a single night. What a wonderful realm of beauty, knowledge, and revelation dreams open up to every human being! No particular place of worship, no tricks are needed. It was not Synesius's intention to write a popular book of dreams and oracles. In dreams the soul is released from its material confines. In the power of imagination it stirs its wings and approaches the source of its true being. Admittedly, there is in dreams the danger of deception and seduction according to the inner condition of the dreaming soul. But a holy spirit, purified by moderation and discipline, quickly leaves behind these demonic possibilities and the theurgic experiments of manticism. It rises, light and dry, on the wings of divine grace to the types of the eternally true and real and comes to know the supreme reality: the suprasensual essence, the bright eternal meaning of spiritual things, and its own natural rights in a world which no time can destroy. When interpreted aright, the world of dreams testifies to the intellectual-sympathetic unity of the world beneath its chaotic surface and proves the immortality of the soul. This is admittedly no pabulum for a half-educated public. The 'teachers of the people' in the cities who, encouraged by their own lack of education, disputed about God with everyone, would have liked to gain the allegiance of Synesius; but he adhered to the judgment of Hypatia alone (*Ep. 154 ad Philos. Magistr.* [Hercher p. 735]). He kept his distance from and thereby expressed his contempt for the 'Christian philosophy' of the proselytizing bishops, but he did the same in regard to certain pagan 'sophists'. He wanted to remain independent of all parties and faithful only to the supreme truth known to man.

Soon after his return home Synesius had to participate in a far-reaching undertaking of his fellow-citizens. Seriously damaged by the repeated incursions of desert tribes, cruelly exploited by incompetent officials and only inadequately defended, the province needed a remission of taxation which could be obtained only at the imperial court itself. Synesius undertook this mission, and it was to keep him in Constantinople for three years, which he later recalled as horrible, lost years which he would much rather have spent at home with his 'books and the chase'. Even so, they were not without influence on his development. The rich, intellectually outstanding notability now became at home in the highest society. He learned how to make his way in the labyrinth of court diplomacy; he made influential connections and found admirers and recognition. Synesius was allowed to make a speech 'About the Empire' before the young Arcadius and his court. Despite its conventionally rhetorical style, it expresses certain features of his character and outlook. Synesius not only summoned the courage to protest against corruption and the abuse of power but made himself the spokesman of the anti-Goth movement. He declared that it was a disgrace that the defence of the frontiers and the most important administrative posts in the Empire were being transferred to the barbarians, the ravenous wolves, instead of the 'watchdogs' prescribed by Plato. He lived to see a change in favour of the national 'Roman' court clique. Synesius described the change in the mystifying language of a treatise entitled *The Egyptians or: On Providence* which records the fall and the return of his patron, the City Prefect Aurelian, who appears in the mask of Osiris, who has been persecuted by his evil brother Typhon. This is a work that tries to be philosophical, mythical, and historical at one and the same time, and is typical of the Baroque taste of 'society' at that period. Another little treatise of this time describes an ingenious astronomical instrument which Synesius presented to a highly placed personality. To appreciate his humorous side, one should read the 'adoxographical' joke, *In praise of Baldness (Calvitii Encomium)*—another typical example of rhetorical improvisation but executed with the utmost elegance.

It may reasonably be doubted whether Synesius was well advised, in the long run, to protest against the allegedly destructive and unnecessary German troops. But he was still a genuine romantic nationalist, for he matched his words with deeds. When he returned home he immediately attempted to organize the frontier guard. He put a strong militia force on its feet, took the field himself, invented a new missile, and strengthened the frontier fortifications against the 'barbarians'. He co-operated with the government commanders and officials, often gave them instructions, and where they were obvious failures replaced them. Once again, Platonism was making practical demands and inspiring political activity. As soon as peace was achieved, Synesius returned to his 'philosophical' life. We find him on his country estate among his books and writings, with his friends and occupied with the education of his nephew. He sings the praise of leisure, of study, spiritual devotion and composure, and he also sings the praises of God's glory. The hymns which we have already mentioned represent the finest and most solemn expression of this mood.

Synesius's hymns are carefully elaborated works of art composed in all possible classical rhythms, full of literary allusions, but also full of bold linguistic innovations. They are genuine religious lyrics, 'philosophical' lyrics of radiant majesty, based on the doctrines of the Neoplatonic philosophers. Admiration for the beauty of the cosmos, prayerful ascent to the inexpressible One, the soul's yearning for purity and perfection, are expressed in a stream of high emotion.

> Unto the King of Gods our voice we raise:
> To him a crown we weave, and bring
> A sacrifice of words, a bloodless offering.
>
> (Hymn. 1 [3], 8–11)

Spiritual praise has taken the place of the old devotional conventions, which the law forbids and which the philosophical man of prayer no longer needs. Probably the nine hymns were written in the period before Synesius was made a bishop and before he became a member of the Church. Nevertheless, Christian concepts already appear alongside purely pagan and mythological conceptions. One of the hymns obviously extols Christ's descent into hell and his Ascension; in another the author has in mind the adoration of the Magi. One senses a progressive approximation to the specifically Christian in the constant stream of feeling. The divine 'offspring' and 'hero' is transformed into the 'Logos', the 'Son', and the 'Son of the Virgin'; the Neoplatonic triad of the One, the Creative Mind, and the World Soul becomes the threefold power of the Christian Trinity. But it is questionable how far one should evaluate the hymns in this way as personal confessions and interpret them biographically. Synesius senses the affinity of the images and concepts, he does not scruple to use the Christian 'mythos', and he pays homage to its truth. For him, paganism and Christianity stand alongside one another like two related 'denominations', and the truth which they share is greater than that which divides them. The poet who lives with a Christian wife in the happiest of marriages differs from the Christian view of life on quite a number of points and is not inclined to join the Church. But that does not prevent him from paying his tribute to the truth in all the forms in which it appears. His letter to a Christian friend who has been converted to monasticism is typical (*Ep. 147* [*146*] *ad Johann.*). In themselves the coarse 'black-coats' (monks) are not very attractive to Synesius, but he has no desire to cast doubts on the seriousness of their contemplative life and he heartily congratulates his friend for having attained with a single step what he has striven and is still striving after for so long in his white philosopher's mantle. 'I praise everything that happens for the sake of the Divine.'

That is the position of the man who was elected Bishop of Ptolemaïs in the summer of the year 410, and thereby became the leading cleric in the whole of Cyrenaica. To understand how this happened it must be remembered that at this time a bishop was legally and traditionally the most important and influential person in public life and was by no means restricted in his activities to the purely religious sphere. He was the man in whose hands the tasks of social welfare and to some extent the administration of justice converged, the only speaker whom no one could prohibit from speaking, the champion of the oppressed against the arbitrary actions of the tax official and the political bureaucracy. It is no accident that higher officials were often transferred to an important episcopal post. How much a vigorous metropolitan can achieve and signify is shown by the life of Basil and of any great bishop in our own time. It was therefore quite natural for the Christians of Cyrene to want to put in charge of their ecclesiastical administration the most energetic and influential feudal lord of their country who was also the most outstanding man intellectually, as well as the richest.

Did Synesius wish to be elected or was he taken by surprise? In his intimate letters he later emphasized more than once that acceptance of the appointment was a great sacrifice, that he would rather have died a thousand deaths than bear the burden of such an office, and he appeals to the 'God who honours philosophy and friendship' to testify that he is telling the truth (*Ep. 96* [*95*] *ad Olymp.* [Hercher p. 691]). He explains that an obstinate refusal would have made life impossible; he could only accept the office or renounce his beloved homeland. Such utterances are perfectly credible, but a man of his kind cannot be judged solely by the criterion of his own feelings. Once before Synesius had been considered a possible candidate for a political office, and at the time he had declared himself ready not to refuse—although he was not really cut out for that kind of appointment. He now had to face the problem a second time and in a new and more serious form, and it appears that he considered it in just the same light as before: the fatherland needed him, and Synesius could and would not wantonly evade the service required of him. The decision that he now had to make was, however, no longer a purely external one. The bishop is also the moral and religious leader and teacher of his people. He should represent publicly what true philosophy demands. It was just this responsibility which evidently made such an impression on Synesius. He regarded the call to office as no mere accident: it was not man but God himself who demanded this service of him. And 'with him, it is said, all things are possible, even the things that otherwise seem impossible' (*Ep. 11 ad Presb.* [Hercher p. 648]).

On the other hand, however, the difficulties were also quite obvious. Synesius had never been baptized and was not a Christian. He did not feel able simply to disown his previous convictions. He did not want to arouse any false hopes. Above all, his future superior, Bishop Theophilus of Alexandria, who would have to consecrate him, would have to be told beforehand in all frankness what he would be doing. The way out of the dilemma which Synesius chose was to explain his views at great length in a letter to his brother, clearly stating the things he would and would not be prepared to do if appointed. This letter was intended, as he emphatically pointed out, to be read by everyone and to make the situation clear to the patriarch. It was therefore a very carefully conceived 'open letter', every word of which was important (*Ep. 105, ad Fratrem*).

'It would', the letter begins, 'be extremely difficult to understand if I were not very grateful to the citizens of Ptolemaïs for considering me worthy of a task which I am unable to believe myself capable of undertaking'. The dignity of this new spiritual office requires an utterly composed, immaculate soul of priestly sanctity, and Synesius is far from being satisfied that he is worthy. A declaration of one's own unworthiness is the usual procedure in such cases, but Synesius underlines the conventional statement with a reference to his previous, thoroughly secular life, so unsuitable as a preparation for the life of a public teacher of the laws of God. Synesius is, however, clearly prepared to make the sacrifice required of him, for the sake of the cause. The joys of the chase, of sport, and even of private study will have to cease. But he is not prepared to give up his marriage. In his view it would be equally wrong to part entirely from his wife or to maintain his relationship with her in secret. 'On the contrary, I want many, well-bred children.' Synesius no longer has any hesitation about joining the Church and accepting baptism: that is a precondition of episcopal office which he now takes for granted. More important are a number of reservations on dogmatic matters which he is careful to make quite clear. He will have to be allowed to conceive the Faith in philosophical terms, and where the barriers between his beliefs and current ecclesiastical dogmas are insurmountable he will have to be allowed to remain loyal to his previous views. The eternity of the world, the pre-existence of the soul, belief in its immortality and not in physical resurrection were some of the points of difference on which he refused to yield. Synesius was prepared, however, not to attach too much importance to them. He should not be expected to contradict them and in private he should be allowed to remain a philosopher; but he would 'speak mythologically' in public, as required of him. For a Neoplatonist an offer of this kind was not treason. He knew that the ultimate truths about the Divine should not in any case be revealed to the masses. Nevertheless, as a bishop he would never say anything but what he thought, since God and sincerity belong together.

The purpose of the letter is obvious: Synesius wants to make it impossible for him to be reproached later on or for action to be taken against him for heresy. If his conditions are accepted, he is willing to be consecrated. Unfortunately, we do not know how the decisive negotiations with the patriarch proceeded. Synesius had known Theophilus from the time of his sojourn in Alexandria; Theophilus had even solemnized his marriage. He can hardly have been very happy about this letter and the situation that it created. He of all men should not have been prepared to consider such proposals, having set himself up as the strong man of faith in the fight against heretics and Origenists. But evidently he did not like to refuse; he did not want to incur the displeasure of either the celebrated candidate himself or the province of Cyrene, which lay at the outer edge of his province. We only learn that Synesius stayed no less than seven months in Alexandria before returning as a consecrated Christian bishop. Possibly he agreed to renounce his marriage in the end, for his wife is never mentioned in the subsequent period. It should certainly not be assumed, however, that Synesius sacrificed his philosophical convictions. Not a word of the open letter that he had issued was withdrawn and it remained in force.

The picture we get of the activities of Bishop Synesius is all the more astonishing. Although he had refused to surrender his convictions, he appears to have been in every respect a loyal, conscientious, and completely orthodox bishop, differing outwardly not at all from his Catholic colleagues. We see him travelling about his diocese, settling disputes, founding monasteries, conducting ordinations. He submits queries to his patriarch, seeks for spiritual counsel from the holy monk Isidorus of Pelusium, and where a heresy such as that of the radically Arian Eunomians appears he takes vigorous action against it. The fragments of his sermons that have survived are of irreproachable doctrinal correctness, and he now quotes from the Bible with a zeal and accuracy which were quite alien to him earlier on, compared with his knowledge of Plato and the old poets.

All this was required of him by the service which he undertook, to lead the people and to lead them to the worship of God. Synesius did not change his faith: he merely translated into the forms prescribed by public life the attitude which he had cherished throughout his life as a philosopher and a private individual.

It goes without saying that Synesius did not cease to participate in the political struggles of his homeland. More than ever before he set all the machinery in motion to prevent a military disaster in the struggle with the desert tribes. The situation had worsened and at times seemed almost desperate. Synesius was determined to hold out to the last. He refused to take flight, but if all resistance should prove in vain he was ready to embrace the columns of the altar and await the final blow in church. Even now he sees to the enlistment of recruits and all the measures which can be taken for the defence of the country. He makes impassioned appeals to the public. But he now has even more effective weapons at his disposal for use against the disloyalty of those responsible for the country's weakness. The first excommunication of which we hear in the history of the Church was imposed by Synesius on the Duke Andronicus who had been responsible for a great many cases of blackmail and brutality. A notice went out to the sister churches throughout the world stating that he and his accomplices must be barred from every house of God and that all who shared a roof or a table with him were to incur the same dire penalty. Synesius forced the proud criminal to repent and brought him to heel. Who would have suspected the gentle Neoplatonist of former days to be capable of such medievally stern action?

Yet Synesius had not really changed. He suffered unspeakably from the tasks and burdens he had to bear. He complained that everything had changed and the pleasure, honour, and happiness that formerly filled his life had gone. In his family affairs too he was dogged by serious misfortune. His brother had to escape from the country to avoid being elected *Decurio*, that is, the public guarantor of the receipt of taxes, a post which

would have ruined him financially. Synesius saw his three beloved sons die one after the other, and the grief broke his heart.
But in public he proudly repressed all his private suffering and
gave vent to his complaints only in occasional, brief notes to
his old friends. He believed that it was not for nothing that the
dream oracle prophesied that death would come in the year of
his accession to office. He felt as though he were dead already.
One of his last letters, full of grief and weariness, was addressed
to Hypatia, his 'lady' and teacher. Soon afterwards, in the year
415, she herself was seized by the Alexandrian rabble on account
of her paganism, dragged to a church, and torn to pieces.
Synesius does not appear to have lived to learn of her ghastly
end. He may have been dead by 413.

Had Synesius succeeded in achieving his service in the new
Christian community, as he had hoped, 'not as a decline but
as an ascent to the heights of philosophy' (*Ep. 11 ad Presb.*
[Hercher p. 648]; *96* [*95*] *ad Olymp.* [Hercher p. 696])? No
word has survived that would suggest that he repented or was
even troubled in his conscience. As bishop, Synesius knew that
he was in the place to which his God and his native land had
called him and where it was his duty to stay. Like Basil, he
deliberately sacrificed his leisure and philosophy to the demands imposed on him by the common weal. He was more
faithful in this respect than Gregory of Nyssa, who was never
able to overcome the individualistic rhetorician in him.

But one recalls Gregory of Nyssa when one sees how he
secured for himself in the inner realm of his personality a kingdom of his own where he enjoyed more freedom than he showed
to the outside world. How many bishops may there not have
been on the thrones of the Greek Church who were like him?
Classical culture and Platonic philosophy never died out in the
Byzantine Empire, and if Synesius already believed in the possibility of preserving his old convictions even when he had become a Christian and a bishop, the Christianizing of Platonism
and the Platonizing of Christianity became a regular tradition
in the following age. Even where it was impossible to ignore

the differences the Church usually left in peace the philosophers who behaved like Synesius. The real crises and conflicts always began where the theologians tried to take their profession quite seriously and endeavoured to make the peculiar and characteristic quality of the Christian Faith binding on themselves and their Church.

CHAPTER XI

JOHN CHRYSOSTOM

GREEK Christianity knew no conflict between Church and State in the medieval sense. There were struggles for power, but they were always concerned with power inside the Church itself. Even the greatest bishops never demanded to be heard on political questions or to make political decisions. On the contrary, it was the Emperor, as the Christian holder of supreme earthly power, who ordered and supervised the affairs of the Church. Limits were set to his action only in the innermost spiritual and sacerdotal spheres; this did not prevent him from intervening in party disputes and using his authority to decide the issue. The real problem in the East was therefore to get the Emperor on one's own side and, with his help, to disarm one's ecclesiastical enemies. Where that failed, all that remained was the protest of faith, the direct appeal to God's commandment and truth, and the way of martyrdom. The Greek Church never lacked men who were prepared to go that way if necessary.

John Chrysostom was no martyr of the orthodox Faith; questions of dogma played scarcely any part in his life. But he was the prototype of the Churchman who remains loyal to his spiritual mission to the end and who would think it treason to have any regard for political circumstances and the powerful of this world. If it had been possible for him to remain what he essentially was—the indefatigable preacher and interpreter of the word of God, the teacher and true admonisher of his congregation, the friend and helper of all the poor, oppressed, and needy—perhaps his life would have ended peacefully. But the brilliant gifts which he possessed and the love and admiration which his work called forth raised him against his will to the highest position, one of decisive importance in the world of ecclesiastical politics. Here the only man who could hold his own was one who commanded not only the spiritual gifts of the preacher and pastor but also political acumen and tactical skill, which Chrysostom lacked. He was, however, far too conscientious and energetic not to take seriously the duties of leadership and government which his office imposed on him. He thus became involved in problems and conflicts in which he was bound to go under.

The world from which Chrysostom came was different from that of the Fathers we have discussed in the last few chapters. He was born in Antioch, the Syrian metropolis on the Orontes. He was therefore no country gentleman and ruler by descent but a child of the great city and its motley life. The environment in which he was brought up was upper-class and well-to-do. He received the whole of his early education from women, as was the case with so many devout ascetics, since his father, a high-ranking officer, had died young. If we are to take him at his word, he led rather a wild life for a time, 'ensnared by the lusts of the world' (De Sacerd. I, 3). But the examples which he gives—the enjoyment of dainty foods, delight in the theatre, and attendance at public court proceedings—show at once that we need not take these conventional self-accusations too seriously. He spent a well-cared-for youth in the midst of what he calls the 'blazing house' of the life of the great city. At eighteen John underwent baptism, which was in his eyes the seal of a spiritual life, and only three years later, after concluding his general education in rhetoric, he was ordained anagnost, or reader. This might have been the beginning of a religious career, but it was still only a time of preparation in his life. Two forces shaped his further development: the monastic ideal, which had such deep roots in Syria, and the excellent school of Antiochene Biblical scholarship. Chrysostom settled in the neighbourhood of Antioch as an ascetic and devoted himself to spiritual exercises and serious theological work.

Monasticism was already widespread in and around Antioch

at this period. The monks were the saints of the people, who went on pilgrimage to their caves and cells, and they included distinguished theologians in their ranks. They quite often supplied the Church with its leading clergy and bishops. Chrysostom devoted himself enthusiastically to the monastic ideals. The conquest of the base earthly passions, the moral discipline of a selfless love concentrated on God, seemed to him the real fulfilment of the Christian commandment. He complied with the ascetic exercises of fasting, enduring cold, and praying, with an obstinacy which did lasting injury to his health, and perhaps he really did at first consider spending his whole life like this as a monk. On the other hand, he was much too active a character and far too missionary-minded to find lasting satisfaction in the pursuit of ascetic perfection. The inner peace to which the monk aspires, to the best of his ability, is not without a secret egotism (*De Compunct.* I, 6) and can never be achieved by physical exertion alone. Another and more noble fire is needed, the love for Christ which automatically binds us to our fellow-Christians. It is, moreover, a tremendous error to believe that only the monk is committed to the pursuit of perfection. Christ called all men and made no distinction between the ascetic and the secular life. Love, the supreme value, is common to both. Paul has 'required the same love of the people of the world as Christ required of his disciples' (*Adv. Oppugn.* 3, 14). The monk merely finds it easier to attain the goal because he renounces marriage and a thousand other temptations from the very outset. Those are to be admired all the more who stand in the midst of the world as priests, bringing salvation and sanctification to others. Later on, as a young clergyman, Chrysostom wrote a treatise, *On the Priesthood*, in which he further developed these ideas, taking Gregory of Nazianzus as his point of departure. Those who are permitted in fear and trembling to perform the most holy sacrifice at the altar, who forgive or retain men's sins, aware that only God in heaven can confirm their judgment, ascend into truly superhuman spheres. It is not surprising that a monk may well shrink from this dangerous office, but it is the greater of the two religious vocations. 'Anyone who compares the torments of the monastic life with a properly conducted spiritual office will find the difference as great as between a private person and the Emperor' (*De Sacerd.* VI, 5). It is clear that the venturesome path from monk to bishop which Basil the Great had decided to tread, with a heavy heart, was beginning to be a solidly built highway open to all.

Even before the beginning of his monastic life, Chrysostom had entered upon his theological studies. The patriarchate of Antioch had had to take a back seat in the disturbances caused by the Arian controversy and give way to Alexandria and also to the young capital of Constantinople, but the first place in which the disciples were called Christians (Acts xi. 26)—a distinction to which Chrysostom draws attention again and again —still proudly claimed to be the centre of theological activities and education. The traditions of serious scholarship which had been developed in Pergamum were revived in the Antiochene school. At this period it possessed in the great Diodorus of Tarsus a leader of outstanding importance and acknowledged sanctity. Diodorus, who had gloriously withstood the oppression of the 'Arians' under the Emperor Valens, was a dialectician trained in the Aristotelian school and a philologist. He was also a dogmatist who gave precise reasons for the doctrine of the two natures of Christ and encouraged his pupils to discuss all imaginable theological problems. But his main influence on Chrysostom was as a Biblical scholar. It was from Diodorus that Chrysostom learned to value and explore the New Testament as the source of all true knowledge and laid the basis of his comprehensive knowledge of the Bible. He did not, it is true, himself become a scholar. Chrysostom never mastered any language but his native Greek and had to rely on experts for his knowledge of the original text of the Old Testament and its Syriac parallels. But he never disowned his careful philological training. He took it seriously and believed that all historical and psychological considerations must serve to establish the original meaning of the text itself and not be used prematurely to find arbitrary theological interpretations and allegorical speculations of one kind and another. Chrysostom also studied the personal characters of and differences between the various authors of the Bible, and on many exegetical problems his wise judgment still carries weight today. Ultimately, however, all scholarly exegesis must subserve the preaching of the gospel, in which alone, by teaching, rousing, and edifying the hearers, it can attain its full effect and development. In the sermon we hear the voice of Christ and the call of his apostles. It should reveal the forgiving love which God has shown by sending his Son and, by the sacrifice on the Cross, arouse our love for him and awaken us to a new life of discipleship and good works. Chrysostom did not contribute to the dogmatic elaboration of Christological theory nor take much interest in the academic disputes of the day in this field. What interested him was the rousing of men's hearts, the kindling of their moral energy, developing in them pure love and an unfeigned spiritual outlook. It was no accident that St. Matthew's was his favourite Gospel, and his love for St. Paul, of whom he wrote a complete exposition, was directed above all to the devotional and moral aspects of the Letters. The heart of the Pauline doctrine of justification meant nothing to Chrysostom. Pelagius referred to him (Chrysostom) as his authority.

It was probably thanks to the old Bishop Meletius, who attached importance to an educated clergy, that Chrysostom returned to the city from his cave in the mountains in the winter of 380–81. Meletius ordained him deacon of his cathedral before his last journey to Constantinople for the Council (see above, p. 111). Later on Chrysostom was also ordained priest. It is said that owing to excessive ascetic exertions at this time he came near to a physical breakdown, so that to live any longer in solitude was in any case out of the question. We find him engaged henceforth as an organizer of charity, as a preacher and pastor entirely devoted to the practical service of the Church. He also continued to devote himself to literary activities which developed out of his day-to-day work and are sober, realistic, and natural. He wrote a treatise of consolation for one mentally ill, another for a young widow, a treatise on the education of children, a warning against second marriages. He also wrote a special treatise against the monastic abuse of co-habitation with consecrated virgins, the so-called *subintroductae* (spiritual marriage). In a series of apologetic lectures he supplied the evidence, for Jews and pagans, that Christ was the Son of God. By special request Chrysostom also preached on controversial theological problems; but the great mass of his sermons were simple interpretations of Biblical texts, not devoted to a particular subject, but homilies in which the text is paraphrased and applied. In this way Chrysostom often thoroughly discussed and preached on whole books of the Bible. The sermons were then published or incorporated in his *Commentaries*. But even in his purely literary work he preferred the form of the homily.

As a preacher he was indefatigable, and he influenced his own world and posterity above all through his sermons. 'I cannot let a day pass without feeding you with the treasures of the Scriptures' (*Hom. in Genes.* 28, 1; 82, 2). He was not given the surname 'Chrysostom' (golden-mouthed) until the sixth century, but admiration for his preaching was already widespread in his own time. It was not long before he became the most popular speaker in Antioch. Several stenographers used to take down his words, and there was loud applause whenever he spoke, even when he was preaching real sermons, not mere lectures; the charm, freshness, and naturalness of his speech were immediately attractive. In appearance he was plain and homely. His voice was not strong, and he was often in poor health. But preaching was a vital necessity to him. Just as the congregation hungered to listen, so, he said, he hungered to preach. 'Preaching makes me healthy; as soon as I open my mouth, all tiredness is gone' (*Hom. Post Terrae Motum*, Migne 50, 713 f.). Chrysostom spoke a pure, correct Attic, and it was clear that he was a trained orator. But he avoided the usual bombast and ostentation and expressed himself very simply in form as well as in matter. He wanted everyone to be able to understand him. His sermons were usually well-prepared, but he could also digress and take up spontaneous suggestions from his audience without the slightest difficulty. Unaffected contact with his congregation is a mark of the true pastor and was typical of Chrysostom's whole nature. When his sermons were published the personal digressions were usually deleted.

Practical and moral problems were paramount in his interpretation and application of the Biblical texts. His sermons contain a great deal of exhortation and moralizing. He often complained about the lack of moral improvement in his congregation, but he also knew when to encourage and praise them; the supremely important thing was to keep alive in them the delight in goodness. The 'good', however, consists not only in devotional exercises and ascetic training but above all in deeds of love and social service within the Church. How much suffering lurks in a great city; how many cripples and beggars crowd in front of every church door; how many sick there are whose sufferings cry to heaven! Chrysostom gives deeply affecting descriptions of the sufferings of the sick who lie on straw and dung with their ulcers and deformities, who have no clothes to cover them, who freeze and starve. Not everything should be left to the Church and its relief workers. People should themselves go to the baths, to the almshouses and hospitals which the Church maintains, and give a helping hand. The lurid contrast between rich and poor, the senseless luxury on the one hand and the extreme poverty on the other within the one society which calls itself Christian, is a further favourite topic on which Chrysostom dwells with relentless candour. The rich man and poor Lazarus, the sufferings of Job, the injunctions of the Sermon on the Mount, the example of the apostolic Church are biblical examples to which he returns again and again. One of his frequent subjects of complaint is the congregation's insatiable lust for pleasure. The old mania for circuses and the theatre, 'this universal school of dissolution', this 'training-ground of unchastity' and 'throne of pestilence' (*Hom. 6, 1 de Poen.*) are, he complains, still rampant. At the popular festivals in the city part of Daphne there have been desperately few changes since the evil days of paganism. On such days even the churches are empty and the preacher is made to feel his complete powerlessness.

In times of trouble or when disaster threatens, the atmosphere changes just as rapidly and everyone crowds into church for spiritual help. Thus it was in the spring of the year 387 when Chrysostom delivered the famous series of sermons 'On the Statues'. Owing to an increase in taxation the people had, in a sudden tumult, defaced the statues of the Emperor and terrible punishment was expected. The whole city, in which individual executions had already taken place, was paralysed with fear and looked like 'a forsaken beehive' (*Hom. de Stat.* 2, 1). Chrysostom visited the prisoners, went personally to the commander, and tried to comfort the people and prepare them for any eventuality. He emphasized that the immediate responsibility for the disaster lay not with the old, established citizens but with the foreign rabble; but the manifold sins of the people, above all, their swearing and blaspheming, had made them all partly to blame. It was now becoming clear what all the wealth and glory of the world were really worth in time of danger. They must put their whole trust in God and not set the pagans a bad example by cowardice and despondency. The Bishop of Antioch then travelled to Constantinople, and after anxious weeks of waiting the city was granted the imperial pardon mainly thanks to the intercession of monks and clergy.

In the year 397 an important event occurred: the death of the metropolitan Bishop Nectarius of Constantinople. As a layman and praetor he had been promoted to this position by Theodosius at the Council of 381, since the elected bishop, Gregory of Nazianzus, had been unable to ride the storm of the conflicting ecclesiastical groups. The unworthy competition for the succession was now renewed. Candidates and interested parties made their voices heard on every side. In particular, the Patriarch of Alexandria, Theophilus, embarked at once on his usual efforts to secure the influential post for someone agreeable and submissive to himself. The less gifted Emperor Arcadius was utterly unlike his father Theodosius and proved quite helpless, but his all-powerful favourite Eutropius decided to take the matter into his own hands. Without disclosing anything to the various representatives of the Church, he tried to prevent the threatening confusion in the same way as in the year 381, by promoting a man who stood outside the turmoil of ecclesiastical politics, except that this time it was not a layman but a theologian of high standing, capable of satisfying the demands of ecclesiastical decorum and representing the Church at court and in the capital. Chrysostom was already famous as a preacher and writer far beyond the confines of his native city. But care was taken not to drop the slightest hint of the appointment, even to Chrysostom himself, to avoid arousing any opposition in Antioch. One day he merely received an order from the highest official, the Comes Orientis, who resided in the city, instructing him to appear in a small martyrs' chapel outside the gates, for a discussion. A coach awaited him there which he was forced to board, and he was taken post-haste to Constantinople. There the unsuspecting bishops were already assembled for the election, and Theophilus himself was forced, after vain protests, to consecrate Chrysostom. Overnight the powerless little priest of Antioch had become the leading bishop of the East, the spiritual ruler of Constantinople, the preacher whose duty it was to preach before the Emperor and his brilliant court.

Needless to say, Chrysostom had never desired such a turn of events and was not in the least prepared for it. But once appointed, he did not hesitate to tackle the new tasks which confronted him with remarkable vigour. No less than before did he regard preaching and pastoral work as his foremost tasks, and in this respect he fulfilled all the hopes that had been placed in him. His services were the best attended in Constantinople, and soon a large circle of personal followers and admirers

gathered around him, especially from the world of devout
ladies who supported him in his spiritual efforts and put large
funds at his disposal. Chrysostom tried to reorganize and ex-
pand the social relief work and nursing activities. With this end
in view he restricted the building of new churches and submitted the whole administration and system of accountancy to
a thorough scrutiny. He was not at all satisfied with conditions
among the clergy. In Constantinople the system of 'spiritual
marriages' had spread to the parochial clergy, and various unworthy priests had to be deprived of their office. Monastic
vagabonds were banished to monasteries and confined to a
strictly religious life. Chrysostom also took up the struggle
against heretics; he refused to tolerate their conventicles any
longer. For all his personal gentleness and readiness to discuss,
he was by no means 'liberal' in this regard and believed in the
rights of the Catholic State Church. 'The Jews and pagans must
learn that the Christians are the saviours, protectors, directors,
and teachers of the city' (*Hom. de Stat.* 1, 12). Even the special
political needs of his diocese found in him a clear-sighted champion who vigorously trod new paths. The Council that took
place in 381 had made the Bishop of New Rome next in rank
to the Western Bishop of Old Rome, but his relationship to the
neighbouring metropolitans still needed to be clarified—in fact,
all he really possessed was an isolated city without a hinterland
of any importance. Under Chrysostom the importance of the
patriarchate of Constantinople grew. What he had in mind was
the position occupied by Antioch in Syria. Among other things,
he deposed the unworthy Bishop of Ephesus, intervened in
other seriously neglected dioceses in Asia Minor, and created
order. The five years of uninterrupted activity which were
granted to him as bishop laid the foundations for the later
development of Constantinople.

Opposition to his policy, and to the whole spirit of reform
which he introduced, was inevitable. Hitherto the people had
been accustomed to expect the bishop of the capital city to live
in magnificent state and appear as representative of the Church

on public occasions. He was expected to play a part in the social life of the court and keep open house and table for all ecclesiastical visitors to the capital. Chrysostom reduced his entertaining to the barest minimum. He ate alone, introduced the strictest economies, and never tired of stressing that he considered care for the poor and activity in the spiritual and ascetic spheres the essential tasks of his office. He rejected the previous spirit of live and let live at the expense of the Church. He soon made enemies of a number of bishops who were always pottering about the capital and the court instead of looking after their own churches at home. His constant attacks on public amusements and the luxury of the upper classes annoyed many influential people in the city. They came thoroughly to disapprove of this choleric ascetic. Occasions for enmity and intrigue were never lacking in Constantinople. Chrysostom took the noble but dangerous course of ignoring these things and keeping steadfastly to the direction he had set himself. In these circumstances the support which he had and was able to maintain at the court was all-important.

To begin with, he had been received with great kindness and good will. Arcadius, who was regarded as exceptionally devout, received the new patriarch, whose reputation for sanctity had preceded him, with great warmth and joy. But he had little influence on the decisions of the government. It was much more important for the new bishop to establish good relations with the lively and enterprising Empress Eudoxia. She, too, welcomed the new patriarch with high hopes. At one of the first religious ceremonies which he organized, the solemn entry of the relics of Phocas, Bishop of Sinope in Pontus, she condescended to carry the martyr's remains through the city in a procession which took place at night. In the sermon which followed the ceremony the bishop did not fail to draw attention to this admirable expression of supreme devotion on the part of the Empress. When the need arose, Chrysostom could command the extravagant style of courtly rhetoric, and he did not spare himself in praise for the pious devotion to Christ of the

imperial house. It is evident that in the early years his position
at court was not at all bad. When Eutropius was overthrown
in the year 399, it was the intercession of Chrysostom that saved
him. Eutropius fled to the altar in the cathedral. Once again
Chrysostom took the opportunity of pointing out to the congregation the frailty of all earthly greatness, and he mercilessly
reproached the miserable man with a list of his sins. But he was
able to save his life. Ill-feeling against Chrysostom began among
some of the gay ladies-in-waiting and seems then to have clouded
his relationship with Eudoxia. Hostile tale-bearers did not fail
to misinterpret and falsify certain innocent remarks which he
made in his sermons. In particular, he is said to have harmed
himself by taking an interest in a widow who had been wrongly
deprived of her possessions by Eudoxia, and in this connection
it is possible that he really did compare her with the Old Testament Queen Jezebel (I Kings xxi). All these things led to disaster, however, only when his enemies in the hierarchy were
able to join forces with the court and so outmanœuvre him.

   The jealousy of the Alexandrian patriarch toward Constantinople was of long standing and was constantly receiving fresh
nourishment from Chrysostom's activities. The hostility came
to a head when an action was brought against Theophilus in
Constantinople by a large group of monks, led by the four so-
called 'Tall Brothers', who wanted to lodge a complaint against
the high-handed rule of the patriarch and the injustices that had
been done to them. Theophilus had branded them off-hand as
malignant heretics because of their Origenist training, and he
had finally banished them from Egypt. Pursued by his spiteful
circular letters, they now appealed to Chrysostom for help.
Chrysostom was by no means blind to the dangers of the situation and tried to calm and put the brake on the angry men,
whom he lodged outside the official church hostel. He wrote a
polite and correct letter to his Alexandrian colleague and did all
he could to prevent the conflict from spreading. But Theophilus
refused to negotiate, and the monks got in touch with the
government, which accepted their writ and called a Council to

settle the matter, at which Theophilus was to appear as defendant and Chrysostom was to sit in judgment. His embittered and aggressive colleague was thus unwillingly pushed to extremes, and the situation moved on to a final catastrophe.

Theophilus did not consider appearing straight away, but he fully grasped the situation and wasted no time in dealing with it. He had inquiries made in Antioch about his rival's early life, but they failed to reveal anything to his discredit. He urged on a narrow-minded enemy of the heretics, Bishop Epiphanius of Salamis, to go to Constantinople and propagandize against Chrysostom. He got in touch with the bishops who had been reprimanded by Chrysostom and spared no money to encourage the anti-Chrysostom party at court. The dissemination of more or less forged sermon notes containing personal attacks on the Empress and the luxury of her life at court proved to be particularly effective. When Theophilus finally arrived in Constantinople he brought with him, against express instructions, a whole host of Egyptian bishops and made a pompous entry into the city escorted by this entourage. He took up residence in a palace belonging to Eudoxia. He turned down an invitation from Chrysostom. He did all he could to exchange the role of the accused for that of the accuser. In spite of the menacing omens, Chrysostom took no action for the moment. This was correct enough but undoubtedly the most stupid thing he could have done. Indeed, when Arcadius, who evidently still supported him, finally gave orders for the hearing to begin, Chrysostom declared himself incompetent to preside, out of exaggerated respect for legal propriety and perhaps also in the hope of propitiating and assuaging Theophilus. But he thereby only made it all the easier for Theophilus to take further arbitrary action.

In September of the year 403 Theophilus held a synod of his supporters outside the city gates in a monastery by an oak tree, and summoned Chrysostom to appear before them. Needless to say, Chrysostom refused to appear, but he did not merely protest and leave it at that. With an excess of humility and conscientiousness he declared himself ready to appear provided his proven enemies were removed from the group that purposed to pass judgment on him. A further delegation which Chrysostom sent to the 'Synod of the Oak' was soundly flogged, and proceedings against him were opened in his absence. A decision was reached in the shortest possible time. We need not quote all the forty-six points of the indictment. The complaints about the extension of his sphere of influence were specially significant. But generally speaking, it was all a frantic mixture of libel, childish or deliberate misunderstanding, and political accusation, the purpose of which was clear from the start—to prove Chrysostom guilty of bribery and corruption: 'he eats on his own and lives like Cyclops; he has committed acts of violence and insulted the Imperial Majesty'. The judgment was nevertheless confirmed by the weak Emperor. The people were exasperated, and if Chrysostom had wished he could probably have resisted. But he was not the man to exploit opportunities for revolution, let alone organize resistance on his own initiative. Calmly and quietly he gave himself up to the soldiers and allowed himself to be taken from the city in the dead of night. It seemed as if his role as Bishop of Constantinople were over.

Suddenly, however, the tide turned. The haphazardness and capriciousness of the Imperial Church administration become all too obvious when we learn the reason why the alleged criminal was recalled, only a day after his banishment. Eudoxia, who had clearly been pulling wires behind the scenes during this whole episode, had a miscarriage. In her horror, she believed that it was a judgment from heaven and gave orders for Chrysostom to return at once. He had trouble in securing a more or less legal annulment of the sentence passed against him. Everything was to be forgiven and forgotten. But once disturbed, it was not easy to restore the relationship. Only a few weeks later the tension had reached menacing proportions again and disaster loomed ahead. During the dedication of a statue in honour of the Empress the noise of the popular rejoicings had upset divine worship. The irritated comments

about the disturbance which escaped from Chrysostom naturally reached the ears of Eudoxia. Then, on the festival of John
the Baptist, he began his sermon with a reference to Herodias,
who was demanding the head of the Baptist 'once again', and
his enemies were probably justified in interpreting this as another hostile allusion to the Empress. The old opposition was
not dead. It is true that Theophilus had decamped, but the
court's episcopal advisers now took the position that the proceedings against Chrysostom had never been concluded.
Eudoxia took the matter up and declared that she would not
attend the cathedral again until the case had been concluded and
the bishop cleared of the charges preferred against him. In fact,
it was scarcely possible to carry out this proposal. The intention
was obviously to get rid of Chrysostom without further recourse to violence, and he again proved quite helpless in the face
of the intrigues which were set in motion against him from all
sides. On the one hand, he resolutely refused voluntarily to
leave the flock with which God had entrusted him. On the
other hand, he did nothing to prevent a new and completely
unauthorized assembly from conspiring against him. When the
situation was still not cleared up by Easter in the year 404, the
government tried to prevent by force of arms the baptisms
which were normally conducted by the bishop at this season,
and their action led to bloodshed. In the end, the unwilling
Emperor was forced once again to sign a decree of banishment.
Chrysostom called together his faithful clergy and bishops for
a final prayer in the sacristy and exhorted the faithful deacon-
esses and female assistants not to grow cold in spiritual zeal. He
then took the necessary measures to prevent disturbances, and
for the second time he went quite calmly into exile and cap-
tivity with a military escort.

A confused situation that had become quite intolerable had
thereby been brought to an end. It is clear that Arcadius's in-
dolence and susceptibility to outside influences were mainly
responsible. He had been incapable of taking any vigorous
action, leaving all decisions to his wife and the partisan clerical

advisers who crowded around her. Chrysostom himself had scorned to enter the fluctuating ground on which alone the battle might have been won. He was bound to be defeated in the end, although fate had twice appeared to offer him a chance of victory. He was to complete the way that still lay ahead of him not as a prince and ruler of the Church but as a martyr to his office and his Faith.

By banishing Chrysostom the Emperor had probably merely wanted to terminate a desperate situation, with no desire to hurt either him or his followers. But his enemies saw to it that this was not the end of the matter. Immediately after his departure, Chrysostom's cathedral went up in flames for reasons which were never explained, and, needless to say, his followers were made responsible. For their part, some of his supporters refused to have anything to do with the new bishop, and they were cruelly persecuted. The treatment and reception which Chrysostom received on his long journey also varied according to the attitude of his brethren of the Church. The numerous letters which he wrote to his old friends give a vivid account of his situation and his feelings. Letter-writing was considered an art at this period, and these letters therefore still retain a slightly self-conscious air which no educated Greek of the post-classical age ever completely lost. Above all, however, they move us by the humanity and purity of thought which they reveal. Chrysostom felt very weak and did not deny that he sometimes suffered greatly from bad treatment, lack of sleep, cold, lack of medicines, and so on; but again and again he tries to comfort his correspondent with the assurance that he is feeling better. He tries to encourage and console his friends, and even from a distance he remains their pastor.

When he arrived at his destination, inhospitable Cucusus in Lower Armenia, his situation began to improve a little. His greatest grief was that he hardly ever had a chance to preach. But his friends saw to it that he did not lack money, with which, once again, he tried to help others. His friends kept him supplied with news and informed him of all the efforts that were

being made on his behalf. Chrysostom took an interest in everything, and gave warnings and advice. Letters were his greatest
joy; nothing worried him more than when they failed to arrive,
and when his former friends no longer wrote to him owing to
their laziness or fear. But his thoughts were by no means concentrated entirely on Constantinople and his followers, his
clergy, and his poor. He sought out new tasks for the Church.
He had formerly concerned himself with the conversion and
care of the Goths who lived in Constantinople. He now turned
his attention to nearby Persia and pondered on the possibility
of a thorough-going Christian mission in that country—a problem to which hardly any other leader of the Greek Church had
given any thought. He also tried to keep in touch with the
Bishop of Rome and other influential representatives of the
Western and Eastern Churches. He did not abandon his cause,
and he continued to hope for peace in the Church and the
victory of the right.

The fact that these efforts were not a complete failure probably contributed to his ultimate destruction. Only a year later,
in the late summer of 405, he was forced to leave Cucusus,
which was threatened by barbarians. He came to Arabissus, and
here too he was followed by a stream of pilgrims who wanted
to see, visit, and speak to him. In the high summer of 407
instructions arrived to move him to the farthest corner of the
Empire: to Pityus, on the Black Sea. According to his own
admission, nothing tired him out so much as travelling, and it
was evidently intended to kill him by making him trudge
through the roughest tracts of country. He was refused any relief. The seriously ailing man was exposed to the heat of the sun
and the driving rain; he was given no chance to rest; he was
driven on relentlessly. Even on the eve of his death he was
forced to march, with a high fever, five miles to the town of
Comana. There he was lovingly received by the little congregation, but he had to travel on the very next morning. After
nearly three and a half miles of walking, he collapsed completely. He was taken back to Comana, wrapped in a white

shroud, and given the holy sacrament for the last time. Chrysostom crossed himself and died with a word of praise for his whole life: 'Glory be to God for everything! Amen.'

The struggle around his name and right continued. The Western world refused as obstinately as ever to recognize the validity of his deposal and banishment, and in the Greek world too it became increasingly difficult to hush up the obvious injustice that had been done. In the year 438 the son of Arcadius, the Emperor Theodosius II, had the saint's remains solemnly interred in the Apostolic Church of Constantinople. Chrysostom's posthumous fame was immense. The writings of no other Father of the Church were read so much or disseminated in such a wealth of manuscripts. He was translated early into Latin and various Oriental languages. Even today John Chrysostom enjoys the love and veneration of all denominations. He whose life was embittered and destroyed by his enemies now has no enemies at all. As a theologian he was neither profound nor original. He was a typical representative of his school, of his period and its ecclesiastical and ascetic ideals. One can, however, get an impression from him of the moral and spiritual forces which were still alive in the worldly State Church in spite of the many disappointing bishops who brought it no honour.

His sermons show that theology was still able to fulfil its task in the Church to a very large extent. The homilies of Chrysostom are probably the only ones from the whole of Greek antiquity which at least in part are still readable today as Christian sermons. They reflect something of the authentic life of the New Testament, just because they are so ethical, so simple, and so clear-headed.

CHAPTER XII

CYRIL OF ALEXANDRIA

THE struggle between Chrysostom and Theophilus was not merely a conflict between two personalities: two regions, two theological traditions, and two fundamentally different intellectual and spiritual attitudes were competing against one another. In Chrysostom the Greek legacy had become wholly ethical, ascetic, and saintly, and so deeply permeated by the spirit of Christianity that it was unconquerable and triumphed even in his death. But it must not be overlooked that his opponent, the Patriarch of Alexandria, was, at any rate to begin with, the political victor. Egypt, which at this period was not accounted part of the Greek 'East', was ecclesiastically an extremely centralized world of its own, and the tradition of imperious orthodoxy embodied in its 'Popes' (it was here that the word first acquired its official connotation) had never been checked. It extended from Demetrius, by way of Athanasius, to Theophilus and in the following generation was to be incorporated once again in a powerful figure who was not inferior to his predecessors in consistency of effort and surpassed them in the audacity of his intentions. This was Bishop Cyril, the last great Father of the Church, and the most distinguished saint of Byzantine orthodoxy. As a moral character he is more than open to attack. 'I do not believe', said Cardinal Newman, still somewhat ashamed, 'that Cyril would have agreed that his outward acts should be taken as the measure of his inner sanctity.' But Cyril dug the bed through which the stream of dogmatic developments has subsequently passed so deeply that, generally speaking, it has never left it since. With him, whom even the West extols as *doctor ecclesiae*, we may conclude our series of studies of Greek Fathers of the Church.

The typical marks of an Egyptian hierarch were stamped so intensely on Cyril's personality that it hardly seems to matter that we know almost nothing about his youth and early development. He was a scion of the same great Alexandrian family to which his uncle and predecessor Theophilus had belonged. He was probably destined for a career in the Church from an early age. At any rate, he took part in the Synod of the Oak in the year 403, as a member of his uncle's entourage. For the rest of his life Theophilus regarded the removal of Chrysostom from his throne, which resulted from that Synod, as a justified triumph of his Church. The memory of this event determined Cyril's career in the same way as Athanasius had been influenced by his participation in the Council of Nicaea. After the death of Theophilus there was only a brief electoral campaign. The candidate of the highest rank, the Archdeacon Timotheus, had to give way and Cyril was consecrated, on October 17, 412, only two days after the see had become vacant. He cannot have been very old at the time; he occupied the throne of St. Mark for no less than thirty-two years and he carried out his duties with vigilance and unbroken vigour to the end.

It would be wrong, however, to think of Cyril merely as an ecclesiastical politician and spiritual ruler. Far more than his uncle, he wanted to be a theologian, to represent and personify the true tradition of the Faith as a teacher as well as a bishop. Cyril was a preacher and at the same time an uncommonly prolific writer whose surviving works comprise today ten imposing volumes. Literary work gave him pleasure, and the extent of what he produced testifies to inflexible diligence. As a writer he was not without ambition, although his occasional attempts to attain rhetorical effects and elegance of form fall short of their purpose. His strident style is flat, monotonous, and pompous. He goes straight to the goal he is trying to reach with ponderous forcefulness, but he always succeeds in expressing quite unmistakably what he is trying to say. His books show that he had a clear and methodical mind, although he lacked the refinements which result from careful training. He introduced philosophical concepts only occasionally and quite superficially. He despised the pagan philosophers, who so often 'contradicted' one another and, in Cyril's opinion, stole their best things from Moses. Similarly he regarded Origen as a heretic who had been justly condemned 'because he did not think as a Christian but followed the chatter of the Hellenes' (*Ep. 81*, Migne 77, 373). From Chrysostom he was, not surprisingly, unable and unwilling to learn anything. Under protest, and only when it had become quite unavoidable, did he condescend to restore his name in the diptychs, or official lists of bishops. In his exegesis Cyril keeps to the 'historical' meaning of Scripture, as opposed to the disintegrating spiritualistic interpretation of Origen. But in fact his exegesis was entirely derived from traditional allegory and typology and is hardly concerned at all with the direct, human meaning of the Bible story. His main interest is exclusively dogmatic and polemical. He uses the Bible to refute the false doctrines of the heretics, to establish the true conception of the Trinity and the divine-human person of the Saviour, on which true piety is based. Christian sanctity is consummated in the adoration of these divine mysteries, in the reception of the life-giving sacraments, and in the ascetic virtues of the monastic way of life.

In his understanding of the message of salvation Cyril thinks of himself as the heir of all previous ecclesiastical teachers, above all of the great orthodox luminaries of his own city of Alexandria. Athanasius he considers the spokesman of the Church par excellence. One-third of Cyril's first work on dogmatics, the tremendous *Thesaurus*, or treasury of a true knowledge of the holy and consubstantial Trinity, consists of nothing but an excerpt from the corresponding *Orations* of Athanasius. Moreover, Didymus, a blind theologian of the second half of the fourth century, while he was never mentioned explicitly, since he was a layman and an Origenist, was no less industriously exploited, and through him something of the work of the Cappadocians flowed into Cyril's writings. For the rest, he does not concern himself much with recent theological controversies. His tireless attacks are aimed at the old traditional enemies: Arius, Eunomius, and the 'godless' Emperor Julian, to refute whom he wrote a gigantic work consisting of thirty books. He always presents orthodox doctrines as if they were solid, revealed, traditional facts which only diabolical malice could possibly distort and misinterpret. Christ, as the divine Logos, i.e. as God himself, stands in the centre. As a mere man he would have been no use to mankind. The real purpose of his Incarnation is to unite our nature with the Godhead and to lead it wholly into the divine—just as the elements of the Holy Communion must be filled with divine energy, if they are to convey to us salvation and the life force of eternity. To consider Jesus 'separately' as a mere man therefore seems an utterly godless proceeding. It is the one incarnate Son of God who effects our salvation. Cyril does not regard as serious the danger that the humanity of Jesus may be evaporated or curtailed. It is true that he knows from the condemnation of Apollinaris of Laodicea that the human soul of the Redeemer's person must not be denied; but he is not clear about the theological implications of this. When, in the struggles with his Antiochene enemies, Cyril was later compelled to develop his Christology in greater detail, he did not hesitate to use the Apollinarian formulas, which he wrongly considered Athanasian, and he spoke of the 'one incarnate nature of the God-Logos'. In the light of later dogmatic formulations his Christology was quite inaccurate and Monophysite. But Cyril never doubted that belief in Christ could be rightly professed and defended only in the way to which he was accustomed. He abhorred all 'tolerant' dilutions and discussions of the truth, and where he had power he was always ready to use it mercilessly to suppress all opposition to his spiritual dominion.

The outlook in Egypt at the beginning of his régime was stormy. The bestial murder of Hypatia was organized by the clergy and was laid at any rate indirectly to Cyril's charge. He gave orders for the churches of the Novatians to be closed by force, though hitherto they had enjoyed official toleration as orthodox, morally austere sectarians. There followed expulsions of Jews and heretics, and when the imperial governor tried to intercede for them Cyril fought him too. He would never give way. His spiritual authority was as unassailable in Egypt as was his economic power as lord of the corn fleets and the estates of the Coptic interior. The monks whom he visited, kept posted with circular letters, and tried to shackle to himself, formed his strongest spiritual army. Cyril attempted to terminate his predecessor's struggle against Origenism and the Origenist-trained monks, relying primarily on the uneducated Coptic saints. But even he had to condemn the barbaric crudeness of the so-called 'Anthropomorphites', who conceived God himself in the bodily likeness of a man.

But here again despair gave rise to opposition which refused to go down without a fight. In the year 428 a deputation of Egyptian monks appeared in Constantinople to protest to the Patriarch Nestorius against the violent rule of their spiritual overlord. Cyril described them as a pack of bankrupt failures from the 'muck-heap of Alexandria' (*Ep. 10, ACO* I, 1, p. 111, 22). The internal conflict thus spread to the realm of universal ecclesiastical politics, and a catastrophic development had begun the consequences of which were as yet unforeseeable.

It appears that Cyril immediately realized the gravity of the situation. The resemblance to the Chrysostom affair was obvious and was to some extent generally noticed. After a long period of political weakness an Antiochene monk of high intellectual standing again sat on the throne in the capital city, theologically and morally stern and fearless, but, like Chrysostom, hardly equal to the political intricacies of his task. Once again the Patriarch of Alexandria was arraigned before him by his own subordinates. If Nestorius refused to yield of his own accord Cyril was faced with the question whether he would turn the tables and go over to the attack himself and wind up the old struggle for power with Constantinople and secure his own predominance in the East.

Like his predecessor, Cyril maintained a permanent legation in Constantinople. His 'apocrisiaries' were there in order to conduct negotiations with the Emperor and the patriarch, and we still have some of the letters containing the detailed instructions which they received from Alexandria. When Nestorius informed them, in a perfectly correct manner, about the complaints that had been received, they met him at once with challenging insolence. They declared that it was improper to accept any complaints against such a great bishop, their Pope, at all, especially as he had hitherto recognized Nestorius without the slightest reservation and treated him kindly. When Nestorius stood firm, they hinted that it might be dangerous for him if they were to report back to Alexandria. Nestorius answered proudly that he was not in need of the kind of friendship that obliged him to approve or tolerate the wrong. It appears that Cyril had every reason to prevent a thorough investigation of the affair which was in suspense; but this meant departing from the formally correct method of procedure which had so far been followed. The best way seemed to be to adopt tactics successfully used earlier by Athanasius and to transfer the legal dispute to the plane of religious belief. If the man who criticized Cyril's dubious official acts could be brought under suspicion of a secret heresy, this would divert attention from any previous complaints and the troublesome attacker would become the defendant and his proceedings would lead to his own ruin.

It was not difficult to find reasons for a theological charge, and it may be assumed that Cyril did not have to act against his convictions. Nestorius was a typical representative of Antiochene theology and the sharp distinction which it made between the human and the divine nature of Christ, which was an abomination to Cyril. Unlike Chrysostom, Nestorius, with his intense confidence in himself as a dogmatist, felt called upon to elaborate the doctrine and to secure universal recognition for it. He too had already made a name for himself as an enemy of heretics and sectarians in an around Constantinople. His enemies were only too ready to co-operate with Cyril and to put at his disposal incriminating sermon notes and the like. Ill-feeling had been aroused in particular by the fact that Nestorius had publicly criticized the current description of Mary as 'God-bearer' (*Theotokos*). It is true that, as a fair-minded pastor, he had actually admitted that this term could in a certain sense be used quite devoutly and orthodoxly. But fundamentally it was important to realize that the divine nature as such could neither be born nor become a human being nor suffer and die on the Cross. All these statements must refer to the human aspect of the person of Christ, and Mary had therefore born the man Jesus, not the eternal Logos of God. Nestorius recommended, in order to bring this dangerous dispute to an end, calling her rather 'Mother of Christ' (*Christotokos*), which would satisfy everyone. This was quite consistent with the Antiochene view, but the public refused to be fobbed off with such dry, rational-istic distinctions. The alleged criticism of the dignity and glory of the Mother of God touched a sensitive spot in popular de-votion, and Cyril knew what he was doing when he declared this term 'God-bearer' to be the distinguishing mark of all true faith in Christ. From his theological point of view this was not only quite consistent but it thereby assured him of a widespread response from the masses and their support for his further pro-ceedings. From a historical standpoint the victory which he was to gain over Nestorius must be regarded as the first great triumph of the popular worship of Mary.

It was some time before the conflict was fully developed. As was only to be expected. Nestorius, in his irritation and injured pride, showed little diplomatic skill. He wanted to avoid a break, but he exposed himself by various tactical mistakes, in his confidence that he must act properly and remain in the right. Leaving aside all moral judgments for the moment, it must be admitted that Cyril's adroitness and genius were dis-played in a brilliant light. He gave his assent to every method of silent intrigue and propaganda as well as the usual method of large-scale bribery, in the form of promises and costly 'presents'. While his clumsy, morally austere colleague scoffed at the 'golden arrows' (*ACO* I, 5, p. 43, 17) with which he was to be injured, Cyril indefatigably gathered together the 'material' which was to compromise him, got in touch with every group hostile to Nestorius, and, without making any open attack, fomented the increasing popular hatred for the alleged new heresy. He was not greatly concerned with the truth; outwardly, however, he continued to play the part of the anxious, thoughtful leader who refuses to take action for reasons of purely personal spite, leaving the first steps to his friends and go-betweens.

Two courts of appeal were especially important in the impending conflict: the Emperor in Constantinople and Bishop Celestine of Rome. As a Westerner, Celestine I stood to some extent outside the theological controversy and was, as Nestorius quite right said, 'much too simple to be able to penetrate into the finer meaning of doctrinal truths' (*ACO* I, 4, p. 25, 34). But care was taken to see that Nestorius's Christological theses were laid before him in such a grossly caricatured form that he was at once persuaded to take a stand against these 'obvious blasphemies' (*ACO* I, 2, p. 8, 1). The whole dispute arose because certain dogmas were pushed to logical extremes. Nestorius would later never admit as his opinion the assumption of 'two sons of God' of which he was accused. But his letter to Rome, written in a quiet, friendly tone, omitted to include the usual terms of flattery, while Cyril addressed his younger colleague right away as his 'most holy Father, most beloved of God' and put himself at his disposal with the most diligent humility. He soon had the Pope entirely on his side. In a graciously written letter Celestine appointed him his deputy and instructed him to pursue the dangerous dispute with unremitting energy.

Cyril was less fortunate in Constantinople. He attempted to incite against Nestorius not only the Emperor but also the Empress and above all the energetic Princess Pulcheria. But for the present Theodosius II was still convinced that his patriarch

was in the right, and Cyril was suspected of trying to sow dissension in the Emperor's family by dedicating certain theological treatises to different members of the family. Nevertheless,
all was not lost at court. Theodosius was a weakling, like his
father, and in the habit of giving way to his eunuchs and other
unreliable advisers, who were not beyond the reach of Cyril's
letters and his gold. An initial success was marked by the fact
that to begin with only the religious dispute was assigned to
the Council that was summoned to Ephesus at Whitsun, 431,
and further proceedings against individual members were expressly forbidden.

Cyril had not waited for the Council to be called. After
apparently hesitating for a long time, he now realized that only
ruthless speed could assure him of victory. Relying on the unconditional support of Rome, he convened a council of his
Egyptian suffragans in Alexandria which forthwith condemned
Nestorius as a heretic. The 'anathemas' with which the judgment was supported were based so blatantly and one-sidedly
on the complete unity of the person of Christ in the divine
Logos, that they were rightly interpreted as Apollinarian by the
Antiochenes and entirely rejected. But the partisan and precipi-
tate *fait accompli* gave Cyril the chance of treating Nestorius
in Ephesus as a notorious heretic with whom fellowship or
negotiation of any kind was out of the question. The local
Bishop of Ephesus, who was striving for his own independence,
had been persuaded to join the anti-Constantinople party and
put all the churches in the city at Cyril's disposal. Nestorius was
virtually excluded. In spite of the protests of the imperial official
charged with the administration of the Council, the Council
gave up waiting for the missing Syrians and the Roman legates,
and Cyril's followers were recognized as the legally constituted
synod. The Council did not hesitate formally to excommuni-
cate Nestorius as a heretic. The jubilant populace celebrated
in the streets the fall of the 'enemy of the Holy Virgin' and
the honour of the 'great, sublime, and glorious Mother of
God'.

When Bishop John of Antioch and Nestorius's other supporters finally arrived, all they could do was to hold a separate
synod which condemned Cyril and his followers. To begin
with, the helpless Emperor recognized the truth of both parties'
views and had both Cyril and Nestorius taken in custody. Protracted and complicated negotiations began in which Cyril,
with his 'well-known methods of persuasion', namely bribery
(*ACO* I, 1, 5, p. 136, 17), quickly won some points. But the
decisive thing was that Nestorius was the first to give in and
offered his resignation, thinking that he must serve the cause of
peace. His resignation was accepted, and he was allowed to
retire to his old Antiochene monastery. Cyril was also allowed
to escape to Alexandria, where he at once proclaimed on every
side the triumph of truth and victory over his godless opponents, as the result of the sacred synod. With this completely
untrue assertion he finally prevailed, but only several decades
later.

The illegal sessions which he had organized with his followers
are still described as the 'Third General Council of Ephesus',
which honoured the Mother of God and saved the true Faith
in Christ from misrepresentation and distortion. And, as a result of the Council, Cyril himself was canonized.

Did Cyril ever really believe his own account of events?
Probably that is the wrong way to put the question. It presupposes a love of justice and an impartiality of which the passionate
and embittered hierarch was never capable. Dogmatic, violent,
and cunning, full of the greatness of his seat and the dignity of
his office, he never considered anything as right unless it was
useful to him in the furtherance of his power and authority and
accorded with his theological tradition and training. The brutality and unscrupulousness of his methods never worried him,
and the fact that similar methods were still more often used in
later theological conflicts may be pleaded in extenuation. The
most serious charge against him is that in the end he was not
even true to his theological principles, but for tactical reasons,
in order to conserve his outward victories, he really surrendered

most of the points he had maintained in Alexandria and Ephesus. After the abdication of Nestorius and Cyril's escape from Ephesus the opposition party had not given up the theological struggle. On the contrary, under the skilful leadership of John of Antioch, a storm of protest was raised throughout the East against the cynical condemnation of a Christological conception to which the majority of Greek-trained theologians and bishops still adhered. The government supported the protest, and in the end Cyril had to give way. After protracted and extremely disagreeable negotiations he accepted a compromise formula in 433 which simply ignored his most outstanding theses and which Nestorius would have accepted at any time. But this was precisely the point on which Cyril remained inexorable: the case of Nestorius was never reopened. He remained condemned as a heretic, and to the outside world Cyril was still 'the man who had unmasked the blasphemers and led the truth to victory'. Indeed, he did not rest until the unhappy man who had been abandoned by his own friends and supporters was wrenched from his Antiochene refuge and deported to Cyril's own territory. He was interned in a remote spot on the edge of the Egyptian Desert; he survived Cyril and died fifteen years later, inwardly unbroken to the end.

One is inclined to deny the theological significance of Cyril altogether in view of his abominable behaviour, and to see in him merely the coldly calculating power politician who sacrificed everything on the altar of his personal success. We have already said that such an interpretation is not in accordance with Cyril's own feeling. It is not enough to see in this subordination of serious theological interests to purely political considerations merely the expression of partisan subjectivism and passion. It was rather the expression of a particular sort of Churchmanship which was no longer tied to theology and tried to maintain the victory of the Faith by enforcing the acceptance of ecclesiastical authority and the 'true' ecclesiastical tradition.

The old problem of the frontiers of theology, which Athanasius had already sensed and Basil had pondered theologically, is now solved in a way which justifies the corruption of systematic thought and theological conscientiousness. After all, the herd thinks in accordance with the teacher's wishes (*ACO* I, 4, p. 227, 19). The important thing is no longer the clarity and purity of the formulas obtained, so long as the right men, the men of the right party, are in power to enforce them. The peace of the Church which has been won by tactical successes can be defended by the usual reference to the essential unfathomableness of religious mysteries and the repudiation of idle curiosity in favour of the eternal wisdom of the Church and its abiding tradition. 'It is not right to dissolve the ancient traditions of the Faith, which have come down to us from the holy apostles themselves; it is wrong to break them up with our exaggerated cleverness and wrong to try to overcome what transcends reason with inquiries carried to extremes or even frivolously to declare with certain artists in definition: this is right; this is wrong. What is needed and blessed is rather to leave the all-knowing God to make his own decisions and not criticize with wanton audacity what he has deemed good' (*De Fide Recta ad Imper.* 17, *ACO* I, 1, p. 53, 10).

Here we see the limitations, or, if you like, the individuality of Cyril as a teacher of the Church. As we have seen, Cyril in fact wanted to be a theologian. But for him theology no longer is answerable only to itself within the Church. It has become the sphere of the teaching office and must in all circumstances comply with the traditions of the Church. No one before Cyril had emphasized the importance of the 'Fathers' so indefatigably. He was convinced that they had 'not left out or overlooked anything vital' at all and that everyone who accepted the orthodox Faith would find in their 'confessions and interpretations' useful material with which to refute 'all heresy and godless insolence' (*De Symb.* 4, *ACO* I, 4, 4, p. 50, 22). He initiated the practice of deciding questions of belief not solely on the basis of the Bible but with the aid of appropriate quotations and collections of quotations from acknowledged authorities and above all from the great Athanasius. This was the purpose of his own writing, which was based from the beginning so largely on quotations and excerpts. This was now regarded as the truly 'royal way' of theology: 'to defer on every issue to the confessions of the holy Fathers, which came about through the inspiration of the Holy Spirit; and to keep firmly in mind the train of their thoughts' (*Ep. 17*, 3, *ACO* I, 1, 1, p. 35, 12). This meant that the creative age of the theology of the early Church had come to an end. In virtue of this theological programme, Cyril can be called the first of the Byzantine scholastics. In the Greek world he was the last of the Fathers of the Church because, strictly speaking, he no longer had any desire to be one. For that reason, he was regarded, as later theologians said, as the 'guardian of accuracy' (Eulog. Al. in Photios, *Bibl. Cod.* 230) and forms the final 'seal of the Fathers' (Anastas. Sin., *viae dux 7*).

THE END OF THE AGE OF THE GREEK FATHERS

WHEN we review the series of pre- and post-Nicene Fathers we are surprised by the rich variety of quite different characters, independent points of view, individual ways of life, and forms of expression. It was a great field of intellectual life with which they were concerned for three centuries, which they tackled, conquered, penetrated, and moulded theologically. Their work was not done according to a fixed plan but in the awareness of a very definite common cause and with a sense of responsibility to a freedom of belief in which reason was respected. All the Fathers we have studied thought of themselves as members of the one 'Catholic' Church and strove to serve the preaching of the gospel, the truth of God, and of the Faith.

The Bible and the revelation of Christ to which the Bible bears witness formed the natural foundation, the common point of departure, and the norm of all their work and research. Starting from these foundations, they sought to ward off 'errors' and prevent a dissolution and disintegration of the Church from within. At the same time, however, they looked outwards into the world and considered its moral and philosophical problems. Everything had to be won for the Logos of God, purified by him and understood anew in him. Their theology was also intended to be a 'philosophy'; it was anti-heretical and missionary, polemical and apologetic in intention at one and the same time. There is sometimes a touch of naïveté about its fresh confidence in victory, but in loyalty to 'the one thing needful' it remains lively and flexible, advances and, in spite of internal and external difficulties, maintains its superiority over its enemies, and finally emerges victorious.

The age of the Fathers of the Church came to an end for various reasons: general, political, sociological, cultural and biological. As with every ultimate historical question, there can be no completely conclusive explanation. We have already touched on the matter in the Introduction and in the course of our description have given our attention first and foremost to the presuppositions underlying the teaching of the Church. A slow process of change took place in the conception of theology and the position of teachers in the Church, which was the inevitable result of their own work and influence. These changes in any case acquire from our point of view an essential and decisive significance. From the very beginning belief in the Bible as the document of divine revelation and high regard for 'natural' reason had gone hand in hand with a frank acceptance of ecclesiastical authority and tradition. The strengthening of these ties and of their political importance, and the progressive systematization of the theological inheritance, which was becoming ever richer and increasingly complex, contributed very largely to the gradual stagnation of intellectual life and the consequent end of the 'classical' patristic age.

We can do no more here than merely outline this process. The turning-point which was reached with the accession of Constantine and the rise of the Imperial Church, closely bound up with the State and public order, undoubtedly constitutes the most significant moment in the process of development. It brought new political and legal ties which strengthened earlier tendencies, and at the same time brought some dangerous developments which involved a stricter regard for dogmatic unity and ecclesiastical decisions. For the first time, in the East the 'Creed' was put forward as a dogmatic and legal standard binding on the Church as a whole. The victory of Nicene orthodoxy was won 'in this sign'. Both Athanasius and Basil persistently appealed to the decision of Nicaea, but they had no wish to go beyond the Nicene Creed and they assiduously avoided adding any further dogmatic formulations. In Ephesus too (431) the old Creed, which had simply been 'extended' in Constantinople in 381, was retained, and even in Chalcedon (451) a tough battle was fought, which failed in the end, to prevent a new formulation of the Faith. On the other hand, however, efforts had been under way for a long time to define more clearly and make more intelligible the fluid conception of the 'genuine' and authoritative tradition. The Emperor Theodosius the Great took the first step in this direction when he appointed to prepare the reorganization of the Eastern Churches a group of theologians, by whom the rest were to be guided (380–81). Soon afterwards, in 383, reference was made to earlier, no longer living, Fathers who had proclaimed the truth in the 'right' way and were recognized by the Church. Later, however, this summary reference to the Fathers was not deemed sufficient. Particular, authoritative writings of Athanasius and other teachers and Fathers were singled out to serve as criteria. These too were supplanted in the following period by the anthologies, which were easier to handle: collections of quotations on dogmatics the selection of which varied according to the passing needs of theological controversy and which brought together genuine quotations torn from their original contexts with a great deal of adulterated and unauthentic material. It was above all Cyril of Alexandria who used this method in his controversies and made it predominant. For analogous practical reasons the method was also introduced in jurisprudence about the same time. The imperial 'Quotation Law' of 426 bound the administration of justice quite formally to particular acknowledged authorities of the past. The final condemnation of Origen by Justinian in 543 brought the effort of Church and State to achieve a standardization of tradition to a conclusion.

As the process of standardization advanced, so the keenness and capacity for independent theological research and teaching waned. Anyone who wanted to say something really new was most likely to say it under a false flag. Thus, in the latter part of the fourth century, the Apollinarians had covered up their condemned literature with the name of St. Athanasius. About the turn of the fifth to the sixth century a Monophysite put into circulation his mystical Neoplatonic ideas about the Church and the liturgy under the cloak of Dionysius the Areopagite (Acts xvii. 34). At a religious discussion which took place in Constantinople in 532 his writings were still rejected as unauthentic, but in the following age they became established. It was inevitable that thanks to this sanctifying of the ecclesiastic tradition the Bible itself was pushed more and more into the background. Official theology no longer responded to its revolutionizing force. It is true that it was revived in the opening phases of monasticism, and for that very reason the monks distrusted all dogmatics and official theology. The most important critic of previous developments, the leader of the Euchite (Messalian) movement, Simeon of Mesopotamia, who died at the close of the fourth century, was condemned as a heretic, and he survives only under a false name as (Pseudo-)'Macarius'.

Another factor was the confusion and complications inherent in the dogmatic tradition itself. The fiction of an unbroken uniformity is in contradiction to the truth and had to be preserved by an ever-increasing expenditure of formalistic ingenuity. The effect of the Council of Chalcedon was particularly catastrophic in this respect. It meant a serious defeat for the Alexandrian theology which had triumphed twenty years previously in Ephesus. But this fact was concealed, since Cyril, the victor of Ephesus, was lauded in Chalcedon with great enthusiasm and set alongside the totally different Bishop Leo of Rome. And so there arose, soon afterwards, the controversy about the interpretation of the Chalcedonian Definition which was concluded a hundred years later under Justinian in a way (Alexandrian Monophysite) that makes nonsense historically and was then converted into a dogma by a new ecumenical Council in Constantinople in 553.

Similar difficulties and artificial harmonizations affected the propositions and methods of philosophy, as if these were the equally traditional presuppositions for theology and dogma.

The earlier Fathers of the Church had all been, more or less, pure Platonists, and the doctrine of the Trinity had been originally conceived in Platonic-Neoplatonic terms. In the fifth and sixth centuries Aristotelian logic began to make its mark and was combined with the Neoplatonic traditions, inside and outside theology. Thus there came into being a terrifyingly complicated apparatus which, however, did not function according to its own laws but was twisted to suit the particular metaphysical and theological principles which it was intended to justify.

The result of all these changes was Byzantine scholasticism, a scientific theology so heavily armoured that only the most learned specialists, monks, and clerics could find their way about. It took a man like Maximus the Confessor (d. 662), and his vigour of mind and faith, to fight in this armour and still make himself understood, setting the whole Church in motion and revealing the sublime errors of Monotheletism as errors of faith. Normally, dogmatics failed to make any impact on everyday piety. The problems of mysticism and of the controversy about images were artfully, but only at a later stage, linked up with doctrine and so brought to a decision. In this connection, the most important name is John of Damascus, who died in 749, since in him the whole historical development of dogmatic thought came to an end in the East. Under the protection of Islamic power he conducted a controversy against the iconoclastic Emperors of Byzantium and composed in a typical combination of cleverness and stupidity the huge dogmatic collection called *The Fount of Wisdom*, which became the model for innumerable later manuals, even in the West. It includes, before getting down to theology proper, an introduction on the history of philosophical concepts, a 'Dialectic', and a heresiology compiled from innumerable earlier authors. Every feasible question is put in its 'rightful' and due place.

Greek theology was gradually suffocated by its own traditionalism. No more or less justified admiration for its conceptual refinements, profundity, and sublimity can alter that fact. The

Fathers had become so holy that in the end they could no longer beget any sons who were their equals in vitality. Theology lived its own life in constant reference to the past and lost all direct contact with the Bible and with life outside or different from itself. In 529 Justinian closed the school in Athens, and the last pagan philosophers left the Empire. Christian missionaries penetrated only into areas where they were desired on political grounds and where the cultural superiority of the Empire smoothed the way for them. The Church was powerless against Islam, and the enormous losses which it suffered at its hands were by no means entirely due to external military causes. It is most striking that the new theological life that came into being in the West in the fourth and fifth centuries had no influence in the East, whereas the West was always open to the influence of Greek theology. Perhaps it was just this feeling of distance from its origins, the need to listen and grow in awareness of the genuine historical differences, which gave Latin theology its power of independent life, although to begin with it owed everything to the Greeks. But the latter had long since thought of themselves as having attained their final goal. Imprisoned in their own territorial and cultural confines, their Church rested upon its own perfection. It trusted in an unchanging and indestructible continuity with the apostles and Fathers of the past whose achievements it admired so much that it failed to observe the changing nature of the problems which faced theology. It preserved their intellectual inheritance without doing anything to renew it.

CHRONOLOGICAL TABLE

138–61	Emperor Antoninus Pius	144	Marcion breaks with Rome
161–80	Emperor Marcus Aurelius	*circa* 165	Death of Justin
		177–78	Irenaeus Bishop of Lyons
202	Septimius Severus forbids conversion to Christianity	202–03	Clement leaves Alexandria; Origen head of the catechetical school in Alexandria
		230–31	Origen moves to Caesarea in Palestine
		235	Death of Hippolytus of Rome
250–51	Persecution of Christians by Decius		
		253–54	Death of Origen
255–59	Persecution of Christians by Valerian		
		circa 270	Death of Gregory Thaumaturgus
303	Beginning of the great persecution of the Christians under Diocletian		
		309?	Death of Pamphilus
324	Constantine the Great sole ruler		
325	Council of Nicaea		
		328	Athanasius Bishop of Alexandria
337	Death of Constantine the Great		
		339	Death of Eusebius of Caesarea
		356	Antony's death at age of 105

361–63	Emperor Julian		
		373	Death of Athanasius
379–95	Emperor Theodosius the Great	379	Death of Basil the Great
381	Council of Constantinople		
		389–90	Death of Gregory of Nazianzus
		394	Death of Gregory of Nyssa
395–408	Emperor Arcadius	398	Chrysostom Bishop of Constantinople
403	Synod of the Oak	407	Death of Chrysostom
408–50	Emperor Theodosius II		
		410	Synesius Bishop of Ptolemaïs
		412	Cyril Bishop of Alexandria
		415	Murder of Hypatia
431	Council of Ephesus		
		444	Death of Cyril of Alexandria
451	Council of Chalcedon		

BIBLIOGRAPHY

INTRODUCTION

The surviving works of the earlier Greek Fathers of the Church are to be found almost complete in the critical editions of *Die griechischen christlichen Schriftsteller der ersten drei Jahrhunderte*, published by the Berlin Academy from 1897 onwards. For the later Fathers the very often inferior reprints by J. P. Migne are still indispensable: *Patrologiae cursus completus, Series Graeca* (with Latin translations), Paris, 1857 ff. A large selection of English translations is provided in Roberts and Donaldson, *The Ante-Nicene Christian Library* (Edinburgh, 1867–71); Schaff and Wace, *A Select Library of Nicene and Post-Nicene Fathers of the Christian Church* (Oxford and New York, 1886–1900); Quasten and Plumpe (later Quasten and Burghardt), *Ancient Christian Writers* (Westminster, Md. and London, 1946 ff.); Schopp, *The Fathers of the Church* (New York, 1947 ff.); Baillie, McNeill, Van Dusen, *The Library of Christian Classics* (London and Philadelphia, 1953 ff.).

The following is a selection of the most important patristic handbooks which will help the interested reader to explore the subject further. A. v. Harnack's *Geschichte der altchristlichen Literatur bis Eusebius* did not get beyond the preliminary parts I (*Überlieferung und Bestand*, 1893) and II (*Chronologie*, 1897–1904). O. Bardenhewer's assiduous *Geschichte der altkirchlichen Literatur*, I–V (1913–1932), is the most complete of the earlier compilations. There is a concise but excellent *Patrology* by Altaner (E. T., Edinburgh, 1958). Also in English there is, above all, the *Patrology* in several volumes by J. Quasten (Utrecht, 1950 ff.) and there are E. J. Goodspeed, *A History of Early Christian Literature* (Chicago, 1942) and, for the Greeks, J. M. Campbell, *The Greek Fathers* (London and New York, 1929).

The most important complete accounts of the dogmatic history of Greek antiquity are: A. v. Harnack, *History of Dogma*, I–VII (1894–99); R. Seeberg, *Lehrbuch der Dogmengeschichte* (Leipzig, 1920 ff.); Fr. Loofs, *Leitfaden zum Studium der Dogmengeschichte*,

I–II, 5th ed., edited by K. Aland (1950–53); J. Tixeront, *Histoire des dogmes* (1930[11], English translation, St. Louis and London, 1930 ff.).

Reference should be made to the following general histories of the Church: L. Duchesne, *Early History of the Christian Church* (London, 1909–24); K. Müller, *Kirchengeschichte*, I, 1 (3rd ed., 1941, in collaboration with H. v. Campenhausen); B. J. Kidd, *A History of the Church to A.D. 461* (Oxford, 1922); J. Lebreton and J. Zeiller, *The History of the Primitive Church* (tr. from the French) (New York, 1949); H. Lietzmann, *Geschichte der alten Kirche*, English translation by B. L. Wolff (New York, 1937 ff.); and the first four volumes of the Catholic compilation, *Histoire de l'Église*, edited by Fliche and Martin (Paris, 1935 ff.).

CH. I—JUSTIN

W. Schmid is preparing a new edition of Justin's *Apology*. The many existing editions of his writings are inadequate. Research on Justin has usually been associated with more far-reaching studies of the apologists in general or limited to articles. Reference may be made to J. Geffcken, *Zwei griechische Apologeten* (1907), and A. von Ungern-Sternberg, *Der traditionelle Schriftbeweis 'de Christo' und 'de evangelio' in der alten Kirche* (1913). Comprehensive accounts of Justin's theology have been given by M. v. Engelhardt, *Das Christentum Justins des Märtyrers* (1878), and E. R. Goodenough, *The Theology of Justin Martyr* (Jena, 1923). W. Schmid, 'Die Textüberlieferung der Apologie des Justin', *Zeitschr. f. neutest. Wissensch.*, 40 (1941), 87 ff., and 'Frühe Apologetik und Platonismus', *Festschrift Otto Regenbogen* (1952), 163 ff., are important for the light they throw on Justin's historical position.

CH. II—IRENAEUS

The editions of the *Refutation and Overthrow of Gnosis, Falsely So Called* (quoted as *adversus haereses*) by A. Stieren (1848–53) and W. W. Harvey (Cambridge, 1857), which were excellent in their time, are still usable. F. Sagnard has undertaken a new edition with a French translation (Paris, 1952). *The Demonstration of the Apostolic Preaching* was published by K. Ter-Mekerttschian and E. Ter-Minassiantz in 1907 in Armenian with a German translation. It has also appeared in English and French translations in the *Patrologia Orientalis*, 12, 5 (Paris, 1919).

Of fundamental importance for the source problem is the (not uncontested) analysis in Fr. Loofs, *Theophilus von Antiochien und die anderen theologischen Quellen bei Irenäus* (1930). For his theological and ecclesiastical thought cf. F. R. M. Hitchcock, *Irenaeus of Lugdunum, A Study of His Teaching* (Cambridge, 1914), J. Lawson, *The Biblical Theology of St. Irenaeus* (London, 1948), and H. v. Campenhausen, *Kirchliches Amt und geistliche Vollmacht in den ersten drei Jahrhunderten* (1953), pp. 185 ff.

Ch. III—CLEMENT OF ALEXANDRIA

The works of Clement were published by O. Stählin in an excellent edition in the *Griechische christliche Kirchenväter*, 1905–09; see also the Index published in 1936 and the German translation in the *Bibliothek der Kirchenväter* (1934–38) with an Introduction and a new revision of the text. Various volumes of the collection *Sources chrétiennes* (Paris, 1949 ff.) provide a revised text with a French translation. See also the English translation by W. Wilson in the *Ante-Nicene Fathers* (1887). There are English editions of *Stromateis* VII by Hort and Mayor (London, 1903) and *Protrepticus* and *Quis Dives Salvetur* by Butterworth (London and Cambridge, Mass., 1919).

The literature on Clement is immense and ever-growing. The most important contributions are as follows: Bigg, *The Christian Platonists of Alexandria* (ed. Brightman, London, 1913); W. Bousset, *Jüdisch-christlicher Schulbetrieb in Alexandria und Rom. Literarische Untersuchungen zu Philo und Clemens von Alexandria* (1915); J. Munck, *Untersuchungen über Clemens von Alexandria* (1933); G. Lazzati, *Introduzione allo studio di Clemente Alessandrino* (Milan, 1939).

On the problems of his theology and intellectual outlook see: F. R. M. Hitchcock, *Clement of Alexandria* (London, 1899); E. Molland, *The Conception of the Gospel in Alexandrian Theology* (Oslo, 1938); W. Völker, *Der wahre Gnostiker nach Clemens Alexandrinus* (1952); H. v. Campenhausen, *Kirchliches Amt und geistliche Vollmacht in den ersten drei Jahrhunderten* (1953), pp. 215 ff.

Ch. IV—ORIGEN

The old editions of de la Rue (1733–59) and Lommatzsch (1831–48) are no longer adequate and have been progressively replaced since 1899 by the editions of the Berlin Academy in the *Griechische christliche Schriftsteller*. The newly-discovered record of a conversation,

Entretien d'Origène avec Héraclide, edited by Jean Scherer (Paris, 1949) is important.

The literature on Origen is enormous; but there has been no satisfactory complete account of him since the earlier exposition of E. R. Redepenning (1841–46), which contains much material, and the somewhat too elegant, more recent study by E. de Faye (3 vols., Paris, 1923–28).

For the early period see: R. Cadiou (translated by J. A. Southwell), *Origen. His Life at Alexandria* (St. Louis and London, 1944).

Of fundamental importance for his relationship to contemporary philosophy: Hal Koch, *Pronoia und Paideusis, Studien über Origenes und sein Verhältnis zum Platonismus* (1932). A. Miura-Stange, *Celsus und Origenes, das Gemeinsame ihrer Weltanschauung* (1926), is also useful. W. Völker, *Das Vollkommenheitsideal des Origenes* (1931), attempts to interpret Origen from the standpoint of his piety and alleged mysticism. Cf. H. Jonas, 'Die origenistische Spekulation und die Mystik', *Theol. Zeitschr.*, 5 (1949), 24 ff.

French research on Origen has been particularly fruitful: R. Cadiou, *La Jeunesse d'Origène* (Paris, 1935); J. Daniélou, *Origène* (Paris, 1950); H. de Lubac, *Histoire et esprit. L'Intelligence de l'écriture d'après Origène* (Paris, 1950); Fr. Bertrand, *Mystique de Jésus chez Origène* (Paris, 1951); H. Crouzel, *Théologie de l'image de Dieu chez Origène* (Paris, 1956).

The danger lies in too much stress being laid on the specifically ecclesiastical and sacramental 'Catholic' aspects. The best objective introduction is provided by Hal Koch, art. 'Origen' in Pauly-Wissowa-Kroll's *Realencyklopädie*, XVIII, 1 (1939), 1036 ff.

CH. V—EUSEBIUS OF CAESAREA

The critical edition in the *Griechische christliche Schriftsteller* has not yet been concluded. Above all, the edition of the *Church History* (1903–09) by Ed. Schwartz (with Rufinus's Latin translation edited by Th. Mommsen), of which a 'short edition' has also appeared (3rd edition, 1922; reprinted, 1952), is of fundamental importance. Schwartz was also responsible for the masterly comprehensive article on Eusebius in Pauly-Wissowa-Kroll's *Realencyclopädie*, VI, 1 (1907), 1370 ff. There are English translations by A. C. McGiffert (London, 1890), Lake (London, 1927–28) and an important article by Headlam in the *J.T.S.* IV (1903), 93, 'The editions and MSS of Eusebius'.

H. Berkhof's *Die Theologie des Eusebius von Caesarea* (1939) provides an excellent exposition. On the political and theological background cf. also H. Eger, 'Kaiser und Kirche in der Geschichtstheologie Eusebs von Caesarea', *Zeitschr. f. neutest. Wissensch.*, 38 (1939), 97 ff.; Joh. Straub, *Vom Herrscherideal der Spätantike* (1939), and the brilliant but theologically questionable study by E. Peterson, *Der Monotheismus als politisches Problem. Ein Beitrag zur Geschichte der politischen Theologie im Imperium Romanum* (1935). The best English works are Lawlor, *Eusebiana* (Oxford, 1912) and Stevenson, *Studies in Eusebius* (Cambridge, 1929).

Ch. VI—ATHANASIUS

H.-G. Opitz made a start on a new edition of the works of Athanasius in 1934; it is to be continued by W. Schneemelcher. An important guide to the study of Athanasius is provided by Guido Müller's *Lexicon Athanasianum* (1952), which also serves as a concordance.

There is as yet no exhaustive biography of Athanasius. F. L. Cross, *The Study of Athanasius* (Oxford, 1945), provides a good introduction.

The essays by Ed. Schwartz, 'Zur Geschichte des Athanasios', in the *Göttinger gelehrte Anzeigen* (1904–11; cf. also *Kaiser Konstantin und die christliche Kirche*, 1936²) are still important.

A survey of the complicated ecclesiastical political struggles is provided by H. Lietzmann's fascinating exposition in the third volume of his *Geschichte der alten Kirche* (1953²) (English translation, 1937–1951).

The development of Athanasius's views on ecclesiastical law is studied in the Giessen dissertation by K. F. Hagel, *Kirche und Kaisertum in Lehre und Leben des Athanasius* (1933), and K. M. Setton, *Christian Attitude Towards the Emperor in the Fourth Century* (New York, 1941).

For the much discussed *Vita Antonii* it is enough to refer to the most recent study by H. Dörries, 'Die Vita Antonii als Geschichtsquelle' (in the *Göttinger gelehrte Anzeigen*, 1949).

Ch. VII—BASIL THE GREAT

There is no complete critical edition of the writings of Basil, nor is there a worthy biography.

A sound and convenient survey of the present state of research is provided by the Basel theological dissertation by L. Vischer, *Basilius der Grosse, Untersuchungen zu einem Kirchenvater des 4. Jahrhunderts* (1953). There are also a great number of more or less valuable studies of particular aspects of his theology and work, especially his attitude to classical culture. On Basil's ascetic theory, cf. D. Amand, *L'Ascèse monastique de S. Basile* (1949) and Clarke, *St. Basil the Great*, A Study in Monasticism (Cambridge, 1913); on his view of the State, G. F. Reilly, *Imperium and Sacerdotium According to St. Basil the Great* (theol. diss., Washington, 1945); on the Antiochene schism, F. Cavallera, *Le Schisme d'Antioche* (Paris, 1905); and for his stand on dogma, K. Holl, *Amphilochius von Ikonium in seinem Verhältnis zu den grossen Kappadoziern* (1904), and more recently, B. Schewe, *Basilius der Grosse als Theologe* (diss., Nymwegen, 1943) and, particularly important, Dörries, *De spiritu sancto, der Beitrag des Basilius zum Abschluss des trinitarischen Dogmas* (1956). More general is Fox, *The Life and Times of St. Basil the Great as revealed in his Works* (Washington, 1939). The correct Greek spelling of the name is Basileios; it was pronounced by then Vasilios.

Ch. VIII—GREGORY OF NAZIANZUS

In the case of Gregory of Nazianzus we are still dependent on the reprint of his works in Migne's *Patrologia graeco-latina*. The old, no longer adequate biography by C. Ullmann, *Gregorius von Nazianz, der Theologe* (1867^2), has been joined by more recent expositions, especially in French, which concentrate on one or another aspect of his character: M. Guignet, *S. Grégoire de Nazianze orateur et épistolier* (Paris, 1911); P. Gallay, *La Vie de S. Grégoire* (Paris, 1943), and the very systematic study by J. Plaignieux, *S. Grégoire de Nazianze, théologien* (Paris, 1952).

Of the innumerable studies of Gregory's attitude to ancient literature and culture, special mention should be made of H. M. Werhahn's richly annotated edition of Gregory's Σύγκρισις βίων (1953). B. Wyss, 'Gregor von Nazianz. Ein griechisch-christlicher Dichter des 4. Jahrhunderts' (*Mus. Helvet.*, 6, 1949), provides the liveliest description of Gregory's personality, as well as useful information on points of detail. The best theological assessment is still to be found, in my opinion, in K. Holl, *Amphilochius von Ikonium in seinem Verhältnis zu den grossen Kappadoziern* (1904), except that even Holl does not perhaps always pay enough attention to the intensely rhetorical character of Gregory's dogmatic formulations and therefore takes some things all too literally and seriously.

Ch. IX—GREGORY OF NYSSA

Werner Jaeger's critical edition of the works of Gregory (the letters edited by G. Pasquali) began in 1921, replacing the quite inadequate texts that appear in Migne. To some extent, however, I have quoted from Migne, since his columns are also referred to in the margin of Jaeger's edition.

There have been many studies of Gregory's mysticism and religious thought in recent times. In most cases special stress has been laid on the 'Christian' content of his thought, as compared with the obviously Neoplatonic elements. Special mention should be made of: H. F. Cherniss, *The Platonism of Gregory of Nyssa* (Berkeley, 1930); H. U. von Balthasar, *Présence et Pensée. Essai sur la philosophie religieuse de Grégoire de Nysse* (Paris, 1942); A. Lieske, 'Die Theologie der Christusmystik Gregors von Nyssa', in *Zeitschr. f. kath. Theologie*, 70 (1948), 49 ff.; 129 ff.; 315 ff., and, in particular, the comprehensive work by J. Daniélou, *Platonisme et théologie mystique. Essai sur la doctrine spirituelle de Saint Grégoire de Nysse* (Paris, 1954²); and also his article, 'La Résurrection des corps chez Grégoire de Nysse', *Vigil. Christ.*, 7 (1953), 154 ff. A recent work is W. Völker, *Gregor von Nyssa als Mystiker* (1955).

The brilliant study by J. Gaïth, *La Conception de la liberté chez Grégoire de Nysse* (Paris, 1953), suffers somewhat from the one-sidedly philosophical and systematic approach. A limited theme but one that is central in Gregory's thought is dealt with by R. Leys, *L'Image de Dieu chez Saint Grégoire de Nysse. Esquisse d'une doctrine* (Brussels, Paris, 1951), and H. Merki, ʹΟΜΟΙΩΣΙΣ ΘΕΩΙ. *Von der platonischen Angleichung an Gott zur Gottähnlichkeit bei Gregor von Nyssa* (Freiburg, Switzerland, 1952), which is a particularly fruitful study from the philological and historical points of view.

Ch. X—SYNESIUS OF CYRENE

The earlier editions of Synesius have been superseded, for the letters by R. Hercher, *Epistolographi Graeci* (Paris, 1873), 638–739; for the hymns and other writings by the Roman edition begun in 1939 by N. Terzaghi, *Synesii Cyrenensis hymni et opuscula*. English translation by A. Fitzgerald of *Letters* (London, 1926), *Essays and Hymns* (2 vols., London, 1930).

G. Grützmacher provided a solid biography in his *Synesios von Kyrene—ein Charakterbild aus dem Untergang des Hellenentums* (1913) and, more recently, Chr. Lacombrade, *Synesios de Cyrène, Hellène et chrétien* (Paris, 1951), in which all the earlier literature is listed. English studies of his life and works by Alice Gardner, in *The Fathers for English Readers* series (London, 1886); J. C. Nicol, *Synesius of Cyrene. His Life and Writings* (Cambridge, 1887); and W. S. Crawford, *Synesius the Hellene* (London, 1901).

J. C. Pando, 'The Life and Times of Synesius of Cyrene' (Catholic University of America, *Patristic Studies*, Vol. 63, Washington, 1940), is more of a compilation.

Ch. XI—JOHN CHRYSOSTOM

No complete edition has been attempted since the edition by Montfaucon (1718–38), which was reprinted, with additions, by Migne. The editions of particular works are also sparse and unimportant. For much of the text the best edition is still that of Savile (8 vols. Eton, 1612).

A prolix biography in two volumes in which all the literature is listed was provided by Chr. Baur in *Der heilige Johannes Chrysostomus und seine Zeit* (1929–30). Especially important for chronology is de Tillemont, *Mémoires pour servir à l'histoire ecclésiastique des six premiers siècles*, Vol. IX (Paris, 1706). Mention should also be made of V. Schultze's exposition in the third volume of his *Early Christian Cities and Landscapes* (1930), which deals with Antioch. An important source for the biography of Chrysostom is Palladius's *Dialogus de Vita S. Joannis Chrysostomi*, which appeared in an excellent edition by P. R. Coleman-Norton in Cambridge in 1928. English lives by Stephens, *St John Chrysostom, his Life and Times* (London, 1880[2]) and (more popular) Bush, *The Life and Times of Chrysostom* (London, 1885).

There are not many theological studies of his work; one of the best is G. Fittkau's 'Der Begriff des Mysteriums bei Johannes Chrysostomos' (*Theophaneia*, IX, Bonn, 1953).

Ch. XII—CYRIL OF ALEXANDRIA

The only complete edition of Cyril's works, by Joh. Aubertus (1638), was reprinted by Migne in *Patr. graeca*, 68–77.

His anti-Nestorian writings may now be found almost complete in the first volume of the *Acta conciliorum oecumenicorum* (*ACO*), by Ed. Schwartz.

The latter's introductions and scattered treatises have made the best contribution to explaining the political proceedings in the Church. See especially *Cyrill und der Mönch Viktor* (1928).

There is no adequate modern biography of Cyril.

The following is important for the light it throws on his theological position within the Alexandrian tradition: J. Liébaert, *La Doctrine christologique de Saint Cyrille d'Alexandrie avant la querelle nestorienne* (Lille, 1951). A. Kerrigan, *St. Cyril of Alexandria, Interpreter of the Old Testament* (Rome, 1952), deals with his methods of exegesis. There is much material too in H. du Manoir de Juaye, *Dogme et spiritualité chez Saint Cyrille d'Alexandrie* (Paris, 1944).

INDEX OF PROPER NAMES

THE FATHERS OF
THE LATIN CHURCH

BY

HANS von CAMPENHAUSEN, D.D.

PROFESSOR OF ECCLESIASTICAL HISTORY
IN THE UNIVERSITY OF HEIDELBERG

TRANSLATED BY MANFRED HOFFMANN

VENERANDO ORDINI THEOLOGORUM
UNIVERSITATIS OSLOENSIS
HOC LIBELLO GRATIAS TESTATUR MAXIMAS AUCTOR
PIE MEMOR
PRIORIS COMMERCII QUO CUM ILLO AMICE ERAT
CONIUNCTUS HONORISQUE SUMMI QUO FACTUS EST
THEOLOGIAE DOCTOR

TRANSLATOR'S NOTE

PROFESSOR VON CAMPENHAUSEN is well known in the academic world as a leading expert in patristics, and as one of the outstanding Protestant scholars in Germany, but his major works have not until recently been available in English. A beginning has been made to remedy this situation by the publication in translation of two of his books, on the Greek and the Latin church fathers, which are highly esteemed both by scholars and by the educated laity. Although the author expressly renounces 'learned quotations, notes, explanations, marginal citations, footnotes, and appendages of that sort', the expert will recognize behind these biographical sketches a background of exact knowledge of the literary work of the church fathers, of their historical setting, and of their theological impact.

As translator, and a former pupil of the author, well acquainted with his methodological and theological approach, I have endeavoured to preserve faithfully the spirit of this work, and the individuality of the author in it. I acknowledge my indebtedness to my colleagues and friends, Professor John Lawson of Atlanta and Dr. Jack H. Wilson of Athens, Tennessee, as well as to the Rev. L. A. Garrard of Oxford for his editorial work. Above all I owe thanks to the author himself for his intellectual inspiration, and for his warm interest in my own work also.

M. H.

Emory University
Atlanta, Georgia

CONTENTS

THE LATIN CHURCH FATHERS
AND THE GREEKS

AN earlier volume in this series was devoted to the Greek church fathers. What was said there about the expressions 'church father' and 'patristics' will not be repeated here. The present volume may be read independently, although in subject-matter it is a continuation of the earlier one. The Latin patristic literature originated almost one hundred years after the Greek. The Latin fathers were the younger pupils of the Greeks, who were their first teachers in Christian faith and thought, and indeed in their whole theology. This relationship is not made sufficiently distinct by the usual purely chronological arrangement of the Greek and Latin church fathers. Through the early church, as through the whole world of ancient culture, flowed a constant stream of intellectual stimulus from the East to the West. There was no comparable counterflow from West to East to correspond to the large amount of literature translated into Latin. Nevertheless, in the Western world there very swiftly developed a new, vigorous, and independent form of ecclesiastical life and Christian theology, which was ultimately to prove not inferior to the Greek, and probably surpassed it in its effect on world history. The rise of this Latin ecclesiastical phenomenon is noteworthy because it marks the first transformation into a new intellectual mould which Christianity underwent as a whole.

Although Jesus and His first disciples did not speak Greek, but Aramaic, Christianity is no 'Jewish religion'. The church consisted of 'Jews and Greeks'; and the Greek fathers rightly understood their faith as a new truth transcending Judaism as well as Hellenism. The New Testament was written in Greek and, as always, the language is more than an external clothing. The Greek spirit touched and to some extent determined Christianity even in its inception. This factor increasingly and rather one-sidedly influenced the further development at the expense of the Hebraic Old Testament foundations. Even where the ancient church in its missionary activity pushed beyond the frontiers of the empire into the East and apparently reorientalized itself, the Greek presuppositions of the text of the Bible, the creeds, and theological thinking generally remained and proved to be ineradicable. To be sure there were also Oriental church fathers; yet they fell far short of the Latin fathers with respect to independent power and importance.

The 'Latin' West, which alone need really be taken into account for the history of the ancient church, had long been influenced and permeated by Greek culture and Hellenistic thinking when Christianity entered the scene. In fact it was only this that made the rapid intellectual development of the Western church possible. However, if the Roman spirit did not simply dissolve into Hellenism, but preserved its identity throughout the constant interchange with it, and only thereby attained its own intellectual character, the same is true to an even greater degree of the Latin church and its theological independence. As has already been said, the Latin church fathers were instructed and educated by their Greek teachers; but they possessed from the very beginning their own approach to the Bible, especially to the Old Testament. In opposition to the philosophical trend, and the metaphysical and speculative tendencies of Hellenism, they display a restraint and reserve which were overcome only at the end of the fourth century. This led to the Golden Age of theology of the Latin fathers, as exemplified above all in Augustine. Even this new 'philosophical' theology, however, did not lose its foundation in Latin thinking. Not by chance was it linked with a rediscovery of Paul, and with a taking up of the question, so characteristic of Paul, of the opposition of faith to 'law'. This is an aspect which was scarcely ever considered by Greek theology and which in its original meaning, at any rate, remained completely foreign to it. The peculiar affinity which existed between the Roman character and Judaism enabled the Latin church, just because of its sobriety and practical legalism, to understand what the 'gospel' meant.

However, we shall not speak of these things in detail in this volume, which presents only a series of biographical sketches and which does not set out to be a substitute for a history of theology and doctrine. The selection of the personalities portrayed is again strictly limited and does not range beyond the end of the old classical culture, the decline of which marks an epoch for church history too. Yet behind my endeavours lies the conviction that historical life is realized primarily through human personalities, or at least that in them it can be grasped most directly and comprehended most distinctly.

CHAPTER I

TERTULLIAN

A CHRISTIAN congregation already existed in Rome at the time of the apostle Paul, but it was then not yet a Roman congregation. The metropolis contained immigrants from all over the world, and not least from the Greek-speaking Orient, from which also came the first missionaries and adherents of the new faith. The language of the Christians throughout the West was exclusively Greek and remained so for a hundred years. This was not only because the church had originated in the East, but it reflected also the general conditions of the empire, which had become one united empire of the Mediterranean area and its culture. Greek was not only the language of the intelligentsia (as French was at one time in Germany), it was likewise the prevalent language of commerce and travel. In every large town of the West, Greek was not only understood but spoken, probably as the ordinary language of the people. For a religion of townsfolk, a faith which at the very outset dissociated the individual from national ties and placed him in a new community as Christianity did, Greek was the obvious religious and ecclesiastical language.

When this situation slowly began to change toward the end of the second century, we can observe the broadening of this intellectual and social basis and the growing popularity and stability of the Western church. The members of the congregations began to speak Latin among themselves and Greek at most only with the higher clergy. Sermons were preached for the first time in Latin; and we also come across the beginnings of a modest Latin-Christian literature for practical use in the church: translations of the Bible, accounts of martyrdoms, and a catalogue of the Canon have been preserved. Yet when and where did the independent intellectual development begin? The first Latin document of importance is considered by some scholars to be the dialogue 'Octavius', which significantly is an 'apology' written with an eye toward non-Christian readers. Its author is a Roman lawyer by the name of Minucius Felix. In the old quarrel about chronological priority it at least looks as if the scale is tipping in his favour, and against the precedence of his fellow-lawyer, Tertullian. Despite this, we start off with Tertullian and can set aside without misgivings the otherwise unknown Minucius. In any event, the first Latin theologian whom we really know in the West as a distinct personality is Tertullian. Tertullian elucidates through the abundance of his vigorous and original writings the whole world in which he lived and worked. To this extent he stands at the beginning of the entire Latin church history.

Tertullian was an African, i.e. a citizen of Africa, the province colonized by the Romans, which is the modern Tunisia. Here in the capital, Carthage, Quintus Septimus Florens Tertullianus was born soon after the middle of the second century. His father was a subaltern in the army. The Roman outlook is taken for granted, although it is a characteristically African form of the Roman spirit which tends to combine discipline with criticism and a sense of order with scorn and passion and which prefers self-sufficiency even to the point of rebellion, rather than blindly to follow and obey. The young Tertullian, having received a sound education in rhetoric and law, lived for a time in Rome and may have begun a practice as an attorney. That he is identical with the famous lawyer Tertullianus, mentioned in the Digests, is very unlikely. Tertullian was no deep scholar, although he had read and knew much and liked to startle his reader with obscure facts. He was, in Harnack's phrase, a 'philosophizing advocate' in whose mouth the precise language of the lawyer has become a means of rhetoric. His keen intellect was constantly in motion; yet he was unfitted for a contemplative life. Everything Tertullian thought, said, and did was directed toward the real world and pressed for a practical decision. This was the determinative factor also in his intellectual and spiritual life. Tertullian was impetuous, hot-blooded, at times intentionally reckless; he himself complained that he could never learn the precious virtue of patience. Jerome, who had in many respects a similar nature, once called him a man always afire (*vir ardens*). Yet his manner was not primitive; he never lost control of his temper. On the contrary, the more he spoke in anger, and the more passionately and personally he threw his weight behind what he thought was right, the more polished were his thoughts and his style, the more subtle his tactics and the more sparkling his cruelly biting wit. Roman restraint, legal clarity, and military discipline were transmuted into an intellectual and moral force in the ardent, aspiring mind and heart of Tertullian.

We do not know the circumstances which led Tertullian to Christianity. Usually one thinks above all of the effect of the Christian martyrs which, according to his own testimony, exercises the strongest persuasive force, and also of the moral impact of the Christian community generally, imperturbable and united in the midst of the world of urban licentiousness. In addition to this, however, the spiritual impact of Christian teaching and preaching must not be overlooked. The message of the one God, Creator and Sovereign—who is no mere idea but directs the whole course of the world—who has overthrown the demons through Christ, and who now calls all men to the ultimate decision, was the source of the decisive experience in Tertullian's life. Contrasted with this, the artificially constructed theories and wisdom of the philosophers were exposed as vain and ineffectual babble. The truth of God cannot be denied in principle by any intelligent being, and yet obviously it is really revealed and truly made known only to the Christians. They know God's Son and through Him, His teaching, and His word, they know the entire will, nature, and law of God. Tertullian must have come upon the Bible quite early, and he adhered to it throughout his life. He knew it inside and

out and referred to it expressly on every possible occasion, not
hesitating to interpret it independently, when necessary according to the original Greek text. In hearing the direct voice of
God throughout—in the words of the prophets, of the Saviour
and of His disciples—Tertullian was, of course, not original. He
shared this belief in 'the Scripture' with the Christians of his
time. But far more than all of his contemporaries he also had an
immediate sense of the unique character of the Bible. He knew
and stated time and again that it is absolutely different from the
spirit and noble wisdom of the world. His blunt, rough-hewn
realism discovered through a natural affinity the unclassical
ardour and stern sobriety of the Holy Scripture, its concrete,
paradoxical character, unapproachable by any religious-aes-
thetic idealization. And by accepting it in this particularity and
loving it in its strangeness he became the most original and in
many respects the most penetrating exegete of the whole ancient
church, whose detailed accuracy and understanding was out-
done by none of the later theologians. The limitations which
finally defeated him were the limits of his own comprehension
of the faith, namely the limits of his proud and mercilessly rigid
nature.

When we first become acquainted with Tertullian, he was
already a respected member of the Christian congregation of
Carthage. He was in the prime of life, happily married, and
although perhaps not wealthy, in an independent and secure
position economically. Thus he made himself available for the
instruction of the catechumens, the candidates for baptism, and
the newly converted. Moreover, he may have 'preached' occasionally, i.e. delivered spiritually instructive speeches before the
congregation. Above all, however, Tertullian was active as an
independent writer, acting as advocate before Christians and
pagans for the best aspects of Christianity. In part he did his
literary work in Greek—'for the sake of our theatre-aesthetes'
as he ironically remarked (De Cor. 6)—but it is characteristic
that none of his Greek writings have been preserved. The
transition to Latin was most appropriate for an author who, like

Tertullian, aimed at a direct effect and confrontation, and by appeals and lectures tried to reach primarily his nearest brethren and fellow-citizens. But what Latin it was that Tertullian suddenly dared to write! It was without precedent in the literary field. In Tertullian's writings, we come across the living language of the Christians of that time, the Latin of the growing Latin church, a language which accordingly is filled with loanwords and new coinage to describe the new facts and ideas of the Christian daily life. It observes and adopts at the same time even in grammatical details the language actually spoken by the society of Carthage, and by the people whom Tertullian knew, observed and sought out. But above all it was Tertullian's own language, an expression of his violent creative power which left nothing unattempted in order to obtain the new self-imposed goal.

Tertullian well knew what he was doing. He renounced no trick of approved rhetoric, which he knew how to combine with the most telling of surprises, puns, rhymes, alliterations, and rhythmic clauses, and all the peculiarities and idiosyncrasies of the contemporary school of writers. In this respect he seems to show a kinship with his older contemporary and African fellow-countryman, Apuleius. At any rate Tertullian had nothing to do with the polished classical elegance of Minucius Felix, who presents his apology in the style of Cicero. He wanted to strike and unmask the reality of his time; he wanted above all to grip, enchain, and captivate his hearers. Hence he expressed himself in a lively and vivid way which often violently exceeds the bounds of good taste. Nevertheless, his colloquialism is never simply crude, because it is demanded by the subject-matter—i.e., as Tertullian sees it, it is demanded by the truth itself. This gives to the crudeness and apparent vulgarity of his language the dignity of a higher mission and the consecration of real sincerity. This impression of an inflexible, heroic realism even intensifies the intended close-clipped phraseology, the volcanic eruption of his sentences. According to a statement made by a critic in the ancient church, almost every word of Tertullian becomes an aphorism. And this aphoristic sententiousness, this rough conciseness occasionally reminds one of Tacitus. But 'the fervour which Tacitus holds in check with an aristocratically restrained indignation, becomes in him [Tertullian] a tidal wave which carries with it, whirling and swirling, everything in its path'. No other ancient author, says Eduard Norden in this connection, has so incessantly violated the 'highest law of the ancient conception of art, the subordination of individuality to the traditional' as has Tertullian, to whom Christ revealed Himself, as he once said, precisely 'not as tradition but as truth' (de Virg. Vel. 1, 1). Even in ancient times complaints were raised concerning the difficulty of his writings. And another consequence of his style for us is that Tertullian's sentences cannot possibly be directly translated into a modern language, not even into English. Only the original Latin preserves the hard stroke and sound of the metal, the sparks flying as he forges it.

There was scarcely a problem in the church of that time about which Tertullian did not express his view, or in some way offer his opinion. The thirty or so different writings we possess today are as varied as can be imagined. Tertullian liked to arrange a topic thematically and treat it exhaustively without becoming verbose. He did not adopt the literary form of a continuous Biblical commentary which was originating at that time. His publications range from the short, crisp, and clever, pamphlet or essay to voluminous theological treatises which are 'books' even in a modern sense, and are thoroughly scholarly. They are well-organized, and always keep in focus his intended purpose. They skilfully put the reader in the picture and anticipate his possible objections; they draw his attention to the bearing and importance of certain ideas and irresistibly carry him with them. Tertullian possessed an ability rare among theologians: he is incapable of being dull. This is true also of treatises written for purely edifying and instructive purposes which mainly represent the result of his teaching of catechumens. Thus he wrote the famous tract on prayer—'which alone defeats God'—containing a beautiful and impressive exposition of the Lord's Prayer. He instructs his readers about the meaning and right use of baptism and repentance. He describes what a Christian marriage should be; and in a short tract praises patience—which he himself sorely lacked. What he expounds is not always new; but it is always independently considered, handled in a new way, and so presented that everyone can realize the significance of the problem. Even when using other authors he was no mere plagiarist, but adapted himself to the actual reader. And this makes his writings an incomparable source of material on the church life of his time.

Most of his writings, however, are of a different nature. They are polemical in approach and pugnaciously directed outwards against the enemies and persecutors, the heretics and seducers of the church. And it is in these that his gifts and superior talents fully unfold. Tertullian knew how a rhetorician convinces his hearers, wins them over to himself and incites them against others. In every situation he appears as the one who really knows, while his opponents are all malicious, stubborn, and ignorant fellows who scarcely need refutation before a competent audience. But simultaneously he liked to act the role of the noble controversialist who holds his punches because he does not want to condemn someone without examination, and is first willing to give every opponent his due and more than his due. He presents his evidence gradually; he knows how to add to it impressively while leaving the impression that he is offering only a selection of what he has available. Often he releases an already defeated adversary, apparently granting him a new chance by still accepting with reservation a thesis already proven as false in order to crush his position a second, third, and fourth time under this and any other imaginable presupposition, and finally to expose him to disdain and complete ridicule while the victorious truth rises unharmed like a phoenix from the ashes. It is not surprising that such a technique of argument sometimes overreaches itself. Since Tertullian was forever rearranging his very sharply formulated, allegedly incontrovertible statements in different ways, the reader who looks for the

logical, hermeneutical, and theological principles which are
really determinative easily becomes bewildered. His brilliant
subtlety tempts one to take him more seriously and regard him
as a deeper thinker than he really is. Nonetheless, this does not
means that Tertullian is not in earnest about what he defends.
As a rule, ancient rhetoric considered much in polemics legitimate which today would appear as unfair or mere shadow-
boxing. Tertullian made radical use of the possibilities given to
him by his education and his incomparable talent. He was no
cynic; but he was a master of the most cunning dialectics and
pointed irony. Each time when, after such invectives, he returns
to his actual subject with a passion often splendid, never bom-
bastic, even the modern reader has the feeling that the whole
man stands heart and soul behind his testimony. And he realizes
too why Tertullian stands up for his conviction so harshly and
fervently, with such wild vehemence.

The earliest writings which we possess by Tertullian are
aimed at the defence of Christianity against pagan suspicion,
against defamation and bloody persecution. This was the first,
the classic task, so to speak, of a Christian writer in that period.
From the middle of the second century onward, the Greek
'apologists' had composed their more or less voluminous
'apologies' addressed to the emperors. These were in reality,
like any such literature, naturally read much more by the Christians than by the pagans for whom they were intended. Minucius Felix had already joined himself to this group. Tertullian
obviously had studied his various predecessors intensively and
had discovered immediately the reason for their failure: they
were not really directed to their opponents; they all tried to
accomplish too much at once and did not concentrate on the
factually and psychologically decisive points. Moreover, they
did not attain the literary and intellectual level necessary for
such a debate. We can still pursue the stages through which
Tertullian endeavoured to cope with his task in a new style.
We see a first attempt in the work in two parts: *To the
Heathen*, which he later abandoned. Then follows the great

Apologeticum in an earlier draft followed by another, perhaps revised by him, and no longer addressed to an inaccessible emperor, but to his unintelligent governors and government officials. Finally there are original variations on specific topics dating from a later time.

The great *Apologeticum* is justly considered to be the unexcelled masterpiece of early Christian apologetics. It was even translated at once into Greek, a distinction which even in later times fell to the lot only of a very few writings of the Latin church fathers. Tertullian advisedly chose for the apology the form of a speech before the tribunal, something which it had long been impossible for the Christians actually to make. This situation itself, he suggests, shows how altogether objectionable the proceedings against the Christians were. 'Truth makes no appeal on her own behalf, because she does not wonder at her present condition. She knows that she plays the role of an alien on earth, that among strangers she readily discovers enemies, but she has her origin, abode, hope, recompense, and honour in heaven. Meanwhile, there is one thing for which she strives: that she be not condemned without a hearing.' This surely could not threaten the prevailing legal system, he adds sarcastically, for the authorities would be able to have an even higher opinion of themselves if they could hear the truth and then nevertheless condemn it (*Apol.* 1, 2 f.; *FC*, 10, 7).

So begins his defence. Tertullian, in his own way, tears apart the whole legal proceedings, and demonstrates that it is insane to prosecute the most trustworthy citizens of the empire in the name of a religion which, itself founded on falsehood and deceit, is no longer really followed or taken seriously anywhere. He is never tired of pointing out that all the atrocities and crimes falsely attributed to the Christians have long been perpetrated and tolerated by the pagans. Yet he now abstains from the clumsy attempt to connect these polemics with positive propaganda for Christianity and conversion. This conclusion may be drawn by the reader himself when he has learned of the teaching, rules of morality, and behaviour of the Christians as

they actually are. The necessary evidence and proofs for such a
conclusion are to be offered at their proper place. Tertullian has
not abandoned any of the traditional material of the old apologetics; he has even materially amplified it. Yet by holding
on to the last to the framework of a simulated court-speech,
everything now appears much more concise, more clearly
arranged, exciting, and distinct. Holding his breath, the reader
follows the surprising demonstrations and disclosures and,
before he is aware of it, he has reached the summary with
which Tertullian, seemingly all too soon, breaks off the speech
for the defence as though he regarded all further efforts as
pointless: 'But, carry on, good officials; you will become much
better in the eyes of the people if you sacrifice the Christians for
them. Crucify us—torture us—condemn us—destroy us! Your
iniquity is the proof of our innocence. For this reason God permits us to suffer these things. . . . Yet your tortures accomplish
nothing, though each is more refined than the last; rather, they
are an enticement to our religion. We become more every time
we are hewn down by you: the blood of Christians is seed
(*semen est sanguis Christianorum*).' We are just thankful to you
that you end the trial so rapidly. It seems as if two courts con-
front each other in God's and man's fight, and 'when we are
condemned by you, we are acquitted by God' (*Apol.* 50, 12 ff.;
FC, 10, 126).

The decisive thought with which Tertullian turns upside
down the state's proceedings is consequently not of juridical but
theological origin. It is the conviction of the emptiness of polytheism and of the reality of the one, revealed God. What the
authorities and the crazy masses venerate is based upon a lie,
upon man-worship, and vain folly; behind this, however, stand
the dangerous demons as the really operative, beguiling, and
misleading force. These are the natural enemies of the truth, and
they have for that reason set off the insane actions against the
Christians. Therewith at a single blow the combination of
religion and politics, the present state religion, until then
unquestioned, collapses. How can one possibly still demand

pernicious sacrifices to idols and demons by those who have come to know the true, almighty God? How can one reproach those with the charge that they lack loyalty and fidelity, who wish only to avoid participation in the falsehood perpetuated by the state, and instead of harming the emperor with a devilish adoration wish rather for his sake to invoke the true God, and who are truly devoted to him in every respect? This is why the good rulers have all along been well-disposed towards the Christians, and only the bad ones have persecuted them. This old tendentious legend, which tries to make real an unfulfilled wish of the Christians, attains, as stated by Tertullian, a little more probability and importance. For out of loyal sentiment he is able to appeal over the heads of the local authorities to the good emperors who may not have been informed about the actions of their executive agencies and the malpractice done in their names.

All these tactical declamations, however, bear in addition a more far-reaching and basic significance. Here we find ourselves at the beginnings of a new understanding of the state, and of obedience to it, which had not existed in the world prior to Christianity and which points to a distant future, at that time completely unattainable. The rulers and the state as such lose their direct religious power. There arises instead a concept of a concrete, this-worldly obedience to the state which becomes, in a new sense, binding and inevitable because it is carried on in the name of the true God. 'What betters man is the worship of God' (de Paen. 2, 7). Despite a liberal interpretation in practice the state was still in principle considered sacred. The essentially religious understanding of the state, which had existed until then, appears now simply as untruth and hypocrisy. It sheds its demonic elements in the light of the new radical faith and the obedience flowing from it. Who, asks Tertullian, really regards the emperor as a god in a serious, i.e. in the radical Christian sense? And who still is faithful to him if not the Christians? He does not shrink from alluding to the constant Palace-revolutions and murders, and suggests that if the breasts of the citizens and politicians were made of transparent glass, some thoroughly undesirable things would doubtless be seen! And is it not after all an absurdity to dictate religious convictions by order of the state? Is faith not free by its very nature? The attempt to demand worship by force is against human and natural law, 'and it also is not religious to wish to enforce religion' (ad Scap. 2, 2). We sense here contact with ideas of philosophical enlightenment. Yet the new faith in a revealed God acting in this world not only liberates the individual from the external authority of the 'tyrant'. It also threatens to arouse doubt regarding the entire combination of religion and politics, and to change it radically in a manner which philosophical teaching on politics and criticisms could neither have sought nor effected.

Furthermore, Tertullian presents the fact in such a way as to indicate that the recognition of the Christians by the empire would impose no practical problem at all. They are not surely —as suggested—'the enemies of mankind', but rather enemies of 'error' (Apol. 37, 10). Therefore, there are no better subjects than they. Christians do not commit crimes, not even those not punished by law. They obey any just order, pay taxes without defrauding, and do not join in subversive activities. Quite childish are the fancies regarding the social and economic dangers of their way of life. The Christians participate in all civic activities of commercial and economic life like everybody else. They are to be found everywhere—except in the temple! 'We are neither Brahmins nor Indian gymnosophists, nor hermits of the forests, nor cranks who run away from life.' He who believes in the Creator does not despise his gifts but only excess and debauchery. 'We are supposedly destroying your commerce although we live with you and are dependent on you, this somebody else may understand' (Apol. 42, 1 f.). Theologically those sentences are interesting; yet in the concrete political situation, they reveal Tertullian—as apologist. In reality, he knows very well that this living together with the pagan society of which he speaks is by no means so easy. Indeed, strictly speaking, it is impossible for Christians. Pagan life is the

domain of the demons; one cannot participate in it without
encountering their influence, cult, and symbols everywhere.
When Tertullian addresses the Christians, he is the first to
arouse their consciences as much as possible against all compromise, unfortunately so often attempted, and does not draw
back from any consequence. Only in the case of pagan education does he make a characteristic exception. 'The emergency
serves here as the excuse.' Christians cannot avoid secular instruction, because even religious culture cannot manage without
it, and also because they will refute the pagan poison all the
better since they are at the same time being instructed about the
true God. Yet this excuse is valid only for the pupils, not the
teachers, who could not possibly deal with the pagan religious
mythology and everything connected with it (*de Idol.* 10). The
limits to what may be allowed are set as narrowly as possible.
A Christian craftsman or businessman must not manufacture
or sell anything which in one way or another could be used to
the possible advantage of idolatry, votive offerings, or even the
immoral and luxurious pagan way of life. In no circumstances
whatever is one allowed to accept a public office; for how could
anyone in such a position escape the prescribed ceremonies and
festivities, the libations and smoke of incense always connected
with it? Moreover, how could a soldier avoid honouring the
idolatrous banner? A judge, in addition, has to inflict tortures
and decree capital punishment. Tertullian does not want to say
that these offices are simply unjust and should be either re-
formed or abolished. The world must be as it is, and 'the
Romans, i.e. the non-Christians' (*Apol.* 35, 9) naturally need
their administration, their civil officials, and their emperors.
But what has this to do with Christians who do not become
Caesars, just as the Caesars of necessity are not Christians?
(*Apol.* 21, 24). One may continue to persecute and martyr
them; it will be evident on doomsday who has made the
more prudent decision and sworn his allegiance to the better
flag!

These are the old, primitive Christian views of believers as strangers here, and of the necessity of their affliction in this world, and of the all-determining future of God. These notions spring to life in Tertullian with new vigour—only that they attain now a one-sided tone, polemical, grim, and irreconcilable, and an accent which cannot be missed and is almost politically threatening. This is partly intended—Tertullian would like to deter the persecutors by his warnings if he can; yet it also at the same time conforms to his inner nature which fights rather than loves, breaks rather than bends, and which has accepted with joy the 'service', the *militia Christi*. He loves to conjure up military metaphors just because it is not a matter of agreement but of decision. Paganism is to Tertullian no foolishness to be enlightened, no prejudice or mistake to be dispelled or brought to reason. It is the 'world', and as such a great demonic unity to be recognized in its entirety, and to be rejected and condemned.

It is therefore no mere accident that in the last chapters of his *Apologeticum* Tertullian comes to speak expressly of philosophy, the highest and seemingly ideal embodiment of ancient spirit and life. Even at this point where the Greek apologists had almost without exception taken pains to indicate a certain appreciation and willingness to bring out a positive common basis for ethical criteria and the recognition of truth, he sees only the differences, and the increased danger of a deception and confusion in the essential matter. For Tertullian philosophers are 'Sophists', who are not seeking the truth but rather their own glory and success. Their dialectical and rhetorical tricks are vain, and result continually in contradictions and inconsistencies. Their knowledge is deceitful, and their conduct of life defective. Even the holiest symbol of philosophical independence and freedom, the death of Socrates, does not arouse Tertullian's admiration. The equanimity of his alleged wisdom was artificial and did not come from the certainty of a real possession of truth (*de An.* 1, 2 ff.). There is no common ground 'between a philosopher and a Christian, between a disciple of Hellas and a disciple of Heaven' (*Apol.* 46, 18;

FC. 10, 114) or, historically speaking, between 'Athens and Jerusalem, Academy and Church' (*de Praescr.* 7, 9).

Of course, Tertullian does not overlook the correspondence every educated Christian of the day seems to detect between his convictions and many traditional teachings, particularly the Platonic. He does not wish to deny them (*de An.* 2, 1) and is much too much of an apologist not to refer to them occasionally. However, he then explains them, in conformity with an older, originally Jewish, theory as due to the use of the Old Testament by the philosophers, the 'theft' of God's wisdom by the Greeks. Alternatively, like the Stoics, he traces them back to the *sensus communes*, to the elements of reasonable insight in which everybody participates by nature. The result in any case is a new confirmation of the Christian revelation, and by no means a recommendation of the philosophers or of philosophy. The philosophers always have blended the truth with their faults and errors. It would surely be a wrong and dangerous détour to try to find right understanding from their conjectures, instead of accepting it where the truth is given complete and pure. He who wants to talk about God must be instructed by God. A Christian, therefore, should build his faith 'not on a foreign foundation, but on his own' (*de An.* 26, 1).

What puzzles the modern reader time and again is the fact that Tertullian, in spite of his radical rejection of philosophy, again and again still makes use of his own philosophical education, even when he moves on to thoroughly theological ground. He refers to 'reason' and 'nature'; he speaks of the substance, accidents, and 'status' of a thing; he establishes methodological principles and makes dialectical distinctions—not to mention the countless instances in which he takes the presuppositions of his proof consciously or unconsciously from philosophical, and especially from Stoic, traditions of his time, and considers them more or less self-evident. For instance, he takes up the Stoic teaching of the physical nature of all reality, God's 'person' not excluded. This apparent contradiction, however, is based on

a misunderstanding of what Tertullian understands by philosophy. Faith and philosophy designate to Tertullian the possession of fundamentally analogous knowledge distinguished
primarily with regard to their content, which is sought and
adopted in different ways. Faith clings to what God has revealed, while the philosopher lives under the illusion that he is
able to solve by himself even those problems which lie beyond
the human horizon. What Tertullian demands is not really a
sacrificium intellectus but an appropriate limitation of the intellectual *hubris* of man according to the criterion of God's
word. God certainly never acts unreasonably (*de Paen.* 1, 2);
but he has made man to hear and obey (*ibid.* 4, 4 ff.). The
question is that of the relationship of revelation to philosophy,
but not yet that of the later formal distinction between faith
and reason, or the issue of 'believing and thinking'. By acknowledging the divine revelation, the believer does not think less
logically, reasonably and 'scientifically' than a philosopher; it
is only that, as a matter of fact, he reaches the goal in his own
way. To that extent Christianity can be called the true or
'better philosophy' (*de Pall.* 6, 2), although Tertullian generally avoids this conception, which is so common in the writings
of the apologists. On no account, however, can a philosophy
which is not willing to accept God's wisdom be equated with
'natural reason'; for unspoiled nature agrees entirely with
Christianity in acknowledging God. Tertullian tries to illustrate this in a little apologetic essay on *The Testimony of the
Soul*, the most charming piece he ever wrote. It is possible, he
thinks, to demonstrate readily from those things which are
'self-evident' to human common sense, and also from spontaneous exclamations and expressions, that the 'soul' truly
knows only one God, and that it fears his judgement and tries
to find refuge with him against the power of demons. For that
reason it testifies more effectively to faith than any erudite
apologetics. It should, however, be noted: this is true only of
the soul 'in its natural state, plain, uncultivated and simple' a
schooled and educated soul which 'belches' the academic

wisdom of Attica is no longer Christian, and there is nothing that can be done to make it reasonable (*Test. An.* 1, 6 ff.).

To understand these views it is useful to remind oneself that Tertullian was a Westerner; philosophy never obtained in the Latin West the publicly approved position and independent activity it had in the Greek world. Here, it could easily appear in fact as dead book-learning and mere rhetoric, as superficial culture without content, and as mere entertaining small talk. But to understand Tertullian's anger fully we must not stop here. We must envisage the actual theological adversaries of whom he instinctively thinks as soon as he talks of the useless hollowness of philosophy. They are the heretics, pompous heads of schools who believe in the fantasy of an 'educated', allegedly higher wisdom and knowledge, which leads even Christians astray and corrupts all true belief. The philosophers are 'the patriarchs of the heretics' (*de An.* 3, 1); only when one recognizes this is the full abomination of philosophical nonsense revealed once for all.

As a mere matter of bulk, the fight against heresy occupies the largest part of the works left behind by Tertullian. These are at the same time the writings which more clearly present his earnestness and objective interest, despite the polemical strife and exaggeration. Of course, the modern reader easily takes offence at his immoderate polemics. Tertullian does not take pains to understand his opponents from the point of view of their own presuppositions or to do justice to their 'concern' at the moment; he seeks to expose them and time and again pours forth against them his biting sarcasm. Yet he would hardly have seen anything blameworthy in this fact. Precisely because he is really concerned about the cause, the truth, and existence of the Christian faith, he seeks to fight and destroy the heretics with every available weapon. The only question which matters to him in these circumstances is whether the caricature of the heretics which is what he undoubtedly gives is 'right' as such, i.e. whether it unveils and strikes at the essential weakness of the hostile position, and so attains a deeper and basic significance.

The answer must be 'yes'. Tertullian is no slanderer, no mean pamphleteer inventing cheap reproaches. He has understood the essential common elements of the heretical position, presented and combated them in their general aspects, long before modern scholarship brought the countless groups and currents of the heresy of the period together under the single designation of 'Gnosticism'. What is Gnosticism to Tertullian? It is a destructive syncretism appealing to man's innate spiritual nature, his inclination to overestimate his own spiritual and idealistic nature, and obliterating the fixed boundary between creature and deity. It is at the same time a 'nihilistic' hostility to the God of reality who has created the world and has revealed himself concretely in the flesh.

As was the case with his Greek predecessors, what stands out is the strong emphasis on the ecclesiastical and doctrinal instability, the permanent inconstancy and fluctuation of the Gnostic congregations and their speculation. The heretics rely only on their own whims and not on God's word. The basic factor of insatiable curiosity and conceit, *curiositas*, establishes the inner relationship and connection with philosophy. Already with good cause Paul had forewarned Christians of philosophy (Col. ii. 8). They should 'seek the Lord with sincerity of heart', as Solomon had taught (Wisdom of Solomon, i. 1), and not invent a new 'Stoic, Platonic or dialectic Christianity' (*de Praescr.* 7, 11). The fantasies which follow are worse than all philosophy. It can be positively painful to see how Plato is forced to 'season' each soup of the heretical kitchen with his thoughts (*de An.* 23, 5). Because of what he reasonably says, Seneca also does not belong to them but rather, as so often, 'to us' (*de An.* 20, 1). There is no New Testament passage which the heretics are so fond of quoting as Christ's advice: 'Seek, and ye shall find' (*de Praescr.* 8, 2). Yet they only refer to it to spread their 'endless fables and genealogies' (I Tim. i. 4), their unproductive questions, and their talk which crawls at a crab-like gait to confuse innocent hearers (*de Praescr.* 7, 7). The heretics will not listen and understand that a search is sensible only when one does not yet know the truth, and that with Christ and His gospel we have reached the end and goal of our seeking. True faith is always simple (*adv. Marc.* V, 20). Tertullian is indignant at the speculative and problematical basis of heresy which is unable to hold on to the one thing that matters. 'Any Christian workman' knows precisely what is at stake, and on what everything for him really depends. 'He finds God, makes him known and then puts a practical seal on all theoretical questions about God with his action' (*Apol.* 46, 9). Obviously Christ was gravely mistaken when He 'commissioned simple fishermen rather than sophists to proclaim his gospel' (*de An.* 3, 3).

The heretic does not know what it means to believe. He takes pride in understanding. He wants to know instead of letting himself be taught by God, and would rather follow human teachers than be satisfied when God does not want to speak any more and is silent. He thinks always that he knows in advance who God is, what God does, can, and ought to do, and what is appropriate for God, and what is not. Therefore, he also fails to understand the meaning of God's Son becoming man. Tertullian comes to the decisive point of the contemporary discussion: Gnostic spiritualism denies the incarnation. It seems to it unnecessary and unworthy of God. The Gnostic can concede only an apparent ('docetic') acceptance of the flesh by Jesus; for he knows only of an imagined, unreal, 'God of the philosophers' —this expression originates from Tertullian (*adv. Marc.* II, 27, 6)—who changes and saves nothing but remains distant and transcendent. He takes offence at the ugly, humiliated, inglorious figure of the Saviour; he considers this kind of revelation and immanence an insult to the divine majesty. He does not see that in no other way would God really have reached us and that his dignity is of a kind different from human honour. 'Nothing is so worthy of God as man's salvation' (*adv. Marc.* II, 27, 1).

The incarnation, and no less the crucifixion, which embarrass the docetic theologians, are the real mysteries of our salvation. With reference to these doctrines, and not, as he makes plain, the general proclamation of God and his commandments, Tertullian is therefore quite justified in appealing to the Pauline expressions of God's 'foolishness' which frustrates human 'wisdom'. His famous statement '*credo, quia absurdum est*' is usually not quoted accurately and still less understood in the context which he envisages: 'God's Son was crucified—this is not a matter for shame, because it is a disgrace; and God's Son has died—this is credible because it is a foolishness; and he was buried and is risen—this is certain, because it is impossible' (*de Carn. Chr.* 5, 4). These forceful paradoxes are intentionally so formulated to be provoking; the Christians know and want their God like this—and this God does not forsake them, least of all when they must confess Him in an apparently hopeless situation and the 'outward man' perishes under tortures.

Religion is for Tertullian nothing other than life in the sphere of reality. For the heretic, on the other hand, it is the realm of self-satisfied speculation and pious dreams. Faith can make nothing of this. He who will follow Christ in life as in death asks for a God who is real and encountered in history; a God who has died and lives forever. The human existence, the full reality of Christ's 'flesh', is the guarantee of the actuality and seriousness of our redemption, as our bodily existence at the same time determines the inescapable necessity of our personal responsibility in this world. As for the man who denies the reality of Christ's flesh, and wants to think of himself as being not flesh, but as existing in the unfettered state of an otherworldly spirituality, he is forced because of his own nature to compromise with this world in the actual situation of temptation and affliction—to compromise with the wisdom and immorality, the deities and demons of the world. The reluctance to undergo martyrdom shown by so many sects is the crucial test. Tertullian composed a writing *The Antidote Against the Scorpion's Sting* in which he rebuts the various excuses wherewith some try to depreciate martyrdom in favour of a transcendant or inner testimony of the spirit! To him every Gnostic is a potential denier, a lax shirker, and an arrogant despiser of the church's command. This is indeed an exaggeration and an unfair generalization. Yet the history of Gnosticism shows that Tertullian's contention was not so wrong, after all. Almost all their societies perished in the course of time in a vague syncretism, which corresponded to the vagueness and boundlessness of their impersonal and unhistorical concept of revelation.

The Catholic church has received the revelation also in externally clear and binding fashion. She lives by the one, certain, and real principle ordered by Christ and contained in the Holy Scripture. She possesses the two-edged sword of God's word in law and gospel, the divine wisdom, 'the enemy of the devil, our armour against spiritual foes, all malice, and carnal lust, the sword which can cut off from us for the sake of God's name even those whom we love most' (adv. Marc. III, 14, 3). He who does not want to understand the truth will not be disputed with. The church knows God's word and does not need to fight with Marcionites, Valentinians, and other Gnostics about its meaning, which they distort. Tertullian has attempted to form this thought into a strictly juristic mould in a monograph, Prescriptions Against the Heretics. This has had a far-reaching effect on the later development of Catholicism. The Catholic church, according to the work, received its teaching as well as its Scripture directly from the apostles at a time when all present heresies had not yet arisen. She has preserved the original truth faithfully and is also able to prove it against later aberrations; for she stands even today in undisturbed communion with the old churches founded by the apostles in Asia Minor, Greece, etc., or in the West, with Rome. And whence should the harmony of all orthodox Christians in the whole world derive, if it was not originally given? Against this the favourite Gnostic insinuation regarding the apostles avails nothing, that Christ had not entrusted everything to them or they had misunderstood or falsified his teaching. They could not all have confused the truth in the same manner. 'What in so many congregations always is recognizable as the very same cannot

be erroneous: it must be tradition' (*de Praescr.* 28, 3). It thus
suffices if we remain faithful to the ecclesiastical teaching and
understand the Bible in a sense which corresponds with the
Creed. (In Tertullian, the Apostles' Creed occurs for the first
time in this normative sense, as a 'rule of faith' binding the
congregations.) The heretics, on the other hand, have no place
in the church, and no right to appeal to the Scripture. 'Who
are you, when and whence do you come? What are you doing
on my property without belonging to me? Who gives you
the right, Marcion, to cut my timber? Who gives you permission to divert my springs, Valentinus? Whence your claim,
Apelles, to remove my landmarks? . . . The property belongs
to me; I have always possessed it, I have possessed it prior to
you and have reliable title-deeds from the actual owners to
whom the estate belonged. I am the heir of the apostles' (*de
Praescr.* 37, 3 ff.).

This is typical of the way Tertullian goes to work; he proves
his point from every possible point of view. Tertullian first
claims every right for himself alone and denies everything to
his opponents. Yet we should not be concerned with Tertullian if he had been satisfied with such an external, formal
assurance. So he closes the already 'summary' plea with the
assurance that he would, if God wills, return again in detail to
the heretical doctrines, and during the course of his life he
energetically fulfilled this promise. Above all, his major five-
volume work, *Against Marcion*, must be mentioned in this connection. Tertullian has here summoned all his strength and
ability, for he has found in Marcion his most dangerous enemy.
It is admirable how he understands the way to combine in this
polemical masterpiece the keenest logic and dialectic, all the
arts of rhetoric and irony, the most earnest, embittered passion,
and the finest accuracy and exhaustive thoroughness in dealing
with the subject-matter. To Tertullian Marcion is the arch-
heretic. As a matter of fact, he had in the middle of the second
century founded his own church, which had now spread everywhere. Marcion's nature was similar to Tertullian's in that he

likewise regarded the most radical solutions and the strictest positions as the best and most genuinely Christian. Like the Catholics he despised the unconfined indiscipline and fantasy of the ordinary Gnostics, and for his part aspired to be nothing other than a faithful disciple of Jesus and student of his greatest apostle, Paul. Yet Marcion and the Marcionites denied any connection between the Christian message and the previous revelation to the Jews in the Old Testament, behind which he saw another God, strict and hostile, the moralistic 'just' God of this world with whom on this account the true gospel by its very nature has nothing at all to do. According to these principles, Marcion drew up his own Bible, consisting only of texts of Luke's gospel mutilated in accord with his principles, and of the Pauline letters. In opposition Tertullian demonstrates the impossibility of this piece of editing with a clarity which would do credit to any modern theologian. In his usual manner he declares forthwith his willingness to show that even the falsified Marcionite Testament still contradicts Marcion and testifies to the Christian truth. He also systematically consolidates his own position and confession of God's unity by proving that God's righteousness and grace, the sovereign transcendence of the creator and his merciful descent into the world, are not to be separated within the Christian understanding of God.

We cannot examine in detail the anti-Gnostic writings of Tertullian. The question they deal with has become unfamiliar to us, in so far as Gnostic thought takes up and answers the problem of reality and divine revelation from the side opposite to that to which we are accustomed, so to speak. The Gnostics as a group do not deny the transcendence and reality of the divine spirit, but the reality and significance of the material, earthly world. They do not question the necessity of redemption, but the divine origin of creation, and similarly they do not deny the divine but the human nature of the Saviour, his corporeality and his flesh. This way also leads finally to the ethical consequence of a certain 'nihilism', and we can easily understand that Gnosticism could hardly have

found a more bitter enemy than Tertullian. To Tertullian anything merely intellectual and theoretical, poetic and aesthetic,
i.e. anything he cannot directly come to grips with practically
and morally, is as such an abomination. As we have seen,
he is a materialistic thinker and as a Christian predomi-
nantly a man of law, of the divine command, and of unconditional obedience. What he defends is the Catholic church and
the Christian demand of faith in its inflexible reality; yet we
can easily understand that the harsh rigorism of such a personality was, just because of its intellectual superiority, not always
comfortable and easy to endure even to his fellow-believers.
This was bound to lead in the course of time to friction,
especially in practical questions of church discipline and of
everyday morality.

We have already come across Tertullian's difficult attitude
where he deals with the Christian's relationship to the world
and its sins. 'Everyone is a denier who does not show himself
openly upon every occasion and who lets himself be taken for
a pagan' (de Idol. 22, 4), and everyone, likewise, who profits in
any way whatsoever from pagan worship and pagan immorality. We are bound to ask what profession a poor Christian
could possibly take up without being reproached by Tertullian
with indirect assistance to idolatry, which is the fount of all
vice. He storms in the same way against all pagan pleasures, the
civic prize-fights, the circuses, and the theatre, which not only
was founded in honour of false deities, as he demonstrates with
archeological scholarship, but in his day still remained the
breeding place of all immorality and excess. A Christian should
likewise renounce all luxury, cosmetics, finery, and costly
adornments. If God had pleasure in colourful garments, why
did he not then create purple and sky-blue sheep? The Christian theatre-goers seem to have been especially stubborn in
their resistance. They even tried to find Biblical support: where
is it written that God condemns plays, since he tolerates them
and lets them go on? Did not even David dance in front of the
Ark of the Covenant? And did not Elijah drive to heaven in a

fiery chariot? But there is no getting round Tertullian with such
ad hoc exegesis. He tears them apart with caustic irony and
approves in the end one play only, which will reward the
Christians for all earthly abstinence. This is the spectacle of the
last judgement! 'What a panorama of spectacle on that day!
Which sight shall excite my wonder? Which, my laughter?
Where shall I rejoice, where exult—as I see so many and so
mighty kings, whose ascent to heaven used to be made known
by public announcement, now along with Jupiter himself,
along with the very witnesses of their ascent, groaning in the
depths of darkness? Governors of provinces, too, who persecuted the name of the Lord, melting in flames fiercer than those
they themselves kindled in their rage against the Christians
braving them with contempt? Whom else shall I behold? Those
wise philosophers blushing before their followers as they burn
together, the followers to whom they taught that the world is
no concern of God's, whom they assured that either they had
no souls at all or that what souls they had would never return
to their former bodies? ... Then will the tragic actors be worth
hearing, more vocal in their own catastrophe; then the comic
actors will be worth watching, much lither of limb in the fire;
then the charioteer will be worth seeing, red all over in his
fiery wheel.' And then the Lord appears in His glory amidst
angels and risen saints, before the false Jews and other persecutors, the Lord who was ridiculed, beaten, spit at, given gall
and vinegar to drink! Such a spectacle no praetor, consul, or
priest in the world can produce, and today already we have it
in a sense before our eyes even before 'what no eye has seen
nor ear heard' (I Cor. ii. 9) begins in the eternal realm of God,
'things of greater delight, I believe, than circus, both kinds of
theatre, and any stadium' (*de Spect.* 30, 3 ff.; *FC*, 40, 106 f.).

Only Tertullian writes like this. No Greek, nor even a
medieval Christian, has ever put on paper such a description,
wild to the point of sadism, dreadful and grandiose. Nothing
can shock Tertullian. He likewise dismisses offhand the economic worries of those whose livelihood is endangered by his

rigorous demands. 'What do you say: "I am being reduced to penury?" But the Lord praises the poor as blessed . . . the disciples he called never declared: "But I cannot make a living!" Faith does not fear hunger; it knows that for God's sake it must despise death by starvation even as any other kind of death' (de Idol. 12, 2, 4). Such cutting answers reduce the hearers to silence; but their apathetic resistance nevertheless cannot thereby be overcome. Tertullian himself feels this. He complains ironically and bitterly of the fate 'peculiar to him', to which he has grown accustomed, that he has no success with his books. And yet he fights for nothing to which truth itself does not point, and against the witness of truth no difference in the times, no human authority, and no local custom have any sanction! (de Virg. Vel. 1, 1). Yet the worst he cannot even express; Tertullian himself is too good a dialectician not to see the gaps in his proofs, not to anticipate the objections which can be raised against his arguments, if anyone is unwilling to accept the right teaching because of laziness, cowardice, or lack of understanding. Tertullian is attempting something fundamentally impossible; he wants to decide on the basis of a legalistic standard the ultimate questions of credal obligation and spiritual obedience. Hence he becomes ever more stringent in his demands, and finally would like to declare everything prohibited that the Scripture does not explicitly allow (de Coron. 2, 4). But he himself feels that not even the strictest interpretation of the Scripture, nor adherence to the creed and tradition of his church, much less still the knowledge of 'natural law' not yet illuminated by revelation (de Spect. 2, 5) can ever reach the point of that complete certainty which a Christian needs, if he is to take and maintain a firm stand in the difficulties of daily life which arise anew each hour. This agonizing experience 'peculiar to him' forms the background of the last portentous change in Tertullian's life.

In the second half of the second century there burst forth a revival movement, enthusiastic and apocalyptic, in Phrygia deep in the hinterland of Asia Minor. Its prophets, Montanus and the women who accompanied him, thought of themselves as instruments of a new outpouring of the Holy Spirit, the 'Paraclete' promised in John's gospel, and they preached the speedy coming of the kingdom of God on the mountains of their homeland. They demanded repentance, renewal, and the surpassing of the current morality. They distinguished themselves particularly by their eager readiness to be martyred. The movement spread abroad speedily and had reached Africa by the beginning of the third century. Tertullian joined it and soon became the most ardent pioneer of the 'new prophecy'. Like many whose nature inclines towards rationalism and drives them to action, he had from the beginning a special liking for the parapsychological, visionary, and ecstatic phenomena of the religious life. In the revelations, exorcisms, and other miraculous signs of the Montanists he now believed that he had encountered anew in increased strength the living spirit of early Christianity. And here, in the Montanist circles, he finally arrived at a complete determination to stand for God's cause without reserve. He found unrelenting severity against all sinners and lax members in the congregation, new regulations for the ethical conduct of life, and above all an ultimate spiritual authority able to secure all this by its inspired testimony. The oracles of Montanus and of the prophetesses were even then collected, and had an unlimited and virtually canonical validity for their followers.

When Tertullian joined the Montanists, their ecclesiastical position was not yet clearly decided. The Western church still hesitated until first the bishop of Rome, and then also the bishop of Carthage and the remaining African bishops followed the example of their colleagues in Asia Minor and pronounced the 'Cataphrygians' a sect. This decided their fate for the future. The movement did not possess enough religious content and originality to prevail by its own strength. It was henceforth a sectarian church gathering together members of morally intransigent reactionary circles—the first of such phenomena, which were to accompany from now on the popular development of the ancient Catholic church. Tertullian of course remained faithful to the movement. External failure did not matter to him, and he soon made the Montanist conventicle the basis of a new, even more definite attack against his old enemies. Only through him and his writings did Montanism gain something like a theology and an 'intellectual profile'.

As a Montanist Tertullian did not become other than he had always been. We can see this from the themes with which he now deals, and equally from the conclusions at which he arrives. From this second period of his activity comes, for example, his famous polemic treatise *Against Praxeas*. As a 'Monarchian', Praxeas had gone so far in emphasizing the divine unity in his refutation of Gnostic speculation that he denied altogether the difference between God the Father and the Son. In opposition to this Tertullian advances Scriptural proof and, above all, effectively disarms his opponent in respect of his appeal to the 'Monarchian' sounding passages in the gospel of John. In this connection he now attempts to clarify the systematic conceptions of the developing Trinitarian theology more precisely, and frames the symbols and ideas which have become determinative for the further Christological and Trinitarian controversies, especially in the West. His formulae turned out to be so useful and convenient just because they remain entirely formal in the legal and logical precision of their definitions and distinctions. Yet they never get to the real root of the theological and metaphysical problems which are bound to arise here. Tertullian deals exclusively with the unity in the Trinity, but not with the later problem of the equality of rank between the divine persons; and to that extent his rough draft is still deficient, compared with the final dogma. Nevertheless, his teaching on the Trinity represents for his time an achievement for orthodoxy. The incidental combination attempted by Tertullian of the anti-Monarchian with the Montanist polemic remains wholly superficial, and was no obstacle to the spread of his thoughts.

It is, moreover, also Tertullian's personal conviction, which he repeats time and again, that the Paraclete never changes the old doctrines of the church, but only endorses them and thereby adduces proof of his legitimacy. Real progress is made—even as earlier from the Old to the New Testament—only in regard to ethics, inasmuch as the new revelation now finally demands the ultimate sanctity and unqualified fulfilment of all command-ments. This is a condition which at the beginning of the church the apostles could not yet demand. Tertullian outlines on this basis a new scheme of salvation in three phases and not two. As the New Testament revelation is prophesied in the Old Cove-nant, and then simultaneously confirms and transcends it, so 'the new prophecy builds on top' of the older order and at the same time brings it to its goal. So we come to the typical idea of a third revelation and a 'third Dispensation' of the church, such as was brought up again in the High Middle Ages by Joachim of Flora and since then has often been repeated. This is always possible only when one envisages as the essential point a higher, 'spiritual' order (or knowledge) of life and when the belief in the saving deed of Christ by itself no longer seems to suffice. This is obviously also the case with Tertullian.

Looking through his Montanist writings we frequently come across praise of the revelations and miracles provoked by the new spirit—'to the infidels a testimony, to believers salvation' (*Pass. Perp.* 1). In a lost tract *On Ecstasy* Tertullian takes ex-pressly under his protection the spirit of the 'new prophecy' against opponents from Asia Minor (hence the tract is written in Greek). For the rest, however, it is still a matter of questions of moral decision. Now finally Tertullian is sure that a second marriage, which he had always advised against, is positively forbidden for the Christian, and must be identified flatly as adultery. The new Montanist orders of fasting must be ob-served, since they restrain excessive appetite, which even in paradise was the cause of the fall and of original sin. Tertullian had previously approved of evading persecution as such; yet 'nobody is ashamed if he makes progress' (*de Pudic.* 1, 12). Now such an attitude means only cowardly denial and escape. All these claims are asserted with the excited emotion of constant moral indignation. Tertullian wrote—as he once claimed of Paul—'no more with ink but with gall' (*de Pudic.* 14, 4). The foil for the new, 'spiritual' ideal was an almost sordid, caustic caricature of a decadent Catholic life where love seems to boil only in the cooking-pot, where faith and hope are intended for the menu, where the indolent let themselves be petted and fattened as though they were martyrs, and brethren and sisters spend the night together after their love-feasts. Yet one thing was the worst of all and decisive. In leaving the original discipline, the Catholic church did not take seriously any more the administration of the ministry of the keys. The last writing which we possess from Tertullian's pen was directed against this abuse. Its ostensible cause was a certain relaxation in the Catholic church of the penitential discipline for carnal sins. The details are disputed and are connected with the difficult problem of the development of penance in general. We are here only concerned with the fundamental attitude of Tertullian, who objected as a Montanist to the possibility of forgiveness of the gravest sins when committed by Christians. The most intimate understanding of Christianity and of the 'holiness' effected by Christ always comes to light in the way in which the question of actual forgiveness is treated.

'What else does God want but that we live according to his discipline?' (*de Orat.* 4, 2). For the sake of this goal of the *disciplina*, the church must, if necessary, be strict in refusing absolution. For 'where pardon begins, fear ceases' (*de Pudic.* 16, 14), and 'where there is no fear, there, likewise is no conversion' (*de Paen.* 2, 2; *ACW*, 28, 15). This logic was compulsive for Tertullian, but it is the opposite of Jesus Christ's treatment of publicans and sinners. But, answers Tertullian, were these people perchance already Christians? Had they already, like us, committed themselves to discipleship, and accepted in baptism the Holy Spirit as their mighty helper? And if one erroneously imagines that the apostles knew of a forgiveness for mortal sins, the answer to this is that they possessed an authority of a kind different from that of any contemporary Christian. If appeal is made, however, to the authority of the Holy Spirit, this Spirit Himself has taught us in the new prophecy, that He never misuses this authority in favour of the sinner, for He is holy. An official of the spirit-forsaken Catholic church deciding otherwise is guilty of usurpation of office, and is meddling with the handiwork of God, who has issued the strictest commandments. This exposé was aimed in particular against a certain bishop whom Tertullian mocks as 'the pagan parson' (*pontifex maximus*), as 'bishop of bishops', and truly blessed father (*papa*) because of his frivolous indulgence and presumption. He was not here aiming, as has often been thought, at the far off 'pope' in Rome but at the Catholic bishop of his own home town, Carthage. Against him, Tertullian appeals to the freedom of the congregation; they, and not a handful of bishops, constitute the church which lives in the spirit and in obedience to God's word. In Tertullian we come across for the first time an anticlerical polemic, which has an almost Protestant sound, with its reference to the universal priesthood, but is nevertheless not at all 'evangelical' in intention. What Tertullian wanted to achieve with his appeal to the laity was just an unbreakable binding to the supposedly Biblical 'law'. To be sure, even Tertullian knew alongside God's 'justice', His mercy or 'grace'; once, at our entry into the church, it had rescued us from the demonic sphere of influence and had cancelled all previous sins. He also knew that because of his weakness the Christian unfortunately cannot do without the daily forgiveness of his venial sins. But first of all 'the whole state of salvation rests nevertheless upon the solid rock of discipline' (*de Paen.* 9, 8). God's goodness shows itself primarily in that He reveals His will, inspires us with His spirit, and calls us to our personal responsibility. Man, as a Christian, lives less from God's mercy and forgiveness, which has its limits, than from God's commandment and man's obedience, which accepts the discipline.

The end of Tertullian's life is lost in obscurity. It is mentioned that he lived long and died very late, in 'feeble old age'. But did he therefore find repose and tranquillity? It is hard to imagine. The vehemence and impatience of his will belonged to his nature and were not the transient expressions of a controllable passion. It seems that Tertullian finally broke with the Montanists, and founded his own sect. Augustine, at any rate, a century and a half later in Carthage came across an independent group of 'Tertullianists', whom he won for the Catholic church. Augustine's remarks about the 'heretic' Tertullian do not sound friendly, and Vincent of Lerins formulated a little later (434) the general verdict that Tertullian had been a serious tribulation to the church, and his later error had destroyed any confidence one might have had in the earlier, approved writings. Yet, Tertullian has remained the only non-Catholic theologian whose heritage was not lost, but has come down to us almost complete. This he certainly deserved. True, he remained a dissenter; nevertheless, the old Latin church had no more educated, more indefatigable, and—despite all exaggerations—more honest champion against her enemies than he. Nor did any by nature belong more to her. 'In him the Western spirit expresses itself clearly for the first time' (Holl). Tertullian has indeed also been called the last of the Greek apologists; but this is true only of his subject-matter and some traditional problems of his dogmatical and apologetical writing. In the powerful non-speculative and practical orientation of his theology, Tertullian appears beyond dispute as the first Latin father of the church. The same applies to the realistic, legalistic and psychological direction of his intellect, to his inclination towards social issues, and towards the congregation and church as a firm, political society, and also to his emphasis on will, standards, and discipline. He merits the title also by his affirmation of the authority of the Scripture and his love of the apostle Paul. Tertullian all his life 'loved righteousness and hated ungodliness'—more unselfishly and more purely than Gregory VII. Yet in all this he remains a Christian more of the Old Testament than of the New. Judged theologically, he is almost a Jew.

CHAPTER II

CYPRIAN

THROUGH Tertullian, Christian Africa had gained a voice. This area was now awakened to a new, vigorous life. The African church led the West intellectually for centuries; and only at her decline in the turmoils of the Arab conquest did she become silent forever. The generation which succeeded Tertullian brought forth another personality of extraordinary significance, whose influence went far beyond the African area, Caecilius Cyprianus. Cyprian was bishop of Carthage and never mentioned the dissident Tertullian by name; all the same, his inner relationship to him can be noticed throughout his writings. His secretary reported later that no day went by when Cyprian did not ask for the reading of his Tertullian; he called him simply 'the teacher'. The comparison of the two is instructive in many ways. The uneasiness, the radicalism, the unbalanced nonconformity of the writings of Tertullian were brought by Cyprian into balance and under ecclesiastical discipline. His world of thought has a quiet dignity, steadiness, and moderation which the former neither possessed nor desired. In the view of this leading ecclesiastic the same problems appear in a light different from the passionate partisanship of that individualistic, intolerant, and reckless man of letters. Also, the background has developed. The church has grown rapidly throughout Africa, her organizational structure has consolidated; she affirmed everywhere a distinct tradition which united and bound bishops and congregations. And to this difference in situation and personal position there corresponded, so far as Cyprian is concerned, also a character completely different in constitution and

36

motives, which was in its own way no less definite and resolute, Roman and African.

We have no reliable information about Cyprian's development prior to his election as bishop. However, it is clear that in contrast to the gifted Tertullian, the soldier's child, he came from the circles of higher society, and was from the beginning accustomed to live in easy circumstances. Cyprian had personal connections with the authorities. We hear of his estates and gardens in the vicinity of Carthage. Furthermore, he himself was master of the conventions of high society with an easy self-assurance. Without doubt he had enjoyed a good and thorough education. His style indicates—without the originality and wilfulness shown by Tertullian—familiarity with all the requisites of the 'school'. His writings again remind one particularly of his African fellow-countryman Apuleius; yet Cyprian also knew the writings of Seneca and the traditional positions of Stoic philosophy. Yet he abstained from expressly attacking the pagan authors. 'There is a big difference between Christians and philosophers' (Ep. 16, 55). A new ecclesiastical pride considered it beneath its dignity to engage in a direct controversy such as that into which Tertullian had thrown himself with so much intellectual ardour. Besides Biblical quotations no wider 'literature' appears.

Although Jerome presumed that Cyprian had begun as a professor of rhetoric, we should perhaps suppose rather that he envisaged the career of a higher government official. He shows himself quite familiar with all constitutional laws and political ideas, and transferred them later quite naturally to the sphere of his ecclesiastical activity. With Cyprian began the line of 'curial' bishops who attempted to perform their ecclesiastical office in the magisterial style of the consuls and pro-consuls, with whom he did not shrink from being directly compared (Ep. 37, 2). Compared with the Greek East this was a novel and specifically Western type of Catholic priesthood. In any case, Cyprian cannot have gone very far in a secular career. His conversion put an end to all such efforts and directed his wishes and abilities completely into the new ecclesiastical path.

A presbyter named Caecilius (or Caecilianus) is supposed to have won Cyprian for the church; indeed, it was said that the latter had assumed the *cognomentum* Caecilius only because of this personal, spiritual relationship (while the derivation of his surname 'Thascius' remains completely obscure). If this was the case even his turning to Christianity indicated a close connection with leading ecclesiastical circles. Soon afterwards this newly converted member of the congregation published his first literary essay, addressed to a friend, Donatus, about whom we know nothing else. In a conventional, rhetorical manner, and with much artificial pomposity, he expounded the reasons for his conversion. The world torn to pieces by wars is in a frightful condition; the abominable gladiatorial fights, the immoral theatre, and the excesses in public and private life indicate clearly enough to him who can see, how things are. The rulers are unrestrained, even the administration of the law is corrupt; the whole social order is empty and undisciplined. There is only one port of peace, which is the life to come, and there is only one way leading to it, the God-revealed pure and simple virtue of the Christians. The man who is baptized is rescued at a stroke from all pagan abominations. He feels the stream of the influences of heavenly grace poured out upon him, and can, if he be willing to preserve and augment them, face the last judgement well-equipped. The material of these declamations, reminding one to some extent of Minucius Felix, consisted of the commonplaces of apologetics, although applied, one might say, individually and biographically. There can scarcely be deduced from this anything definite about Cyprian's inner experiences and intentions. It is nevertheless noteworthy how strongly the consideration of political and moral factors is placed in the foreground; theological questions, strictly speaking, are not introduced.

More significant theologically is another work which was probably written soon afterwards: the first two books to 'Quirinus', which were called later *Books of Testimonies* (*testi-*

monia). They contain a collection of Biblical quotations, an 'anthology' arranged topically under short sentence headings, and intended for practical use. We can see that for Cyprian theology consists basically in the exposition of Scripture. With this attitude no specific problems and difficulties occur to him. Later, for instance, he once just simply filled up the last page of a tract with Biblical texts. It suffices if God's word is always heard, learned, and known. Here, Cyprian saw himself already in the role of the superior teacher, who knew his Bible well, expressly trying to perform his task not only for himself but for others. In the first book there is a collection of material for the ever-present controversy with the Jews, and the second brought together texts Christologically significant. This kind of *pons asinorum* evidently met a widely felt need. Cyprian added later a third part to this compendium, concerning the practical ethics of the church, and after the outbreak of the persecutions he produced another Biblical manual. Similar to the others, it contained quotations regarding the vanity of idolatry, the necessity for making witness, and the promises for martyrs. From a post-Cyprianic time several other reference books of this kind have been handed down. Contemporary juristic literature seems to have known similar works. The beginnings of the ecclesiastical testimonies may go back as far as the second century; they continued the tradition of the oldest Christian apologetics against scholarly Rabbinic Judaism. But with Cyprian the old method now underwent an essential extension, and thus was introduced for the first time to the Christian public.

Although Cyprian, as he mentioned in his first preface, simply wished to facilitate the preaching and homiletical preparation of others, he had already certainly been ordained presbyter, if not bishop. It is said that he was still almost a neophyte when elected bishop; and even if this may be an exaggeration, nevertheless his rapid promotion as bishop of the leading and largest African congregation remains extremely unusual and surprising. Had Cyprian counted upon such a thing right from the beginning, on account of his position and intellectual superiority, and perhaps even aimed at this himself? We do not know; but it is certain that his election provoked misgivings among the older members of the clergy of Carthage over whom he had been promoted. And, unfortunately, the young ecclesiastic was not given much time to establish his position and prove himself peacefully. He had held the office for scarcely a year when the first extensively-organized persecution began and severely shattered the whole ecclesiastical order. Cyprian's authority had to undergo the test of fire before it had been really firmly established.

The persecution put into operation by the new emperor Decius in 249 at first appeared to be only a general festival in which prayers were said and sacrifices made for the benefit of the emperor and the empire, in which every subject had to participate. Anyone who refused was to be forced to comply in all circumstances by violent measures, degradation, confiscation, and tortures. When the offerings had been made, certificates to this effect were issued. Evidently this enactment was aimed against the Christians from the beginning. Decius hoped to bring about their apostasy and the destruction of the church. Two reasons chiefly prevented success. On the one hand the military and bureaucratic system of 'survey' was unavoidably defective, and since the persecution came to a halt one year later because of the emperor's death, it did not succeed in breaking up the congregations completely. On the other hand, the church in the critical moment revealed an elastic adaptability to the new situation which had not been calculated upon. The whole plan relied on the presumption that a Christian once brought to renouncing the church was lost to it once for all. In reality, however, those forced to sacrifice at once streamed back into their old congregations, and here means and ways to accept them were soon found, first as penitents, then even as members with full privileges. In retrospect, this development clearly appears comparatively simple and almost necessary. Only if one reads Cyprian's letters of this time is one aware of all the actual difficulties, the human dilemmas and embarrassments, and the apparently impenetrable darkness of the situation which those who lived through it had to face. In these crises and conflicts the young bishop and rhetorician finally matured into a man and became the leader of the church, superior and able to cope with all its miseries and sorrows.

After the sudden beginnings of the persecution the apostasy in Carthage was shockingly great, as everywhere else. 'At the first threatening words of the enemy, an all too large number of brethren betrayed their faith; they were not felled by the violence of the persecution, but fell of their own free will' (de Laps. 7; ACW, 25, 18). Others went straight to jail, while still others tried to escape to remote places. The presbyters still free had their hands full holding together their frightened lambs, pacifying and protecting them as far as possible. Cyprian was no longer in their midst. Obviously he had received notice of the dangerous events in time and retreated to the country with a few chosen companions. From here he attempted to retain the reins in his hand. While the people shouted, demanding 'Cyprian to the lions', the authorities had to be satisfied with an ineffective proscription of his person and initiated a confiscation of his property by public proclamation. He himself was in safety. This decision to evade the violent storm had serious results—most of the difficulties in Cyprian's remaining time in office were connected with this in one way or another. How has this step to be judged?

Without doubt, Cyprian was in more danger than others. Everywhere the police sought primarily to get hold of the bishops and make them recant; the congregations would be deprived of their leaders. In this way the bishops in Rome, Antioch, Jerusalem, and Caesarea were martyred in the very beginning of the persecution; only in Alexandria had Bishop Dionysius miraculously escaped arrest. Had Cyprian stayed in Carthage, the same fate would doubtless have overtaken him. But was it not all the same his duty to accept martyrdom? Escape in times of persecution was considered generally permissible, for the opposite and stricter standpoint of Tertullian and the Montanists had not prevailed. Yet, could a pastor with the care of his congregation's souls leave his flock in the lurch? Had he not to stay with it, particularly in the time of trouble and, if he was of no other use to it, still by his death to leave behind an example of a confessor's spirit and faithfulness? This was evidently the opinion not only of some firebrands and personal opponents of Cyprian. We can see the embarrassment in a letter sent to Carthage by the Roman college of deacons after the death of their own bishop. Cyprian is not mentioned in the address. The letter remarks only in a preliminary statement that 'pope' Cyprian might as an official have had his reasons for his conduct; the Roman clergy, however, would feel themselves compelled to endure to the end according to Jesus' word and commandment (Ep. 8, 1). Therefore, they would be inclined to keep in suspense a judgement about someone else's bishop; yet we can detect that people had reservations and doubted the purity of his motives. Cyprian's reaction was no less plain. He acknowledged the receipt of the letter and congratulated the Romans 'with rejoicing' upon the splendid and glorious 'consummation' of their bishop, who had indeed all along lived and reigned flawlessly. But then he noted that the form and content of the Roman letter had made such a strange impression on him that he must question its authenticity and returned it to the senders for examination (Ep. 9, 2). Only later did there follow another letter in which he explained more in detail why he had considered it right to retreat, not for his own sake, but in the interest of public tranquillity and for the sake of the congregation. The Romans had obviously been informed (by a subdeacon of Carthage!) but not 'quite accurately and correctly' (Ep. 20, 1). Cyprian did not tolerate his authority being held in question even at a distance—already any explicit defence of his actions would have been a sign of uncertainty—and he categorically maintained that he was fully right. To this second letter is added as supporting evidence a bundle of thirteen letters of his correspondence with Carthage. It proved that Cyprian did not wish by his escape to save his own life, but was thereby enabled to perform the duties of his office 'being absent only in body but not in spirit'.

Indeed, everything now depended on the close ties with the distant congregation. We find the messengers perpetually travelling to and fro between Carthage and Cyprian's hiding-place. The letters they carried were on the part of Cyprian not limited to pious admonitions and abundantly flowing praise of the steadfast confessors; it was necessary also to make practical decisions and to take urgently necessary measures. Even prior to his departure Cyprian had provided money from his private fortune. Now he sent from the 'little' he had available considerable sums by which the congregation's faithful poor—and only they—were to be supported. They were not to sink into distress, lest that which could not be achieved by the frontal attack of the persecution might be brought about finally by hunger. The brethren in the jails were to be visited by the deacons regularly—but cautiously and in alternate turns in order not to attract attention. The released needed clothes, food, and work. The bodies of the martyrs were to be secured and all the execution-dates collected for future liturgical commemoration. It seems that the ecclesiastical machine at first functioned well and remained equal to the manifold problems. The actual difficulties began with the question of the attitude toward those members of the congregation who had yielded to terror and fear, and had obeyed the state order in one way or another. The earlier practice of the church had been in this respect, for the most part, very strict. But could the isolated, unthinking, and weak apostasy of former times possibly be compared with the temptations now being brought upon all Christians by cunning state action? As always the widespread nature of the lapse alleviated the feeling of its sinfulness, while the unlucky traitors themselves everywhere intensely desired forgiveness and readmission to the congregation. The responsible clergy showed themselves uncertain, and the situation became even more confused by the role which soon began to be played by the steadfast confessors, who were generally considered as saints, enabled by the Holy Spirit himself to resist so gloriously. So their decisions were hailed as miraculous testimonies of the inspiration of the Spirit of God, and with them the penitents seeking help at first obtained a sympathetic hearing. As could be expected, things were handled frequently in an all too human manner. The new saints, who included some dubious figures, too readily welcomed the role offered to them of infallible judges, and the opportunity of making themselves popular by accommodating mildness without further investigation. True evangelical readiness to forgive was combined with a naïve, officious desire to dominate, with pious gullibility, and sometimes with worse things still. The 'letters of peace' for readmission into the congregation in the jails were obtained from one's friends and relatives, even in other congregations; appeal was made to the oral absolution of an already 'perfected' martyr and wholesale declarations issued for the sinners and their whole family were produced as well. All supervision and control were lost, and the situation threatened to become impossible.

Cyprian certainly realized the seriousness of the situation. He understood that a certain amount of accommodation was inevitable, yet, as things stood at the moment, it seemed to him impossible to commit himself definitely. He sought therefore to postpone the decision on the penitential problem to a later time, after the end of the persecution. He decreed that the lapsed should not be lost sight of, but for the time being they were to be treated as penitents and in no case to be readmitted. Similar provisions had been made in Rome, with whose clergy Cyprian was now again on the best of terms; and in order to fall into line with their order, he granted as an outward sign of accommodation the desired ecclesiastical readmission of penitent sinners on their death-bed. Above all, Cyprian tried to treat the holy confessors with indulgence so far as possible. He merely asked them to show a little more consideration and caution, and he accepted their decisions as in principle not readmissions, but only pious recommendations for a future readmission left to the responsible ecclesiastical leadership, i.e. to the bishop. It was certainly risky to have to make such decisions from afar and by letter. The longer the persecution lasted, the more difficult it must have become for Cyprian to keep in hand the reins of leadership. Nevertheless, it might have been possible to carry through his directions if he could have relied completely upon the loyalty of his clergy. Yet in this tense moment, the old irritations and rivalries also revived. A section of the clergy renounced obedience to him and made common cause with the confessors. The apostates themselves dared to send Cyprian in the name of the church a letter containing their demands, which he immediately repudiated sharply. The bishops, and they exclusively, he affirmed, are called according to the Lord's word to act in the name of the church. They, together with the clergy and the Christians who remained steadfast, represented the church. He was astonished at their overbearing insolence, whereas a humble, quiet, and ashamed attitude alone would have been appropriate (*Ep.* 26, 1). The situation became critical. Without himself surrendering Cyprian could not recognize a readmission carried out by them against his explicit order. An attempt was made to send two friendly bishops to Carthage, to intervene, to pacify, and in particular to arrange the distribution of the subsidies according to his wishes. The effect, however, was just the opposite. A certain Felicissimus, who had been ordained deacon against Cyprian's will, and had taken charge of the congregational purse, dared to take a stand against him publicly, and when Cyprian excommunicated him five other presbyters eventually joined the opposition. Cyprian had now to appoint new officials, and call upon the congregation to refuse obedience to their own rebellious ministers. In these circumstances he pointed time and again to the bishop's office as the one decisive ministry, which sustains the church. He who leaves the holy altar of the bishop and changes his allegiance to the wicked party of Felicissimus is lost to the people of Christ, and can never again join them. Yet the division of the congregation could no longer be avoided. The apostate group held its ground, and finally there was even a formal election of an anti-bishop. But this happened as a final, desperate step after the end of the persecution, and when after an absence of a year and three months Cyprian had returned and could begin to assemble and build the congregation anew.

Decisive for his victory was a synod of bishops which he called probably in the spring of 251. It not only supported him personally, but also established principles in the question of the lapsed which confirmed his previous attitude. Against open opposition from the 'left', which had granted admission to all the lapsed, and in spite of the misgivings from the 'right' originally shared by Cyprian, they agreed now on a central course. The aim was to graduate penitential punishments in accordance with the gravity of the lapse. The Christians who had not really sacrificed, but who had only obtained the necessary certificates by bribery were considered sufficiently cleansed by the penance already undergone, and were admitted again. Those, on the other hand, who had actually made sacrifices to demons should remain under penance; and the 'letters of peace' of the martyrs were no longer to be acknowledged. But to these penitents too absolution was to be administered when they were in danger of death and not taken away again if they recovered. The doctrinal aspect of these decisions remained essentially unclarified. The bishops obviously wished to retain a certain freedom of movement, and when a new persecution drew near two years later, they resolved offhand to accept into the community all penitents who had remained faithful. So they were able to face the threatening danger with a united front. Cyprian emphasized particularly that the penitents must not be deprived any longer of the Eucharist, and of the Spirit who lives in the church, if they were to withstand new afflictions. For additional security in the case of such decisions he referred to the heavenly signs or illuminations given to him, as he often did at other times.

The principal outcome of this turbulent time had been reconstructed by Cyprian earlier in two important writings: *Con-*

cerning the Lapsed and *The Unity of the Church*. The latter work
was perhaps begun while he was still in hiding, while the tract
on the lapsed must have been written immediately after his
return to Carthage. It represents a comprehensive justification
of the standpoint repeatedly advocated by Cyprian on this
question, now somewhat more distinctly and resolutely than
before. Cyprian was not among those of tender-hearted nature
who, from indulgence or uncertainty, are willing, once victory
and success begin, to leave behind and forget a painfully maintained position. But it must be a victory of the cause and not a
personal triumph. A true pastor 'weeps with the lamenting',
and feels himself affected and humbled by the defeat of his own
congregation. 'Believe me, my brothers, I share your distress,
and can find no comfort in my own escape and safety' (*de Laps.*
4; *ACW*, 25, 16). The glory of the steadfast members of the
congregation stands inviolable, and Cyprian did not neglect
once again to pay the respect and praise due to all confessors
and steadfast brethren; yet the attitude of a substantial section
had disappointed him bitterly. The worst part is, however, that
some had still not fully realized their guilt; indeed, that there
were tempters encouraging them therein and deceiving them
about their true salvation by false flattery and assurances. Only
immediate repentance and conversion could save these. The unruly presbyters and confessors signify 'to the lapsed that which
hail is to the crop, tempest to trees, to the flocks the catastrophic
pestilence, and to ships a violent storm' (*de Laps.* 16). Only
with the bishop is salvation, not with the unauthorized who
lightly assume the privilege, reserved by God to Himself, of
forgiving sins. Even little children trying to deceive their bishop
by coming to the Lord's Supper unreconciled, have been punished terribly by God. Others when they sought to receive the
eucharistic elements got instead only ashes in their hands (*de
Laps.* 26). Cyprian used all available means in order to paint as
black as possible the danger to the impenitent sinners, and to find
hearing and obedience to his appeal for spiritual responsibility
and submission. He was for the most part successful in this.

Even more significant historically is Cyprian's writing on the unity of the church, in which he brought to an end his controversy with the schismatics. Here no tactical considerations were necessary, no doubts and vagueness existed. The security of the institutional church meant for Cyprian the security of salvation, and of Christian faith itself, for which he suffered, lived, and fought. The church is the Bride of Christ, the 'mother church' for all faithful; 'you cannot have God for your father unless you have the church for your mother' (de Un. 6). Outside her there is no salvation. But there is only the one church founded by Christ and entrusted to the apostles as leaders. She remains one even after having spread throughout the world—'just as the sun's rays are many, yet the light is one, and a tree's branches are many, yet the strength deriving from its sturdy root is one. So too, many streams flow from a single spring' (de Un. 5; ACW, 25, 48). These are illustrations used already by Tertullian to render the mystery of the triune God intelligible. They were now transferred to the church, eternally one in its multiplicity, in order to demonstrate from this the impossibility of a schismatic 'church'. One cannot separate a ray from the light, a branch from the tree, a creek from the spring without its vanishing, withering, drying up. This unity of the church, however, exists because of the bishop's office. The church is in the bishop as the bishop is in the church (Ep. 66, 8). Woe to those who will not recognize this! They are become the company of Korah, and they tear apart the seamless robe of the Lord. Satan invents schisms, and the schismatics stand under his power. Cyprian did not hesitate at once to brand everybody leaving the 'Catholic' community as a morally depraved individual having to answer for countless sins. A Christian can only turn away from him with disgust.

The bishop's office, that which upholds unity, was for Cyprian no mere concept or religious idea. In the confused situation which now obtained in all the congregations after persecution and lapse from the church, it was vitally important that at least the bishops should stand together, remaining united with each other, and following the same practical principles. Cyprian assembled his colleagues at various synods and sent to them his messengers, letters, and encyclicals. He laboured for exchanges of opinion, for joint declarations, and for mutual confidence. It was not only his African colleagues who congregated round him, thus protecting each other mutually by their decisions; Cyprian likewise corresponded also with the newly elected bishop of Rome, Cornelius, who had to hold his ground against a rigorous opposition (from the 'right') led by an important theologian, the former presbyter Novatian. In the name of the priestly college, Novatian himself had earlier addressed letters to Cyprian and received answers in agreement with his views. Now, however, the situation had changed. Cyprian stood firmly by that bishop for whom the majority had decided, and sought to recommend him in all instances as the only valid bishop, the only one worthy to be regarded as holder of 'Peter's chair'. So the unity of the Catholic church became a tangible, firm, and canonical reality in church politics, which determined the order of the Western church as far as Spain and Gaul.

Cyprian's strength of will and drive were not exhausted by these problems of ecclesiastical government. In these years he turned again to literary work with increased success. He became a productive writer of devotional literature, the model of the episcopal teacher and preacher. The topics and even the thoughts of these writings were frequently derived from Tertullian. Yet the impatient fiery verve, the moral radicalism and the enthusiasm of the 'master' had disappeared, and issues of systematic or dogmatic significance no longer came to view. There remain a sturdy rationalism and moralism, and a practical reasonableness of argument, which were simple, easy to understand, and popular. The dominant tone is one of instructive persuasion, versatile admonition, and lively earnestness, full of impressiveness and dignity. Cyprian's style is never harsh and sarcastic, but solemn and grave; in the words of a later writer, it always flows smoothly like pleasant oil (Cassiodorus). He loves to describe the same thing two or three times

over in synonymous words, and repeats certain idioms, illustrations, and thoughts. In short, Cyprian speaks the language
of the experienced preacher, which is what he is. His rhetorical
passion does not sound, as in the case of Tertullian, artificial and
hollow. It had taken shape in the practical use of daily church
life, and had been united with the clear expression of the trained
official, and with the vivid plainness of the African Bible, into
a new Latin religious style, whose echo we hear again and again
from now on throughout the centuries.

Alongside the empirical ecclesiastical demands and decisions
which had to be expounded to the people of the church, Cyprian dealt by preference, in his pastoral letters and tracts, with
practical problems of life concerning religious education and
individual virtues. For this the Bible always served him as an
inexhaustible treasure of illustrations. He poses the problems
plainly and simply without any individualization and refinement. Cyprian pays special respect to the devotion to asceticism
of the consecrated virgins in the congregation, to the praise of
abstinence as such and the glorious example of the holy martyrs. Peaceableness, humility, and modesty are virtues especially
esteemed, for they uphold peace in the congregation. Also
'love' viewed in this way attains the character of a chief social
and ecclesiastical virtue, which is injured most severely by the
arrogance, quarrelsomeness, and insubordination of the schismatics. The benefit of good works is stressed everywhere with
startling naïvety. God has 'given man his freedom and made
him dependent on his own will; he himself has to strive either
for his death or his salvation' (*Ep.* 59, 7). For that purpose it is
necessary to perform with fasting and prayer 'righteous works',
which bring salvation from the punishments of hell. Alms in
particular extinguish the flames of the sins of the Christian, as
baptism has washed away the previous offences of a pagan life.
Such admonitions were heeded. When Numidia was devas-
tated by invasion, its bishops asked Cyprian to help their
congregations. He arranged a collection and received 100,000
sesterces to send for the ransom of prisoners. In times of hunger

and of great pestilence the congregation was ready to make sacrifices in the same wonderful manner. 'Practical Christianity' was certainly no meaningless phrase in Cyprian's church.

In these troubled times Cyprian also composed apologetical writings. The old accusations against the Christians were revived, and against this weaker Christians needed strengthening, instruction, and encouragement. 'We must, dear brethren, consider well and continually ponder the fact that we have already renounced this world and as foreigners and strangers have only to live in it for a short time. Let us welcome with joy the day which leads each one of us into his home, carries us away from these surroundings, releases us from the bonds of the world, and restores us to paradise and the kingdom of God. We see paradise as our homeland; even now we begin to have the patriarchs in some measure as our fathers. Why then do we not hasten and run, so that we can see our home-country and greet our fathers?' (*de Mort.* 26). The way this political and eschatological longing is put is truly Cyprianic. The old, early Christian expectation of the coming kingdom of God was combined with the consciousness that we face a lost and senile world which is beyond help. Nature has also grown old; rain and sunshine fail to come, the earth is exhausted, population has decreased, people die sooner, business and trade have become stagnant, the state and society, the arts and science are declining (*ad Demetr.* 3 f.). All these are signs of the divine anger towards the ungodly, while the Christians who are being accused because of these events are the least guilty. By them the time of trouble must be welcomed as a time of probation.

Cyprian's ecclesiastical position was strengthened further during these difficult years. He became an authority even far beyond the borders of the African church. Everywhere in the Latin West his letters and books were read; people from afar turned to him for information and advice. The answers he gave were always delivered in a friendly, polite, but firm tone, and it can be seen from them that Cyprian was by now used to his directions always being observed. It could not be long before the difference of ecclesiastical principles between the various provinces came up for discussion in such a correspondence. Cyprian avoided demanding impossibilities in such cases. He put his confidence in the 'cement of concord' which, despite all, united the bishops in the whole *Catholica*, and made them stand together against all external and internal foes of the church. With this we have the background of the serious ecclesiastical conflict which broke out once again and embittered the last years of Cyprian's life. His opponent was the only bishop of the West who, on account of the traditional significance and power of his see, could still dare to defy the 'pope' of Carthage, the newly elected Pope Stephen I of Rome.

Until this time the ecclesiastical leaders in Carthage and Rome had co-operated well, as we have seen. Cyprian could refer to a corresponding Roman procedure when regulating the problem of penance; moreover, Cornelius owed a good deal personally to Cyprian in his contested position, and seems to have acknowledged the intellectual superiority of his senior colleague without question. But Stephen, who had now taken over the helm of his church, was quite another man. He felt Cyprian's advice as an unwanted tutelage and evidently considered it time to make powerful and effective once again the independence and ancient superiority of the Roman church. There was, in addition, a definite difference of opinion of considerable importance. The efficacy of baptism administered outside the true church had occasionally been discussed in earlier times. The divisions and confusions brought about in the aftermath of persecution posed anew the problem of the proper attitude toward 'baptism by heretics'. For Cyprian the decision had already been quite clearly made in accordance with his whole conception of the church. All sacramental acts performed outside the one Catholic communion of salvation are in his opinion null and void. How could apostate persons, possessed by the devil, confer the gifts of the Holy Spirit which they themselves had lost? In this opinion, Cyprian was in agreement with the ancient tradition of his home-country. Tertullian had already demanded rebaptism of heretics. A generation earlier Cyprian's episcopal predecessor Agrippinus had decided likewise at a council in Carthage of seventy African bishops. On the other hand, in Rome they had earlier gone over to the other side and had affirmed in principle the validity of heretical baptism. Now, they declared themselves willing in addition even to recognize the 'Novatian' ordination in case of conversion. This had the great advantage of making considerably easier the return of the schismatic clergy. Stephen with great determination put his weight behind the Roman practice, which he quite calmly pronounced to be an 'old' custom (and this could at most mean 'customary at Rome'). 'No innovations—stick to tradition' was the effective battle-cry, which he sent down the ranks.

The alarming aspect of this issue for Cyprian was above all that it did not confine itself to Rome or Italy. There were bishops in Africa, too, who, under the pressure of necessity, were willing to conciliate the schismatics, or had already decided for this course. They were now backed up by Stephen, at least indirectly, against Cyprian. Yet he still hoped to come at least to a practical settlement, without giving up in the least his own definite opinion. He called his adherents together to a council in Carthage, which endorsed the accepted African practice, and addressed a letter to Stephen informing him as usual about the decisions. They expressed their expectation that Stephen, known as a pious and truthful man, would likewise agree to what had clearly shown itself as true and pious to the assembled bishops. Cyprian, however, who had naturally composed this letter, added at once that they knew well that some brethren in office found it very difficult to change a decision once made, and that in such cases they preferred to adhere to the existing order 'for the preservation as colleagues of the bond of peace and concord'. 'We on our part do not wish to put pressure on anybody or to give him directions. Every leader of a congregation has the right to decide for himself freely according to his own discretion; he will have to answer for his actions to the Lord alone' (*Ep.* 72, 3). Cyprian was thus aware from the beginning that he had neither the ability nor the right to carry his point of view to complete victory, and here, if you like, was a dogmatic weakness of his position. As a matter of fact, there was then really, as things stood, no other way to sustain the peace and unity of the church.

Stephen had a different opinion. It is open to doubt whether he had a clearer theological understanding of the whole bearing of the decisions than Cyprian. We get the impression rather that for his part he was more concerned to pick holes in the arguments of his colleague, and so he began with a frontal attack. Of course, we know his utterances only from the echo in Cyprian's correspondence; nevertheless, it is evident that amongst other 'presumptuous, irrelevant and contradictory matters' which he 'scribbled ignorantly and thoughtlessly' ... (*Ep.* 74, 1) Stephen also demanded that in dealing with heretics in Africa there should be compliance with the 'traditional' Roman proceedings. And for proof Stephen referred to the 'primacy' (*primatus*) which was his to claim as the holder of Peter's throne. The other bishops were thereby placed expressly in a lower position, subordinate to the Roman bishop, and were to be obliged to pay allegiance to him.

This was a hitherto unheard of demand, and it is understandable that Cyprian was indignant at the 'insolent and arrogant' attitude of his younger colleague. He felt the impudent claim of 'tradition' in this case to be an impertinence. It will never do, he averred, with tacit reference to Tertullian, for directions to be issued at will, and with reference to a mere 'custom'. They have to be supported by reasonable arguments. Above all he was insulted by the improper reference to Peter, who neither had claimed 'primacy' nor demanded the obedience from his younger fellow-apostles who joined later (*Ep.* 71, 3). Cyprian, in common with the whole early church, regarded Peter as the first holder and representative of the episcopal office in general, in the authority of which all bishops, each in his own area, participate 'in solidarity' (*de Un.* 5). When the Lord at first founded the episcopal ministry solely on the one rock Peter, he only intended to emphasize symbolically the necessary unity and concord of the entire episcopate. But the other disciples were not therefore inferior to Peter, and they possessed the same authority and dignity as he (*de Un.* 4). The idea of a legal priority for Peter's local Roman 'successor' does not fit into this train of thought. If this nevertheless seems to be present today in a striking special edition of Cyprian's book on the *Unity of the Church*, this is hardly likely to be the text that Cyprian wrote, but is a tendentious emendation introduced later along Roman lines. However, we need not concern ourselves further with this very controversial special problem; for the picture of what Cyprian, on the whole, meant is clear in any case. In Stephen and Cyprian there are opposed for the first time two fundamentally different ideas about the nature of the Catholic hierarchy and church. Stephen with his 'monarchic' conception of the entire church is, so to speak, the first pope. On the other hand Cyprian, with his idea of a firm but free union in love of bishops having equal authority, is the classical representative of 'episcopalism'. We can see now how easily a unity of the organized church so conceived could actually be upset by conflicts between ecclesiastics. But the peculiar greatness of this concept should not be overlooked. The unity of the church was no simple, secure matter of fact to Cyprian, but appeared as the spiritual calling, and, at the same time, as the ethical task of her leaders. In any emergency they have to demonstrate and prove their faith in the church by their personal decision.

Cyprian proved to be equal to the serious situation. On September 1, 256, a new council gathered in Carthage at which he brought together no less than eighty-seven bishops. It developed into a protest on the grand scale against baptism by heretics. Nobody mentioned the Roman bishop; his declarations were treated as if they did not exist, and yet it is evident against whom this demonstration was politically directed. We still possess the minutes with the votes of the individual participants. After the decisive letters of Cyprian had been read, he, as the chairman, called upon those assembled to proceed to a final vote. Everybody should declare his conviction openly; nobody would be subjected to any unpleasantness in consequence. 'For no one of us has created himself bishop of bishops or tries violently to force his brethren in the ministry to an absolute obedience by despotic pressure. Every bishop possesses definitely the freedom and right to hold to his own opinion as he pleases and is to be condemned as little by another, as he himself can condemn. Rather we all together await the judgement of our Lord Jesus Christ, who alone has the power to raise us to be leaders of the church, and to pass judgement on what we do.' All assembled bishops then assented, with shorter or longer arguments, to Cyprian's standpoint, and—appealing to his earlier pronouncements—he cast his vote last.

The delegation which was to deliver the council's decision to Rome was not even received by Stephen, and was left without quarters. He considered that communion with the African churches was broken. Stephen did not shrink from abusing Cyprian personally as a false Christ, a false prophet, and a deceitful worker (II Cor. xi. 13). Cyprian now no longer remained on the defensive, but conducted a sharp and extensive propaganda campaign for his point of view, and against the unbrotherly attitude of his reckless Roman colleague. Even the Christian East was involved in this controversy, and since the Christians there also frequently repudiated baptism by heretics, and did not at all acknowledge ecclesiastical centralism in the Roman style, Cyprian found some support from them. Among his correspondence is found a letter, undoubtedly translated and circulated by Cyprian himself, from bishop Firmilian of Caesarea in Cappadocia which agrees completely with Cyprian in this matter, and further expresses in strong language indignation at the 'open and obvious foolishness' of Stephen who boasts about the privileges of his episcopal seat, and thinks he possesses the succession of Peter (*Ep.* 75, 17). Dionysius, the influential bishop of Alexandria, finally tried to mediate, and admonished Stephen to peace, but in vain. The controversy was ended by outside factors. In the summer of 257 persecution by the state set in anew. Stephen died as a martyr, and in the following year the same fate overtook his successor, Xystus. Cyprian too was no longer free by then. The deadly seriousness of the church's situation pushed aside the quarrel of the parties, and made it a matter of secondary importance. So, as it appears, the relation between Rome and Carthage was restored of its own account; the differences of baptismal practice were not further mentioned. This was in substance a complete victory for Cyprian, who had in truth never asked for anything else. Only much later, and in a time when circumstances had changed, did the Roman church succeed with governmental help in putting into effect as law even in Africa her principles regarding the baptism of heretics. Over this issue the church split once again. The issue in these later Donatist controversies was still Cyprian's heritage; but Cyprian himself and his general ecclesiastical authority were no longer affected by this.

By and large Cyprian had served as bishop for one decade at most—ten years full of cares, of almost uninterrupted conflict, and of difficulties from without and within. However, Cyprian was not one of those natures who wear out and exhaust themselves in such trials. On the contrary, he felt himself to be in the right place, and under the burden of overcoming all his difficulties became more and more fully his resolute true self. Cyprian knew that in his activities he was a fellow-worker with God, who sustains his church. The bishop did not doubt his rights and even in obscure situations always knew what it was all about and what had to be done. By this he remained master of the situation and held his ground. At the start he was a beginner sitting on a swiftly won episcopal throne, supported only half-heartedly and insufficiently by his assistants, in hiding from persecution in voluntary exile, while 'rebels' fought about the leadership in his congregation. Yet he emerged to be the spiritual head of the entire African church, enjoying the confidence of distant colleagues, a teacher to the whole of the West and respected and honoured even in the East. A Numidian bishop wrote to Cyprian that through his letters the wicked were corrected and the pious strengthened. His writings built up the faith, converted infidels, and set the example of his own character before the reader's eye without his knowing it. 'For more than anybody else you are a great preacher and a master of speech, wise in counsel, and plain in your wisdom, generous in your works and holy in your abstinence, humble in obedience and unselfishly ready for any good deed' (*Ep.* 77, 1). Only one thing was lacking: the glory and crown of the highest perfection, which is what he himself considered martyrdom to be. This too was now to be his portion.

Cyprian was arrested on August 30, 257, but it was deemed sufficient to remove him from Carthage. He was therefore banished to Curubis, a small place not too far away. It seems as if he was able to make an appeal to the emperor for clemency some time later, and that this appeal succeeded. Through a personal letter Cyprian received permission to return to Carthage, and he was assigned as his lodging his own gardens, which he was not to leave! This mild arrest lasted a long time. Then the situation changed. A new edict of the emperor Valerian ordered stricter measures everywhere, and in particular that the lives of the clergy should no longer be spared. In the course of time Cyprian was informed of what was to be expected by messengers who had gone on his behalf to Rome, perhaps even before the newly appointed proconsul himself. He now saw the situation clearly, and made his last arrangements swiftly and quietly. Not only did his own clergy have to be notified, but also his episcopal colleagues 'in order that everywhere, by their exhortation, the brotherhood may be strengthened and prepared for the spiritual conflict, that every one of us may think less of death than of immortality; and, dedicated to the Lord, with full faith and entire courage, may rejoice rather than fear in this confession . . .' (*Ep.* 80, 2; *LPNF*, V, 408). There is no more talk of escape. Without doubt it would have been possible, but this time he could be sure of his congregation. He was resolved to give them an example of how one should suffer martyrdom as a Christian and as a bishop, and he trusted completely in the merciful support of his Lord. The new proconsul apparently wanted to avoid disturbance, and to have Cyprian transported to Utica for execution. When this was known Cyprian left his quarters secretly, to return later. 'For it is proper that a bishop make his confession to the Lord also in that place where he heads the Lord's church and that the whole congregation be glorified by their leader's confession in their midst.' The words expressed by the confessor-bishop in the moment of his testimony are spoken by God's inspiration 'in the name of all' and as if 'through the mouth of all'. As they had so often been directed, the clergy were instructed to observe that complete peace was to be kept 'and that none of the brethren was to incite a tumult or to surrender himself voluntarily to the heathens' (*Ep.* 81).

Cyprian was arrested in proper form and taken into custody by two high officials. The congregation followed him, and the house in which he was accommodated for the night was surrounded by a vast crowd which wanted to 'die with him'. The interrogation on the following day was formal and short: the sentence was to be carried out at once. Having arrived at the place of execution, Cyprian took off his robe and knelt on it for his last prayer. Then when he had undressed completely, he stood there in silence with his eyes turned toward heaven until the executioner was at his post. As a final lordly gesture of superiority, Cyprian ordered that he be paid five and twenty gold pieces for his pains, and then he was blindfolded by two of the clergy while the people spread linen cloths in order to catch the precious blood of the martyr. The body was at first buried at the place of execution 'to remove it from the curiosity of the pagans', but was the same night brought in by the people carrying torches and candles and solemnly buried, 'accompanied by the prayer and loud jubilation of many of the brethren'.

No Latin church father can compare with Cyprian in popularity until Augustine. The account of his death rapidly circulated in many different editions and copies. A panegyric of his life and death, supposedly written by his deacon Pontius, is the oldest Christian biography. His writings and letters are all preserved in various collections and arrangements—the Roman collections, of course, omit now and then the embarrassing sections dealing with the quarrel about baptism by heretics. An old record lists Cyprian's works immediately after the writings of the Scripture. Even more significant is the great number of books falsely attributed to his name, which often, however, breathe his spirit and clearly display his influence. The sober use of the Bible, and practical moralism combined with a strong churchmanship, which his writings display, evidently corresponded to what the Latin Christianity of the time accounted eminently Christian and edifying. In the integrity of his faith Cyprian appears as the embodiment of the ecclesiastical *disciplina*. In his fidelity and steadfastness as an ecclesiastic, he is the very model of an independent bishop of the old Catholic period. His dedication to the new reality of Christian life does not lack warmth. It is genuine and of a striking practical seriousness. It is, one could say, the single-mindedness of the Roman official, now become a Christian, who has affirmed and accepted the saving faith simply and without question in order henceforth to fulfil his duty as a man in the Christian community justly and without compromise. We are surprised what polished ecclesiastical Catholic thought confronts us in Cyprian at a time when in the older and more developed Oriental congregations so much was still unclear, disputed, and in flux. Yet it is precisely this well-rooted moderation which explains the rapid formation and compactness of this ecclesiastical world. Latin Christianity is indeed not represented by Cyprian in its maturity, but only at the beginning of its development, not yet having attained to its real, full possibilities.

CHAPTER III

LACTANTIUS

In the whole early church being a Christian and a Catholic meant belonging to the church, and to belong to the church usually meant to belong to a certain ecclesiastical province and congregation. In Latin Christianity there were missing the representatives of that class in the East which had always preserved a certain ecclesiastical independence and freedom to live where one liked on account of one's profession, the Christian 'philosophers' and scholars like Justin and Clement of Alexandria, or even Julius Africanus and Methodius. This was due to the slight moral significance which higher learning and philosophy as a whole possessed in the Latin world. In place of the philosophers there here appeared the public figures of writers and rhetoricians, who as a rule had only a very superficial knowledge of philosophy. When they became Christians, they retained no further respect for their former occupation. They entered the service of the church as instructors of catechumens or clergymen, and at least inwardly bound themselves, like Tertullian, completely to the new tasks imposed by the Christian community. On this the rigid simplicity of the Western theological tradition is based. From the pre-Constantinian period we know of but one single exception, Lactantius, and it is no accident that he is found at the transition to the new period. Like Tertullian and Cyprian, Lactantius was an African. While still a pagan he was driven to the East and witnessed there after his conversion the beginnings of the 'Constantinian' revolution. The new position of Christianity offered novel possibilities, especially to an apologist and rhetorician. So far as we know, Lactantius was the first theologian to make the most of this chance. Through Constantine he received an excellent and independent position, and a new field of action. Having become a Christian in the time of persecution, he enjoyed for the first time in old age, as an imperial favourite, the advantages of the new-found union of state and church just beginning, of Christianity and the dominant culture. Yet outwardly Lactantius remained what he had always been, a teacher or professor, an aesthete and Christian writer without ecclesiastical ties and office. This role in life gives his personality and development an interest for the history of the church, as well as of ideas; otherwise, despite his unusual literary talent and pure and estimable character, he cannot be placed among the great.

We are indebted for what little we know of the biographical facts of his life almost exclusively to a short account and occasional remarks by Jerome. From his name Lucius Caecilius Firmianus—Lactantius is his personal Christian name—little can be inferred. In Sicca Veneria, a large country town in the neighbourhood of Carthage, Lactantius received his rhetorical education from Arnobius, a renowned teacher of his time, who was also later converted to Christianity. He also had a good knowledge of the law, yet according to his own testimony never appeared publicly as a practising lawyer or speaker. Lactantius was interested in rhetorical training for its own sake, i.e. with the intention of becoming, so to speak, an academic teacher of rhetoric. He succeeded. Already by the end of the century, the emperor Diocletian had called him to his residence at Nicomedia, the imperial capital prior to Constantinople on the Sea of Marmara, in order to contribute to the glory of the new capital as *rhetor Latinus*. He was thus transferred into purely Greek surroundings. He was needed, however, because Latin was still the official language of the empire and its legislation. Anyone who wanted to have a public career had to learn it at least in some measure.

We can only guess how Lactantius then thought of religion. His early writings are lost, only the titles being handed down. The *Symposium* may have discussed some educational themes in the usual manner; a travel book *From Africa to Nicomedia* was composed in hexameters—for poetry was in those days appropriate to a representative of higher rhetorical education. Undoubtedly no Christian influence was yet to be noticed in these works. Nevertheless, it is possible, even likely, that Lactantius had already gained his first impressions of the church in Africa. For a long time the Christians there could not be overlooked; even pagan ridicule and polemic brought them to notice. Perhaps Lactantius never was in real opposition to them, for as a Christian he still held to the principles of his pagan religious world-view. He lived in the tradition of a Platonism understood more devotionally than philosophically, which attempted to base all truth on a higher revelation and illumination, and upheld the recognition and veneration of God as the true goal of human life. The supposedly very ancient writings of '*the divine Hermes*', translated from the Greek, are the most important testimony to this piety, which was already adopted to a certain extent by Apuleius, and then by Arnobius too. It is surely no accident that Arnobius, and then Lactantius, and after him Flavius, a grammarian, who like him was called to Nicomedia, all became Christians in turn. These men represented a religious and philosophically coloured education, and half-education, which was seeking a religious focus. Only in the church, with its clearly revealed doctrine and actual ethical community, which at once imposed obligations and helped in their fulfilment, could their religious longing, when taken seriously, be satisfied. This ideological derivation probably also explains the gradual and growing approach which we must presume to have led to Lactantius' conversion. In his own opinion, naturally, only the baptism which he must have received in Nicomedia counted as the decisive event of his life, which imparted salvation.

The promoted rhetorician may at first have felt lonely and isolated in Nicomedia. It seems as though Lactantius never really learned Greek. His studies were limited to 'our', i.e. the Latin authors, and so later when dealing with Christian literature he took notice only of the church fathers who wrote in Latin. Lactantius knew even classical philosophy only through the medium of Latin. He knew the 'shrewdest of all Stoics' (*Inst.* II, 8, 23) Seneca, and above all Cicero, 'the prince of Roman philosophy' (*Inst.* I, 17, 3), completely and thoroughly. He modelled himself primarily on Cicero so that his writings, according to Jerome, could be considered in form an 'abstract' of all the Ciceronian dialogues. In the matter of style also Cicero remained his ideal all his life. Most likely Cicero had been recommended to him as a pattern by Arnobius, but the latter's own undisciplined vehemence always remained foreign to Lactantius. He strove for a high-minded, lively, and at the same time, in the traditional sense, elevated style. He was a classicist and in this respect really no 'African'. He consciously repudiated the careless colloquialism and vigour of Tertullian, whose literary style appeared to him as difficult, obscure, and uncultivated. Yet he also criticized Cyprian's brilliant eloquence because in choosing his words he did not show enough consideration for non-Christian readers. Lactantius did not forget that an outstanding pagan rhetorician had once mocked this first teacher of the Christians, calling him a 'Coprianus', i.e. dirty fellow (*Inst.* V, 1, 27). Of course, Lactantius also could not entirely evade barbarous loan-words and neologisms when he came to speak of Christian conceptions and things. But he employed them as little as possible, and if he realized their strangeness tried to paraphrase and explain them. Here the academic, and keen apologist, comes to light, openly deploring to his educated audience the low literary ability shown in Christian propaganda. It was, however, no mere artificial tactics, no forced new expression of his thoughts which he desired, for the cultivated and well-balanced manner of Lactantius' writing was natural to him. It corresponded to his genuine, unobtrusive, cool and restrained nature, and therefore in his writings appears appropriate and pleasant.

We have, however, been anticipating with these observations. In his own words, in Nicomedia Lactantius first trained the young men, as he had done formerly in Africa, 'not to virtue, but rather in cunning wickedness' (*Inst.* I, 1, 8); that is to say, he imparted to them a pagan education, and the usual devices and tricks of rhetorical presentation. This met his teaching obligation. The persecution now breaking out under Diocletian first brought a change. The very first edict against the Christians, issued in February 303, denied them any public office and dignity, and accordingly forced Lactantius to make a decision. It became even more inescapable when the campaign of anti-Christian propaganda presently spread to his immediate vicinity. Not only Sossianus Hierocles, the governor of Bithynia, but also an unnamed philosopher—as it appears a close colleague of his—placed themselves at the disposal of the government in this attack, and supported it with pamphlets hastily written against the sect of the Christians, who were henceforth publicly outlawed. In view of the brutal governmental measures this was an attitude which was to some extent felt to be ungracious even in pagan circles. In spite of this, Lactantius may still have hesitated for a while; but then he drew his conclusions. A formal renunciation of his conviction would never have entered his mind. But he also did not want to be regarded directly as a 'slave of his time' (*Inst.* V, 2, 10) and therefore he resigned his appointment as teacher. The general remark of Jerome about the financial distress of Lactantius, and his lack of tuition fees, apparently has to be related primarily to the years that followed. Lactantius, he says, had always remained so poor in his earthly life, despite his brilliant rhetorical talent, that he often lacked the necessities of life. One might add to this his own words which he had formulated on the dangers of wealth: men who could pander to concupiscence, to ambition and to avarice, and who had never run into need, would not enter the way of truth. And 'so it happens that the poor and humble more readily believe in God' (*Inst.* VII, 1, 19); for they need not carry the luggage which burdens the rich and makes them unfit to march. From such statements there perhaps speaks not only the experience of the period of persecution, but also the general conviction of one who is concerned more about moral than about material values, and who therefore has an ear for the Christian message. At any rate, readiness to help and to suffer remained a fundamental requirement of Christianity for Lactantius all his life. If we really want to do God's will, he says, we must 'despise money and "deposit" it in the heavenly treasures. There no thief digs it out, there no rust destroys it, and no tyrant steals it, but under God's protection it remains reserved for us as an eternal treasure' (*Epit.* 60, 9).

We must not imagine that Lactantius wanted to make a noisy demonstration as he left. Against this speaks the fact that he could still remain undisturbed in the capital, although he was known personally and was to some degree prominent. Lactantius affirmed explicitly the ecclesiastical rule according to which nobody was permitted to give himself up for arrest in time of persecution, and press for martyrdom. It was sufficient if he remain faithful to his belief and 'does not evade what he then has to suffer and bear' (*Inst.* IV, 18, 2). It would seem that he refers to himself when he speaks, in relation to that philosopher who is a slave to the state, and to avarice, of the Christians who, in view of the present circumstances, had contented themselves with inwardly 'mocking at him', that they therefore had not really and outwardly separated themselves from the world (*Inst.* V, 2, 9). Yet however that may be, Lactantius, now free of his teaching office, found all the more time for literary pursuits. Only now did his Christian literary work begin. The first treatise we possess by him deals with providence in God's work of creation, *On God's Workmanship*. It is dedicated to a pupil named Demetrianus. He may here discover the occupation in which his former teacher is now engaged in this time of trouble and so will not be entirely deprived of instruction. This instruction now covers 'a more precious subject matter' than before 'and in a better system' (*Opif.* 1, 1). Demetrianus had obviously also become a Christian; but in distinction from Lactantius, he continued his occupation. All the more urgently he is admonished not to succumb imperceptibly, for the sake of worldly goods, to the devices of temptation which the devil has put into operation everywhere.

In form this treatise appears to be a mere expansion of Cicero's writing on the state, and as to the subject-matter, it simply contains an extensive description of the human body and its relation to the immortal soul. The care and providence of God, although foolishly and blasphemously denied by the Epicureans, is evident, it is argued, from the glory of the creature. This is not original, for Lactantius most likely obtains the material for his statements from the current medical and philosophical textbooks, and one might almost think that he has no specifically Christian purpose in mind at all with this little study in anthropology. This, however, would be a misunderstanding. Providence remained for Lactantius at all times a central point in his Christian teaching, and is to this extent a theological conception. In reality, he wants to defend the Christian belief in creation, and to take under his protection the despised 'Philosopher of our school' (Christ) (*Opif.* 1, 2) against all others, including 'Marcus Tullius' (Cicero), whom he mentions, of course, only with the highest respect, for even Cicero 'had already been often vanquished' (*Opif.* 20, 5) by certain people void of learning and eloquence, who nevertheless knew how to fight for the truth, namely the Christians. As he himself admits, it is only in consideration of the perilous times that the author feels compelled at present to express many things more concisely and obscurely 'than is really proper' (*Opif.* 20, 1). Lactantius was certain that he had now found his calling and life's work. Eloquence mattered no more, but something more serious, namely truth and life itself. He would know that he had not lived and laboured in vain if he should succeed in 'freeing some men from errors and directing them to the way which leads to heaven' (*Opif.* 20, 9).

Meanwhile, the horror of persecution took its course. Lactantius also lived outside Nicomedia for a considerable time— where, we do not know; soon after 310 we find him again in 'Bithynia' as the witness of the last measures of oppression.

During these years he composed his principal book, which he had already envisaged in his first treatise. It looks as if it were put together by placing one after another a number of such thematically limited essays; yet in this way it finally became a well-arranged whole. The *Divinae Institutiones*, '*Seven Books of Divine Institutes*', are even in modern print an imposing volume of several hundred pages. It is the most comprehensive apology which Christianity created before the end of the time of persecution. As a manual of religion it is modelled even as to the title on the *Institutes* of Ulpian, or similar manuals of the lawyers. The subject-matter here too is 'justice' and Christian law. Educated pagans are envisaged as readers, the representatives of just those circles to which Lactantius had himself belonged, and who in their conceited superiority are pleased to regard Christianity as contemptible. To them the work is explicitly addressed. Lactantius knew that it was not easy to win a hearing in this society. He 'knows the obstinacy of the people' who would much rather prove themselves to be in the right than learn the truth, and who 'enjoy themselves with the flow of blood rather than the flow of words of the righteous' (*Inst.* V, 1, 18). Yet the truth is nevertheless stronger than all lies, and one must not faint-heartedly despair. At least some, at least the better, among his readers must allow themselves to be won. As always, however, the Christian apologist thinks also of his own fellow-believers who, hesitating and unstable, need spiritual help. When they begin to rise into educated circles, and when they have acquired a taste for the reading of the pagan philosophers, rhetoricians, and poets, just then are they especially exposed to danger. They should learn that true knowledge does not necessarily destroy a man like the former false instruction, but rather makes him wise and just. The idea is to combine the good old form with the new good content, to make men devout by understanding and learned by true piety.

Lactantius began as usual with the refutation of false pagan religion. Monotheism is to him the only true and reasonable form of belief in God; the general conception of perfection itself excludes of necessity the idea of several divine beings. On this account man possesses his reason and for this God has created him, in distinction from the animals, erect with a face turned toward heaven, that he might know his almighty Creator, pray to him alone, and follow and confide in his providence and guidance. Faith in providence is, as already observed, a basic truth to Lactantius, which only Epicurus and his school have dared to deny. Whenever he comes to speak of it—and for this the opportunity offers itself in the very beginning of the book—he separates himself with indignation from this religious 'arch-pirate and robber-chief' (*Inst*. III, 17, 41). Also monotheism should be a thing natural to man; Sibyls and prophets have again and again testified to it. Despite this, polytheism has become a common evil. In the manner of the enlightened criticism of Euhemeros (*c.* 300 B.C.), Lactantius explains it from the deification of deceased leaders and rulers, and then from the malice of wicked demons which reveal their nature sufficiently in the abominations of the ancient cults. Here he follows even to the details of his description the Christian apologetic tradition. In doing so, however, he endeavours, more than do his predecessors, to understand the power of evil as a unity, as a single great principle of perversion 'always hostile to the truth' and knowing but one goal, namely to darken the minds of men so that they do not come finally to 'look to heaven', and to desire to live according to their nature (*Inst*. II, 1, 13).

The third book on 'The False Wisdom' leads to the centre of the discussion: it contains the refutation of philosophy. Lactantius distinguishes between serious philosophical research and mere rhetoric. The latter is designed for external beauty and earthly success, and therefore is not an adversary worth fighting. Yet philosophy also does not contain what it promises. Even in the Bible its ideas were already rightly rejected as folly. The eagerness with which some philosophers strive for truth deserves no blame at all, to be sure, and it must also be conceded

that some of them have made real sacrifices for virtue, by renouncing lust and wealth. But, nevertheless, they did not find
the truth, but at best fragments of the truth, which without a
trustworthy criterion can never be joined together into a unity
(*Inst.* VII, 7, 4 f.). This was further prevented by the perpetual
quarrel between the philosophical schools. The reason for the
failure is simple: human endeavours could not succeed from the
outset, for 'the truth, the mystery of the highest God who has
created all things, cannot be comprehended by one's own mind
and reason' (*Inst.* I, 1, 5). Hence, the philosophers 'could as
learned men make clever speeches, but not true ones, for they
had not learned the truth from him who is alone the master of
it' (*Inst.* III, 1, 14). This answer is firmly adhered to and constantly repeated anew. Lactantius is a theologian of revelation.
Even when he refers to the nature and reason of man, it is
always God who must make accessible the way to real cognition. Man is a religious being, who finds truth only in finding
and venerating God. Without God self-knowledge too is impossible, and 'the ignorance of oneself' remains the source of
all evil (*Inst.* I, 1, 25). This inclination toward revealed truth
was prefigured by his pagan understanding of religion, as we
have seen. Yet now he knows only the one Christian answer.
All philosophers have erred because they remained attached to
the earth with their inquiries, teaching, and volition. Even
Plato occasionally appears as a sheer atheist (*Inst.* II, 4, 26), and
Socrates, admittedly the wisest of all, ended notwithstanding
with the 'desperate' confession that he had come to know
nothing else than his own ignorance (*Inst.* III, 28, 17). Christianity is no more understood—as it could appear to be in the
early work—as a new or more perfect philosophy. It is commissioned to outdistance all philosophies, and to replace them
as the truth itself.

God did not leave mankind to its self-earned misery. He
showed it the way of life, and in such a way that it is really
open now to everybody, without distinction of age, education,
or sex. 'There is only one hope of life for men, one harbour of

salvation, one castle of freedom.' One must open one's eyes and
look at God 'who is the only home of truth'; one must despise
the earthly and regard philosophy as nothing—in this way one
attains wisdom and by wisdom, i.e. by piety, immortality
itself (*Epit.* 47, 1). Immortality is seen everywhere in Lactantius
as the real meaning of salvation, or philosophically speaking, as
the highest good (*summum bonum; Inst.* III, 12, 18), given by
God to the pious as a reward and fulfilment of their life. At the
same time, immortality is also an attribute of every created soul,
imperishable by virtue of its spiritual nature. As so often,
Lactantius did not succeed at this point in fully reconciling
these two types of ideas, the Biblical-Christian and the philo-
sophical-religious tradition.

The following book, *The True Wisdom and Piety* (they belong inseparably together!), reveals even more strangely the
combination of the academic philosophical debate in its tradi-
ditional form, with a completely heterogeneous, and in part
fantastically enlarged, Christian soteriology and mythology.
The difference is concealed and brought into a seeming harmony by the constantly streaming flow of a Ciceronian eloquence, always correct. The heavenly origin and redeeming
work of Christ are described, and pagan objections against the
meaning and possibility of the incarnation, and especially of the
crucifixion, are rebutted in many ways. Generally speaking, in
Lactantius Christ appears as above all the teacher of the true
religion and virtue. One can trust him all the more safely, because he convinces us at the same time by his pattern and
example. The fifth and sixth books deal with Christian
'righteousness' and the true worship. The golden age described by the poets existed as long as people still venerated the
one God. With polytheism righteousness departed and the only
righteous ones, the Christians, are persecuted with incredible
fanaticism. Yet the Christians disprove all accusations by their
heroic patience. With the Stoic emotionalism of a Seneca,
Lactantius talks about the martyrdoms but emphasizes at the same
time that only with God's assistance is it possible to prevail

over such agonies. The action of the persecutors is in any
event just the opposite of all true veneration of God. God desires brotherly love and humanity among men, a pious thought,
and moral conduct of life. In the religious field this corresponds
to the renunciation of every act of worship performed reluc-
tantly, and thus to a practical attitude of tolerance. Lactantius
finds once more an opportunity of attacking the merely external
cult of the pagans, the foolishness of idolatry and sacrifice with
which God is supposed to be receiving a favour of extraordinary value, when the altars drip with blood. True service
'does not come from the purse, but from the heart; it is not
offered by hands, but by the spirit, and the truly agreeable
victim is to be found whenever the soul sacrifices it from its
own property' (*Epit.* 53, 3). This is the worship known to the
Christians. Lactantius practically never mentions the social and
sacramental side of the church's life.

The last book deals with the 'Happy Life' and once again
enters systematically into the problem of immortality. At the
end, the Christian teaching of the 'Last Things' is expounded.
The astonished reader realizes with what enthusiasm our seemingly enlightened author clings to the particulars of the cosmic
eschatological drama. He is far from interpreting spiritually the
statements of John's apocalypse, and even adds further apoca-
lyptical material. In two hundred years at the latest the millennium will begin. Christ will descend from heaven with His
angels and will establish His throne in the middle of the earth.
He will furnish the just who have risen with new bodies and
will put the anti-Christ in chains. But toward the end of the
seventh millennium anti-Christ will regain his freedom, and
over the city of God a terrible fight will take place, until the
'last wrath' of God breaks out and brings all things to an end.
Heaven will be rolled up, the earth changed, and the unjust
will be condemned to eternal torment, while the just now
attain the nature of angels 'dazzling as the snow' (*Inst.* VII, 26,
5). 'Therefore let us strive after justice; for it alone, as a faithful
companion, will lead us to God. Let us, "while a spirit rules

these limbs'' (*Aeneid*, IV, 336), render untiring military service
to God. Let us stand guard and watch, and boldly take up the
fight against our familiar foe, in order that as victors and heroes
we may then obtain from the Lord the reward of virtue
promised us by God Himself' (*Inst.* VII, 27, 16).

When we look at the whole, we see clearly what sort of man
has composed this comprehensive work. He is an old experienced scholar, thoroughly at home in Latin literature, who now
places all the resources of his long-standing rhetorical experience at the service of the Christian 'truth' (*Inst.* I, 1, 10). God's
spirit, says Lactantius, assists me, for without it the truth could
neither be comprehended at all nor described (*Inst.* VI, 1, 1). The
material he is working with, however, is, for the most part, not
of Christian but of pagan origin. With his proof from prophecy,
to which he attaches great importance, this is particularly evident. It is almost exclusively built upon actual or supposed
pagan testimonies, above all on the (Jewish or Christian inter-
polated) Sibyllines, on the revelation of 'Hermes' and passages
from oracles and poets of any provenance. Later, Lactantius
considered Virgil also to be a prophet, for he had already foreseen and prophesied the last persecutions of the Christians.
Lactantius stands here at the beginning of the Christian interpretation of Virgil. Only where it was wholly indispensable, in
the Christological passages of the fourth book, does he quote
to any considerable extent the Old Testament, and here he
follows mostly Cyprian's collection of testimonies. But one
must not without further ado conclude from this that he had a
correspondingly superficial knowledge of the Scripture. A man
who acknowledges the divine authority of the Holy Scriptures
as decisively as Lactantius does, has certainly read and come to
know them. But Lactantius is now writing in order to win a
pagan audience. He realizes what aversion the 'vulgar and
common' language of the Bible causes, especially 'with wise,
educated, and authoritative personalities', and therefore tries to
refer to known and accepted texts. They are indeed in accordance with the Bible and therefore equally true. The truth is

finally able 'to illuminate by virtue of its own light even where it cannot be verified by divine testimonies' (*Inst.* VIII, 7, 5).

What Lactantius accomplishes in this way is more than a mere apology. His work, as he himself emphasizes, is not intended merely to refute, but also to instruct (*Inst.* V, 4, 3). For this, it is necessary to present the entire content of the Christian faith and life; it was likewise necessary to deal with 'hope, life, salvation, immortality, and God' (*Inst.* I, 1, 12). The church had not until then possessed such an over-all study in Latin, and furthermore the systematic work of the Greek church most comparable to the *Institutes*, that written by Origen in his early years, was differently oriented, and remained 'Dogmatic' in a much stricter philosophical and esoteric sense. One might think of Clement of Alexandria, who had attempted but not completed something similar in his great trilogy. A comparison with him is instructive in other respects too, for Lactantius reveals the completely different nature of the Latin theological attitude—even when both are connected by similar Gnostic-Platonic traditions. It is significant that Clement recognizes his pagan predecessors as such, loves, and to some extent approves of them. On the other hand Lactantius contents himself with stressing time and again the frustration and final failure of all philosophers. The tone in which he speaks of them is seldom respectful, never friendly, and almost everywhere decidedly hostile, at any rate in substance. Different likewise are the ways by which both seek to win men for the Christian teaching. Clement dares to approach the mysterious reality of God only hesitatingly, if at all, and this he does in various ways by a certain diffident dialectic. He stresses that an inner maturity and a special understanding is needed really to comprehend it. Such difficulties and detours are completely unfamiliar to Lactantius' thoroughly realistic and rational understanding of revelation. Christianity is the truth; i.e. it should really be intelligible immediately to every unbiased person. God has given it; one need only learn it, and one can then also defend it by means of reason. The decisive proof lies in the moral effects it accomplishes. On the other hand what is the use of a philosophy if, as the lives of the philosophers show, it does nothing to make men better? (*Inst.* IV, 3, 2). This is the point at which the alleged wisdom of the world must undergo its trial, and here Christianity finally shows its superiority. This is a thought not unfamiliar to Clement also, and known more or less to every Christian apologist. But with Lactantius, it is the crown of his theological endeavours. Clement understands the free, glorifying 'Gnosis', the association with God which enables one to love and to see him as transcending and perfecting all human knowledge, whereas Lactantius points to the clear demand of the 'righteousness' which surely is 'the highest virtue, or the fountain of virtue itself' (*Inst.* V, 5, 1). This righteousness is a markedly moral and social conception. The religious ideals of late Platonism are thus interwoven with the practical emotion of the Stoic and in particular the Roman-Stoic tradition. The old demands of ecclesiastical Christian ethics can then be easily attached to it. The five chief commandments of true humanity now read: hospitality, redemption of prisoners, care for widows and orphans, nursing of the sick, and burial of the poor and strangers. The virtue of justice includes above all 'humanity'. Indeed, with Lactantius it is sometimes almost identical with 'mercy'. Christianity was evidently adjusting itself to the sad changes of the enfeebled and impoverished ancient society in its decline. It is no accident that the new teaching on virtues is rooted in the religious sphere; 'almost all the ties of humanity' which bind us together, says Lactantius, really arise from 'fear and the consciousness of our own frailty' (*Opif.* 4, 18).

If, on the other hand, we inquire concerning his theological views in the narrower sense, the result is disappointing. Everything Tertullian and Novatian had achieved for a systematic teaching on the Trinity is forgotten by Lactantius. What he has to offer instead is a massive mythological genealogy of divinities. We hear that God—even before he created the multiplicity of angels—had brought forth as the 'Second' a dearly beloved Son. That means that Christians worship 'two Gods'; but this need not disturb anybody, because a 'Father' and a 'Son' always belong together in their nature, and a complete harmony exists always between these two. Even Plato, taught by Hermes, speaks almost 'like a prophet' of a first and a 'second God' (*Epit.* 37, 4). God created, however, yet a third spirit, in whom the 'nature of his divine genus' failed continuously to prevail (*Inst.* II, 8, 4). Followed by a part of the angels, He rebelled out of jealousy against the second and therefore became a wicked anti-God, the '*antitheus*' (*Inst.* II, 9, 13). This quarrel within the divine family is interpreted by Lactantius in terms of the philosophy of religion with the help of Stoic teaching on the elements. The condemnation of the devil is no mere fate which he has brought on himself, but was foreseen and planned by God from the very beginning. As God wanted to create and effect all good things through His Son, so He destined from the very beginning the third as His opponent. 'The one spirit is his right, the other is his left hand' (*Inst.* II, 8, 6; *LA*, 2). For no life exists without opposition: two principles govern the world, and the good has evil as its indispensable presupposition. There is no warmth without cold, no light without darkness, and also in the ethical life no victory without an adversary and a preceding fight. How foolish are the people who accuse the divine world order of defect and injustice! So long as he lives, man is confronted with the necessity for decision and for good reasons. His body is earthly, and in it dwells evil. His soul is heavenly and must prove itself in its freedom. Evil does indeed cause many to fall, but on the other hand, it is also defeated by many, and thrown to the ground (*Opif.* 19, 8; *LA*, 5). Truly, the whole world, a thing in essence disunited in itself, was created only for the sake of man, in order that man, who is not to remain a child for ever, might learn virtue by struggle and 'that his virtue might reward him with immortality' (*Inst.* VII, 5, 27; *LA*, 17). As we can see, Lactantius, the student of the Roman Stoa, feels no difficulty in combining in this way his monistic theology with a sharply dualistic ethic, and this theodicy now serves as justification for a traditional speculation more Jewish than

Christian, about the struggle and fall of the angels! He may perhaps have later had theological misgivings about these bold statements, for without change in the over-all conception, the most daring passages of this kind are now deleted in the majority of the manuscripts.

In his writings Lactantius fails to mention the Holy Spirit as such. The 'third' was indeed the devil! In a letter Lactantius is even supposed to have later denied expressly the 'substance' of the Spirit, and to have treated him as referring simply to the person of the Father or that of the Son, whose 'sanctity' was sometimes designated by this 'name' (Jerome, *Ep.* 84, 7). Such slips by Lactantius were of course taken amiss in later times. An index of the early sixth century lists his books explicitly among the 'apocryphal', i.e. among the more or less disreputable literature not ecclesiastically approved. Yet this is in fact only the weakness of a self-taught man, who collects his theological ideas from wherever it suits him, or creates them himself without, as a moralist and practical apologist, being really much concerned about the details of his 'system'. Far from his home country, and all the more isolated in his Greek surroundings, Lactantius personally at all events feels himself to be completely orthodox. He is offended as a good Catholic that the 'unity of the holy body' (of the church) is torn apart by sects, reckless, ambitious, or simply foolish and lacking in judgement. At times he planned to write a book of his own to refute them (*Inst.* IV, 30, 14). Fortunately for his later reputation, this was not written! Even Jerome, who is well disposed toward him, cannot suppress a sigh that such a successful fighter against pagan error had shown so little skill in describing his own belief (*Ep.* 58, 10). His theology, superficial, and more rhetorical than philosophical, would definitely not have been equal to such a delicate task.

In spite of this, one must not underestimate the Christian content of his convictions. Occasionally there are interesting transitions between the ancient and the Christian elements of his thinking. A small monograph on the *Anger of God*, written after the *Institutions*, show this particularly clearly. It again deals with an apologetical problem. The passionate, personal, temperamental action of God, as it is described particularly by the Old Testament, was in ecclesiastical preaching always obnoxious to feeling determined by Greek thought. Is it not just the nature of the deity, not to have any 'emotions' like man? Tertullian had in opposition to this rightly emphasized God's purpose of salvation, and hence a compulsive attention to the world and its 'afflictions'. Wrath meant to Tertullian, as it were, only the reverse side of the divine mercy. Lactantius knew the explanations of Tertullian, yet approached the problem in a characteristically different way. He sees in God's anger above all the expression of the penal justice, of the '*iustitia*' emphasized so strongly in all his works. In his opinion, therefore, God is the 'Father', just because He is simultaneously '*dominus*', the Lord, and as such exercises the '*imperium*'. His merciful and just government has to inflict evil also where necessary and let His sovereign wrath rule. This is an interpretation of the Biblical idea of God which precisely corresponded to Roman feeling. Indeed, it might be expressed even more strongly; here we come across an extensive, true 'commensurability' of Biblical and Roman thought (Kraft). The Roman understanding of legal lordship and governorship, also characteristic of the '*pater familias*', is completely thought through to the end when it is applied to the sovereign God of Christianity. The Bible on which Lactantius here rests is still primarily the Old Testament, and indeed the Old Testament narrowed down to its most moralistic.

The negotiations, favourable to the Christians, of the emperors Constantine and Licinius, and the decline of Maximin, the last persecutor, ended oppression in 313. Lactantius must by then have been elderly, perhaps, as Jerome thinks, a very old man. Like all Christians, he welcomed Constantine's victory and rise with rejoicing. In him—at first in common with Licinius—he saw the divinely elected saviour of order and justice, the protector and liberator of the Christians, who had been unjustly oppressed for such a long time, and presently praised him personally as the worshipper of the true God. He was most likely acquainted with him already from earlier times. Before the outbreak of the great persecution, Constantine certainly stayed for some time at the palace of Diocletian in Nicomedia as a kind of hostage for his father. It is a likely guess that the young foreign prince had at least already met the equally foreign rhetorician of distinction. Now he appointed him tutor to his oldest son Crispus, and Lactantius gladly accepted this honourable summons which brought him again to the Latin West, to Gaul. The writer, for years proscribed and without financial support, now suddenly again held a position, and a more splendid one for a man of his standing could not be imagined. Constantine felt it to be a matter of importance that he be taken as a patron of the Christians and a promoter of religious education and culture. One may imagine how Lactantius was received as a celebrity in the palace of Trèves, or how he lectured to his imperial pupil in one of the beautiful villas of the Moselle valley. Trèves may have been his usual place of residence, but it is not impossible that he occasionally accompanied Constantine himself on his journeys. We cannot give details of this, because it is not the way of Lactantius to write about himself in his books, and other data are not available.

In his new position Lactantius had also enough time for his literary work. Perhaps it was only now that he finished his *Institutes* or edited them anew with an enthusiastic dedication to the emperor. Later, as a work written in his old age, an abbreviated version of this book in one volume was published. This '*extract*' (*epitome*), the condensation of his main thoughts, eliminating all meandering details and repetitions, is an especially successful achievement which reveals Lactantius' undoubted talent and his calm nature in a particularly pleasant light. The little work is dedicated to 'brother Pentadius', who set great importance upon being named by the famous man in this way. Also a part of the literary work of Lactantius the rhetorician, which is, so to speak, professional and not actually

Christian, is undoubtedly a product of this period. Lactantius is the first Christian letter-writer, who published a number of collections of letters, certainly not only for the sake of their content, but also as a pattern of a good epistolary style. Jerome still had those collections available, as well as a *Grammaticus* and the earlier writings already mentioned. In these letters, to be sure, theological problems were also discussed, yet only 'seldom', and mingled with a broad variety of items of general interest, in the manner approved by ancient culture. At any rate Pope Damasus, who borrowed the collection from Jerome, considered them verbose and boring, and at best interesting to schoolmasters, with their anecdotes about philosophers, and their information about metre and geography. Lactantius tried once more to write poetry, by dealing in his own way with the traditional material about the phoenix. This was most likely intended by him as a Christian allegory, but would be scarcely understandable to an outsider in this connection. Incidentally, a conjecture in Virgil handed down under the name 'Firmianus' seems to go back likewise to our Firmianus Lactantius.

Lactantius' further activity, however, was not exhausted in the fostering of old interests in this new environment, now favourable to Christians and completely peaceful. As a matter of fact, his horizon had widened in this new situation and surroundings. The Christian and the theologian began to be interested in the fate of the empire. The old learned apologist still showed surprising open-mindedness and inner versatility. In a certain way, Lactantius always had been a conscious, practical Roman. When in his main work he censures the past of Rome, and when he prohibits the Christian from military and judicial service (*Inst.* VI, 20, 16), he has traditional and specifically theological reasons. It is not an expression of any particular attitude of hostility to the state, and of renunciation of the world. Lactantius likewise shows an interest in social and political problems and regards it as quite right that Cicero 'gives preference, above teachers of philosophy, to men employed in public life' (*Inst.* III, 16, 2; *ANF*, VII, 85). He distrusts the superficial and gossiping manner of philosophizing Greeks who have always 'esteemed the most trifling things as of great consequence' (*Inst.* I, 18, 7; *ANF*, VII, 31) and insists upon order and justice. It is hardly accidental if this side of his nature seems to be intensified in the later 'extract' of his handbook. Full justice is now done to the courage which protects the homeland (*Epit.* 58, 4), and the teachings of many a philosopher are also criticized politically. 'How could states exist', it is asked, if for instance the principles of the Cynics were to find general acceptance? (*Epit.* 34, 5). Lactantius now lived at the court of an emperor friendly to Christians. Political tasks now automatically appeared in a new light, and the matter did not rest with such theoretical discussion.

With his essay on *The Death of the Persecutors* (*de Mortibus Persecutorum*) Lactantius takes for the first time a step into contemporary political literature. As long as Christians were still excluded from public life this sort of study did not come under consideration. To be sure, Lactantius even now wrote as a theologian—if you like, as the first representative of a Latin Christian theology of history. As to the content, his book presents a piece of 'contemporary history'. After a short introduction concerning the older persecutors, he describes the measures of all emperors since Diocletian against the Christians, and portrays the horrible punishments which the persecutors thereby without exception brought upon themselves. Fortune regularly deserted the rulers whenever they allowed themselves to be carried away into the 'defiling of their hands with the blood of the righteous' (9, 11). Even their wives and daughters were stricken by ruin, and only the pious rulers inspired by God could hold their ground, or can now enjoy undisturbed peace and glittering fortune. The lesson resulting from this is obvious, and it is emphasized. It is the special duty of the historian to hand over the truth to posterity, so that future generations may be warned. God protects justice and leads all ungodly men and persecutors without fail to their deserved punishment. This is just as much a theological as a political

truth. Lactantius had dedicated his book to a surviving confessor whom he knew personally, but it is evident that he
envisages not Christian readers alone. He is thinking not least
of the emperor Licinius himself, who was then beginning to
turn again toward the party hostile to Christianity. Unfortunately, we cannot date this writing accurately. At any rate, it
belongs to the years of the beginning of alienation between
Constantine and Licinius, who is portrayed with noticeable
criticism, i.e. the time of the beginning of the 'cold war' between the Western and Eastern halves of the Empire, which
turned some years later into a hot war and ended in 324 with
Constantine's undivided sovereignty. We may assume that
Lactantius published this book with the approval of Constantine, or at least after indirect contact with him. Seen in this way,
the apologetical tract attains almost the character of a religious
and political pamphlet with a particular aim.

On the whole, the historical statements of this small volume
are entirely reliable. Lactantius is, of course, writing a polemical
and partisan work, as is usual in such cases, but he guards against
consciously distorting the truth anywhere. As to form, the essay
is a complete success. The strong personal involvement in the
events makes the rigid, academic style unusually lively. Sometimes the description becomes almost dramatic. Nevertheless,
in places it is almost intolerable to the modern reader. The
glorification of the bloody martyrdoms has a repulsive effect,
and the merciless triumph over the cruelly overthrown enemies
of Christianity is rather offensive; it reminds us of Nietzsche's
interpretation of the Christian 'inferiority complex'. In former
times the attempt was frequently made to deny completely
Lactantius' authorship of this book, in order to attribute it to
some unknown 'pupil' of his, in accordance with the familiar
means of escape of the philologist from embarrassment. The
'fanaticism' and hostile tone did not seem to match the noble
humanity, culture, and love of one's enemies which Lactantius
at other times displays. But Lactantius is not the last Christian
humanist to change his view and lose his vision in this way

when passing over to the ground of politics and of real controversy. With his natural, logical morality, and its corresponding
political theology, he stands unconsciously at the threshold of
a new period with a 'dominant' church, to which the demands
of tolerance and intellectual respect for the enemy will have
hardly any practical weight.

His book is most interesting if understood as a document of
the growing political consciousness of a church destined to
govern. The basic idea has already been prepared to some degree in the older apologetics: 'He who persecutes justice can
only be a blackguard' (de Mort. 4, 1). Tertullian's thesis, that
the tolerant emperors had always reigned happily, while all persecutors have been accursed both as men and sovereigns, is taken
up by Lactantius, and for the first time based upon a corresponding historical narration. Out of a tactically and polemi-
cally adduced argument of apologetic conflict has now arisen
a principle of the theology of history, to which the Christians
will henceforth refer, and upon which they will rely for edification! It is indeed they who represent justice on this earth, and
he who attacks them takes God himself as his enemy and must
bear the consequences. In this temporal framework the Christian idea of judgement, however, now also links up with the
older Roman political ideology. According to this, the victories
of Rome from time immemorial had been the result of Roman
virtue and justice. Now, however, it is the one, true God of the
Christians who takes under his protection this justice, moral,
religious, and political in the person of the pious emperor.
God's hand shelters Constantine (de Mort. 24, 5) while the
wicked, persecuting emperors appear throughout as incompetent 'tyrants' suppressing simultaneously with Christianity
justice also, and introducing 'barbaric' morals. They are evil
'beasts', which can tolerate the truth of God as little as the old
Roman freedom, virtue, and discipline. Such exaggerating
statements must not be condemned as adulation or hypocrisy;
they are understandable enough in the mouth of a Christian
who experienced the change under Constantine. Lactantius,

however, stands here at the same time under the shadow of a primitive pagan tradition, against which his Christianity has not really any counter-weight to offer. Scarcely had the revolution been completed, when the old church ideology of martyrdom and persecution vanished, and changed almost to its opposite. The Christians are no longer strangers in this world, and do not suffer through holding to a truth essentially different from that demanded and known by the world. The only connection with the past which, one would like to hope, will never come back, is the glorifying remembrance of the old fighters and their sufferings. One must not overlook the positive elements in this point of view, for combined with the over-hasty optimism and moralism of this outlook there is an unquestioning readiness for political co-operation and an affirmation of public life within the framework of a very definitely understood new 'justice'.

All this is just beginning to be delineated in this last work which we possess from Lactantius. The menace of, and triumph over, the 'persecutors' is still more strongly present than the promise and praise of the pious emperor who respects the Christians, and the traditional Roman political feeling is more evident than a Christian ideal of the empire. All the same, the new line of political thinking is announced. The common de-nominator for state and church seems to be found in the idea of 'justice' as Lactantius had developed it already in his *Institutes*. Constantine had an ear open to such statements. Further-more, Lactantius' fundamental theological ideas in the strict sense agreed largely with his own politico-religious ideas. The stress upon the monotheistic belief in providence and upon ethical culture, the demand for religious tolerance and a better morality, and the emphasis on the old Roman greatness and tradition fitted well into his policy of renewal for the empire, which intended to extend patronage to the Christian and yet not give offence to the pagan majority. Constantine's decrees and speeches are in such close agreement with Lactantius' con-ceptions in principle, and sometimes even in formulation also, that this can hardly be an accident. To all appearance, he had occasionally called upon his son's tutor for his own instruction. If the missionary preaching of Lactantius in Constantine's version occasionally sounds somewhat more neutral, vague, and general, this is understandable in the circumstances and must not be seen as a lack of inner agreement. Perhaps Constantine was more of a theologian in his political ideas than Lactantius had become a politician.

We should probably know more about these things if development had not led so rapidly from these Western beginnings to a new politics, though not yet in the later sense the politics of a state church. Lactantius did not follow the emperor to the East. With new ecclesiastical and theological problems, new advisors soon took his place here. The detailed theology of the Christian empire was created only by Eusebius, who has therefore in this area almost completely overshadowed his older predecessor in the eyes of posterity. We do not know how Lactantius would have reacted to the Arian controversies, and to the resulting ecclesiastico-political decisions. He certainly would not have become an Athanasius. He did not have the theological requisites for this. But he might perhaps not have yielded so thoughtlessly to the 'opportune' necessities as did Eusebius, whom he otherwise closely resembles in his basic political and apologetic attitude. The whole nature of Lactantius was not that of a church politician, and he belonged to the older generation. Moreover, we do not know the exact date and detailed circumstances of his death. He probably did not witness the terrible end of his pupil, who was sentenced to death by his own father (326). Otherwise one could bring the deletion of the enthusiastic addresses to Constantine into relation with this incident; it is closely parallel to the dogmatic eliminations already mentioned. Yet these are vague assumptions which we must leave at rest. There was certainly no public break with Constantine. Lactantius was no courtier and no careerist; but, always cautious rather than bold, calm, and considerate in his attitude, he probably preferred to conclude his days in quiet retirement.

His immediate effect was at first small. Only Jerome, as we have seen, occasionally mentions him sympathetically; Augustine also must have known him well and has made use of his writings. The great enthusiasm for Lactantius began only with the Humanism of the fifteenth century. The Salerno *editio princeps* of his works in 1465 was the first book printed in Italy, and in the same century there followed a good dozen further editions. Pico praised the perfect literary form of the 'Christian Cicero'; Erasmus and Zwingli esteemed him because they saw the ideal union between Christianity and ancient culture accomplished in his writings. Right up till the Enlightenment Lactantius remained a frequently read author. The attempt to become free from the burden of theological traditions by appeal to the ancient humanities today is certainly a very different thing from the attempt of Lactantius to accommodate himself to the ancient society, to which he himself belonged, in order to convert it to the new 'Christian Way'. Lactantius indeed had hardly an idea of the difficulty of such an undertaking. He did not take seriously the intellectual power of philosophy, and he thought that he could control the historical revolution of which he had become a witness theologically with a general teaching of retribution. He therefore reflects only the first naïve reactions with which educated Christian circles met the new era at the time. They were as superficial and unreflective as they were honest and serious in intention. It took almost two generations' time, with new experiences, and a theology more profound than that of Lactantius to do justice to the new situation.

CHAPTER IV

AMBROSE

With Constantine in sole power (324), and with the foundation of Constantinople, the weight of ecclesiastical decision shifted again entirely to the East. Here the alliance between empire and church was firmly established in the next years; here began the Arian controversy with its violent commotions; but here also began a general rise of ecclesiastical and theological life. The West did not participate herein and created nothing comparable. Always 'behind the times' compared with the East and intellectually backward, the development of the Latin church seemed to stagnate for almost a generation after the death of Lactantius. Only after the middle of the century did it begin slowly to wake up. The impulse was given by external ecclesiastical circumstances which brought the West once more into connection with the Greek church.

After the death of Constantine the Great (337), the administration of the empire was divided among his sons. The relative political independence of the West intensified its intellectual isolation from events in the East. They would, to be sure, have decided in favour of Athanasius; but even decades later educated Christians had not heard anything about Nicea (325) and its creed. This situation changed only when Constantius, the emperor of the East, was able to take control of the West also in 353, and at once tried to establish here too his ecclesiastical government which was directed against Athanasius and the Nicene Creed. He succeeded superficially; only a few firm confessors had to be deported into exile. Yet the majority of the Latin church nevertheless wanted to remain 'orthodox'. The pressure which she had to suffer here and there at the hands of the new imperial bishops determined her further development. The Arian controversy—nobody really had much idea of its theological presuppositions—appeared to the West from the beginning as a dispute concerning the independence of the church, and its freedom of decision in creedal matters. Under Julian the Apostate (361–363) all schools of opinion were tolerated, and the Nicene party rapidly gained the upper hand. In spite of this, his successor Valentinian I, who was orthodox in his personal beliefs, was not yet successful in restoring full unity. The Arian bishops of Constantius remained in office and the synodal decisions which were made against them were not executed. The government was weary of the ecclesiastical quarrels, and it seemed simplest just to ignore them and 'put them on ice'.

This confusion of ecclesiastical relations was accompanied by the continuing obscurity of the intellectual situation. The Arian controversy was based on the data of Greek theology, particularly as created by Origen one hundred years earlier. The problem was to combine the idea of Christ's divinity with monotheism, and to fit it rationally into the setting of a metaphysical view of the world. This was a systematic task in which the West had until then barely taken any part. Even now there remained a widespread inclination here to be satisfied with a plain acknowledgement of the unity of nature of the Father and Son, and to cut short all the further questions that were sure to arise by simply referring to the Nicene Creed. The renunciation of a theologically responsible solution of the problems threatened to separate the West from the like-minded 'Nicene' circles of the East, which were still involved in fierce fights and controversies with the dominant Arian parties. Old differences, bygone misunderstandings, and countless practical and theological difficulties everywhere stood in the way of a general 'Catholic' termination of the church struggle and blocked the way to the desired peace. Only this much was clear: a final settlement had to be accomplished on a firm dogmatic basis, and could not possibly succeed without a positive relation to the political power, or without a re-ordering of the state establishment of the church.

Ambrose was the man who accomplished this task intellectually and politically. Prior to him, there can be named only one who at least understood and aimed at the same goal in a similar way: Bishop Hilary of Poitiers. In many respects he was a forerunner whose work was now completed by Ambrose. Hilary belonged to the inflexible Niceans who had been banished by Constantius to the East. Here, outside the circle of all Western prejudice, the full implications and theological complexity of the quarrel became gradually clear to him, and from then on he tried to enlighten his Western colleagues by continually writing new treatises, 'white papers', and pamphlets about the existing ecclesiastical and theological connections, and to mediate between them and the 'new-Nicene' leaders of the East. Having returned home, he began to establish a practical union in ecclesiastical affairs and forced the remaining Arians more and more on to the defensive. Nevertheless, even Hilary finally failed because of the resistance and indifference of the governmental agencies. His attempt to overthrow the influential bishop Auxentius of Milan ended with his expulsion from Italy, and soon afterwards he died. The new organization of the state-church on a Nicene basis was first accomplished by Ambrose. He brought to an end the intellectual controversy with the Arians. Yet he too could obtain his goal only gradually, and then only with the assistance of the state, and had to maintain it in ever-renewed and wearing contests until at last the new order was firmly established for all time.

Ambrose was the first Latin church father to be born, reared, and educated not as a pagan, but as a Christian. He was likewise the first descendant of the Roman high aristocracy to stand up publicly for the church, and to have found in it his life-work. Both elements were important for his historical significance and decisive for his activity itself. In Ambrose there was an inner confidence and imperturbability of nature which appeared only the more clearly during the crises and storms of his outer life.

Of superior intelligence, energetic, a born diplomat and where necessary an extremely adroit tactician, he seems never to have faltered in his real purpose and in his religious and ethical convictions. He was thoroughly genuine in what he demanded, and for all the hardness of his conduct was never rigid, inhuman, or unscrupulous. Detest as we may the aims and method of his actions, the man himself continues to command respect, just as even his adversaries could not withhold respect and recognition in his lifetime. The same clarity and integrity distinguished Ambrose as a theological teacher. His numerous writings, practical, devotional, and dogmatic, are neither particularly original nor especially brilliant, but they display in their objectivity and straightforwardness something earnest and trustworthy which carries conviction. Like all fathers of the Latin church, Ambrose was well trained in rhetoric. Wherever it seemed appropriate, he did not hesitate to use the appropriate devices of passionate overstatement, emotion on display, and highly coloured language and imagery. Yet none is basically less of a rhetorician than he. One realizes that Ambrose stood under the double responsibility as preacher and political leader of his congregation. His speech is always aimed at the essential and the decisive for practice. It is uncomplicated, realistic rather than studied, yet it keeps the entire man in view. Its earnestness moves the conscience, and reveals not the slightest vanity or desire for applause, despite a well-founded self-assurance, which grew over the years.

Ambrose was born in 339 in Trèves. His father, Aurelius Ambrosius, who had risen to the high rank of the prefect of Gaul, resided here. An early death terminated his career, and his widow moved back to Rome with the three children. Even in later years, Ambrose had friends and relatives among the first families here, and perhaps he really did belong, as his family name may indicate, to the famous line of the Aurelians. In these circles of the Roman aristocracy education and culture, which had become rare elsewhere in the West, were still alive. This explains how Ambrose came to learn the Greek language

thoroughly and not merely as a school subject—an advantage
which proved very useful to him in his later life. As was natural
for a man of his ancestry, he at first entered on a career in the
Civil Service. Toward the end of the sixties we find him working together with his brother Satyrus as *advocatus* at the central court in Sirmium, then the most important metropolis of
the Balkans. Around 370, when he was approximately 30 years
of age, he was already appointed governor of the upper Italian
provinces, Liguria and Emilia. His residence was Milan, the
capital of upper Italy, which had already repeatedly served as
residence for the emperors of the West.

Ecclesiastically, Milan was still governed by Bishop Auxentius, a Cappadocian by birth, who had been brought into this
office by Constantius after the dismissal of his orthodox predecessor Dionysius. Auxentius, of course, like his whole party,
strongly repudiated the name of 'Arian', but he refused to
acknowledge the Nicene Creed, and would not promote those
who accepted it in Milan. Otherwise he tried to evade any
dogmatic controversy and so to maintain his ecclesiastical
power; but his opponents already considered him a back number. We do not know what Ambrose's attitude toward him
was. The position of Ambrose as a civil official prohibited him
from recklessly revealing his personal conviction. On the other
hand, his strongly Nicene orthodoxy certainly could not have
remained completely unknown during his years in Milan. With
Auxentius dying in 374, the Niceans believed their hour to have
come; now at last the heresy was to vanish for ever. Against
them the adherents of Auxentius fought no less enthusiastically
for their ecclesiastical existence. The election campaign threatened to degenerate into a tumult, and Ambrose hastened to the
church to establish the necessary order. There—it is related—a
child raised his voice to the complete surprise of all, and called
'Bishop Ambrose' into the room, and thereupon as by a
miracle those present agreed spontaneously and unanimously
to his candidature (*Vita*, 60). The prophetic voice of the child
may be a legendary addition; otherwise it appears to be quite

conceivable that the quarrelling parties realized it to be the best solution at this critical moment to create as bishop a Nicean, to be sure, yet to a certain extent 'neutral' personality, who was not prejudiced by the previous controversies. Ambrose assures us that he was completely surprised, and sought at first to avoid election. From his career up to then he could certainly not be regarded as prepared for this high ecclesiastical office—he was not even at that time baptized—and without imperial consent he could not possibly accept the appointment. He asked for his ordination at least to be postponed; but when the unconditional consent of Valentinian I arrived from Trèves, he no longer resisted. Before the end of the year 374, the 35-year-old government official was consecrated bishop of Milan.

If government and people had expected from him above all the preservation of the peace of the church, Ambrose did not disappoint them. He naturally insisted upon receiving first baptism and then ordination from a Nicean, and one of his first official acts was the solemn return and burial of the bones of his predecessor, bishop Dionysius, who had died in exile. The change in favour of the Nicene Creed was thus publicly demonstrated. On the other hand, Ambrose showed himself willing to take over into his service the entire staff of Auxentius' clergy. He thus avoided engendering conflict and carrying differences too far. The period which followed justified his generous procedure, for from now on the Milan clergy firmly and faithfully gave their support to their episcopal lord in all disputes.

The abrupt change 'from the platforms of this vain world and the clamour of public acclamation to the chants of the psalmist' (de Paen. II, 8, 72) is somewhat reminiscent of the similar rapid rise of Cyprian; but times had changed since then. This change in the now Christian Roman empire meant much less to Ambrose than to Cyprian any denial of his former interests. The office of bishop of Milan was certainly not inferior to that of the governor of the province in public influence, authority, and responsibility. Indeed, in the precincts of the church he could now find a new, and yet entirely appropriate, sphere of activity for his aristocratic Roman traditions. On the other hand, it is not to be doubted that Ambrose was a convinced and determined Christian already prior to his election. Orthodoxy belonged to the tradition of his family. There was a martyr among his ancestresses, and prior to his elevation to the episcopate his only sister, Marcellina, had vowed life-long virginity. It is hardly accidental that he himself and his brother were still unmarried. Celibacy was esteemed by Ambrose at all times as a higher form of life, particularly appropriate to the Christian ideal, and its maintenance had never, it seems, caused any difficulties to him. If Ambrose was still unbaptized this was nothing unusual, and speaks for rather than against the seriousness of his conviction. An official had at times to decree enactments involving bloodshed and also tolerate opinions and customs in his environment which seemed to be irreconcilable with the idea of a perfect Christian life. Ambrose had possibly already occupied his mind with theological, or at least semi-theological, matters before his change of office. There is something to be said for the view that he was the author of an edition of Josephus' *Jewish War*, and of a paraphrase of the Biblical books of Kings mentioned there but no longer extant. These would then belong in his early years. The choice of a politico-historical subject would fit Ambrose well, and an early literary activity would explain at the same time how the young bishop succeeded in becoming a significant writer so shortly after his election.

To Ambrose, the most essential task of a bishop was at all times Biblical instruction and preaching. However many duties his office imposed upon him in the course of the years, duties of administration and pastoral care, the education of his clergy, and ecclesiastical and civil politics, Ambrose never neglected or failed in his obligations as a preacher. In this, above all, he saw the meaning of his spiritual calling. Although he had a soft voice, he was yet esteemed everywhere as an outstanding preacher and was therefore, as we know from Augustine, heard with pleasure not only by the faithful members of his congregation, but also by outsiders. This admiration applied also to the matter of his sermons. Modern readers may be surprised at this, but the allegorical interpretation used by Ambrose with a credulous and unsuspecting neglect of any literal meaning, was then something new in the West. There were any number who breathed freely when all at once they saw the Old Testament in particular liberated from all apparently meaningless externals, such as painful human weaknesses otherwise beyond comprehension, and many conceptions of God and of the divine nature which to the educated way of thinking appeared unworthy. Instead they found everywhere unsuspected spiritual mysteries and wonderfully profound revelations. Ambrose did not himself invent this method of spiritualizing reinterpretation, but adopted it in essence from his Greek models and particularly from the Alexandrian theologians. Their writings were continuously drawn upon for his sermons, and for the writings resulting from them. Ambrose had no ambition to appear original, and he took the material which he needed from wherever he found it. Entire Biblical books were explained as a whole or in selections by means of the Greek commentaries. Ambrose preferred series of sermons. He began, as it appears, with the first book of the Bible, for which he had an especial liking all his life, and later published tracts on Paradise, on Cain and Abel, on Noah and the ark, etc. Besides Origen, his main source was the Jewish theologian Philo, although recent Greeks as well were called upon. The later exposition of the *Work of the Six Days*, popular and voluminous, was chiefly compiled on the lines of Basil. His one-sided inclination toward spiritualization is here kept in check by a strong affirmation of God's creation and its visible beauty. Older Stoic and other classical traditions have obviously contributed. All the same, the adoption of the material was never carried out uncritically; in the course of time Ambrose revealed an increasing independence also of his Greek theological models. The practical and ethical admonition of the congregation occupied increasing space, and in the beautiful expositions of the Psalms and Luke's gospel,

which date from the last ten years of his life, teaching on redemption and the devotional proclamation of Christ in particular appeared in a new, vividly personal form. However,
Ambrose retained all his life a certain inclination toward speculative explanation and mysterious discoveries on the basis of the
divine word. Allegory seemed to him the higher and proper
theological form of Scripture exegesis, and he took its conclusions especially seriously. In this there is revealed perhaps a
sort of need of his otherwise very practical and realistic nature,
with its inclination to plain faith and morals, for spiritual
expansion.

With these remarks about Ambrose the preacher we have
already anticipated further developments, and must turn back
to the beginning. The first writings which the young bishop
published were two memorial addresses for his brother Satyrus.
Satyrus had also left the public service after Ambrose's election,
and had taken over for Ambrose the administration of his household, but he had died a few months later. The elaborate description of his virtues and career, and of the inseparable love
of the brothers, his grief over the loss, and the exultation at the
thought of his abiding memory of the deceased, all these followed the primitive Roman aristocratic tradition. Only everything has now become at the same time a sermon, being
set in a light of religious edification, and connected with a
corresponding instructional purpose. The orthodox zeal of the
deceased is emphasized, and the whole meditation ends in a
proclamation of the certainty of resurrection, by which it lifts
itself beyond the purely personal. The traditional grounds of
solace thereby attain a far more earnest background. Both
speeches were actually delivered before publication, and are of
interest as to the form of contemporary Christian memorials of
the dead. Soon afterwards, Ambrose took the liberty of paying
a similar spiritual tribute to his sister. He concluded his work on
virgins with the speech which Pope Liberius is supposed to have
delivered at her initiation as a nun.

In the same way, Ambrose had already expressed himself

repeatedly on the topic of virgins and virginity orally as well
as in writing during the first years. This was an aspect of the
practical life of the congregation which he took especially to
heart. His ascetic recommendations are directed almost exclusively to the female sex, to the virgins and 'widows' consecrated to God, who were then not yet grouped together in
convents, but had their own status in the church. Ambrose
shows himself still untouched by the new impulses which monasticism had brought to the old ideal. In its content his ascetic
preaching barely went beyond what was already taught by
Cyprian in this respect. There are basically three stages of
chastity in the church: marriage, as far as possible only once,
widowhood, and the holy virginity of the 'brides of Christ'.
Voluntary virginity is a virtue first brought into the world by
Christianity; its value and special merit are considered as un-
questionable. However, Ambrose was no friend to exaggerated
competition or asceticism. The virgin should lead a quiet, secluded life, and within her family dedicate herself above all
to prayer, fasting, and sanctification; the inner disposition of
humility and dedication is the decisive thing. Nevertheless his
ascetic preaching aroused a stir and some anxiety. Women
came to Milan from afar in order to receive the veil from his
hands. On the other hand, he also met resistance, especially
within his own congregation. Many parents preferred to see
their daughters well settled as wives, and sought therefore to
dissuade them from their ascetic enthusiasm. Yet these were
wishes of which Ambrose had not the slightest understanding.
In such cases he firmly took the more pious children under his
protection against their parents. In all this, he is the authoritative representative of a fourth-century tendency which was
growing in other ways also. Ambrose is a typical defender
of the contemporary Christian and late classical ideal of life,
which recognizes spiritual seriousness and ethical discipline in
matters of sex almost solely in the form of renunciation.

In the long run, the new bishop could not content himself
with practical theological tasks. The dogmatic situation in

upper Italy and the areas adjacent urgently required, as we have
seen, a settlement, and Ambrose was not the man to withdraw
for long from the expectations fixed on him by the Niceans
from all sides. Their position was far from being firmly established, especially in the neighbouring Illyrian provinces. Their
adversaries were frequently predominant, and spread their influence from there to Italy too. As a first victory, Ambrose and
his fellow-believers were successful in promoting the election of
an orthodox bishop in Sirmium. In addition, the validity of the
Nicene faith was solemnly endorsed anew at a Council held
there. In these controversies which were to accomplish the final
victory of the Nicene party, it would be wrong to regard
Ambrose only as a church politician. Faith and church policy
completely coincided in him. Acknowledgement of the unqualified and consubstantial divinity of Christ was in accordance with the nature of his personal soteriology. It was therefore
for him also the only possible foundation for a truly Christian church. The earnestness of this claim made of him a dogmatic theologian in the years that followed. Ambrose did not
rest until he had worked through the whole range of the Trinitarian problem, section by section, and had established it anew
in public. Going beyond Hilary he followed here the modern
Neo-Nicene theology of the East, yet did not renounce the older
traditions of his Latin homeland. Independently and preg-
nantly they were united with the results of the more advanced
Greek theology into a new system. By this means Ambrose
brought the Arian controversy to an end in the West intellectually also.

The study of the most important writings did not cause him
any difficulties, owing, as we know, to his knowledge of Greek,
and he undertook it with zeal and earnestness. Moreover, he
also got personally in touch with Basil the Great. The old
Western distrust of 'academic' theology was out of the question to a man of his type; the frequent suspicion of the Greeks
that the Westerners were incapable of differentiating at all
between Father and Son would have been entirely unfounded

in his case. The distinction between the one inseparable 'substance' of God, in which alone rests the divine unity, and the three 'persons' of the deity, not to be confused one with another, was a matter of course to Ambrose, and from the outset made any confusion impossible. All this had long ago been formulated into concepts by Tertullian. The problem now was to vindicate against the Arians also the equality of the Persons, and to exclude finally that subordinationist doctrine of the emanation of the Son from the Father, and of the Spirit from the Son, which lessened their rank. All three are equally eternal, equally original, in their respective special natures indissolubly united one with another. From this point of view, the adoption of essentially Athanasian and 'Neo-Nicene' ideas caused no further difficulty. Ambrose unfolded his teaching on the Trinity—always in the medium of sermons—first in a voluminous work *On Faith* published in two parts. There followed a three-volume treatise *On the Holy Spirit*, the position of the third Person having been until then only inadequately dealt with in this connection. The circle closed finally with Ambrose's great examination of *The Mystery of the Lord's Incarnation* in which the consequences of the Trinitarian theology are drawn in respect to the Person of the God-man. In this important book Ambrose went most decisively further than his Eastern predecessors, and began to examine new problems.

The determination and confidence with which Ambrose dealt with this complex of problems within a few years (378–382) is astounding. It would be incomprehensible if in respect of philosophy his mind had been a *tabula rasa*, as was the case with most of the Latin theologians of the time. From the outset of his ecclesiastical career at the latest, Ambrose must have come in contact with that Platonic and Neo-Platonic philosophy which, for a deeper systematic understanding of the doctrine of the Trinity, could hardly be neglected. The priest Simplician, who instructed Ambrose as a catechumen, lived in these traditions. If he nevertheless condemns the philosophers in the usual way, he is thinking of the Epicureans and Stoics, and above all of Aristotle. The Platonists are tacitly excepted; at any rate they are nowhere explicitly attacked, and of Plato it is said once again that he derived his theological knowledge from the Old Testament. This concept of philosophy would have been nothing new in the East. In the West, however, it signified a change, which was to prove decisive in Augustine's conversion, and pointed to the future. As to Ambrose himself, this statement needs yet again a proviso. Indeed, it is just the limitation of his philosophical interests, and of his philosophical ability, which makes the speed and general success of his dogmatic work understandable, although he hardly could have accomplished it without philosophical education. Ambrose was willing to learn from the Neo-Platonists. He adopted, for instance, their conception of substance; yet what he was looking for was not a new metaphysic. Problems of this kind he did not pursue. All that mattered to him was to define the revealed Christian truth in an intellectually neat and consistent form and thus make it unassailable. His knowledge of God as such is not a conclusion of his systematic thinking, but is based on the Holy Scripture. Proof from the Scripture is with Ambrose not something adventitious, but an absolute necessity. It receives the most attention in his dogmatic writings. Inasmuch as it deals with God, all theology is for Ambrose exclusively a theology of revelation, and must not seek to be anything else but this. The radical and, if you like, Neo-Platonic emphasis on the distance separating the divine from every created being, has the purpose of making impossible any analogical, speculative bridge built from the side of the creature. Only God's own work and word can span this gap. This ontological dualism is also the presupposition for the essential understanding of Christ's divinity, and for the corresponding extremely 'dyophysite' construction of his doctrine of the Person of the God-man, which sharply separates the two 'natures' of the Saviour. There is no emanationist and gradual combination of divinity and humanity, or of the supernatural and natural worlds.

This once established, it is comparatively easy for faith to be

satisfied with a few concise formulae. It will show how much
it is in earnest from the religious point of view by the very fact
that it prefers to fear rather than comprehend the depths of the
Godhead (de Fid. V, 18, 221). In this renunciation of all speculative reason, and this stress on faith, and the obedience of faith,
as the essential element of religion, Ambrose is a true Westerner.
In this his thoughts remind one of Tertullian's religious position. Also reminiscent of Tertullian is the close relationship
between revelational theology and a determined, almost massive rationalism. Nobody has expressed so inflexibly, so forth-
rightly, and so powerfully the logical force and form of
Trinitarian thought as Ambrose himself. There is therefore
something to be said for the view that he was also the author
of the so-called 'Athanasian Creed', the typical Western profession of faith in the Holy Trinity which endeavours to close
once for all with its forty stereotyped and rhythmically formulated clauses any conceivable gap in the construction of the
doctrine. This also is characteristic, that Ambrose after having
once developed his doctrine of God in the controversial years
of his youth, never later returned to this area of dogmatic
theology. The truth is considered as already found and finally
established. The only concern henceforth was to preserve it
immovably and to defend it and, furthermore, to deal forth-
rightly with the manifold spiritual and practical problems of the
church's daily life and to solve them.

As has already been said, Ambrose's attitude to church politics was in complete accord with his theological convictions.
His goal was the public recognition of the one, true Catholic
church, standing on the immovable foundation of the one
orthodox, and therefore also only legitimate, creed. This ideal
marked an innovation in so far as the imperial church as such
had scarcely been a real 'Confessional Church' until then.
Indeed, in the course of the Arian controversy different creeds,
among them also the Nicene, had been formulated and proclaimed; but the church policy of the state had for tactical
reasons again and again put them aside, changed them, and

finally endeavoured to save the unity of the church by eliminating all question of a creed. Now a new period began. As the outcome of the Arian controversy the Nicene Creed was understood as the dogmatic and 'confessional' solution of the problem of the state-church, and no weakening or exception was any longer tolerated.

We misjudge the religious meaning of the contemporary Catholic ideal of the imperial church if we place it, in this form, in direct opposition to the idea of freedom of conscience, and try to understand it merely as a result of priestly love of power and intolerance. The decisive thing is the underlying faith in the clear objectivity and general accessibility of the dogmatically formulated truth, which must therefore remain in force 'ecumenically' for the whole world. Ambrose himself indeed was a convinced exponent of freedom of faith and gave it unrestricted scope in practice in the personal relations of individuals. If he unconditionally defended the Nicene foundation of the Catholic church, he did not have in mind the individual believer. His concern here was to protect the independence of the church as a whole against the illicit interference of the political powers, whose lack of dogmatic scruple had been sufficiently experienced in the early disputes under Constantine. In view of the despotism and caprice of the imperial religious policy, this was a very understandable concern, with the West having an absolute Nicene majority. Everything taken into consideration, the conflicts in which Ambrose carried his demands clearly prove his moral superiority too. Yet the contest for the 'freedom' and 'rights' of his church, which he undertook in the name of 'faith', was of course always simultaneously a fight for ecclesiastical supremacy, i.e. it was a power struggle which, as such, he attempted to win by co-operation with the state, and with use of governmental measures against all 'heretics' who thought differently. Ambrose did not sense the contradiction arising at this point. He still held to the old ideals of the period of persecution, and liked to stress that faith must remain independent, and can be accepted only in freedom. He abhorred

external pressure. For instance, he indignantly broke fellowship with the Gallican bishops, because they had for the first
time, with the help of the state courts, had ecclesiastical opponents executed. Nevertheless, Ambrose the church politician
sought to secure as far as possible the predominance of his
church. In his actions even Ambrose could not always escape
the ambiguity of all ecclesiastical power policy.

We will not pursue in detail the complicated incidents of the
church politics of those significant years, in part so difficult to
grasp. They were in their perpetual ebb and flow determined
in no small degree by the over-all political situation. In 378 the
Goths had decisively defeated the Roman army, and overflowed
almost the whole Balkans. Only with much trouble were they
gradually calmed and settled in the newly conquered terri-
tories. For the most part the Goths were still pagans; however,
in so far as they had been converted—by Ulfilas—they had not
become orthodox, but (in the opinion of the Niceans) 'Arian'
Christians. Wherever they came, Arianism raised its head again.
Ambrose recognized the gravity of the danger to the church
and was, not without reason, convinced that the political
fidelity of the Roman heretics too, now allied religiously with
the Goths, could not be trusted. From this standpoint he tried
to warn the rulers and arouse them to ecclesiastico-political
resistance. He observes that the Goths are the people Gog, of
whom Ezekiel had prophesied (Ezek. xxxviii f.). He who
wants to fight them has to stand fast in the true faith and can
then be certain of the victory. On the other hand, 'belief in the
Roman Empire was first overthrown, where faith in God gave
way' (de Fid. II, 16, 139; ANF, 10, 241). With disgust Ambrose
describes an Arian bishop who dared to appear 'in front of the
Roman army, defiled with Gothic ungodliness, and dressed like
a heathen with collar and bracelets'. Such conduct, he thinks,
is not only sacrilegious for a priest, but must be regarded as
altogether unchristian, for it is 'contrary to Roman custom'
(Ep. 10, 9). Even as a bishop, Ambrose remained wholly a
Roman; 'Germanic' and 'Arian', 'Roman' and 'Catholic-

Christian' become almost synonymous expressions. Fidelity to
the empire is a Christian obligation. Ambrose commends it not
only to the Roman citizens but also to the barbarians living
outside the empire (*Vita*, 36).

Nevertheless, under pressure of emergency the government
felt at times urged to compromise ecclesiastically with the
Balkan Goths and those who shared their views. Ambrose had
to tolerate the requisition of a church even in Milan, evidently
in order that it might be offered to the Arians if necessary. But
the political stabilization also restored the old ecclesiastical
order. The young emperor Gratian, to whom Ambrose had
dedicated his book on faith, took up his residence in Milan, and
willingly allowed himself to be advised in questions of religion
and church politics. His more important co-ruler, the Spanish
general Theodosius, at the same time brought the Nicene Creed
to recognition in the Orient also. The conclusion of these uneasy years came in 381, in the East at the great Council of
Constantinople, and in the West at the Council of Aquileia,
which stood completely under the leadership of Ambrose.
Here, the last adherents of the older system of the state-church,
who did not want to acknowledge the Nicene Creed, were
arraigned in due form, and then dismissed from their episcopal
sees by the agencies of the government. The minutes of the
sessions are preserved. It is obvious that the proceedings at
this religious convention were quite stormy. The condemned
bishops, who came from Illyrium, had been deceived about the
true purpose and character of the synod. Instead of the promised
general and free discussion there awaited them a one-sided
interrogation by their declared enemies who recklessly, and at
last even violently, brought the transactions to an end without
heeding their protests. In his official report to the government
Ambrose set the proceedings in a considerably milder light. At all
events the victory was won, and orthodoxy had officially attained
exclusive control in the whole of Italy and also in Illyria.

In the following years Ambrose became a leading personality in the Privy Council of the Milan court and we find him

repeatedly entrusted with political tasks. When Gratian was defeated in 383 by a co-emperor from Gaul, and then murdered, Ambrose together with the leading army officers took over the protection of his 12-year-old brother, Valentinian II. The bishop was twice sent to Trèves for diplomatic negotiations where he succeeded in saving Italy at least for the young emperor. The usurper later saw in Ambrose his real opponent, who had halted the eagles of his legions at the borders of the Alps (*Ep.* 24, 7). It was then still most unusual for the clergy to undertake political missions. Ambrose was no medieval hierarch. He would rather have understood his political services from the viewpoint of the bishop's traditional privilege to intercede for the weak (*Ep.* 24, 5). The emperor's mother, leading young Valentinian by the hand, had personally implored for his assistance (*Obit. Val.* 28). How could he then have refused? He wanted to act only in the framework of the duties of his office (*Ep.* 57, 12), for the protection of the faith and of his church. Ambrose tried to keep to this line also in his later years. He liked to emphasize that it was not his task to intervene in matters of state. But on account of his position and abilities political decisions came to him almost automatically, and the more his reputation grew with the years, the less could Ambrose withdraw from responsibility when things became serious (*Obit. Val.* 24). In his opinion, where peace, humanity, and justice are at stake, in the last resort even a bishop must not remain neutral. The line between spiritual and political competence naturally could not be drawn easily. It required a great deal of human tact, and of political acumen and responsibility, and all the cleverness and prudence of an Ambrose to give the right ecclesiastical verdict at the critical moment; that is to say, to make it not only morally convincing, but also politically effective. At any rate such action has nothing to do with opportunism in the usual sense. Ambrose never forgot whom and what he had to represent as bishop, and that is why he acquired the greatness and dignity of a churchman who really possesses authority.

It is not possible here to discuss all the political and ecclesi-astico-political happenings in which Ambrose came forward in this manner, and occasionally almost seemed to play the role of a 'Chancellor' or clerical Minister of State. We restrict our-selves to the most famous examples. The insecure political situation in which the Milanese government found itself after the fall of Gratian soon showed its religio-political implications. One after another, paganism first, and then Arianism too, sought to improve their situation, and to win back positions already abandoned. To be sure, the old Roman religion was neither forbidden nor had it disappeared under the Christian emperors, yet it was nevertheless more and more driven on to the defensive. Perhaps on Theodosius' instigation Gratian was, just shortly before his death, about to strike a new blow. The pagan Roman priests were deprived of their government sub-sidies and privileges, the altar and statue of Victory were re-moved from the Senate house, and from among the imperial titles there vanished the traditional designation of *Pontifex Maximus*, the highest pagan sacerdotal office. These decrees were of a far-reaching symbolical significance, for the new imperial régime, confessionally committed, now relinquished once and for all its still to some extent 'impartial' attitude to the old religion, and people had simply to accept this. True, the senate, in which the Christians did not yet have a majority, wanted immediately to protest against these enactments which especially affected Rome; but its delegation had not even been received in Milan. Now, after the change in government, an opportune moment seemed to have come to venture a new attempt.

The leader of the rejected delegation, Quintus Aurelius Symmachus, had in 384 just become the holder of the prefec-ture, i.e. the highest imperial office in the city of Rome, and was authorized to write the petition. He was the most famous writer and rhetorician Rome then had, educated in Neo-Platonic philosophy, himself a senator of a very old aristocratic family, and, in addition, a relative of Ambrose. We cannot read his petition even today without being moved: it was the swan-song of the proud, Roman religion. Symmachus defends the memories and institutions under which the venerable Rome had once become great. He emphasizes that Victory had earlier been protected even under Christian emperors, and had been of service to their rule. He speaks of the unselfish service to the general public of the priests, and particularly of the chaste vestal virgins, and thinks that the revenues for this have long ago changed from a free demonstration of favour to a historical legal claim. He even dares to recall at last the famines, and the terrible end of Gratian, who probably had not known at all of the fateful order issued in his name. Not a single disrespectful word occurs. Symmachus strains every nerve in order to make retreat as easy as possible for the emperor, but basically he himself feels that he is fighting for an order whose historical day has passed. He contents himself with begging for nothing more than tolerance for the ancestral religion, and as a philosopher refers to the heritage common to all religion: 'What difference does it make, by what pains each seeks the truth? We cannot attain to so great a secret by one road; but this discussion is rather for persons at ease, we offer now prayers, not conflict' (*Rel. Symm.* 10; *ANF*, 10, 415).

As a matter of fact, the advance seemed to have succeeded. Pagan and Christian members of the Privy Council alike voted in favour of this application, by which they hoped to put the leading circles of the eternal city in their debt. At this moment, however, Ambrose learned about the negotiations, and his intervention forced a decision the other way. In such a case, he declared, the bishop is directly responsible, for this is a matter of God's business, and a question of religion. Without going through the 'official channels' or waiting for special authorization, he wrote a letter to the emperor as his spiritual adviser: 'All people who live under the Roman government serve you, you Emperors and Princes of the world. You yourself, however, serve the almighty God and the holy faith' (*Ep.* 17, 1). There was no more to be said. 'I am surprised how it came into

the mind of certain people to think you were obliged to renew
the altars of the pagan gods' (Ep. 17, 3). The emperor is a
Christian and has as such—no matter what his political advisers
might wish—to represent the cause of the faith in the empire
too. In such matters he must at least never seek to retract a step
he has once taken. After Ambrose had received a copy of the
petition on his request, he answered it in detail once more in a
second writing directed to the wider public. In this he takes up
to a certain extent the neutral position of his adversaries—
although there can of course be no question in principle of an
equality of religious rights. But this is precisely how he makes
it possible for himself to repudiate most effectively the complaints of the pagans. The church does not have to fear a comparison of her rights with those of her opponents. When they
complain about the removal of the altar—what shall the Christian senators say when they are again forced to participate in
an idolatrous sacrifice? When they lament the lack of subsidies
for their few priests and vestals—what about the countless
Christian nuns and clergy who receive not one penny from the
public funds and cannot even accept legacies? As a matter of
fact, the church, having become great under persecution, was
at the time still living essentially from her own strength, while
the ancient cult, having been connected with the body politic
from the outset, would because of its very nature go to pieces
without public support. Ambrose naturally also protested
against the superstitious conjuring up of an alleged anger of the
gods and declares, contrary to his usual manner, that political
successes or disasters are completely independent of the question
of religion. In an interesting historico-theological excursus, he
describes progress as the actual power that moves nature and
history, and he mocks the nostalgic complaints of the Roman
senate. Rome is in reality not senile and is by no means ashamed
to make a change for the better. 'Only this I had formerly in
common with the Barbarians: that I had not yet come to know
God' (Ep. 18, 7).

Ambrose had composed a refutation which was also a

masterpiece, more popular and robust, less considered and polished as to detail than the refined work of art of his opponent, whose nobly suppressed emotion is of a peculiar charm. But he is more powerful and fresh in what has to be said and is said, supported by the force of conviction of a determined faith, which is fully sure both of itself and of the victorious power of its reasons. Ambrose later represented it as though purely spiritual reasons had decided the issue of this matter. The young emperor had risen 'like a Daniel' against his advisers, and made the decision in the power of the Holy Spirit (*Obit. Val.* 19). Yet this has undoubtedly to be regarded as an idealization. In reality, the men of the Privy Council must have decided to yield. There was no ignoring the emphasis with which Ambrose referred among other things also to the older co-emperor Theodosius, whose hostile attitude to the pagans was sufficiently known (*Ep.* 17, 12). Indeed, he went even further: 'At any rate', he says, in his first letter to Valentinian, 'if a different decision should be made, we bishops cannot by any means accept it calmly or ignore it. You may come to a church—but you will not find a priest there, or if you find one, he will resist you' (*Ep.* 17, 13). 'We are not in a position to share in the errors of others' (*Ep.* 17, 14). This was an open threat of excommunication, and the government could at this time risk a church struggle even less than a humiliation of the pagans. Ambrose had prevailed, but the disposition of the authorities to him certainly had not become friendlier. In the following year, this became evident.

The last reaction with which Ambrose had to cope of the Arianism which had infiltrated with the Goths, was virtually insignificant with respect to the whole ecclesiastical development. It was not supported by any strong religious movement, and did not possess any popular power. The foreign adherents of the defeated Illyrian heresy who had gathered in the shadow of the small Milanese court did not as formerly seek leadership in the church. They wanted merely to obtain the right to exist of their ecclesiastical separatist group, and relied in this entirely on the assistance of the secular power. But just for this reason this conflict becomes important from another aspect. The church struggle of the year 385–386 was the crucial test of the stability and the duration of the new system which no longer tolerated any loosening or breaking of its dogmatic order. Here, therefore, also the secular power met a limit which it had indeed once drawn by its own authority, but could no longer itself overstep. Ambrose was the embodiment of this new order. He defended it against the crown, and reduced the quarrel immediately to ultimate principles, theological and canonical. Therein lies its permanent importance.

Without doubt, the beginnings of the conflict did not originate in a general framework of church politics, but solely in the personal desire of a single personality, temperamental and accustomed to domination, namely the emperor's mother Justina. Theologically and politically, the wife of Valentinian I still lived with the viewpoint of an earlier period. Gratian, under whom the change had taken place, intentionally kept his mother away from governmental affairs. On the occasion of the bishop's election in Sirmium, there had already arisen a conflict and on that occasion Ambrose had remained victorious. In the early part of the reign of Valentinian II she had of necessity restrained herself, for it was none other than Ambrose himself whom she had to beg for support in a humiliating scene. Now finally, Justina felt herself again free to foster, at least in the environment of her own palace, those ecclesiastical ideas which appeared correct to her. Her Illyrian court chaplain Mercurinus was chosen as the anti-Nicene bishop of Milan, and he assumed thereupon the significant name 'Auxentius'. The emperor was a child and submitted to her desires, and the court was so indignant at the dictatorial bearing of Ambrose that it wanted him to be humiliated. The demand directed at first to him in the spring of 385 could be considered as moderate: it was desired that a small church only, situated outside the city wall, should be placed at the disposal of Auxentius. We remember that Ambrose had to tolerate a similar action of the emperor

Gratian only a few years earlier. However, times had changed since then, and so he bluntly refused the request. Ambrose knew that public opinion, i.e. the whole Catholic population of Milan, shared his convictions and stood firmly behind him. How, he asks, could he as a priest of God deliver up the temple of God to the heretical wolves? He himself has described to us the dramatic scene in which the controversy took place. He had been ordered personally to the Privy Council to negotiate the conveyance. There, face to face with the authorities, he was, however, not at all abashed, and insisted on the right of his case 'with the steadfastness of a priest'. Suddenly there was a tumult outside. The people, who had been informed about the proceedings, broke into the palace, and the guards were unable to stop them! All were ready 'to let themselves be killed for the faith of Christ'. Frightened, the emperor waived his demand. Ambrose himself had to be asked to calm the crowd, which he succeeded in doing immediately. So the matter seemed to be happily settled. But, as Ambrose complains, disfavour was now aroused against him more than ever (*Serm. Aux.* 29). Neither the empress nor the government was willing to accept such a defeat. The court absented itself from Milan for a long time. The main object was to prepare the attack better and to furnish it above all with a formal legal basis.

In January 386 there was issued a regular imperial edict which granted the right of public assembly to all adherents of the faith, as formerly decreed 'under Constantius of blessed memory', i.e. of the anti-Nicene, so called 'homoean' theology of Auxentius. Those, however, who presumed upon 'having the exclusive power of such assembly' were at the same time threatened with death as instigators of revolt, as breakers of the church's peace, and insulting the emperor's majesty (*Cod. Theod.* XVI, 1, 4). According to this, the government seemed to be willing to renounce the unity of the state-church, yet combined this completely new regulation with sanctions the severity of which were entirely unheard of, compared with anything previously in force. Significantly, the responsible

official had declined to draw up the law, and had therefore lost
his position. However, this strange decree should not be taken
at its face value. In reality, it was only issued to secure the
desired public recognition for Mercurinus-Auxentius, and the
exaggerated threats of the second portion were also aimed at
one man only, namely, Ambrose, who was intended to be
intimidated by this. Yet nobody could then know how far
such an attack so menacingly opened would actually lead.
Ambrose realized that only courage and inflexible consistency
could save him and his cause in this situation, and made his
preparations accordingly.

In order not to have to weather the storm upon his own
responsibility only, he hastily gathered a handful of bishops
from the surrounding area, who stood by him with admirable
courage, and on their part unanimously encouraged him to
persevere. When the imperial delegate then again demanded,
not long before Easter, the surrender no longer of the outlying
church, but of the larger new basilica, Ambrose had it occupied by the faithful populace, while he himself retreated to the
church outside the wall. The congregation was inspired and
held by sermons, addresses, and hymns. Ambrose had distri-
buted gold-pieces among the crowd adhering to him, and after
—very much against his directions and desire—an Arian presbyter had been thrashed soundly in the open street, very soon
no partisan of Auxentius dared any more appear in public. The
whole city, even to the street-gangs of youths, sided with
Ambrose. In spite of the soldiers on guard the people streamed
in masses into the church. These were days of enthusiastic
exultation and of a general readiness to fight and suffer which,
the young Augustine also, among others, lived through, and
which remained unforgettable to all those participating in it.
These were events simply unheard of in the declining years of
ancient society. How far off were those times when the population of a city could yet be summoned to act upon its own
political responsibility!

The soul and centre of the resistance was naturally Ambrose

himself. He restrained himself from public action and instead made 'the congregation' act—as though spontaneously. He declared, 'I have not stirred up the people. It is God's business and not mine, to calm them down, if he wishes' (*Ep.* 20, 10). Nobody wished to resist government measures if enforced; but still less could the possibility of yielding, or of approval of the injustice, be considered. Ambrose assured them time and again of his readiness for any kind of martyrdom: Christ desires the suffering of His disciples, and 'I know that whatever I must suffer, I shall suffer for Christ's sake' (*Serm. Aux.* 8). The emperor may do 'whatever royal power is customarily used for; I am willing to accept that which has been all along the fate of priests' (*Serm. Aux.* 1). Ambrose clearly understood that in his situation everything depended on keeping the fight on this spiritual level, for a violent riot would have had disastrous effects. On the contrary, the general readiness to suffer was his real weapon. They reproach us, he says, with a 'tyrannical' attitude: well then, 'we have our despotism; the tyranny of the priest is his weakness; "when I am weak", says the apostle (II Cor. xii. 10), "then I am strong"' (*Ep.* 20, 23). Ambrose had here made a discovery which he, of course wrongly, refers to Paul. Passive resistance, here for the first time exercised in the grand style, will remain henceforth the most important weapon of the church in all controversies with the secular power. It is in fact a weapon which Ambrose handled with calculation, and which opened to him possibilities of public propaganda even in the sphere of developed late Roman despotism. But this weapon demanded from the congregation which was to use it a high degree of readiness to make sacrifices and of moral energy, and from him who wished to manipulate it an extraordinary courage and cold-blooded determination. Moreover, Ambrose did not hesitate to make strong attacks against the heretics 'who make common cause with the imperial power' (*Exp. Luc.* VIII, 17). Auxentius appears as a bloodthirsty 'Scythian' barbarian wanting to move the church around as if it were a gipsy caravan (*Ep.* 20, 12); and that raging woman, the empress, takes the part of a tempting Eve, an Herodias or a Jezebel.

A direct assault upon the churches occupied by the people was in these circumstances impracticable for the government, so they tried another way. Shortly before Palm Sunday, the imperial tribune Dalmatius came to Ambrose and at first expressed his surprise still to find him about, for they had wanted for a long time to banish him. He then invited him in the name of the emperor to negotiations at the palace. The conflict with the anti-bishop had now to be brought to an end. Auxentius had already chosen his judges (evidently leading personalities of the court, among them even some heathens) and Ambrose had the same right. If he would, however, rather avoid such a court of arbitration, then he would be allowed to quit the field of his own accord. The carriage was ready, he could travel under safe conduct, and not a hair of his head would be touched. The government now obviously renounced half-measures and went all out. So much was clear: Ambrose could not agree to the offer of a court of arbitration at the palace without giving up as a lost cause what had been his case from the very beginning. The very alternative proposal of a voluntary retreat made this clear. But how could he now avoid the air of intransigence and open disobedience if he did not agree to a settlement which seemed such a fair compromise? Ambrose once more took up his pen and answered with one of his great political letters, addressed directly to the person of the 'most gracious Emperor and most blessed Augustus Valentinian'. First, the situation and legal order until then existing are depicted in a few concise lines. For this, Ambrose skilfully refers simply to Valentinian I. This emperor, he says, had always refused to transgress the limits of his political commission. 'In matters of faith, and in any problems of the ecclesiastical constitution, the judgement can be passed only by a person who is appointed to this on account of his office, and who is legally in the same position, i.e. bishops can be tried only by bishops' (*Ep.* 21, 2). Nobody is forcing the people to stand by Ambrose—they themselves have decided for him as their legitimate bishop, and for the cause of the faith (*Ep.* 21, 6 ff.). Ambrose, however, could not possibly appear before an alien political court of arbitration. Under the shadow of the new anti-Nicene law, this would in any case at the moment be a farce. Auxentius may act as a bishop in a city where he is considered to be one. Besides, were the emperor not so young, he himself would realize 'what kind of a bishop he could possibly be, who leaves to laymen the decision about his legitimacy as priest' (*Ep.* 21, 5). All this is said with the highest reverence and due respect for the imperial majesty. 'I have not learned', the letter ends, with a side-glance at his former activity as ambassador, 'to represent in the Privy Council anything other than your interest. I am no courtier and cannot participate in political intrigues at the court' (*Ep.* 21, 20).

As we see, the dogmatic inviolability of the church is now completed and supplemented by this further claim of the indispensable independence of her clergy, deduced from her legal structure. This is an essential product of the struggle which at first had begun as a conflict about the property of a single church building. The principle was not directed against the congregation as such, for as things stood its consent on the contrary could be presupposed without much ado. Hence, it needed for proof not a special divine law, and particularly no reference to the Old Testament. The bishop simply counts as the competent, elected, and authoritative representative of his church. If his right and independence in case of emergency were not to be respected, then the 'freedom' of the church was a deceitful word and an illusion. Seen in this light, the clerical claim against the secular power was simply necessary and consistent. Yet this implies that the imperial authority also was restricted by the right of the church. This is the second consequence of the controversy, drawn with full vigour by Ambrose. To the emperor, he says, naturally belong the palaces, but not the churches (*Ep.* 20, 19). As a Christian, he stands within the church and not above her. In the church the bishops are accustomed to rule over the emperor and not the emperor over the bishops (*Ep.* 21, 4). If therefore the emperor is designated a 'son of the church'—here Ambrose coins a new expression which will never again be lost sight of—this is no insult, but an honour (*Serm. Aux.* 36). Thus prior to all the popes, Ambrose already taught and defended a sharp, 'Western' distinction of the 'powers', and he did it with full awareness of its fundamental importance.

For him these ideas were set against a still broader background. Ambrose was not satisfied with securing the independence of the church. He claimed rather a quite general moral and legal control of all, even the imperial power. To be sure, he is told 'that everything is allowed to the emperor and everything stands at his disposal' (*Ep.* 20, 19), yet this insidious claim is false. In his own person, even the emperor is obliged to keep the law; even the emperor must never illegally bring under his power even the smallest hut. Yet the people, if necessary, must bear injustice in such instances, although they cannot approve of it (*Serm. Aux.* 33), while the rights of God remain completely unassailable, and the obedience of faith has absolute validity. Ambrose basically still thought in a republican way. As he understood and defended his own position and responsibility in the church in the spirit of the old Roman official, so he conceives of the authority of the monarchy—the mere existence of which is already to some degree a sign of political decadence (*Exam.* V, 52)—as by no means despotic or 'Byzantine'; it would otherwise become a 'tyranny'. Of course, one may say that we encounter elsewhere in the rhetorical tradition similar points of view and classical reminiscences. They are natural to Ambrose from the first, in consequence of his aristocratic Roman education and descent. But the decisive factor in the seriousness of his claim is that it is now brought forward in the name of God and backed by his commandments. Not in vain does the story of Naboth's vineyard (I Kings xxi) stand in the Bible. For the churchman God's word converts the ideal which cannot bind into a real obligation. 'God's law has taught us what we ought to do; human laws cannot teach this. They compel timid souls to change their mind by force; but to inspire faith, this they cannot do' (*Ep.* 21, 10). 'Trusting in God, I do not shrink from telling you emperors what in my opinion is right' (*Ep.* 57, 1). And behind such statements stands not merely an individual, private conviction, but the living social reality of the church.

On Maundy Thursday in the year 386, the government decided to break off the hopeless quarrel. Quietly and without bloodshed, the imperial colours were removed from the vainly besieged basilica, the punishments already decreed were annulled, and the prisoners released. There was no other way out. In the end even the soldiers to whom Ambrose had directly appealed in his speeches had left their posts and taken the part of the faithful people. This looked like the end of the exciting contest, when some weeks later on the occasion of the dedication of a newly built church the relics of two 'martyrs' were found, decapitated giants, 'such as the old days produced' (*Ep.* 22, 2). Saints 'Gervasius and Protasius' were transported triumphantly to the basilica, soon to be generally called 'Ambrosian', and here solemnly buried. There followed the expected miracles and healings. Ambrose conducted the service, and his sermon for the occasion directed the common enthusiasm into the desired direction: 'Now you all see; these are the comrades whom I choose. . . . Such men have I won for you, my holy people, as your helpers, men who are profitable to all, and harmful to none! . . . Lord Jesus, thanks to thee, that thou hast raised up again at such a time the strong spirit of the holy martyrs; for more than ever thy church needs thy protection today' (*Ep.* 22, 10). The tense situation was not to last much longer. A civil war between the Western rulers, which Ambrose tried in vain to prevent, drove Valentinian II to flight. After the overthrow of the usurper, the victor Theodosius took over the control of the whole empire practically alone. In strained co-operation with him, the life-work of Ambrose came to an end during the years that followed.

Theodosius 'the Great' was not only an excellent general, but also as sovereign an independent and by no means insignificant personality. He was the first emperor to adopt for himself the ideal of a dogmatically fixed state-church, which he had realized already in the East. This policy was at the same time in conformity with his personal, strongly Catholic piety. Yet the changing necessities of the day forced him also to proceed flexibly, and where necessary to show consideration for opposing groups. Personally, Ambrose had a proper understanding of such difficulties. Despite this, however, it was inevitable that the political interests of the emperor and the ecclesiastical interests represented by Ambrose should occasionally come into tension one with the other, and then their good relations were disturbed. Ambrose, like all his contemporaries, did not recognize any separation between the political responsibility and the personal religious duties of the ruler, and he considered the protection and advancement of the church in all circumstances an obligation of faith. In the years 388–391 Theodosius resided principally in Milan. It is fascinating to follow in detail the ebb and flow of the relationship between the two men during these years. We restrict ourselves, however, to the best known and most important incidents.

Theodosius also, as the new lord of Rome, was soon confronted with the question whether he should again grant to the city the cancelled religious revenues, for the senate had again forwarded the old petition. 'I did not hesitate', said Ambrose, 'to put my point of view publicly and immediately before the most gracious Emperor' (*Ep.* 57, 4). On account of its long history, the matter had grown into a question of ecclesiastical prestige, in which compliance had become impossible. Ambrose gave the emperor to understand that if necessary he was resolved to go to the utmost lengths, and he ostentatiously stayed away from the palace for some days until the problem was settled in his way. Even more dramatic was the course taken by another conflict. In the Far East of the empire, the bishop of Callinicum had instigated a tumult, and had allowed gangs of

monks to set on fire the synagogue of that place. In great anger
Theodosius vowed duly to punish this breach of public peace,
and decreed rebuilding at the cost of the guilty persons. Yet
again Ambrose raised a protest. It was, he declared, virtually
blasphemous to permit such a triumph to the God-forsaken
Jews. 'Which is more important, the idea of law and order or
the cause of religion?' The penal law must take second place to
the commandment of faith (*Ep.* 40, 11; *LCC*, V, 233). When
Theodosius still hesitated, he was addressed by Ambrose during
the worship before the assembled congregation. The bishop refused to offer mass until the emperor had expressly promised
the revocation of his order. Thoroughly angry, Theodosius
arranged henceforth to leave Ambrose uninformed about
transactions in the Privy Council (*Ep.* 51, 2).

Yet Ambrose did not always appear in such a questionable
role. There were also cases where he exercised his ministry less
as a church politician than as a real pastor, and called the emperor to order as a 'son of the church'. The famous 'penance of
Theodosius' belongs in this connection. In order to avenge a
bloody riot in the Macedonian city of Thessalonica, Theodosius
had had several thousand unsuspecting inhabitants enticed into
the theatre, and one and all massacred by the soldiers (390).
Even in a period accustomed to barbaric punishments, this
butchery provoked general horror. Too late Theodosius himself had regretted his order, and vainly tried to revoke it. Now,
the act was done. Theodosius belonged to Ambrose's congregation—what should his attitude be to this matter? Ambrose
was well known for observing very strictly the obligation to
require penitence after a crime. Was a horrible mass murder
pardonable, because it was committed in the exercise of imperial power? Penance was at that time invariably a public act,
and was, in case of murder, usually life-long, or at least a matter
of years. At first Ambrose let some days go by, during which
he left Milan and assured himself of the consent of his colleagues
in the area. He then wrote a letter to Theodosius, with his own
hand, as he emphasizes, in order that no third person would

have to read it. As always, this piece of writing is composed
with thorough consideration, carefully aimed at the person
addressed, and it is, if you like, a 'political' document. Yet
dominating everything is the intention to exhibit the religious
meaning of the penitential order as such, and to make the in-
escapability of the divine commandment theologically plain.
With deep earnestness the rigour of the 'law' and the consolation of the 'gospel' are brought into their correct relationship.
God is merciful and does not give up even the sinner; but He
forgives his sins only when he really regrets them, and is willing
to bear the consequences. 'Sin is taken from us in no other way
than by tears and repentance' (*Ep.* 51, 11). Nothing can be
changed in this divine order. It is not a matter of what Ambrose
wants, or does not want. 'I would of course like to enjoy the
imperial favour, and to act according to your wishes; but the
matter does not permit it' (*Ep.* 51, 15). 'If the priest does not
tell the truth to him who is going astray, he will die in his sin,
and the priest will be guilty of his punishment, because he did
not admonish him who erred' (Ezek. iii. 18) (*Ep.* 51, 3). There
is no question of destroying the imperial reputation. The emperor also is a man, and may fall into temptation. He must now
do nothing else but what had been done long before by king
David, or by the pious and mighty Job. If he does this, he then
rises to the same level as the great saints of old, just as Ambrose
stands with the old prophets (*Ep.* 51, 16). 'He who accuses himself when he has sinned is just, not he who seeks to praise himself.' If the emperor is a Christian, he will not make the vain
attempt to excuse his sin (*Ep.* 51, 15). He must decide himself
what profits him. However, if he refuses, Ambrose will here-
after never be able to offer for him a sacrifice in the church. 'If
you believe, follow me! I say, If you believe, acknowledge thus
what I say! If you do not believe, pardon me for what I do—I
must give the honour to God!' (*Ep.* 51, 17).

The words Ambrose used were perfectly clear. He was
threatening the emperor with excommunication, but he did it
in a way which did not violate the obedience of the subject, and

which made it as easy as possible for the emperor to take the bitter step. Theodosius found himself in a desperate situation and capitulated. But it seems that he did not act solely under compulsion, but that he also gave inward assent to the penance and willingly took it upon himself in true contrition. It is certain that at least once he appeared without the imperial regalia as a penitent in the church, and there, as custom required, confessed his sin in front of the assembled congregation. One can see in this a first 'Canossa'; yet contemporaries saw in this event something other than the later medieval legend, which distorted the outward events to suit its purpose. They saw no bending of the secular power, nor triumph of the sacerdotal government, but a spiritual incident and a decision of conscience on the part of the emperor, who honoured himself by acknowledging the inviolability of God's commandments. Seen thus, the ecclesiastical penance of Theodosius is the final stage in the process of the Christianization of the imperial power, which had begun with Constantine the Great. Now the church had ceased to be merely the instrument or beneficiary of the governing power. She had also taken possession of it inwardly, and now tolerated public disrespect of her ethical principles as little as denial of her dogmatic commands.

This ecclesiastical penance had also brought Theodosius and Ambrose together again personally. When the emperor again moved to the East in 391, he left Ambrose behind in Italy as his most trusted supporter. Ambrose did not disappoint him. Soon afterwards, there arose in Gaul a usurper, not acknowledged by Theodosius. He sought immediately to establish contact with Ambrose and to win him over to himself. It is amusing to observe how calmly and inconspicuously Ambrose was able to evade all attempts at approach, and only came forward with an open rejection when he was able to support it ecclesiastically. Later on he withdrew to Florence to elude a personal encounter with the usurper, who had marched against Theodosius, and for a full year he did not see his Milan congregation again. A happier man, he hastened to meet Theodosius after his victory, and by his supplication procured clemency for the defeated. The emperor, moreover, declared publicly that he had been saved 'by the merits and prayers' of this bishop (*Vita*, 31). When he died soon afterwards, Ambrose delivered the funeral oration. Here he once more celebrated the dead ruler as the model of a truly great and pious prince, and did not miss the opportunity on this occasion to bind the soldiers' loyalty to his sons. A few weeks later an edict was issued, in which the new regents gave the explicit assurance that they were determined to take away from the church none of her rights, but for the future rather to augment their respect to her to the best of their ability.

Ambrose could thus finally feel himself at the goal toward which as a church politician he had striven during the whole course of his life. From now on we find him indefatigably active as preacher and teacher, as a theological writer and as the conscientious counsellor of all who turned to him, often from afar. His secretary Paulinus, who later, urged by Augustine, wrote his biography, assures us that five bishops would not have been enough to conduct the baptismal instruction given in his lifetime by Ambrose alone. On the return home from the consecration of a bishop abroad, he contracted a fatal disease. He was asked to pray for his recovery, but Ambrose refused: 'I have not lived among you in such a way, that I would have to be ashamed to live longer; but I am also not afraid of death, for we have a good Lord' (*Vita*, 45). In a barely audible voice he made his last arrangements. The 'good old man' Simplician, who had instructed him prior to his baptism, should also become his successor. Ambrose spent his last hours in silent prayer with his arms extended to form a cross. Immediately after he had received the Lord's Body for the last time, he passed away on the 4th of April, 397. He was buried in the Ambrosian basilica. The powerful Stilicho is supposed to have said at the time that the death of this great man would start the decline of Italy. Ambrose was spared from experiencing the collapse of the empire which from an early age had been his world, and which as a bishop he had served in his own way. Only the church of the empire, as he had designed and built it, was still to remain even in a changed world.

Anyone who wishes to understand and judge Ambrose must not overlook the basic practical and political bent of his nature. Ambrose knew himself to be called by God to look after the rights and interests of his church, and this obligation he fulfilled as a matter of course, just as any statesman or official would do for the state. So far there was no problem for him at all. All the same, it would be utterly wrong to consider Ambrose a politician who was, as sometimes happens, accidentally driven from state to church politics. The goals Ambrose truly wanted to serve, and which inwardly determined him, did not lie in the realm of this world. They were given to him morally and spiritually. Whenever he extols the glory of the church—and this happens quite frequently—Ambrose is not thinking of her visible structure and constitution, but is thinking rather of her mysterious spiritual nature. The church is the bride of Christ, the holy city of God. She is the store-house of the peoples and lives at the same time in every individual pious soul. Her organization is never compared to the state. The people of the church are not a nation in the sense of Egyptians, Jews, and Arabs. Her nature is best seen in her worship. The Milanese church gained under Ambrose an ever richer liturgical life. In his sermons and writings he delighted to explain the meaning of the different customs. Ambrose was a productive theologian of the sacraments and sacramentals, the first definite upholder of a mysterious teaching regarding transubstantiation in the Holy Communion, which, however, he never developed before profane ears.

Yet, the church does not exist merely for the sake of the 'mysteries'. She should above all proclaim 'faith' and teach the people to know God's holy will. God has redeemed us in Christ and forgives us our sins. He demands that we now likewise forgive, and as Christians conduct a life of rigid discipline and sanctification. The church and the Christian have also a social task. They must help all the world's oppressed to obtain their rights, and seek to relieve the distress of the poor to the best of their ability. The rich are continually admonished to charity, and Ambrose himself sets a good example. In the troubled times of the Gothic invasion he unhesitantly had the precious church vessels melted down, and is not concerned about bitter criticism (*de Off.* II, 28, 136). The poor are the real treasure of the church; it is unnecessary that she be also rich herself. According to Jesus' words the first task of the Christian is the support of one's own parents; the next in order are the poor. Only then, after that, in the third place, the priest also might receive his share. Mercy is demanded, and not sacrifice (*Exp. Luc.* VIII, 79).

As to the canon law, Ambrose is an episcopalist, like all the ancient Latin fathers; i.e. the bishop elected by the people is the supreme pastor of his congregation. As such he co-operates well with the bishops of his own area, and acknowledges the common decisions at synods without question; but in principle he has no metropolitan or patriarch as lord above him. Even Ambrose, as bishop of the first city in Upper Italy, exercised only moral authority over other bishops. He conferred with the Pope on completely equal terms. The Roman church is certainly the focal centre of ecclesiastical unity and communion for the whole world, but this does not imply a legal primacy. 'I wish', says Ambrose with reference to the ceremony of foot-washing, usual in Milan, 'to follow the Roman church on every point. Yet, we too have our sound common sense, and what other places have done well to retain, we too do well to maintain' (*de Sacr.* III, 1, 5). In the last analysis, Peter only made the first confession to Christ (Matt. xvi. 16), and on the strength of that did not claim any supremacy: 'He exercised the primacy of faith and not a primacy of legal order' (*de Incarn.* 4, 32).

The classical document of Ambrose's conception of the ministry is his work *On the Duties of the Church's Servants*, or simply *On Duties*. It grew out of addresses to his spiritual 'sons', the clergy of Milan, and is most closely linked in construction and train of thought to the work of Cicero with the same name, from which he copies extracts almost verbally for pages at a time. As Cicero's philosophical ethics were designed for the Roman citizen and statesman, so also the first Christian 'ethics', represented by this book, is intended to serve in a similar way as vocational ethics, instruction in virtue, and as a handbook to the clerical office. A churchman also must do in all respects what is decorous, useful, and just, and show a dignified, serious appearance. The man of God must not have a 'popular' demeanour; 'for how can he maintain respect from the people, if he possesses nothing that distinguishes him from the crowd' (*Ep.* 28, 2)? The ancient historical examples are so far as possible replaced by Christian and Biblical ones, especially from the Old Testament. But it still remains astonishing how naïvely the book is now presented as 'Christian' in distinction from its philosophical model. Ambrose was so deeply involved in the classical tradition that he did not yet realize his own relationship to it. In spite of this, we can sense in the slight variations and additions here and there the rising of a new spirit, which changes the heritage from within. The Highest Good is no longer considered as virtue, but as eternal blessedness, which lies in the future, and in communion with God. Its promises stand at the beginning of the teaching on duty, as the Beatitudes introduce the commandments of the Sermon on the Mount. The soul, which is the seat of the man's real life, is more and more distinguished from the body, and from the world of visible things. A special excursus, going beyond Cicero, is concerned with the value of silence. Ambrose was, so far as we know, the first figure in antiquity no longer to read books aloud but only silently and in meditation. To be sure, he had a weak voice which he protected by this practice; yet beneath this new exercise which he inaugurated is hidden a deeper change of literary apprehension and general intellectual enjoyment.

These 'unclassical' changes of consciousness and intellectual style, which point to the Middle Ages, must not be explained at once as 'Christian'. They are a general symptom of the time, and with Ambrose most likely due to Neo-Platonic influences.

But religious thinking is not satisfied with a general 'spiritualization' of life and the world. The force of a longing for personal salvation transcends the philosophical level of consciousness, and seizes upon the historic Biblical statements on Christ
as the actual living reality which redeems and saves man. It is
precisely the traditional questioning of the old Latin theology,
psychological and anthropological, which here rises above its
hard moralism and legalism. Ambrose catches something of
what is really meant by the freedom of the spirit, faith, grace
and the dwelling of Christ in the faithful. Christ's coming into
the world remains useless if He does not also come into the
heart, 'and live in me, and speak in me' (*Exp. Luc.* X, 7). Christ
must dwell in the human senses if not only sin is to disappear
from them, but also the desire to sin (*Exp. Ps.* cxviii, IV, 26).
God makes the will receptive and ready for the good (*Exp. Luc.*
I, 10). Therefore 'I will not glory that I am righteous, but I will
glory that I am saved. I will not glory that I am free from sins,
but that my sins are forgiven.' Christ who died for me has also
become my intercessor. 'Guilt has brought more blessing than
innocence; innocence had made me proud; but guilt has subjected me anew' (*Jac.* vi. 21). One only needs to compare such
words with any of the statements of Cyprian to feel immediately what spiritual discoveries have been made since his time,
and what new, mighty developments have been put into
motion. Ambrose has really read Paul, and we already stand
quite near to Augustine. Certainly we have here only isolated
utterances. The new view does not present a theological programme in Ambrose; it announces itself only involuntarily, and
allows all the traditional conceptions to coexist with it. Yet by
this very means we perceive that it is a matter of genuine experience, whose power dwells within the soul to touch and
change the real religious life.

Even today we come closest to Ambrose through his hymns.
Although their original melody can hardly be reconstructed,
these verses still speak distinctly of the nature and piety of this
man. For Ambrose was a poet. He was certainly not a poet in

the modern more subjective meaning of the word. Nor did he write poetry in the sense of the formal art of his time. Yet he was a genuine poet of almost classical originality in the way he harmonizes task and accomplishment, the form and content of his message. The hymns are the songs of the congregation. Here for the first time the spiritual feeling of the old Latin church achieved an adequate expression, great and strong. From now on 'Ambrosian' meant a whole new kind of poetical style which inaugurated the ecclesiastical hymnology of the Middle Ages. The first hymns are supposed to have originated in the days of oppression during the church struggle of 386, when the task was to gather the people in the besieged churches, and strengthen them spiritually by these 'magic melodies'. The model of this innovation was most likely the congregational singing of the Syrian Greek church, which had already existed for a long time. Ambrose, however, succeeded in what Hilary, himself a man of a remarkable poetic talent, had attempted in vain before him. He rendered into the ethos and spirit of the Latin ecclesiastical language both the genuine and simple thought of the people, and the completely different genius of the East. As to form, the hymns consist of faultless classical verses ('acatalectic iambic dimeters'), now arranged in stanzas of four lines, but they avoid any complication, and thus the natural stress of the word regularly coincides with the accent of the verse. Like the pillars of a sunny, spacious basilica, the plain stanzas join in a steady rhythm, and express what the Catholic congregation believed and felt. Acknowledgement of the Triune God is combined with different Biblical themes, and harmonized with the experience of the time of day and its changing light. A wonderful simplicity and strength lives in these hymns. No less a man than Augustine has described to us how these plain verses alone were able after his baptism to infuse a new, sweet happiness into his uneasy heart (*Conf.* IX, 6), and after the death of his mother the frantic pain found release in liberating tears with the harmonies of the Ambrosian evening hymn:

Maker of all things, God most high,
Great ruler of the starry sky,
Who, robing day with beauteous light,
Hast clothed in soft repose the night.

That sleep may wearied limbs restore,
And fit for toil and use once more,
May gently soothe the careworn breast,
And lull our anxious griefs to rest.

We thank Thee for the day that's gone;
We pray Thee now the night come on;
O help us sinners as we raise
To Thee our votive hymn of praise.

To Thee our hearts their music bring;
Thee our united praises sing;
To Thee our rapt affections soar,
And Thee our chastened souls adore.

So when the parting beams of day
In evening's shadows fade away,
Let faith no wildering darkness know,
But night with faith effulgent glow.

O sleepless ever keep the mind,
But guilt in lasting slumber bind!
Let faith our purity renew
And temper sleep's lethargic dew.

From every carnal passion free
O may our hearts repose in Thee!
Nor envious fiend, with harmful snare,
Our rest with sinful terrors share.

Christ with the Father ever one,
Spirit! the Father and the Son,
God over all, the mighty sway,
Shield us, great Trinity, we pray.
                    (tr. John David Chambers, 1854)

Incidentally, Ambrose is the only church father of whom we still possess a portrait today. It is extremely expressive, by no means idealized, and can claim with good reason to be regarded as 'authentic'. It is a mosaic with his name in the chapel of the Ambrosian basilica dedicated to his brother Satyrus, and was made at the beginning of the fifth century, and therefore only a few years after the death of its subject. Before us stands a lean, slender figure in a long tunic, and the simple but elegant cloak of a man of distinction (there was as yet no special 'clerical' dress). The face, slightly tilted, long, and not entirely symmetrical (an examination of the relics has confirmed the slight dislocation of the left eye) is framed by short-cut hair, while above the puffy lips and the almost invisible chin a small moustache is visible. The characteristically distant and almost melancholy expression of his face is fully apparent in the wide open eyes. They seem to look penetratingly upon the assembled congregation, yet the deeply earnest, calm gaze looks right through it and beyond it into infinity. Naturally we cannot now make out how much of the inner life of this picture really goes back to genuine, historical recollection, and how much is perhaps based on a later artistic interpretation. But at any rate this picture portrays Ambrose more nearly as he really was than do the countless sensational pictures from later times, which glorify the proud Milanese prince of the church or the learned bishop.

drawn to
this
book
5/23/2003

a quote
good
5/24/2003

CHAPTER V

JEROME

EVERYONE knows Dürer's engraving 'Jerome in His Study': a comfortable, well-furnished scholar's chamber in which a silent old man, completely absorbed, writes in a book by the light of his halo, undisturbed by the panting of the little dog and the purring of his lion, with the warm sun shining through the roundel windows on to his fur. The whole is a symbol of inner and outer peace, of perfect harmony between scholarly work and true spiritual composure. This is not a picture of the historical Jerome. He was indeed a scholar and a theologian, but the wildly, agitated, baroque portrayals of the 'penitent' old man in front of the rock-cave give in this case a far better idea of the real temper of the man, although the external setting here is also not quite typical for him. Only for a short time during his youth did Jerome make the attempt to live as a hermit, and he did not persevere with it. Despite his ascetic zeal and his scholarly interests, he was never really able to turn his back upon the world around him. Passionate and craving for recognition, he sought its appreciation, applause, and response, even when he thought he despised it, and poured upon it his reproaches. Jerome was always occupied with himself; he knew no inner peace, and made enemies for himself everywhere, whom he then pursued with fervent indignation and personal hatred. Alongside his brilliant qualities, the weaknesses of his character were always manifest. This was already seen by his contemporaries, and to this day his biographers have not found it easy to narrate his life without polemic or apologetic prejudice. If we want to understand the interest and historical importance of this man and his influence we must suspend moral and theological judgement.

129

Jerome was a child of his country and of his time. In the second half of the fourth century a new intellectual life began to stir in all northern Italy. It was not only on account of the influence of Ambrose that, in areas where Christianity had until then been without any intellectual significance, and had probably been quite weak outwardly as well, preachers, theologians, and writers now everywhere took up their pens. We can sense the altered situation after the conversion of Constantine, the new ecclesiastical and cultural possibilities within a Christian order now favoured by the state. Jerome was born around 347 in the otherwise unknown little town of Strido(n), in the remote corner of Italy which bordered Dalmatia, or, on another view, still further to the south-east, in Dalmatia itself. The population of this place hardly recognized any intellectual, let alone spiritual, interests. As Jerome puts it himself, 'their gods is their belly'; anyone who was rich was also counted as pious, and the bishop was the lid you would expect on this pot (*Ep.* 7, 5). Jerome's parents belonged to this world, and, according to all appearance, were in no way exceptional. They were well-to-do, good Catholic people, but did not provide for their son any serious stimulus. After he had learned reading, writing, and arithmetic, they decided to send him to Rome to acquire higher education there, and make a career in one or other of the secular occupations. Jerome was apparently in full agreement with this. Together with a school companion from home, he received the usual education in Rome. Even as a grown man his student days came to him in nightmares, and he had to stand in his toga before his teacher, and as part of his rhetorical exercises make a speech. He heard the great grammarian Donatus, but also listened as a student to the lawyers in the public courts, and light-heartedly participated in students' jests and amusements. Even at that time he began to lay the foundations of his dearly-prized library of classical Latin authors. Jerome was, we may suppose, from an early age a diligent, untiring reader. He possessed an astonishing memory and even in old age could quote without effort from Virgil, Horace, and

many other poets. He also read Quintilian, Seneca, and various
writers of history; but for him, as for Lactantius, the real teacher
and model of good style was the incomparable Cicero.

Jerome occasionally lamented in his later years the way in
which he frequently slid on the slippery paths of vain and sinful
youth. This does not surprise us from an ascetic convert! Jerome
was open-minded, eager to get the most out of life, and receptive. That he was well acquainted with the temptations of the
sensual side of life, his later writings sufficiently indicate. Yet
there is no real reason to take his retrospective and quite general
statements too seriously. At the same time, the ecclesiastical life
of Rome had also impressed him vividly. The rich congregation no longer occupied a position of obscurity; imposing
church buildings and palaces testified to the beginnings of a
Christian Rome. Jerome participated with pleasure in the magnificent, well-attended services, and also visited the catacombs
outside the city gates, rich in memories and at that time not
well cared for. As it seems, all the friends with whom he associated, Pammachius, Rufinus, and others, appear later to have
turned to a markedly Christian, ascetic life. At the end of his
studies, when he was approximately 19 years of age, Jerome
decided to receive baptism together with his school friend
Bonosus, whom we have already mentioned. This was, as we
have seen in the case of Ambrose, not then usual for a young
man with ambitions in public life. In 367 the twenty-year-old
student set off on a long trip to Gaul. He presumably meant to
apply for a well-paid position in Trèves, the imperial capital.
However, he was now interested in ecclesiastical and theological as well as classical literature. In Trèves he experienced his first
conversion. Jerome renounced a secular career and decided instead to dedicate himself completely to pious meditation and to
spiritual work. He also induced the faithful Bonosus to consecrate himself in the same way to the service of Christ. It would
be a mistake, however, to see in such a decision the monastic
ideal in the later meaning of the word; an inner crisis must not
be presumed. Jerome was committing himself as a Christian to

a new form of life, intellectual, and to a certain extent also spiritual. This meant, however, neither 'poverty' nor strict subordination and 'obedience'. It would just provide him rather with quiet, and with personal independence for his studies and intellectual hobbies, in addition to the enjoyment of friendship, and exchange of common interests. At any rate, that is how it appears in the light of the way in which it worked out. It is a typical change of career, frequently to be observed in other cases in these decades. For an intellectually active man political life had become uninteresting. The normal activity in schools and academies likewise appeared as formal and empty, showing no sign of any stirring and vital new ideals. It was different in the realm of the church and her religion. Having suddenly attained recognition and influence, she needed everywhere men who would take up the new tasks imposed on her, preserve her inner resources, and carry on and fill with new life the spiritual traditions she possessed. Some, like Ambrose, must pass directly into the service of ecclesiastical government and administration. To others new 'inner' tasks and possibilities revealed themselves, which had only to be grasped in order to lead to a higher life of freedom, meaningful before God and men. The injuries, upsets, and contempt which earlier menaced the Christians had now gone forever. The Christian writer, saint, and scholar, needed to be neither lonely nor unproductive, and could count on general recognition and admiration if he now proudly claimed that henceforward he served Christ alone, and wished to take his truth seriously. In doing this he even became a helper and example to the church and the world.

After a stay, probably only short, in his home-town, Jerome found in Aquileia the surroundings and society he sought. Here in the house of the priest Chromatius he again met his old friend Rufinus, and a large number of clergy interested in asceticism, with whom he was soon at one in lively spiritual friendship. Years later he casually erected a memorial for his friends in his chronicle, by making a note under the year 373, that the clergy of Aquileia resembled a choir of angels. He also established relations with the neighbouring town of Concordia, and with a community of devout ascetic women in Laibach. Unfortunately, we do not know anything in detail of these years; but we may suppose that in those days all the elements had already come together which we find again in Jerome's later life: the common cultivation of ascetic and theological interests, the human exchange with like-minded friends and the pious admiration of spiritually inclined women—all perhaps still somewhat more primitive, provincial, and youthfully immature than later. And this phase of his life ended for Jerome, as so often in the time that followed, not peacefully, but with personal disputes and quarrels. We do not know whence the 'sudden whirlwind' came, which tore apart almost the whole circle of friends; it may be that self-conscious ascetic zeal had upset the people of a church not yet used to it, and perhaps also the higher clerics. Jerome was not the only one to be affected; but he felt himself even more disgracefully defamed than others. Even in Laibach the devout would have nothing to do with him, and the good relationship with his parents and relatives, who were probably not impressed by their offspring's change of career, was now completely destroyed. The fact that Jerome succeeded in arousing in his younger sister an enthusiasm for asceticism, and bringing her under the influence of a deacon who was a friend of his, may have been a contributory factor. We still possess a letter crammed with quotations from the Bible, with which he tried to reconcile an angry aunt—evidently in vain. After this Jerome never mentioned his parents, and he never saw them again.

The young ascetic genius, for whom his native soil had become too hot, now decided to travel to the East (373-374). Jerusalem and the Holy Land were already by then the goal of countless pilgrimages, and anyone who wanted to distinguish himself in practical holiness could find in the deserts of Syria or Egypt patterns of the monastic life, which was known in the West only from hearsay. Moreover, the Greek Orient was still the land of education and higher theological learning. Jerome

thought of himself as a pilgrim and future hermit, but there can
be no doubt that the intellectual treasures and stimulus which
he could expect there also attracted him. Having arrived in
Antioch on the Orontes, he did not think of proceeding at once
into the desert. He felt himself ill and overworked—a complaint which appears time and again in his letters both now and
later. His 'poor body', which in reality was to remain unusually
tough throughout his long life, feels itself to be suffering 'even
when it is in health' (Ep. 3, 1). Jerome already believed that
he was near death (Ep. 6, 2). He met with a hospitable reception in the city, and on the estate of his friend Evagrius, and
soon revelled in all the excitements offered him by the intellectual life of the metropolis. Jerome now tried hard to learn
Greek thoroughly; he went to lectures, and plunged into all
available theological literature. His studies of the Aristotelian
dialectic also probably belong to this period. It was not long
before his own first literary attempts appeared. At the request
of his friend Innocent who was at his side, he described a striking criminal case of the recent past: a young wife, falsely
accused of adultery and sentenced to death, was wonderfully
preserved alive, and finally saved by Evagrius' intercession. The
little narrative, arranged like an account of martyrdom, concludes with an encomium of his host at Antioch. It is no masterpiece—in spite of, or rather because of, the rhetorical splendour
and bombast which Jerome bestowed upon it. Much the same
seems to be true of an exposition of the prophet Obadiah, which
has not been preserved. After twenty years Jerome recounts,
when commenting on the same text, how embarrassing it was
to him afterwards when immature readers tried to praise to its
author's face the supposed profundity of this elaborate piece of
work. He saw in this little writing a youthful folly which he
simply could not acknowledge any longer.

The earliest letter preserved gives direct, and still more indirect, information about the state of mind in which he found
himself at that time. It is addressed to the head of a community
of hermits with whom he had stayed during his travels, pre-

sumably a letter of thanks after safe arrival, which takes the form, however, rather of a letter of confession and a cry for saving intercession. The pathos with which Jerome contrasts his woeful state in the wicked world with the happy solitude of the holy recipient produces a thoroughly artificial effect. Jerome 'does not want to retreat and cannot advance'. There has obviously been a discussion about his ascetic plans during his visit, and he therefore 'incessantly' assures his correspondent that now as ever his heart possesses the burning desire to pursue the prescribed way. Yet he still lacks the strength to decide, and only the intercession of the hermit can ensure that perhaps one day his aspiration will be followed by fulfilment (*Ep.* 2). The young rhetorician wanted to be a Christian saint, and the decision once made was not abandoned; yet he had still not found the way by which he was able to find a place for his ambitious dreams and his literary inclinations and abilities within the framework of a monastic way of life. He hesitated, and he suffered from his own hesitance, while at the same time he let the bright, rich life, the friends, and the unexpected possibilities of work and study in Antioch have their effect upon him.

Meanwhile the conflict lay not only in externals: Jerome felt it also in the intellectual field of his actual work and interests. His heart still clung to his old loves, and was by no means inclined to tie itself exclusively to the Holy Scripture and theological research to which his life was now to be solely dedicated. The uneasiness torturing him is reflected in the famous dream which probably took place at about this time. To be sure, it was only recorded ten years later. The account is found in a letter of ascetic instruction, and it is obvious that Jerome had written it up in a stylized form to fit the purpose of this tract. The miraculous conclusion, also, is to be evaluated in this way, and not, of course, to be taken seriously in a literal sense, although that is what Jerome intended. All the same, there is no conclusive reason to deny the reality of the dream altogether. Jerome writes (*Ep.* 22, 30): 'Many years ago I renounced home, parents, my sister and my relatives and, what is much more difficult, the familiar good kitchen too' (this, coming right at the start, is a surprising confession, yet characteristic of Jerome!); 'for I had made myself a eunuch for the sake of the kingdom of heaven (Matt. xix. 12), and I wanted to move to Jerusalem to perform the military service of the spirit. Yet I could not part from my library, which I had brought together in Rome with so much labour and diligence. So miserable was I: I fasted —to read Cicero afterwards! I lay awake many nights, I wept with all my heart thinking about my former sins—and then I took Plautus in my hands. I then repented and began to read a prophet; but I found the uncultured language detestable and, because I could not see the light with my blind eyes, I thought the sun was to blame and not my eyes. As the old serpent thus played his tricks on me, a consuming and ceaseless fever came over my exhausted body during the fast, which so wasted my unfortunate limbs, that I finally—it sounds almost incredible— really consisted only of bones. They were already making arrangements for my burial; my body was quite cold, and only in my frozen breast was there fluttering a little spark of the natural warmth of life. I was then all of a sudden seized and in the spirit dragged before a tribunal. An awful light shone upon me, and from those standing around it there went out a flashing brightness—I threw myself to the ground, and did not dare look up. Then I was asked about my calling and answered, I am a Christian. You are lying! said the One on the throne. You are a Ciceronian, and not a Christian! (*Ciceronianus es, non Christianus*): Where your treasure is, there is your heart also (Matt. vi. 21).' Jerome described furthermore how under the terrible blows raining upon him, he kept begging for grace. The bystanders also interceded in his favour, that a lenient view be taken of the lapses of his youth, and opportunity be given him for improvement. He vowed never again to wish to possess secular books: if he read them once more, this might be considered denial. So he was released, and returned to life, to the surprise of everyone. These were, Jerome assures us, no mere dreams. When he awakened he still felt the blows, and his shoulders had blue marks. From this time on, he turned to the divine writings with a zeal which he had never known yet for the 'mortal' authors.

Cicero—in this name Jerome included the whole 'classical' cultural heritage. He did not, like Lactantius, think of Cicero primarily as a philosopher. Jerome never had any interest in philosophy itself, and he did not find it hard simply to thrust aside its representatives as ignoramuses and babblers. Jerome thought of Cicero the orator, the master of cultivated language and of a noble style, Cicero the teacher of general education and culture, Cicero who belongs in the succession of Plautus, Virgil, Horace, Seneca, and the historians. The school education of late antiquity, of which Jerome is thinking, had a strong bias to the study of language. It was the advantages of its formal expression which—besides his lively need for conversation—above all made him enthusiastic for the ancients. There is no need to think of deeper, human, and aesthetic values: despite all the sensitivity and versatility of his temper, Jerome had basically a prosaic or, at any rate, a totally unpoetic nature. That is why the external advantages of a perfected cultural language played such a paramount role, while in contrast the Bible appeared to him raw, tasteless, and almost unbearable. But Jerome knew now that with this attitude he was on the wrong path, and he was determined to change direction. From now on his literary work and his whole will concentrated exclusively upon the Bible, exposition of the Bible, and theological studies pertaining to it.

Is this claim correct? Later, when their friendship had broken up and had turned into bitter hostility, no other than his intimate friend Rufinus openly raised the accusation that Jerome had in reality been disloyal to his vow made in the dream, and had constantly broken the oath not to read the profane authors. He collected the evidence: he referred not only to the innumerable quotations, but also to copies of such proscribed books, which Jerome as an enthusiastic collector of books had again and again ordered and paid for at great expense. The petty and insincere manner in which Jerome defended himself against these reproaches did not improve his position. In the long run the 'vow' was obviously not kept in a literal sense. Nevertheless Rufinus did Jerome an injustice; for in intention and conscious purpose Jerome never returned to profane studies in the old sense. He used the pagan authors henceforward only as a help to Biblical exegesis. He no longer read them for their own sake, for mere pleasure. Even pagan historians he quoted 'not from caprice, but only because of cogent necessity'—namely in order to demonstrate that the Biblical prophecies are true and have really been fulfilled (*Comm. Dan.* prol.). That did not mean, of course, that Jerome hid his rich knowledge under the bushel, or meant to renounce the rhetorical elegance of his style. On the contrary, he was just as fond as ever of showing it off: occasional phrases assuring the contrary are simply part of a rhetorical convention, and are not to be taken seriously. It was his secret ambition to vie with his pagan models, and wherever possible to outdo them, but this was done now only in the interest of God, and of higher, holy culture. According to the precepts of the Bible (Deut. xxi. 11), the hair and nails of the unclean slave girl are to be cut first, and her whole body must be washed and cleansed from idolatry and sensuality before she can find admission to Israel (*Ep.* 70, 2); i.e. the good things of pagan culture are not accepted directly, but are assimilated into a new context. 'What has Horace to do with the psalter, Maro with the gospels, or Cicero with the Apostle? . . . Certainly "to the pure everything is pure!" (Tit. i. 15), and nothing is objectionable that is enjoyed with thanksgiving (I Tim. iv. 4). Nevertheless, we shall not "at the same time drink the chalice of Christ and the cup of the demons" (I Cor. x. 21)' (*Ep.* 22, 29). Jerome preferred to depict the situation as though Christian culture was already perfect in itself, and had no need at all of such borrowing. 'Our Simonides, Pindar, and Alcaios, or Flaccus, Catullus, and Serenus' is king David (*Ep.* 53, 8). A man like Theophilus, Bishop of Alexandria, unites in himself the talents of a Plato and a Demosthenes (*Ep.* 99, 2). Our Athens, that is to say, the university of Christian learning, is Jerusalem (*Ep.* 46, 9).

The brief outline of the history of literature written by Jerome after the model of Suetonius, on _The Illustrious Men,_ i.e. the writers of the church, serves the sole purpose of setting forth the rank and significance of the intellectual giants of Christianity, so that the pagan libel-mongers may be put to shame, and instead of asserting the philistinism of the Christians may realize their own ignorance (_Vir. Ill._, prol.). Yet, of course, Jerome is quite aware that this proud attitude is premature, that Christians cannot possibly dispense with pagan education, and so, in defence of his borrowing, he refers again to the men of the Bible who from Moses to Paul were supposed to have acted in this same way (_Ep._ 70, 2). This is precisely his task, and that of all Christians with the same intention, to make up at last for the church's backwardness, and to justify the public glory she has attained, by corresponding intellectual achievements.

Tertullian and Clement of Alexandria had previously been concerned with the problem of ancient culture, namely, whether or no the indispensable pagan education was allowable to Christians. It was no accident that the problem now in the fourth century assumed an increased importance. Jerome is unique only in the intensity with which he experienced this conflict as his personal fate. His dream was hence of deep symbolical importance. The solution he found was comparatively external and unrefined just because he only saw the advantages of the ancient culture quite externally, in the richness of its knowledge, and above all in the beauty of its language. His decision to forgo its enjoyment was forced; it was typically ascetic and led to a purely external and thematic limitation of his work and reading, measured according to the Christian or pagan content. Not without pain, yet with a bitterness all the stronger, and almost scornful, the converted Christian repudiated the pagan authors, just because he still loved them, and could never really dispense with them. On every possible occasion, and often enough more passionately than truthfully, he assured others that he had studied them all and knew them well —and just for that reason he did not need them any more, and professed himself interested only in God's word. But in the service of the truth of this he hoped now the more to be a Christian Cicero, an equally comprehensive teacher of Christian culture, and in addition to be a monk and a saint. The inconsistency of this ideal reached to the roots of his being, and had a decisive influence on Jerome as long as he lived. It drove him to restless work, and to his, on the whole, astonishing achievements. It explains at the same time his human weaknesses, his inordinate vanity, and his frequent failure in the realm of ethical and personal relations. There was no real theology behind this ascetic cultural ideal, for which he fought with such conviction. He remained attached to the traditions which he endeavoured to suppress and conquer. Jerome was as much a monk as a humanist. Projected on world history, this has determined the whole cultural tradition of the Western Middle Ages proceeding from him—in so far as it did not draw from other sources, or obtain by Augustine's mediation a deeper understanding of what Christian humility, spiritual life, and Biblical truth and culture really mean.

After about a year and a half Jerome had come to the point at which he could say good-bye to his host, and actually go into the desert as a hermit. He chose an area not too far off, the desert of Chalcis, situated south-east of Antioch and outside the gates of Chalcis on Belus, the last important town of the Syrian fertile zone. For a long time, the rock-caves of the deserted valleys had been inhabited by hermits living apart from each other, among whom the newcomer at first attracted no further attention. Jerome most likely moved into a vacant cave. It must have been quite spacious, and for the desert 'comfortable'; for he could provide a place for his whole library here, he could copy books and occasionally receive visitors. The hermits were not totally secluded from each other and from the outside world: Jerome regularly received and dispatched his letters. From this time, a number of early letters are preserved which were sent to his friends all over the world, and almost every letter contains the earnest admonition to write to him and write again, no matter what they wrote—they must write! Jerome praises the stillness and saintly life he had found—but the silence did not make him silent. Of a thoroughly sociable nature, he welcomed solitude only to organize his thoughts and to set them in the right form. This accomplished, he was the more consumed with impatience to communicate them to others, to have intellectual exchange, and to maintain at least a correspondence with like-minded persons.

Jerome undoubtedly took upon himself the ascetic exercises belonging to the life of a true hermit, but one does not get the impression that he was particularly happy in them. Jerome was not a man to whom renunciation could be an enjoyment and the opening of new emotions. Even in later years we hear scarcely anything of the exaltations, illuminations or ecstasies of his inner life. The hard bodily achievement as such is what stands out. Asceticism was to him a means of discipline and of sanctification, in this respect meritorious and indispensable, yet also always a strain, wearisome and unpleasant. So he himself described in thoroughly realistic terms the beginning of his monastic strife, laying the colour on thick in his usual way: 'Ah, how often I took myself to Rome in my thought, to all the splendours I had once enjoyed—in those days in the desolate, lonely desert which, parched by the glowing sun, furnished a frightful home for the monks! There I sat alone, my heart full of bitter despair, my limbs stuck into an ugly sackcloth, my skin like that of a negro, dark from the dirt. Day after day I had to cry and sigh, and once, falling asleep against my will, my fleshless bones lay nakedly on the bare soil. I do not want to talk about eating and drinking! Even sick anchorites drink only cold water, and a cooked meal is regarded as an excess. And he, who in fear of hell had banished himself to this imprisonment, and had company only with scorpions and wild beasts—he notwithstanding this found himself time and again in company with dancing girls! My face grew pale with hunger, yet in my cold body the passions of my inner consciousness continued to glow. This human being was less alive than dead; only his burning concupiscence still continued to boil' (*Ep.* 22, 7).

The hidden instincts of the ambitious zealot did not change direction. Jerome continued to work indefatigably. He had new books sent to him, and soon he also won friends to copy them. He was proud not only to augment his library by this 'manual work', but also to be able to make his living himself like a real monk. At this time, Jerome began to learn Hebrew from a Jewish convert. Otherwise, he testified, he could not keep a tight rein on his thoughts. He had to combine bodily fasting with intellectual toil. 'I knew the brilliant style of Quintilian, the eloquence of Cicero, the dignified loftiness of Fronto, and the soft charm of Pliny, and now I learned the ABC again, and memorized the hissing, jarring words. What a labour! What difficulties! How often I was about to despair, and then began anew from the start, driven by the ambition of learning! I have gone through all this, and can testify to it from experience; and those who then shared life with me know it too' (*Ep.* 125, 12).

However, one must not only consider those complaints. Jerome also realized the advantages of this life. He could place it in an ideal light, and then like an outsider rhapsodize over the poetry and calm perfection of the monastic solitude. The most charming fruit of such moods is the small volume on *The Life of Saint Paul, The First Hermit*, which was written in those years. Until then, the anchorite's calling had been intimately known to the general public only through the famous biography of Anthony written by Saint Athanasius. Evagrius, Jerome's friend, had translated this into Latin for Western readers: an earnest book, reporting the demonic temptations and heroic purification and trial of the wonderful saint, who was supposed to have founded the new monastic way of life. In his book Jerome competed to a certain extent with this model. His Saint Paul, it is explicitly maintained, is older and more perfect than Anthony, who had hitherto been unjustly counted as the beginning. Apart from this, however, the little book is quite different. Its aim is primarily to entertain and recount the story

in an edifying way. To achieve this, it restricts itself to the first
and last days of the hero's stay in the desert, which lasted one
hundred and thirteen years. We hear how, persecuted and forsaken by the world, he finds an enchanting solitary refuge in the
wilderness. A palm-tree grants him food and clothing; a raven
brings him daily the necessary portion of bread. The whole is
an idyll, nor does Jerome avoid the usual classical convention-
alities: a friendly centaur and a Christian-minded satyr show the
way to Anthony, who has been ordered in a dream to go to
Paul. Both men then humbly converse at a bubbling spring
under the palm-tree. Finally the deceased Paul is covered with
a coat once given to Anthony by Athanasius. The burial is performed by two pious lions, who beg and receive from Anthony
his Christian blessing for this task. The religious content of this
little romance is modest, but nobody can fail to recognize its
charm. Jerome proves himself to be a brilliant popular story-
teller who, according to the occasion and need, knows how to
tell his story in an edifying, exciting, humorous, and even quite
piquant manner, without transgressing the limits of good taste.
It is idle to inquire for the 'historical' core of this story; it is
probably at best no more than the name of the hero. Later
Jerome composed biographies of two other monks, which are
somewhat more trustworthy with regard to their content.
After all, he drew here from partly recognizable sources, and
one of the saints he even knew personally. In spite of this, the
harmless sketch of the *Vita Pauli* yet remains his most perfect
writing from a literary point of view. Jerome became in the
course of time more scholarly and impressive, probably more
theologically serious, and in his way, more important. His
talent as a writer, however, was finally developed when he was
thirty years of age, and he never reached again the gentle charm
of this little work of his youth.

The little book closes, quite like the monastic literature of the
Middle Ages, with the supplication to the reader to be mindful
of 'the poor sinner Jerome', and with the assurance that Paul's
tunic would be much more precious to him than all that royal

purple which provokes divine punishment. In reality, his own life as a monk was, as we have seen, by no means an undisturbed idyll, and with time the dissensions began to increase. The dogmatic controversies, which even in the quiet colony of monks he could not evade for long, caused him particular trouble. The whole Orient, then in the last stages of the Arian controversy, was split into different parties attacking each other. All intellectually important personalities of the Greek church, and also Westerners like Ambrose, were involved in these quarrels, and were passionately interested in their outcome. Jerome, however, considered them only an annoying disturbance of his personal peace, and found that the whole quarrel of the Greeks was fundamentally of no concern to him as a Roman. He was indignant at their tactlessness in refusing to leave him in peace, and in expecting his theological judgement and support. What possible concern could he have with the new sophistries regarding one or three hypostases? Jerome was not interested at all in questions of speculative theology and metaphysics; if necessary, he was willing to accept any solution which did not directly contradict the decisions already made. When he saw no escape, he resolved upon an unusual step: he wrote a letter to the new Roman Pope Damasus, who was completely unknown to him personally, and asked for brief information as to what faith he had to confess, which formula he now had to affirm, and which of the opposed bishops of Antioch he had to follow. He stressed that he was a 'Roman' by virtue of baptism by Damasus' predecessor, and he wanted to remain such. The Pope shall therefore make the decision for him—however Arian it might sound, Jerome will nevertheless accept it as his orthodox instructions. Now the sun of righteousness no more rises in the East, but in the West. 'For the moment, I only exclaim: "He who is installed in Peter's chair, he is my man"' (Ep. 16, 2). When he received no answer, he wrote a second letter imploring the great shepherd with most flattering phrases not to leave his 'black sheep' in the lurch. But Damasus had no intention whatever of committing himself in such a naïve manner in the difficult ecclesiastico-political situation then existing—least of all to an uninfluential and virtually unknown writer and hermit.

A little later, Jerome left Chalcis forever. It was probably hardly two and a half years altogether that he endured monastic life in his cave. He himself tried to give the impression that the dogmatic quarrelsomeness and obtrusiveness of his companions had spoiled his further stay in the desert, and even made it impossible. But this is not a very convincing excuse. Jerome had had quite enough of this form of striving for sanctification. Otherwise nothing could have hindered him from seeking out another, quieter refuge, in any other place East or West. In reality, he longed again for the world, for people, for communication, and for intellectual stimulus. In a deeper sense, Jerome was probably right in breaking off his monk's career, which at first sight appears somewhat embarrassing. His development was not yet concluded, and the scholarly possibilities for which, without admitting it, he longed could not be offered by the wilderness. Only many years later did he succeed in finding the appropriate combination of intellectual work, asceticism, and community, to which he then remained faithful. Now, the great cities of Antioch and Constantinople were the goal of his wishes.

In Antioch Jerome finally had to choose his ecclesiastical party. He joined the side of the extreme 'orthodox' theologians, represented by the old-Nicene, Western-looking Paulinus, whom Evagrius also followed. Jerome considered it all his life safest and most convenient to follow the most definite-sounding theological slogans—just because they did represent nothing else but slogans of ecclesiastical orthodoxy. For his scholarly interests, however, he resorted to any book, however much under suspicion, and where he could learn or experience something concrete, he did not shrink in certain cases even from dubious acquaintances. Thus in Antioch, for instance, he heard the exegetical lectures of Apollinaris, bishop of Laodicea, whose Christological teachings were condemned as heresy despite his anathema

being acknowledged as a Nicean. Yet Jerome shielded himself against suspicion by also signing if necessary, i.e. as soon as anyone wished it, any dogmatic sentence of anathema. He let nobody excel him in orthodoxy and ecclesiastical devotion. It was during this period that Jerome was ordained priest by Paulinus, in gratitude for his support. Jerome felt himself now as much as ever a monk, and expressly insisted that this freedom must not be restricted in any way. But on these terms, as in no way binding him, but simply an 'honorary promotion', his new rank was welcome to him. Jerome always thought and taught, even regarding the ministry, in tones of an uncomplicated 'Catholic' piety. The priests 'make' the Lord's body, they guard the Bride of Christ in her chastity, only by them can we be Christians at all (*Ep.* 14, 8). Yet he was far from ignoring their weaknesses, and—despite his assurances to the contrary—from keeping his sharp tongue in check where they were concerned. Whenever he was personally upset or provoked in his vanity, any form of affront and insult seemed allowable to him even against spiritual—in such cases only apparently 'spiritual' —enemies. All this needs to be taken into account if we are to understand his human and theological attitude in later struggles.

Jerome stayed in Constantinople from 379 to 382, years important in world history, as the great change under Theodosius was modifying the appearance of the whole Eastern church in favour of the Nicene Creed. He was presumably a witness of the famous 'theological speeches' of Gregory of Nazianzus, he experienced at close quarters the turbulent Council of 381, later called 'ecumenical' and stayed on for some months afterwards in the city. In spite of this, he never mentioned these happenings. This is characteristic. To be sure, Jerome, as a Westerner and adherent of Paulinus, could not be very pleased with the result of this Council; yet on the other hand he was in the closest personal relationship with the leaders of the victorious, Neo-Nicene party. He repeatedly designated Gregory of Nazianzus as his 'teacher', who had disclosed to him the understanding of the Holy Scriptures. In the days of the Council

Gregory of Nyssa, Amphilochius of Iconium and others came into the circle of his acquaintance. But Jerome was not concerned with the controversies of church politics. He wanted to advance his theological studies, and this meant above all, even then, instruction about the correct interpretation of the Scriptures, a solid knowledge of Biblical exegesis and philology. Under the overwhelming impression of the superiority of Greek theological education, he became for the first time aware of his calling and his real life-task, of which he would never again lose sight. 'I wanted'—he confessed at the end of his life —'to dedicate myself completely to the exposition of Scripture, and to impart Hebrew and Greek learning to the people of my tongue'; but the devil, he added bitterly, did not wish it, and interrupted and again and again disturbed his longed-for peace (*Hierem.* III, 1, 2). It was as much as anything the devil of his own perpetual unrest, of his quarrelsomeness, and vanity. But we will speak later of the scholastic achievements of Jerome.

At first Jerome occupied himself with the modest task of a translator—an activity to which during his whole life he returned time and again, an activity second only to his own writings inspired by Greek theology. He attempted to translate into Latin the chronicle of Eusebius, or, more strictly, the second part with its table of parallel dates, and so to create a solid source-book and manual, particularly for Biblical history. According to his own testimony, this was a pure translation as far as the fall of Troy; for the later centuries he sought to amplify and correct the work with the help of Latin historians, and finally he carried it on independently up to his own time. He chose to conclude with the year of the dreadful battle with the Goths at Adrianople (378); for now 'barbaric hordes rage through our lands, and everything is uncertain' (*Chron.* prol.). Jerome was at all times a naïve Roman patriot. It is to his credit that he now immediately applied his scholarly passion to such decidedly delicate and difficult material. Unfortunately, the characteristic weakness of almost all his scholarly enterprises is already revealed here. He himself called it a 'tumultuous' work,

and one not completely organized on account of his haste, and
he excused himself on the ground of the special difficulties of
the subject-matter. As a matter of fact, he adduces an abundance of scholarly data, but it is hasty and full of errors. In the
later parts the subjective partisanship of the author in praise and
blame alike is obvious at once. His assurance that if necessary
he was not afraid to tell the truth about living personalities
could have been omitted. Jerome envisaged also a history of his
own time—but this was one of the many plans of his life never
accomplished. About the same time he began, perhaps at the
instigation of his 'teacher' Gregory, the translation of certain
homilies of Origen. Origen was for Jerome, as he was for
Ambrose, indeed even more than for the latter, simply the
great Biblical scholar, the only one who like himself was master
of the Hebrew language, and who always carefully observed
the differences in the textual tradition. Jerome followed him
without hesitation even in the allegorical method of interpretation, which was to him, especially in the Old Testament, the
accepted bridge to deep understanding and 'edification'. On
the other hand, the methodical and systematic presuppositions
of Origen's hermeneutics scarcely interested him; even as a
follower of Origen, Jerome was primarily concerned with the
material. Concrete questions of exegesis were to his philological mind the real theological problems.

After Gregory of Nazianzus and the various members of the
Council had left Constantinople, the city lost its attraction for
Jerome. He decided to follow the two bishops whose sym-
pathies looked to the West, and who for this reason had failed
to make their case at the Council. He travelled with Paulinus
and Epiphanius from Salamis to Rome. Here a new Council
was to meet which was to do them justice. Already his knowledge of languages must have given Jerome some importance,
and he was no longer the unknown hermit of earlier days, but
a personality of literary renown, whose connections with the
East must have recommended him as an adviser. With a sure
eye Pope Damasus recognized the importance of the man whom

he had not answered some years ago. He appointed him his private secretary to prepare difficult letters, and at the same time custodian of the papal archives and of his library. Ecclesiastical rank played no role in this: it was medieval legend which first exalted Jerome into a cardinal of the Roman Church and adorned him with the broad-brimmed red hat. But now began the happiest and at any rate outwardly the most splendid and richest years of his life.

Damasus loved the grand style and presence. He was a great builder, and under him the papal household first assumed a 'princely' appearance. He was no narrow-minded Maecenas, and he placed the keeper of his archives and counsellor in an appropriate position, with suitable remuneration. Thus Jerome for the first time participated in luxury and the social life of the great world. Although he had a hard despotic nature, and was ruthless with his adversaries, Damasus nevertheless had a feeling for human intercourse, and was by no means without intellectual interests. He enjoyed the society of a man like Jerome, who was soon complete master of the manners of the curia. We still have some of the long and short letters exchanged between them. The Pope demanded books or precise theological information; he asked with condescending humour why Jerome was so long silent, whether he was 'asleep' or hugging his books. Jerome sought to satisfy his impatient master as far as possible, and promised him the dedication of his latest translation. But Damasus knew also how to put tasks before his protégé which were appropriate to his abilities. We have him to thank for the first impulse towards an enterprise which has made Jerome's name immortal in the Western church: the renewal of the Latin Bible, the text of the philologically reliable *Vulgate*, which put an end to the chaos of the older traditions. In these days at Rome, it is true, Jerome hardly went beyond a first revision of the gospels. He added to it a translation of the Eusebian *Canones*, i.e. synoptic tables which made it much easier to find the parallel pericopes.

Jerome was also soon drawn into the contests of church

politics against sects and theological parties, and his skilful pen
and his extensive knowledge proved themselves useful. At this
time (?) he therefore wrote a pamphlet against the Luciferians,
a small rigorist sect of extreme anti-Arians, whose obstinacy
gave the Catholics in Rome much trouble. In this he cleverly
found the happy mean between the tone of breezy popularity
and the calm superiority of objective and learned argument.
This little *Dialogue* between a Luciferian and an 'orthodox' is
written as though it were an official report of a disputation
which really took place. All the emphasis is laid upon the
'objective' side of Catholic churchmanship, which not only
forbids a deliberate schism, but also, when correctly understood,
makes it senseless and unnecessary. The sacraments of the
church, her ministry, and her apostolic tradition are efficacious,
even if, like Noah's ark, she also contains impure animals. This
should be understood even by the 'snarling eloquence' of the
Luciferians, although experience shows that 'they are easier to
refute than to convince' (*Dial. c. Lucif.* 28).

A deeper matter was his controversy with Helvidius regarding the perpetual virginity of Mary. This pamphlet was probably likewise instigated by Damasus, or at least, as Jerome
emphasized, explicitly approved by him. Helvidius was a layman who by reference to the Scripture, which knows and
mentions the 'brothers of Jesus', disputed the theory that Mary
remained a virgin even 'after the birth' of her first Son. He was
conscious of defending along with this the older Western tradition, which had certainly declined in popularity since Ambrose,
and he protested against a more recent one-sided prizing of
celibacy at the expense of matrimony. Here Jerome was in his
element. His whole Biblical scholarship came into motion in
order to save Mary's honour against all alleged distortions and
forgeries of the text by the slanderer. The exegetical proofs he
brought out are essentially the same as those the Catholic
church still maintains today. They were effectually reinforced
by a drastic caricature of the opposite point of view. Behind
this stood the real, personal concern: the conviction of the clear

religious and moral superiority of virginity. It was justified by
the entire tradition and practice of the church, as Jerome saw it.
Already the 'virginal Christ' and the virgin Mary had laid the
foundation of virginity for both sexes. The apostles were celibate or, if they had been married, abstinent in their matrimony.
Bishops, presbyters, and deacons are chosen from the celibate
or widower's class, or at least they live in perpetual chastity
after becoming priests (*Ep.* 49, 21). The whole idea of merit
depends for the ascetic on this distinction between the two
modes of life according to achievement and rank. It would be
a peculiar God who punishes sins, but will not also reward
good works! (*adv. Jov.* II, 3). Jerome guarded against prohibiting
marriage as such, but it was a matter of course to him that it
was of minor value, and consequently receives less reward.
Marriage is to virginity as the mere avoidance of sin is to doing
good, or 'to express it a little more mildly: as good to the
better' (*adv. Jov.* I, 13). 'Why should we lie to ourselves and
make ourselves angry? If we are continuously greedy for the
embrace of women, the reward for chastity must naturally be
denied to us' (*Ep.* 49, 21). This is the answer he gave to a later
critic of his inflexible ideal, which all his life appeared conclusive to him in its logic. He lacked any faculty for the more
serious problems of the monkish idea of sanctification, which
other Western theologians of that time did nevertheless recognize. Jerome was the most zealous, but also the most indigent
ascetic theologian the ancient church produced. Yet in what he
said in these controversies he was completely serious.

Moreover, Jerome did not restrict himself to propaganda
with his pen for the ascetic life. He also made a personal stand
for his ideals. Soon we find him as the intellectual centre of a
circle of aristocratic and wealthy ladies, to whom he became
teacher and counsellor. His special liking for a female audience
which admired and understood him, and which he could
instruct, educate, and admonish was, as already stated, a lasting
feature of his nature. Next to the protection of the Pope, the
circle of aristocratic ladies in Rome evidently constituted his

strongest support. Otherwise, his ascetic preaching and learning seemed to have found little echo. The palace on the Aventine in which the widow Marcella lived with her mother and her daughter Asella was the centre of the new ascetic movement. A number of other young women and widows who were no longer satisfied with the social life of Rome congregated around them. The earnestness of the ascetic demands gave their life a new meaning. They all felt themselves to be more or less like nuns who wore the veil, and renounced adornment and the vanity of the 'world'. They rarely appeared in public, fasted much, held devotions, and were very generous to charity, to the annoyance of their relatives and heirs. Even before Jerome's arrival, some had decided to make pilgrimages and a settlement in the Holy Land. The new ideas he imparted to this circle were, besides a more intimate knowledge of the strict Eastern exercises, the concentrated and regular pursuit of Bible reading and Biblical studies. Soon Jerome delivered before a select female audience his own lectures which found enthusiastic acceptance. Some began to learn Greek and even Hebrew themselves. They assailed him with more or less learned exegetical and theological questions. They borrowed books and translations, so that he had trouble in doing justice to all their wishes. To Marcella alone he wrote no less than sixteen letters which, from their content, were of course aimed also at a wider public. Jerome edited them himself, and considered them to be a complete 'book'. This evidently important woman dared on her part to educate the uneasy man a little, and tried to win him from his delight in slander and polemics. Paula was primarily interested in a 'mystical', i.e. allegorical-devotional interpretation of the Scripture. To her daughter Eustochium Jerome dedicated his famous letter on the right form of ascetic life.

At first Jerome had barely the courage, he asserts, to raise his eyes in their presence, such was his respect for these high-born ladies (*Ep.* 127, 7). But with time the relationship became more cordial and unconstrained. Jerome felt increasingly at home in the 'house-congregation' of his students, who were 'truly happy in their bodily and spiritual virginity'. 'The teaching made us stay together continuously; being together made me unself-conscious, and unselfconsciousness gave me confidence' (*Ep.* 45, 2). For Saint Peter's Day, Eustochium sent to Jerome, with a 'spicy' little letter, bracelets and doves which he did not re-ject, in addition to a little basket 'full of cherries, blushing with virginal modesty'; Lucullus could not have offered them better (*Ep.* 31, 1, 3). Another time, Marcella gave him a new robe, an arm-chair, candles and chalices. It is amusing to see how Jerome every time combined in his answer (of the elegance of which he is obviously proud) social and personal thanks with edifying reflections. The hairshirt, he thinks, signifies fasting; the arm-chair points to domestic decency; the candles to the light with which we await the bridegroom; the chalice to mortification and martyrdom. In his case this interpretation, however, is too favourable—here the arm-chair is rather a sign of laziness, the chalice signifies revels, etc.! Yet in respect to the donors he nevertheless believes himself to have revealed the 'mystery' of that which is veiled (*Ep.* 44). We see that the allegorical me-thod, once learned, could be made useful for any purpose. With Jerome begins the dubious history of the theologian's 'pro-fessional joke'. What shall we say for instance, when he gal-lantly greets Paula, whose daughter had taken the veil, and now had become 'the wife not of a soldier but of a king', as the 'mother-in-law of God' (*Ep.* 22, 20)?

Jerome appears as the first example of the spiritual coun-sellor and confidant, almost in the manner of the later domestic chaplain of noble and aristocratic society. This too is a sign of the times, and lends his candid descriptions a more general interest. He had all his life avoided concerning himself with simple people. Being himself of common descent, in his social intercourse he always sought connections with those above him. But we must not adapt the picture too much to the analo-gies of modern times, for example, to the French salons of the *ancien régime*. The world-renouncing atmosphere was too strong for this and the gloom of a by no means aesthetic asceticism

brooded over the whole. It was supposed to be an expression
of a special love to Christ, but the physical side of virginity was
primarily emphasized, and in a way highly embarrassing to
modern feeling. To be sure, Jerome had at his disposal the
entire assurance and flexibility of an ancient rhetorician and
preaching pedagogue, but his rough ascetic cure of souls had
not yet progressed into the more sensitive regions of feeling.
'If in Rome any respectable woman would conquer my heart,
this is the only way! She would have to mourn and fast, she
would have to be caked with dirt and almost blind with tears.
Her song would be the psalms, her speech the gospel, her burden
abstinence, and her life's occupation fasting' (*Ep.* 45, 3).

Despite this it was inevitable that in the course of time mistrust and rumours arose out of these meetings and this correspondence. They were borne on a wave of opposition which
the new ascetic propaganda was arousing everywhere. We detect it at the same time in Milan, in Gaul and throughout the
West. The Romans were furious about the 'disgusting brood
of monks' who gave themselves airs with their ascetic demands,
the 'impostors and Greeks' who entrapped rich matrons, but
otherwise were satisfied with nobody and nothing. Jerome was
unwise enough usually to meet his opponents only with haughty
wit and sarcasm. The critics of his Biblical text are 'two-legged
asses'. Anyone who 'throws stones at' his ascetic tracts must be
a dissolute person, a worldling and a hypocrite, and there are
more than enough of those, he assures us, even among the
monks and clergy. If anyone felt himself touched, things became even worse for him. We still have a letter in which
Jerome makes fun of such a priest, with the ridiculous name
'Onasus': he will operate on his evil-smelling nose, and can
only give him the advice not to let himself be seen any more if
he wished to maintain his reputation as a handsome, eloquent man
(*Ep.* 40). Even this little satire is, like everything with Jerome,
embellished with a flood of classical and Biblical quotations.

It seems that Jerome scarcely had any real friends among the
men of Rome besides the Senator Pammachius, the son-in-law

of Paula, and Damasus himself, 'who has my lady's ear', as his
enemies said. Of course, Jerome's quarters were daily visited by
many; they kissed his hand in public, and struggled for the
favour of a man who was esteemed the right hand and mouth-
piece of the Pope, but they did not forgive him 'that he exposed
with his filthy invectives the whole of Christian society, every
rank and class, in short the whole church', so that everything
appeared to be far worse even than their pagan opponents
claimed (Rufin., *Apol.* II, 5). And so, when Damasus died on
December 11, 384, catastrophe occurred. On all sides hostility
burst out. The change was all the more bitter to Jerome, since
he, as it appears, was at times naïve enough to have had his own
hopes for succession. The new Pope, Siricius, had no understanding of his scholarly work. It even seems that the 'Senate of
Pharisees'—as Jerome called the Roman presbytery—had explicitly expressed itself against him. At any rate, he was out
of his profitable position. Unfortunately the young Blaesilla,
whom Jerome had converted to a strict asceticism, died during
these weeks. It was said that fasting had broken her. Her own
mother, Paula, was near to collapse. The letter of condolence,
which Jerome then wrote to her, praised the deceased to the
skies, and at the same time met the mother's grief with barbaric
harshness. This is probably understandable only in the light of
the difficult situation in which Jerome actually found himself.
Blaesilla, it says, is now blessed and enjoys the company of
Mary and Hannah! How hurt would she be to see that her
mother is provoking Christ by not controlling her sadness!
Paula must not in any circumstances appear weak. Tears on
account of such a happening are not allowable to a Christian,
and even less to a holy nun. The Scripture teaches us the right
behaviour. Moreover, a traditional theme, the remembrance
of the departed will live on, and in this lies an earthly consolation too. With every line that Jerome will write in the future,
Blaesilla's spirit will be before his eyes, and with his books her
name will travel through the world and can never more die
(*Ep.* 39, 8).

At times Jerome thought of navigating his 'leaky ship' into a calm harbour, and awaiting the storm on some near-by country estate. Why should he be concerned, he wrote, about Rome, her luxury and theatres, and even about the pious circle of his dignified friends? To cling to God—that is sufficient. And again a picture emerged before him, gleaming in Virgilian colours, of the happy rural life. There he may be satisfied with cabbage he has grown himself, with country bread, and fresh milk, and be frugally happy in the shadow of the trees and the meadow-bank dotted with flowers (*Ep.* 43, 3). Yet then he realized that such an evasion could not serve him. For the second time, Jerome made the decision to go to the East—and now finally: 'he returns from Babylon to Jerusalem'. His farewell letter to Asella (*Ep.* 45) is a true reflection of his mood at that time. He is evidently determined to silence his envious enemies, the 'priests and Levites' of the ungrateful city, and to refute especially the slanders concerning his female company; yet at the same time his whole personal exasperation and irritation once again forces its way in. He is supposed to be a libertine, a filthy sneak and intriguer! And even the people, who had once treated him with so much love and respect, say this! But the hypocrites, the worldly-minded society ladies may ridicule his holy life! He has learned to enter the kingdom of heaven 'in ill repute and good repute' (II Cor. vi. 8). Before Christ's tribunal it will some day be revealed who has had the right way of thinking. In its impulsive candour this letter is an astonishing document. The West had hardly known anything like it until then. It is as though Ciceronian cultural expression had combined with Paul's passionate scorn of the world. We hear the language of a reckless ascetic, who in his bitterness is neither free nor great, yet is at any rate a man really alive, through and through.

At first Jerome went to Antioch, where he again took lodging with Evagrius and Paulinus. Yet it was not for long. It was probably agreed from the outset that Paula and Eustochium should follow him by another route. He presently called for them at the house of Epiphanius, Bishop of Salamis, and then travelled in their company through Palestine—a pious pilgrimage which was quite customary in those days. Furthermore, this was for Jerome a new opportunity to broaden his Biblical knowledge. Jerome was the first theologian to emphasize the scientific importance of archeology and personal inspection in this way. 'He who has seen Athens learns to understand Greek history better, and he who has sailed from Troy, by Leucas and Acroceraunia to Sicily, and farther to the mouth of the Tiber, understands the third book of Virgil (i.e. the *Aeneid*). In the same way one looks at the Holy Scriptures with different eyes, if one has visited Judea and knows the old sites and landscapes, whether they have kept their old names or changed them' (*Paralip.* prol.). We owe to Jerome the revision of an old dictionary of Hebrew proper names, and above all of the Eusebian *Onomasticon* of Biblical geography which, supplemented by his own observations, is still an indispensable source today. Besides Palestine, the monastic settlements in Egypt were no less popular as a destination of spiritual and educational journeys. To these places also their learned guide joyfully accompanied the ladies and 'thus learned much, which was unknown to him until then' (*Apol.* III, 22). Above all, he now came to know Alexandria, the last metropolitan centre of theological education which Jerome had not yet visited. He made the acquaintance of the blind Origenist Didymus, his 'clairvoyant' teacher, whom he 'could ask about everything that seemed to him doubtful in the Scripture' (*Ephes.* prol.). Didymus' work on the Holy Spirit is the only dogmatic writing Jerome translated from Greek into Latin; he himself, however, seems to have questioned him primarily about exegetical problems.

In the summer of 386 the travels came to an end. They decided to settle down finally not in Jerusalem, but in the quieter Bethlehem. Jerome had means of his own, and later converted into money the property he had inherited from his parents, in order to help finance the colony planned, and 'not to be laughed at by his envious slanderers' if the enterprise failed

(*Ep.* 66, 14). The greater part, however, was without doubt paid for out of the immense fortune which his women friends put at his disposal. In the course of the years a large convent arose under Paula's leadership, divided into three departments in which the nuns were accommodated according to their social position. Jerome was head of a monastery, smaller than the convent, but in time also counting about fifty inmates. Besides all this there was a hostel for pilgrims and a school in which Jerome also imparted secular education in rhetoric to students. He had again refused to take over regular religious duties: the cloister had a chapel, but for worship the monks went to the church in the town. Jerome was satisfied to preach occasionally before his monks, at times even in Greek. Almost all the monks were Westerners. From the West came more and more visitors and pilgrims, with recruits for the cloister as well. Others occasionally travelled back into their home-country for visits, or on business. Permanent residence (*stabilitas loci*) was not yet considered by the monks of that time as an inescapable obligation, and there was still no question of strict solitude and silence either.

For thirty-four years, i.e. almost half his life, Jerome lived at this place, and did not leave it except for short visits in the neighbourhood, until his death. Besides new polemical treatises, all his long Biblical writings and translations originated here. This was his real life-work, in comparison with which his earlier scholastic achievements appear negligible in extent and weight. Undoubtedly the favourable external conditions contributed a great deal to this productivity. Almost like a modern scholar, Jerome complained, to be sure, of the many disturbances and the crowd of visitors who left him no other choice but to close either his books or his door. He says he does not want to boast of his hospitality—but he must excuse himself, that his work does not make better progress. Only in 'stolen' hours of the long winter nights, burning the midnight oil, does he find time for his commentaries (*Comm. Ezech.* VII prol.). Furthermore, he complains as ever about his weak eyes, which especially while reading the Hebrew manuscripts refuse to work; and in principle it is only possible to formulate thought correctly if one writes down the words oneself (*Ep.* 21, 42). On the other hand, he had in Bethlehem everything he needed at his disposal: his countless books, readers, secretaries, and assistants, students eager to learn, and not least important the interest and sympathy of his devout women friends who clung to him and cared for him with ever constant devotion. Whoever visited him received an indelible impression of his restless energy at work: 'He is constantly at his studies, completely absorbed by his books; neither by night nor day does he grant himself relaxation; he is constantly engaged in reading or writing' (Sulp. Sev., *Dial.* I, 9, 5). That Jerome nevertheless could not find permanent repose is due less to the small disturbances and dissensions, which even in a monastery cannot fail to arise, or to the slanders and envy of enemies, whom he imagined always and everywhere to be at work, but above all to the uneasiness of his own incorrigible temper, which could always be provoked to controversy and defence.

Jerome's greatest remaining accomplishment of these years is the translation of the Old Testament from the Hebrew. This was probably begun in 390, and substantially concluded about 406. Besides this, he was engaged in other work which was partly related to it. He had earlier started upon a new translation or revision of the text by use of the Septuagint, the old Jewish-Greek Bible which in the church had replaced the original text, and which was very much in repute and honour. In the library of Caesarea in Palestine Jerome had come across the original copy of the *Hexapla*, in which Origen had in his time put together the text of the Septuagint with further translations, and with the original Hebrew text. Jerome started off with the Psalms. This, his first translation from the Greek Septuagint, is even today occasionally used liturgically. Further books followed. Then, however, it became clear to him that for his work, as he planned it, only the original 'truth' of the Hebrew text could be determinative. With admirable energy he set about thoroughly to refresh and deepen his remarkable Hebrew knowledge, which manifestly was not sufficient for such a project. He secured—as he did not forget, with his own good, hard money—as teacher a learned Jewish rabbi, who dared visit him only at night for fear of his co-religionists. Beyond purely grammatical knowledge he owed to him also many an important hint for the interpretation as such. The new translation which resulted turned out—like everything Jerome created—uneven. Upon the large historical books he generally did excellent and precise work; upon others, more superficial. For the translation of Tobit Jerome claims to have spent only one day, for Judith only one night; moreover, both are translated from the Aramaic. A useful innovation, not until then used for prose Biblical texts in Latin, was the arrangement of the text in lines corresponding to the sense, which to a certain extent form a substitute for our modern punctuation. Having perhaps found the suggestion for this from the Hexapla, Jerome referred to corresponding editions of Demosthenes and Cicero and emphasized that these 'cola' must not be understood as 'verses'. Naturally, he could not help relying for his translation to a considerable extent on older Latin translations. This was done in part consciously and on purpose: the faithful reader of the Bible should not be offended by too radical innovation. There is, of course, no lack of faults and errors in the work as a whole—this could hardly be avoided with such a difficult and novel task. Nevertheless Jerome's translation signified a tremendous advance in every aspect, as compared with the state of affairs up to that time, and it remains for those days a very respectable and, on account of the continuous reference to the Hebrew, unique achievement. With regard to the style, Jerome repressed the many vulgarisms and barbarous neologisms of the Old Latin Bible without sacrificing to a dull purism its popularity and vigorous expression. Consequently, the *Vulgate* has justly remained up to the present day the classical Latin Bible. There is hardly a later ecclesiastical translation into a modern language which is not at least indirectly influenced and moulded by it—even the translation of Luther not excluded.

Certainly it was at first far from immediately becoming the *Vulgate*, i.e. the commonly used ecclesiastical edition of the Latin-speaking church. Not until the early Carolingian epoch was this achieved. The new translation could only gradually establish itself against suspicion and all kinds of opposition. His contemporaries felt little gratitude to Jerome for the greatest work of his life. Even Augustine, who still complained about the chaos of older translations, and who tried to control it to the best of his ability, regretted that Jerome had not adhered more firmly to the Septuagint, in whose miraculous, inspired origin he firmly believed. This was, of course, painful to Jerome, who had at one time believed this legend himself. Others went even further in their criticism. As usual, the new and unfamiliar was at first regarded as merely perverse. But having once convinced himself of the *Hebraica veritas*, i.e. of the superior claims of the original text, Jerome could not give way on this point, at least in principle. Finally he attempted also to define the limits of the Old Testament canon on the basis of the Hebrew. Those books and parts of the Old Testament originally written in another language, in Greek or 'Chaldean' (i.e. Aramaic), have no right to be regarded as God's Word in the strict sense. They are 'apocryphal' and are pushed into the margin as more or less 'legendary'—a decision followed later by the Protestant churches, while the Roman Catholic church finally rejected it at the Council of Trent.

What caused Jerome most trouble was the narrow-mindedness of those who found fault with his translations, because, as he says, in their lack of education they had no conception what translation really means. One cannot simply transfer a living sentence word for word from one language into another. Every language has its own spirit and—without being therefore the poorer or more rigid—because of this also its own laws and possibilities. The 'verbal monstrosities' of the earlier translations are simply ridiculous. The problem is not to replace each word with the same word, but to rewrite the sentence in

accordance with its meaning. Jerome, however, was cautious
enough to defend the liberty which he takes primarily for his
other translations from Greek into Latin, and not for the translation of the Bible, although the Latin language is far closer to
Greek, as he well knows, than to Hebrew. In the Holy Scripture, he says, the precise sequence of words as such has in certain
cases a deeper meaning, and must be preserved (*Ep.* 57, 5). This
again is one of the safeguards which Jerome laid down to protect his ecclesiastical impeccability. Fortunately, he did not in
reality by any means always act accordingly in his translation
of the Bible. Jerome also referred to the freedom which the
New Testament authors themselves display when quoting Old
Testament passages, and with regard to the general principles of
translation he relied, along with Horace, above all on Cicero,
yet he was actually more cautious than either. In his translations
taken as a whole, Jerome turned out to be a prudent and experienced scholar, who knows his business and makes no radical
experiments. More profound problems of the philosophy of
language did not occur to him. Here also, only the material
with which he dealt was 'theological', and not the spirit in
which he appropriated it. It would be doing him an injustice to
compare him in this respect with a thinker like Augustine, who
himself ungrudgingly acknowledged the superiority of Jerome's
linguistic talent.

   The largest part of Jerome's heritage comprises expositions
of the Holy Scripture. They are in part detailed commentaries,
in which he tried to present and expound every point, but in
part also more concise comments or glosses, which are restricted to the brief explanation of the more difficult passages
only (*Comm. Dan.* prol.). In addition we have the letters devoted to special problems, the extensive exegetical portions of
his dogmatic writings, and the sermons which, though preached
before monks, nevertheless have a similarly scholarly character.
Jerome could not, for instance, refrain from going into the
various readings in the Greek translations of the Psalms. Even
as a preacher he expressly refuses to present mere declamations,

but offers real 'expositions'. Most of his commentaries are on the Old Testament. The explanations justify and at the same time confirm the underlying translation. The prophets predominate, and Jerome commented on them all in succession. On the other hand, he did not deal with a single historical book, but only some *Hebrew Questions on Genesis* (i.e. of translation) in a special treatise. This seems at first sight remarkable; but Jerome is no historian, only an 'historical-philological exegete', who regularly uses historical information only in order to elucidate the background, the hidden allusions to the history of the time, and above all, of course, the 'fulfilment' of the promises. From the New Testament, apart from a short exposition of the gospel of Matthew dictated in two weeks, which is restricted admittedly to 'historical' matters, he expounded only four of the shorter Pauline epistles. Here Jerome reflects the contemporary Western interest in Pauline theology. Nevertheless, this was only a comparatively modest work done in haste, which is essentially a catena of passages from older Greek exegetes. The projected complete commentary on all the Pauline epistles was never written. By contrast, Jerome's 'Work on the Prophets' had kept him busy for thirty years.

Jerome was a rapid writer, or rather a rapid dictator. He describes to us how once his amanuensis became nervous, and began to play with his fingers and to wrinkle his brow when Jerome stopped in the dictation and tried to reflect. 'I dictate what comes into my mouth' (*Comm. Gal.* III prol.). 'As the hand of the writer runs, so also my speaking' (*Comm. Is.* V prol.). There remained barely time to revise the dictation. It was not without vanity that Jerome was pleased to apologize with the excuse that he had finished this or that work under the pressure of circumstances in so many days, or during one night watch. In such a case, the circumstances are responsible for the fact that he could not concentrate better, that this or that side of the subject could not be more extensively or better dealt with. As mentioned already, Jerome needed these excuses. Almost every one of his works is somehow an *opus tumultuarium*, and bears the marks of his manner of working—not exactly uncritical, diligent in its way, yet always hasty and not very conscientious. It is not at all easy to evaluate Jerome adequately as a scholar. Where his statements can be checked, we again and again come across carelessness and oversight. Yet, although modern exegetes have complained about this loudly and legitimately—they nevertheless cannot get away from Jerome! The material he provides is so rich and manifold that nobody can miss it. Without his countless notes, haphazard and scholarly, there would today be lost to us forever any amount of information, allusions, and philological explanations. However, there is no possible doubt about one thing: Jerome produces his astonishing knowledge chiefly at second hand. Various later Greeks are drawn upon for the older information, and Eusebius particularly for the historical material, and above all again and again it is Origen of whom he takes toll, often repeating him almost verbatim for pages on end. Occasionally Jerome frankly admitted his dependence: 'They say that I made excerpts from Origen's works, and that it is illegitimate to touch the writings of the old masters in such a way. People think that they gravely insult me by this. For myself, however, I see in this the highest praise. It is my express desire to follow an example of which I am convinced that it will please all men of discernment and you too' (*Comm. Mich.* II prol.). In other cases, Jerome carefully concealed his dependence. He manages, for instance, —it may be from sheer hastiness—to present things which Origen had learned from his Hebrew teachers as if he himself had discovered them. The worst thing is the obvious exaggeration of his own knowledge of the sources. Jerome undoubtedly knows a great deal, yet he had not really read or even handled one half of the books to which he refers in the proud tone of a man with intimate knowledge. He can be excused in individual cases. It was then a common literary custom not to cite explicitly more recent authorities from which one drew. Nevertheless, the overall picture of Jerome's personality suffers from his thorough unreliability, coupled with his arrogance. Even in scholarly literature, the 'style' of the man reveals his character.

The exegetical method of Jerome is not uniform. He adopted the allegorical method of the Origenist-Alexandrian school, as well as the realism of the Antiochian philology, and he followed neither consistently. Yet on the whole it is evident that as time went on the 'mystical' interpretation of the texts was increasingly crowded out by the historical-philological exposition. It fitted much better the whole manner and bent of Jerome. He was primarily interested in the concrete meaning of a statement, less in its timeless and allegorical meaning. He was concerned to grasp the natural 'literal' sense, and to understand the special purpose of the text 'in that way in which it was understood by the author himself, who wrote it' (*Ep.* 37, 3). What mattered to him was the so-called 'historical' or 'literal' sense, the content of which he rightly defined so broadly that the figurative and metaphorical meaning also was included in this, so far as it was still aimed at the original, historical context. This did not yet mean to Jerome, however, that he had therefore rejected the 'higher', allegorical interpretation, or even that he considered it superfluous. Like all exegetes of the early church, and like his master Origen, Jerome affirmed the twofold or threefold meaning of the Scripture, and repudiated an exclusively historical interpretation as 'Jewish'. The mere letter 'kills'. What he demanded with increasing emphasis was only that the literal, historical exegesis should not be found inferior to the allegorical speculation, and in principle should precede it. One must not interpret a writing allegorically without any knowledge whatever of the historical content, as he himself had done in his youth (*Comm. Abd.* prol.). It is also significant that the 'mystical' explanations Jerome offered on his own are far more typological than allegorical in the strict sense. That is to say, they do not attempt to deduce general religious knowledge from the words and events of the Old Testament, but take them only as pointers and 'types' of the future New Testament history, which had 'fulfilled' them. Basically, the 'historical' method was to Jerome the really scholarly mode of interpretation, while allegory met rather the devotional, practical, and ecclesiastical needs, and had to be adapted to these. 'History (i.e. the historical interpretation) is precise, and does not permit arbitrary deviations. Tropology on the other hand (i.e. the higher, 'moral' interpretation) is free, and subject only to the one law that it must have a pious meaning in view' (*Comm. Abac.* I, 11). Accordingly, it allows different ways of interpreting one and the same text. When Jerome proceeded 'historically' he basically followed the original text, while he unhesitatingly based the higher, allegorical understanding upon the Septuagint, although at times somewhat 'against his conscience' (*Comm. Nah.* i. 14). But what else can he do, in view of those who consider any interpretation made without reference to the usual translation (i.e. the Septuagint) to be simply incomplete and defective (*Comm. Is.* xxx. 33)? 'We have', he suggests, 'the obligation to expound the Scripture as it is read in church, and yet we must not, on the other hand, abandon the truth of the Hebrew (text)' (*Comm. Mich.* i. 16). This is the genuine Jerome, who did not like carrying arguments on principle to their logical conclusion, and wished always to remain in contact with the ecclesiastical mind and tradition.

Independent theological decisions are not very common in his commentaries. His own judgement was often practically stifled by the many contradictory opinions he reported, and it was left more or less to the reader's discretion. The teachings and expositions of the heretics, or of heathens like Porphyry, were indeed always sharply repudiated (for the books of the Holy Bible are of course dictated by the Holy Spirit, and he who does not have the Holy Spirit, is naturally not capable of understanding it correctly), but the 'correct' understanding itself was equated with the teaching of the church. A critical examination is found only in regard to details. The basis question is never really asked or answered, what the inspiration of the Scripture actually means in relation to critical and philological knowledge, and whether this conception was to be understood literally or in a more general sense. Jerome contented *infallible*

himself with the general acknowledgement that the Scripture contained no contradictions and was infallible, but he was not able to develop a Biblical hermeneutic of his own. Accordingly, his explanations of the Bible fluctuated between dull philology and unauthoritative edification. Useful as these were, they lack theological substance. Only in moral and especially in really ascetic exposition did his personal temper break through. This corresponds to the picture also revealed by his later letters, so far as these have an instructive character. Often in the form of small essays, they discuss specific questions of Biblical exegesis, or as admonitions (and obituaries) glorify and illustrate above all the ascetic 'virginal' ideal.

From time to time Jerome still intervened with his own treatises in the theological controversies of the West, particularly when they were of practical ecclesiastical importance. He remained in later years also consistently silent regarding Trinitarian Christological problems, in face of which he had already been somewhat perplexed at the beginning of his career, as we have seen. It is as if these questions, which kept the whole East around him in ferment, did not exist for him. He had probably not even read the numerous new works on this subject. Everything which happened, however, in Rome, Gaul, or Africa, immediately provoked his excitement, and it was not difficult for his friends there to elicit letters and essays from him, which then produced the natural response. 'I only have to write something', says Jerome in self-satisfied complaint, 'and at once my friends or my enemies are out to circulate my writings among the masses. The intention is surely different, yet the zeal of both groups is identical, and both exaggerate whether in praise or blame' (*Ep.* 48, 2). Conversely, it was felt in the West that Jerome was often lacking in due moderation in his polemic, that he distorted his adversaries' opinion, and that he argued from personal irritation—objections which he always repudiated with indignation. When the views of Helvidius found a certain revival in the 'books drunkenly vomited' by the 'Epicurean' monk Jovinian (*adv. Jov.* I, 1), the two-volume refutation turned out so violent that the effect threatened to be the opposite of that intended. Jerome's praise of virginity shocked many circles, appearing as a defamation of marriage. Pammachius vainly exerted himself to withdraw from circulation the copies published. Things went no better in the case of the priest Vigilantius, 'The Vigilant', than they had with Jovinian. Jerome in his attack called him 'Sleepy head', *Dormitantius*. After Jovinian had 'belched out his spirit between pheasants and roast pork' (*adv. Vig.* 1), Vigilantius represented not only a repetition of his immorality and intemperance, but even aimed his spittle at the holy martyrs also; i.e. Vigilantius had criticized new forms of the martyr cult, and the abuses related to it, which even Jerome could not completely deny without doing some justice to the underlying serious concern of his opponent. He was especially bitter against Vigilantius because he had himself lodged him earlier in Bethlehem, and now presumed him to have secret connections with his Roman enemies.

Such violent invective has done no little damage to Jerome's reputation in the eyes of a more sensitive posterity. It cannot be denied that, like the coarse statements on sexual matters, it belongs to the figure of the man. Jerome in anger readily displayed a vulgar and malicious disposition, which stood in singular contrast to the elegant form and culture of his writings. Nevertheless, it would be unjust to take his methods of controversy as the expression of an unrefined or impure habit of mind, and completely to ignore the contemporary presuppositions of his polemical style. In this, also, Jerome was the successful product of the academic training he had enjoyed. The various forms of bellicose insinuation and mockery, including the exaggerations, misrepresentations of names, and manifold zoological terms of abuse conform to the rules of ancient, and particularly of Ciceronian polemic, in both the juristic and literary field. Tertullian also served as an example. Jerome was not deficient in wit when he was using such weapons. He possessed an innate talent for striking characterization and telling caricature. His descriptions of the vices of society, of the bad habits

of the monks, and of the manifold profanities of the Holy Land
are convincingly life-like and perspicuous. The disturbing factor
is simply that he used his sharp eye, his amusing sarcasm, and
his polemical tricks no longer as a pagan rhetorician, but in the
essentially different profession of a Christian, and that he did
not, like Tertullian, compensate for the all too human side of
his method by deep and truly original thought, and a genuine,
objective passion. His controversies stayed on the level of the
petty, the outward, and the personal. Despite his learned display, his ascetic zeal, and his occasional spiritual unction, they
remained basically inappropriate and not really satisfying; they
were edifying only for his partisans. Jerome was not equal to
the spiritual requirements of his subject-matter, and much too
self-satisfied to recognize the limits of his nature. Thus, for
instance, he let himself be moved in old age to compose a
Dialogue against the Pelagians, from which the modern reader
must conclude with astonishment that Jerome had not the
slightest understanding of the real issue in the controversy, and
stood much nearer in his attitude in the matter to Pelagius than
to his alleged confederate Augustine!

In the permanent private warfare and quarrels the constant
confusion of factual and personal issues had a most embarrassing
effect even on his contemporaries. He was unable to look away
from himself, and his veracity failed whenever his own reputation seemed to be jeopardized. Jerome could not bear to have
any person of rank placed at his side. Basil the Great, whom he
never knew personally, he did not acknowledge because of his
wicked 'arrogance'. Ambrose, his predecessor in appreciation
of the Greek theologians, he declared for this very reason to be
a writer without strength or savour, and he compared him to
an ugly crow trying to adorn himself in borrowed plumes.
For a time he even pursued Augustine, who had approached
him by letter without flattery but with respectful politeness,
with damaging insinuations and treated him as an impertinent
young man. Apart from a small circle of friendly woman
ascetics and blindly devoted adherents, hardly anyone

scrupulous

succeeded in living continuously at peace with Jerome. Once the quarrel started, it was almost impossible again to reconcile this suspicious, choleric and, as an opponent, unscrupulous man. He felt that all means were justified that helped him to achieve moral annihilation of 'the envious'. In one case, this unfortunate disposition not only hurt himself, but also had very serious implications damaging to the whole church—in the so-called 'first Origenist controversy'.

distort

In reality, these struggles which lasted for years, and details of which can hardly be untangled, do not at all represent a unity of subject-matter. Incidental personal and political differences were artificially transferred by Jerome to a dogmatic basis, distorting the real connection, simply because he could best defend himself in the role of the persecuted witness for the truth. In this way, there was a break-up of old friendships, traditions, and convictions which must really have been dear to him, and which in different circumstances would have enjoyed his protection. We must here be satisfied with a short sketch of these disgraceful incidents.

Origen, the great Alexandrian theologian, had not remained immune to attack in his lifetime, and during the century and a half which had elapsed since then, opposition had again and again been registered against individual doctrines of his system which was, strictly speaking, more Hellenistic and philosophical than Biblical. His opinion regarding the origin and end of the world, his teaching on the soul, and his theory of universal salvation and redemption, could hardly as a matter of fact be brought into harmony with the early Christian tradition. Added to this was the use made of his writings by the 'Arian' theologians, and the quite general suspicion aroused against the extremely spiritualizing tendencies of his exegesis and speculation with their various layers, tending to sublimate and evaporate every concrete, historical, and visible element. On the other hand, however, Origen was the real creator of a 'scientific' theology. He was the great systematic Biblical expert and interpreter, on whose immense life-work the following generations lived. In the fourth century the study of his writings and his theology underwent a revival in the East, and thus Jerome was in his early years won over to this master. He saw in him the Doctor of the Church *par excellence*, the like of whom had not been seen since the days of the apostles. Jerome dreamed of an almost complete translation of his works into Latin, and began with the Homilies. During his Roman stay he praised and recommended Origen in enthusiastic terms, and based almost all his own writings on him as the most weighty authority. There is not a word of qualification of his theological authority; on the contrary, the hostility Origen had had to endure from churchmen was to Jerome just an example of the ingratitude of the world, which has always pursued the best with its envy (*Ep.* 33, 5). While Origen was still virtually unknown in the West, this judgement coincided with the conviction of almost all Greek theologians of rank. Only the narrow-minded enemy of all dubious teaching, Epiphanius, Bishop of Salamis, had already declared Origen to be a heretic to be condemned—and with him Jerome had co-operated. At first, however, this produced no repercussions upon his relationship with Origen. The only circles besides this hostile to Origen were in certain monks' colonies in Egypt. The monks felt themselves disturbed in their crude religious notions by his spiritualizing interpretation of the Scripture, but this 'anthropomorphism' was then still despised as a primitive superstition and the patriarchs of Alexandria themselves deemed it important that its adherents should not become too powerful.

The change of position which Jerome made in 393 on the basis of a rather unimportant incident thus appears even more puzzling. Certainly we do not know the background from which a certain Atarbius, otherwise unknown, at that time stepped forward in Palestine and carried on propaganda against Origen. While he was flatly rejected by John, Bishop of Jerusalem, and his friends, he was successful with Jerome in Bethlehem: and the latter was willing without more ado to anathematize all errors of Origen, lock, stock, and barrel. It may be that,

his interests being primarily exegetical and ascetic, he had not
until then considered it necessary to examine more closely the
disputed teachings of the master, and to ponder their theological rightness or wrongness. He had certainly never himself
consented to these false teachings. All the same, this indis-
criminate condemnation, the moment it was demanded from
outside, was irresponsible. Jerome was certainly always anxious
to be seen in the foremost ranks of ecclesiastical orthodoxy and
prone to condemn more or less without examination what was
accounted doubtful, suspicious, and undesirable. To be added
to this is his allegiance to Western presuppositions. He was only
willing to learn from the East academically, not dogmatically.
Jerome hardly imagined what implications this first, and almost
incidental, expression of opinion would have. Later, he explicitly declared that the theological condemnation had by no
means been intended to justify the Philistines who did not read
Origen at all. As a matter of fact, Jerome never ceased to base
his work on Origen, but from now on he necessarily became
increasingly cautious not to refer to him by name, and he no
longer dared to complete the translation of the *Homilies*.

When in the next year the aged Epiphanius visited Palestine,
and unpleasant scenes took place between him and Bishop John
on the question of Origenism, Jerome was already considered
to be his declared partisan. Among the monks at Bethlehem
Epiphanius stormed against the Origenist heresy, and called for
a decision. Here also there were controversies. These disputes
would probably have been forgotten again after a time, had he
not simultaneously undertaken a canonical step which Jerome
welcomed for completely different reasons. Epiphanius ordained
his brother Paulinianus presbyter of the monks of Bethlehem,
in order to make them ecclesiastically independent of the Greek
clergy of the town, and at the same time also of John. By canon
law, this was an affront which the bishop of Jerusalem could
not possibly brook after all that had happened. He refused to
give approval to this encroachment upon his rights, and, when
this did not succeed, changed to means of coercion by barring

access for the unruly monks to the churches of Bethlehem altogether. Jerome now had no alternative, unless he would give
in and admit his guilt, but to transfer the quarrel completely to
the dogmatic field, and to renounce obedience to his bishop
on account of doctrine. He drew up against John a frenzied
pamphlet, in which he presented the case—by no means in
accordance with the truth—as though John, because he had not
permitted the anathematization of the illustrious dead, approved
of all Origen's errors. But, meanwhile, John had turned to
Theophilus, Patriarch of Alexandria, for help and intervention.
The latter substantially took his side, and the government also
threatened Jerome with expulsion on the grounds of continuous disturbance of the peace. Nothing was left to him but
to accept the 'paternal' intervention of Theophilus, and, with
loud praise for his love of peace, and faint complaints about his
'credulity', to reconcile himself again with John (396/397).
That the old relationship was not so easily re-established can be
imagined; yet, fortunately, the discord seemed to have been
resolved outwardly.

The quarrel had another and more intimate and personal
side for Jerome. His old friend and compatriot Rufinus had also
travelled to Palestine, some years before Jerome, likewise
accompanied by a wealthy and aristocratic Roman lady. He
lived in Jerusalem, just like Jerome in Bethlehem, in pursuit of
his ascetic ideals, and the study of Greek theology. However,
when Atarbius appeared, Rufinus behaved very differently
from Jerome. Being an Origenist like him, he at first tried to
keep away from the conflict, and then, when he did not succeed, he came out resolutely on John's side. This firm attitude
must have been all the more embarrassing to Jerome, as a comparison between the two friends was natural. The admiration
which Rufinus reaped from activities similar to those of Jerome
had perhaps already earlier aroused his jealousy. Of course, the
official steps of reconciliation re-established the outward relationship between Rufinus and Jerome, and both friends again
shook hands. Yet, since Rufinus soon afterwards left Palestine

and settled in Rome—Rome which Jerome had left under such unfortunate circumstances!—it is understandable that Jerome's suspicion against a rival barely reconciled to him soon began to stir again. All this constitutes the background for the rapid revival of the unfortunate controversies.

Rufinus had found in Rome, as he thought, the appropriate place to work for the promotion of Greek theological education, and especially for the knowledge of Origen, in the way indeed which Jerome had originally intended, and in a certain way still practised. The Palestinian disputes, however, had meanwhile aroused suspicion against Origen in Rome also. Rufinus tried at first to dispel this by translating the *Apology*, formerly written by Pamphilus and Eusebius in defence of Origen. He then added a revision of *De Principiis* itself, Origen's main systematic work. At the beginning of 398, the two first volumes of the *Beginnings* or *Chief Articles* of the Christian teaching were published for the first time in Latin. Rufinus admittedly proceeded by simply leaving out the dogmatically disputed portions, or by 'supplementing' with orthodox passages from other writings of Origen, a procedure which Jerome in his commentaries largely followed in just the same manner. Rufinus felt himself even more entitled to do this, since he did not consider the questionable passages to be authentic, but— doubtless mistakenly—as later interpolations inserted by the heretics. In the prolegomena to this edition he mentioned, without name, the older and meritorious translation by Jerome which Pope Damasus had formerly sponsored. Since Jerome had meanwhile turned towards other and original projects, Rufinus, urged on by his friends, had now to decide on the continuation of these works despite his own more modest talents. It is not necessary to suspect spite concealed behind these words which are respectful in tone. Rufinus could not very well avoid some mention of the works of his predecessor, and he hardly could have imagined that Jerome would now simply take as tactless any reference to his earlier efforts upon Origen. On the other hand, it is evident that Rufinus with this reference simply

wished to protect himself against the new anti-Origenist sentiment, and the cool tone in which he mentioned his old friend
no longer reveals any trace of the former intimate confidence.
Be that as it may, Jerome, who in this whole matter could not
have had a completely good conscience, felt himself compromised, and he attached the worst construction to Rufinus'
reference, and to the whole work. He took the prolegomena
as a more or less malicious attempt to damage his reputation,
and to cause him new trouble by unwelcome reminiscences of
his former attitude.

Nevertheless, he tried to keep his temper, and his only wish
was if possible not to be connected any more with the regret-
table disputes about Origen. It was the clique of his Roman
friends and associates who first opened the conflict, and who
would have liked to put Rufinus in the prisoner's dock as an
Origenist. The Christian community of Rome had obviously
been split for a long time, and the rival parties were fighting
for influence in the church. After all that had previously
occurred, Jerome, however, could not keep silent for long. If,
as Rufinus maintained, Origen was no heretic, but actually
entirely orthodox, then his own noisy attacks upon John, and
Epiphanius' condemnations which he had translated, were evidently unjust. Such a suspicion he could not let go unchallenged!
Hence, Jerome hastily made a second translation of Origen's *De
Principiis*, complete and literal, which admittedly had no other
purpose than to unmask the author as a notorious heretic. This
made it inevitable that Rufinus' translation and defence appeared unreliable and untrue or at least partial and extremely
questionable when compared with it. A half-hearted concilia-
tory letter written to him by Jerome was intercepted by his
Roman adherents. Rufinus only knew his polemical remarks
from third parties, and must have felt himself attacked with
bias. Threatened from all sides, he on his part now put up a
vigorous resistance. His *Apology* against Jerome expresses the
whole bitterness and indignation he felt at his two-faced attitude. On the one hand, it is charged, Jerome reproaches Rufinus

with his Origenism; he renounces, on the other hand, his own
old love to Origen, and tries to conceal the change of position
which he had quietly made. Rufinus makes a good case in
defence of his method of translation, his personal behaviour,
and his orthodoxy. He no longer shows any consideration
toward Jerome: with painstaking accuracy the unpleasant features of his character, and the contradictions of his statements,
are proved by verbatim quotations. Rufinus is almost completely in the right in his claims. Moreover, his personal honesty is not to be doubted. Yet Jerome was now driven to
extremities: his moral standing was at stake.

Among the many polemical writings composed by Jerome,
the three-volume *Apology* against Rufinus, which did not
originate at a stroke, is the most passionate and spiteful. The
manner in which he hurls at his adversary charges of malicious
intent, conscious lying, and every kind of baseness, is most dis-
pleasing, and shows sufficiently how bad a case he really had.
So is his unvarying prejudice, and the way in which he gets
tied up in his own contradictions and half-truths. It would have
been far better for him to take a stand by the distinction he had
attempted between Origen the exegete and Origen the theological heretic and, in addition, quietly to concede certain
distortions in his own evaluation. But Jerome was incapable of
this. Everything Rufinus had enumerated had to be shown up
as utterly untrue, and his behaviour shown to be determined
entirely by the most sordid motives. Fear for the reputation of
his own orthodoxy now combined with the insulted vanity of
the scholar. The quarrel was theological as well as literary and
personal, and threatened repeatedly to lose itself in mere insignificant corrections, insinuations, and trivialities. Rufinus is
now an ignoramus, with not the slightest idea of how to translate. He is not even able to express himself at all like an educated
person. In his personal life, too, there is not a word to be said
for him. It is simply not true, maintains Jerome, that he ever
had stood up in the church's warfare and suffered for the faith.
Even now this alleged ascetic in reality lives in magnificence

and pleasure. Above all, he is and remains an Origenist, who committed forgeries to protect his heresy, and brings in the most dubious heretics on his side. In the third book, added later, Jerome indignantly rejects Rufinus' olive-branch, and declares further proposals of reconciliations attempted by other parties to be totally unacceptable. So long as the faith is in danger, there would be no peace for him, and least of all would he let himself be intimidated by threats. Jerome wrote letters in all directions, and sent his *Apology* as far as Africa in order to check Rufinus' abominable intrigues, about which, as Augustine disapprovingly informs him, until then nothing had there been heard. Nobody was really interested in this quarrel. The heresies of Origen were still virtually unknown in the West, and Rufinus was the last to attempt to circulate them. When despite this an official condemnation finally took place, it is to be attributed only partly to Jerome's activity. A double change which occurred in the politics of the church as a whole was the decisive thing.

Until the year 400, Theophilus, Patriarch of Alexandria, had protected the Origenists in accordance with his own conviction. He was, however, now confronted with the pressure of the anti-Origenist monks, and was at the same time exposed to serious personal charges raised against him by these monks. This sufficed to cause a complete change of mind. Theophilus condemned Origenism, and since his accusers had turned for help to John Chrysostom, Patriarch of Constantinople, the matter soon attracted further attention. Almost at the same time, a change of pope took place in Rome which also signified a shift in attitude. The deceased Pope Siricius was, as we know, not too well disposed toward Jerome; the new pope, Anastasius, was elected by the opposition, and was also supported by Jerome's friends. So he was readily willing to endorse the condemnation pronounced by Theophilus and compelled the bishops of Milan and Aquileia, to which Rufinus had retreated, to take up the same position. There was no intention to persecute Rufinus personally; Jerome, however, was triumphant at his victory and tried to extend it on all sides. So he put himself in other ways also at the disposal of Theophilus' unscrupulous policy. Even old Epiphanius, who had all along participated in the struggle, finally refused to take part in the intrigues against Chrysostom, yet Jerome did not hesitate to translate into Latin the shocking pamphlet, full of atrocious slanders, which Theophilus had written against Chrysostom. He thereby sided with the mendacious propaganda against one of the purest figures of the old church. His attitude toward Rufinus is similar. The latter had been wise enough not to continue any longer the undignified conflict with such an opponent. For years he peacefully produced his translations of Origen and other literary works, and never again mentioned the name of Jerome. Jerome, by contrast, could never let an opportunity pass without needling anew and complaining about the fat 'grunter', as he calls Rufinus. He was the 'poisonous and dumb beast' like a scorpion, the voluptuous 'Sardanapalus', the wild 'Nero' who outwardly carries himself as a puritanical Cato. With his classically-draped but mean sarcasm his former friend persecuted him even beyond his grave. How far Jerome himself believed in the truth of his invective is difficult to decide. In the bitterness of the controversy he finally lost all feeling of decency and veracity. Disregarding these personal differences which occupied the foreground, the first condemnation of Origenism remains the permanent result of this controversy. However, at first the practical consequences of the official anathema were small. The final proscription of the 'heretic' took place only a century and a half later, at the fifth Ecumenical Council (553). There can undoubtedly be different opinions about the rightness and necessity of this delayed censure—even by the criterion of the dogmatic attitude of the ancient church. For Jerome's agitation, however, there is hardly any real excuse. It was just in the West, which he tried to stir up against Origen, that there was not the slightest ecclesiastical cause for this. The 'danger' of a theological heresy existed only in his head. It was only his own interests, by no means unselfish, his private embarrassments, entanglements, and whims which forced him, almost against his will, to this public polemic and heresy-hunt. Jerome cannot be excused in this case. We can only explain his attitude up to a point in the light of the circumstances, and make it to some extent understandable on the basis of the known facts of his weak character.

The last years of Jerome also were filled with controversy. It is as if he subsequently wished to justify his own behaviour by trying to bring into an artificial connection with Origenism new enemies with whom he had to deal, Pelagius among them. Out of revenge the Pelagians set fire to his monastery in 416. Already before this, however, there were external troubles: the Bedouin of the desert and the turmoil resulting from the beginning of the barbarian invasions were threatening Palestine. Refugees from the West deluged the country, and for a time an escape by sea was even considered. The dangers, however, always passed by. A serious blow for Jerome was Eustochium's death in 419—Paula had died earlier (404). At last his physical strength began to diminish. It is said he had become so weak that he could rise from his bed only by aid of a rope which was fastened to the ceiling beam. Yet his energy was unbroken. His last commentary, on the Prophet Jeremiah, shows no sign of senility; even the continued polemic against Origen's arbitrary allegorism is here well-founded and entirely pertinent. Jerome, now more than seventy years old, was able to carry on his dictation as far as the 32nd chapter. Then he died on September 30, 420 (419?). His bones were buried in Bethlehem. They are supposed to have been brought to Rome in the Middle Ages, but are missing today.

If we wish correctly to understand and classify Jerome's historical significance, we have above all to see and hold to one fact: Jerome was a Westerner, a typical and conscious representative of Latin Christianity. This sounds rather paradoxical in respect to a man who lived the greater part of his life in Greek surroundings, who everywhere carried on propaganda for Greek education, and who became famous primarily as a student and translator of the Greeks. None the less, the man who called himself ironically a 'half-barbarian', and who in distant lands had virtually forgotten his Latin (*Ep.* 50, 2), remained always a *homo Romanus* in nature and purpose (*Ep.* 15, 3). The Greeks were his 'teachers'; but Latin compatriots remained his associates, his friends, and his correspondents. In all Jerome said, wrote, and did, he looked exclusively to the West, and gave his attention to the response he found there. Thus in church politics too he always adhered to the party of the 'right', to the extreme group of Western-oriented old-Niceans who in the East formed a diminishing minority. The problems of theological metaphysics dealt with in the East did not interest or concern him at all. In this, Jerome was far more backward than other Western theologians of his century, like Hilary, Marius Victorinus, Ambrose, or the deacon Chalcidius who had even translated and partly commented on Plato's *Timaeus* for Hosius of Cordova. By nature he was as entirely un-philosophical as any previous Latin theologian, even if he occasionally boasted of his philosophical knowledge: 'What has Aristotle to do with Paul? or Plato with Peter?' (*adv. Pel.* I, 14). His austere moralism, his practical church sense, his real-istic liking for the visible, the actual, and the concrete, his sar-casm and rude wit were also a Western heritage. As theologian, Jerome stuck to his church, to her firm teaching, to the Scripture, and, above all, to the Old Testament. This was completely sufficient for his inner religious life. Yet with a clear view Jerome recognized what his home church lacked, when her modest literature was compared with the rich theological, and above all the exegetical, tradition of the Greek church. Jerome sensed the need for Western Christianity to catch up with the East intellectually, and he summoned all his strength to fulfil this need. The hasty nature of his writings, unbalanced and rushed, can be partly explained by this. He thus imparted to the West a knowledge of the Greek commentaries and homilies. By his own works he aroused scholarly interest in the exposi-tion of the Scripture and acquainted his fellow-countrymen

with the literary, archaeological, and above all, with the linguistic prerequisites for such work. Jerome was, of course, not
the only man to attempt this sort of activity, but he far outdid
all his friends and enemies who were striving for the same goal,
and looked at as a whole completed an imposing life-work.
He gave to Latin Christianity its Bible anew, and provided the
possibilities for further study of its language. Yet one seeks in
vain to find in him solid methodological and theological principles, on the basis of which such research should be conducted.
His own attitude, the perpetual fluctuation in principle, and the
many practical, ecclesiastical, and polemical considerations he
incorporated were not very promising as a theological model.

We do Jerome an injustice if we try to view him as a creative
theologian, as a great teacher of the church, and judge him as
such. In a way it was his misfortune to have been pushed into
this role by the situation of his time and his own convictions.
What kept Jerome all his life bound to his spiritual calling was
his ascetic decision, gained after a painful struggle, and passionately maintained. This ascetic pattern changed his intellectual
world and made him the teacher of an ascetic education, the
theologian of the Holy Scripture. But even in the monk's habit,
he remained himself the late classical scholar and rhetorician,
who with his literary ambition could never get free from himself, and who valued the world and men according to the
success of his own productions. Jerome believed in his ideals,
but his faith remained superficial and never penetrated to the
depths. All his ecclesiastical and theological achievements were
ambiguous and remained problematical in their effect. He
lacked all round the decisive requirement for lasting greatness:
character.

It is different if we evaluate him as a literary figure in the
general history of ideas. Jerome was a successful scholar, the
founder of Western Biblical philology. In his cultural aims,
despite his asceticism, he was almost a humanist. The stimulus
his writings gave to scholarship has had a lasting effect through
the centuries. In their formal skill his letters remain a model of

the elegant art of correspondence, such as the older Christian literature did not yet possess. The whole picture of his personality, never dull, always lively, has made an unforgettable impression upon posterity. Therefore all good humanists, and most humanistically-inclined theologians, have always treasured a measure of friendship for Jerome, in spite of his human limitations.

CHAPTER VI

AUGUSTINE

AUGUSTINE is the only church father who even today remains
an intellectual power. Irrespective of school and denomination
he attracts pagans and Christians, philosophers and theologians
alike by his writings and makes them come to terms with his
intentions and his person. He also has an abiding indirect influence, more or less modified and broken, as a conscious or unconscious tradition in the Western churches, and through them
in the general heritage of culture. It is therefore not easy for the
historian to find the necessary distance and correct criteria for
the study of Augustine. We still stand on the many-fissured
spurs of that mountain-chain, the ridge of which seems almost
to cut off behind us the horizon of church history. If one
approaches it, however, as we do now, from the opposite side,
the impact of the steep height and of the precipitous summit,
of the breadth of intellectual and religious power in this one
figure, so far above all his predecessors, is even more surprising
and, at first sight, overwhelming. The older Western theologians appear, compared with Augustine, small in stature, unproductive, almost insignificant. Yet this impression too is
deceptive, or at least one-sided. On closer examination, one
realizes that the colossal massif is still based upon the old solid
strata of the early Latin church, and that the lesser peaks which
we have so far crossed have often pointed in the direction where
Augustine emerges before us, though still suddenly and independently.

Pre-Augustinian Western Christianity—this has shown itself
time and again—had a fundamentally 'Jewish' character. It was
moral, legalistic, and rigorous. It demanded subjection, it asked

183

for accomplishment, and affirmed ecclesiastical order and discipline. In its earnestness and practical energy it was great, but it dwelt upon the rational consideration of the divine precepts and promises. It lived on the institutions of the past and hope for the future—a religion without a genuine present, without full freedom, and without final dedication and blessedness. It was therefore also lacking in freedom in its relationship toward the natural and the intellectual world. Western asceticism was until Augustine exclusively negative, violently renunciative and defensive in spirit, and the dry rationality of Latin thinking did not tolerate any real philosophy. This means that at the same time it did not tolerate any attempt to come to terms with the spirit of Hellenism, or with the theological vitality of the Greek church. Yet it is obvious that already prior to Augustine this inner seclusion and intellectual inadequacy of Western Christianity had begun to change, so that new vistas were increasingly opened up. Jerome was a straggler of the old brigade, and even he in his own way sensed the necessity of a renewal. With others of his generation, above all with the great Ambrose, a dialogue with Greek theology was already bound up with a deeper understanding of the Biblical proclamation itself. The Old Testament lost its autocratic position, while the individuality of the 'gospel' gleamed and waxed bright. The previous formulation of the anthropological problem, and the old Latin interest in virtue and merit, in forgiveness of sins, penance, and justice, changed meaning in this light. They were united with faith in Christ, and acquired an evangelical direction. The most important symptom of this change was the new interest in Paul's theology which came to have a decisive influence on Ambrose, Marius Victorinus, and the so-called 'Ambrosiaster', sometimes in quite different ways. In the East Paul remained, as with the Gnostics of the second century, primarily the theologian of spiritual and 'mystical' cognition, of speculative enthusiasm, of vision and the purified life. The anti-Judaizing Paul who broke through the law and established 'righteousness by faith' was first discovered by the Western theology of the

grace

fourth century, and never again lost. In Augustine's theology of grace this movement reached its climax, and found a formulation valid for a long time. The period which followed varied in its attitude to his Paulinism; only the Reformation went beyond the Augustinian understanding of Paul, and to that extent in a fundamental sense beyond Augustine himself.

Augustine was a genius—the only father of the church who can claim without question this pretentious title of modern personality-rating. All attempts to find some explanation of the greatness of this man from his milieu, from his intellectual heritage, or from his undoubtedly extraordinary natural talents lead nowhere. Augustine developed more than others. This ability to develop, i.e. to take up new ideas, to change and remould himself, was perhaps the most essential requisite of what he became. His own story and this inner capability he himself understood as no natural gift, nor as his own accomplishment, but as the work of divine grace, and of the inward and outward guidance which was granted him. We will not attempt to analyse his 'nature' in this introduction, but proceed immediately to follow the course of his life, and to mention briefly the accomplishments in which his actions and his 'nature' found expression.

divine grace

Augustine's background—his ancestry, environment and the first stages of his career—is reminiscent of Jerome. Augustine also came from a middle-class, perhaps even a lower middle-class, provincial milieu. He was born on November 13, 354, in Thagaste, a small town with a veneer of Roman culture, in which nevertheless the national Berber traditions were still strong. To outward view, his youth appears banally commonplace. What his family and he himself strove for was rapid advancement, wealth, and reputation. For this reason, the gifted son had to receive the best possible education, yet the circumstances were more straitened and depressed than they were for the son of a notable from Strido, who hardly ever knew serious financial problems. Patricius, Augustine's father, must have been the descendant of some Roman veteran who

had been settled in what is now Algeria, in the interior close to
the Tunisian border. He was a member of the city-council of
Thagaste, and possessed a vineyard and a small competence; but
it was not sufficient to enable his oldest son, who had finished
his schooling in the neighbouring Madaura, to continue his
studies in Carthage. A friendly patron and relative, Romanianus, had to assist. Patricius probably thought of making his son
a lawyer, but Augustine decided to enter the more intellectual,
and, so to speak, 'academic' career of a professional rhetorician.
The ideal created by the Greek Sophists, and transplanted by
Cicero on to Roman soil, of the rhetorician who had mastered
language and classical literature was still central in the idea of
those who cared for culture and general education. Though
rhetoric had long ago forfeited its old political power, and had
become a purely literary activity, its cultivation, which was then
restricted to a small stratum of urban society, was still a part of
public and political life. The intellectual content of its rhythmic
and vocal devices, of its arrangements, definitions, and ety-
mologies, of its dialectic and polemical dexterity, seems to us
today chilly, formal, and wearisome. Nevertheless, this school
developed and refined both the ear and grammatical sensitivity,
with the result that it offered the most attractive possibilities to
a man like Augustine, of linguistic talent and artistic ability.
With his gifts he was quickly able to attain rhetorical self-
assurance, and soon became a master. At nineteen Augustine
became a teacher of rhetoric in his native town, in the following
year in Carthage, the capital, and rapid advance continued
during the decade following. Augustine was well on the way
to becoming a celebrity in his department. He took his calling
seriously, finding it hard to bear the crudity of his students
when they disturbed his lectures with their ill-manners and
only assimilated what he wanted to teach them superficially, if
at all. He could, nevertheless, be satisfied with his successes. In
383 he was called to Rome, where the intellectual conditions
were more propitious. Here he was upset only by the fact that
the students, though listening diligently, absented themselves

from classes at the end of the term, and 'forgot' to pay their
fees. To Augustine this was by no means of secondary importance. He was consumed by a burning intellectual ambition, and
wished to become renowned and admired for his abilities; but
he also wanted to become wealthy, and dreamed then of an
aristocratic marriage, to complete the happiness of his position.
For the time being he contented himself with a concubine for
the satisfaction of his desires and of his need for more intimate
companionship, and this kept him from grosser excesses.
Augustine was faithful to his mistress for fifteen years, and the
words with which he remembered her love and faithfulness
even as an elderly man and a bishop indicate that this irregular
association really meant much to him, although he passed over
her name in silence. Before he was 18 years old she bore to him
a wonderfully gifted boy, as Augustine assures us, who received
the name Adeodatus, 'given by God'. He remained until his
early death the joy and happiness of his father, and this relationship was in no way changed by their joint conversion to a strict
Christian view of life.

Unlike Jerome, Augustine did not interrupt his secular career
prematurely, but pursued it to the climax. But with him the
change signified much more than the more or less arbitrary
result of a moral decision; it prepared for itself gradually, and
progressively and irresistibly made itself known. This, at any
rate, is how Augustine himself later saw and described his youth.
Parallel with the external history of rise and success ran a history
of his inner life which lay beneath the surface and often almost
disappeared, but pushed up and emerged again and again, finally seizing upon his entire existence to give it a new meaning.
Augustine has described this development in his *Confessions*, and
interpreted it as the secret action and guidance of the ever-
victorious divine grace. The *Confessions* are not an autobio-
graphy in the modern sense, but a new, extremely personal,
kind of work of edification, composed with high literary
aspirations and written in the appropriate style. Nevertheless,
it is not fiction. Augustine expressly maintained that the book

was to contain exclusively, and even in detail, nothing but the truth, and wherever we are able to test it, this claim proves to be justified. Mistakes have no bearing on this, and the light in which his own past is seen in retrospect is no deception, but an interpretative unlocking of his life by him who knew it best. Once its purpose is understood we can safely trust ourselves to the guidance of this book. In any event, there is no other, better guide.

Unlike Jerome, Augustine did not stem from the pagan Balkans, with their lack of traditions, but from the soil of Africa, soaked for centuries with the blood of Christians, the only Latin-Christian region which had long possessed an intellectual profile and, in addition, a distinct ecclesiastical individuality. Already in childhood he knew what living Christianity was in the person of his mother Monica, the only one 'not to be imagined as absent' from his development (Guardini). Augustine has depicted her personality in the *Confessions* with tender love, and even reported many trivial features of her life; yet he has not really idealized her. Monica is essentially nothing more than the wife of a typical bourgeois, herself the product of a country-town, intellectually alert yet without higher education, practical and gentle yet at the same time full of womanly energy and determination whenever she wished to follow her motherly instinct and religious conviction. Devoted love for her eldest son became her fate. Only in her care for him and for his eternal salvation, did she rise to true inner greatness and complete freedom. Up to his conversion Augustine's history can be understood, as it was by him, as a story of mother and son, of their indissoluble relationship persisting despite every alienation until they finally came together in the faith. It was a faith which Monica had confessed from the beginning, and affirmed vicariously for her son throughout, while Augustine came to it only late, by long travels and laborious détours. Yet in a certain sense, he was always a Christian. Monica had already taught him to pray in his childhood, and had made him familiar with the customs and practices of the Christians. Augustine could never efface these early impressions, and they had not only to

do with externals. The Bible was all along a holy book to him,
and, according to his own testimony, he had already with his
mother's milk sucked in and preserved the name of the Saviour
so intensely that nothing could really delight him later that was
deprived of this name (*Conf.* III, 4, 8). As Augustine the child
desired baptism when he had indigestion, or prayed that he
would not be beaten in school, so also in later life praying was
a natural thing to him. Yet all this lost its importance at the
beginning of his manhood; Augustine no longer took either
the faith of his childhood or his mother's complaints and reproaches seriously. As a student he plunged into a whirlpool of
love affairs and would like to appear a little more shameless than
he actually was. He began to work intellectually and make
progress, and in this he saw the meaning and content of his life.

The first time this attitude was shaken, it was the result of an
intellectual experience, not through a person, but through a
book. In the same way Augustine's further stages of development were never to occur without some new intellectual perception which then brought in motion his whole personal life
and activity. The curriculum of his studies led Augustine to the
reading of the *Hortensius*—a dialogue, lost today, in which the
ageing Cicero called his readers away from political rhetoric to
philosophy. Philosophy alone was able to make life meaningful,
to make death gentle, and to prepare the soul to pass over to
immortality. The effect on Augustine was striking. In contrast
to the great variety of opinions of the various schools, as he
considered philosophy to be until then, for the first time the
seriousness of the one object of life, the Real and Whole which
is wisdom, dawned on him. 'Suddenly every vain hope became
worthless to me, and with an incredible warmth of heart I
yearned for an immortality of wisdom', and thus I, continued
Augustine, 'began now to arise that I might return to thee'
(*Conf.* III, 4, 7; LCC, 7, 65). This is not a later, reflective interpretation: according to his own testimony, Augustine was
only disappointed by the fact that there was not to be found
any word about Christ in Cicero, and the first effect of this

experience, which was shattering in both its philosophical and its religious effects, was that he reached for the Bible, and began to read it seriously. But the attempt failed. Its words seemed unpalatable, 'unworthy to be compared with the dignity of Tully (Cicero)' (*Conf.* III, 5, 9). We might think we were listening to the young Jerome! At this moment, the spiritually inexperienced and helpless Augustine needed personal guidance and living fellowship. Among his acquaintances up to now he was unable to find it, and hence he soon joined a sect widespread among the intelligentsia of Carthage and also elsewhere: he became a Manichean.

This fellowship, founded by the Persian Mani in the third century, was the last great religious creation of the East between Christianity and Islam. It rejected Judaism and the Old Testament, but had accepted Christ among its forerunners, and in the West claimed to be a higher and spiritualized form of Christianity itself. This was how Manicheism appeared to Augustine too. Always prohibited and suppressed in the Roman empire, its conventicles were thereby surrounded by the attraction of secrecy and mystery. The basic teaching was a rigorous dualism. In Manichean mythology the present world was considered to be an outcome of an original fall, of a fatal mixture of light and darkness. The souls of men were only dispersed sparks of the one divine substance of light, which require to be rescued and liberated from the dark imprisonment of their corporeality. This bringing together and leading home of the elements of light was understood as the real redemption of men, and of God himself. A total separation, attempted by all sorts of fantastic methods, will finally bring about the end of the world, and the consummation of all that is light into the unity of light. The practical implications of this message of salvation could only be a strict asceticism. Yet only the very few set foot on this radical way; these were the elect and perfect. Augustine was satisfied with being a mere 'hearer', i.e. to remain like the majority a member of the broader fellowship, with few commitments. They were fully aware of the value of their new acquisition, and treated the young rhetorician with the greatest politeness. The tragic analysis of his own incompleteness and weakness, the possibility nevertheless of rising up above them intellectually, and the enchantment of the services of common worship, with their psalms and hymns, their liturgical confessions and utterances, all this appeared to Augustine as release and exaltation over mundane everyday activity. It appeared as the true religion glorifying ordinary life. Soon he himself was active as leader and missionary: under his influence his pupil, the son of Romanianus, and he himself became members of the Manicheans, and his relationship to his mother, who was almost at the point of despair over this development, became increasingly unhappy. She could not think of following her son in his new way, and irritated him by her unshakable hope that she would yet see him one day return to her in the haven of the Catholic church. Monica had been a widow for some years, but continuous life with Augustine proved impossible in these circumstances. Temporarily he moved into the house of his patron, Romanianus.

It is a question how far Augustine ever accepted Manicheism without reservation. Its aesthetic and emotional attractions, and its fantastic proclamations and promises could not in the long run cover up the inner difficulties of the system. Augustine was no half-educated enthusiast. He demanded clarity and closely reasoned thought. Instead of the primitive prejudices and superstitions of ecclesiastical Christianity, he had expected to find in Manicheism, as it promised, a real, spiritually-based outlook. Now question after question emerged to which it gave no convincing answer. By this time, 'at twenty-six or twenty-seven', Augustine published his first study, *On Beauty and Propriety*. It seems that he here sought to relate himself to the Manichean metaphysics; but this work, which was soon lost (in his later years it was not available even to him), was already truly Augustinian with respect to the topic and posing of the problem. The nature of beauty remained for Augustine at all times a genuine metaphysical problem, and even then it drove him beyond the consideration of mere appearance. Everything that

metaphysics

is appropriate to its purpose is appropriate only in relation to
something other than its 'purpose'. The beautiful, however, is
beautiful through itself. It is spiritual and thereby lies beyond
the visible, corporeal world. Yet what is spirit and spiritual
truth itself? The materialistic thought of the Manichean metaphysics of light could not solve this problem. Besides, there were
the contradictions of its cosmic and astronomical theories.
These philosophical and scientific objections remained unsolved.
For a long time, the Manicheans consoled Augustine with the
prospect of the visit of Faustus, a bishop with a reputation for
great learning. When at last he came, he proved to be an amiable, rhetorically educated cipher. All that remained was a
fundamental disappointment, which occasioned an increasing
alienation from the sect, and a hopeless discontent with his own
intellectual situation and condition. Augustine now occupied
himself with astrological writings which, on close examination,
likewise turned out to be empty. Finally he came upon the
literature of Scepticism. The denial in principle of any certainty
of knowledge seemed to him the most honest attitude open to
us. But this attitude is really one of despair. Augustine decided
to pray no longer; he forced himself into the sceptical attitude,
against which his whole nature rebelled. The truth he sought
in his sceptical broodings was in reality no theoretical matter
at all: Augustine was looking for a secure centre of gravity, the
basis and meaning of his life itself, and he was unable to find it.
He never actually doubted that there was this saving truth. It
was only that access to it seemed to be forever barred to human
reason. Basically Augustine was still looking for the truth which
he had known as a child: he wanted to obtain knowledge about
God, about divine providence, and judgement, and about his
own immortality, and he felt that all this had now become unattainable to him as an intellectual possession. His life no longer
had any direction, and drifted along. The picture of his mood
may have been painted unduly dark in the *Confessions*. At all
events, it is certain that Augustine suffered as a result of his
unsettled state of mind, and all outward successes offered no

effective solace for these secret troubles.

In the autumn of 384 Augustine reached Milan, with a recommendation from the city prefect Symmachus, and thus he
came to the imperial residence itself. When leaving Africa, he
had meanly deceived his mother: he wanted to be rid of her,
and had departed secretly. Now she followed him to Milan. He
restored their life together, and peace was re-established. The
victim of this reconciliation was Augustine's mistress. Monica
succeeded in having her dismissed, a step which seemed justified
in view of a future marriage, and which in any case had to be
undertaken some time (to marry a concubine was entirely
impossible for legal reasons). Yet Augustine suffered under
this separation: 'My heart which clung to her was torn and
wounded till it bled' (*Conf.* VI, 15, 25; *LCC*, 7, 132). While the
girl, who returned to Africa, remained faithful to him all her
life, Augustine presently took into his house a new concubine,
as though in defiance of his mother. He himself felt this con-
cession to his sensuality to be disgraceful, but he could not resist.
Monica was also obviously unable to help in his deeper spiritual
miseries. The same was true of his friends who loved and admired him, but whom he knew only too well not to be his
equals. Augustine felt frustrated and wretched. A brief scene,
described in the *Confessions* with extreme artistry, reveals his
mood. Augustine was entrusted with the delivery of a panegyric upon the emperor (Valentinian II) at a festive occasion.
Full of uneasiness and stage-fright on the evening before, he
took a walk with his friends through the suburbs. There, a
drunken beggar got in their way, and launched forth into foolish jokes and seemed to feel extremely merry in this. The sight
overwhelmed Augustine. 'What do all our plans and ambitions
mean?', he exclaimed. 'By them we only increase our miserable
burden, which we have to carry in any case! We do not want
anything else but to be happy, after all. The beggar has
achieved it: and we perhaps never shall!' Yet this temperamental
outburst had no results. Augustine went on living in the old
way and, inwardly unsatisfied, continued 'to be greedy for

honours, money, and matrimony' (*Conf.* VI, 6, 9).

Milan brought Augustine more than reconciliation with his mother and new professional successes. The church and Catholic Christianity, which he thought he knew from infancy, met him here in a new form which surprised him, impressed him, and finally urged him to a decision. The decisive thing was the personality of the great Ambrose. Augustine himself describes to us how he first wanted to get to know the famous preacher as a rhetorician, and attended his sermons for this reason alone. But soon the preaching fascinated him also by its content. Augustine realized with astonishment how the seeming absurdities and 'old wives' fables' of the Bible could be understood in their deeper meaning by the allegorical interpretation, and that a powerful and comprehensive idea of God, the world, and man became visible behind the anthropomorphic statements and the apparently primitive ideas of the texts. So Christianity was a spiritual reality which evidently had something to say not only to uneducated and childish spirits; and it was at the same time the reality of an actual fellowship which could lay hold of, transform, and determine men. In his undivided devotion to the service of the church, and in the impact and composure of his commanding appearance, Ambrose appeared the antitype of Augustine, the problem-ridden intellectual, who was still undecided and immature, uncommitted and yet dependent in so many ways. Nevertheless, he was also a person of rank, whom Augustine had to regard as an intellectual equal, indeed, an entirely new experience to him, his superior. In his figure the authority of the church was embodied, firmly established beyond arbitrary opinions and sceptical objections, and demanding that one accept and obey her teaching as the truth of God. With this claim she could face an intellectual test and hold her own under a critical judgement. Augustine still hesitated to give complete assent to her claims; such a *salto mortale* into faith would have appeared to him as capricious and irresponsible. But he slowly began once again to draw near to the church, and decided to remain in the wait-

ing class of catechumens until such time as 'something certain
should shine forth' to him, by which he could then finally
direct his way (*Conf.* V, 14, 25). Several times he tried to speak
to Ambrose personally. There were no external difficulties
about this; for, in spite of his countless duties, Ambrose never
locked his door, and anybody could visit him without announcement. Yet one knew that actually he had not time. Every time
Augustine found the bishop so deeply absorbed in his work and
his books that he did not dare to disturb him, and after a period
of silent waiting returned home unsuccessfully. The pious
Monica, however, had met the great man some time ago. She
realized very well the inner crisis of her son and followed it with
intense hope. Perhaps this was a reason why Augustine could
not overcome his final hesitation regarding Ambrose. Or was
he perhaps afraid that the busy pastor of the congregation would
not consider and understand his complex doubts and anxieties
as carefully and personally as seemed to himself desirable and
necessary? Once Augustine turned to Ambrose's old teacher,
the priest Simplician, who aptly referred him to the example of
the Neo-Platonic philosopher Marius Victorinus. The latter had
sacrificed his teaching appointment and publicly confessed
Christ in the time of the Julian reaction, and had then become
an important theologian.

This was the time of Ambrose's fight against the Arian policy
of the empress Justina. The whole city was excited and sided
with its bishop. But it is characteristic how superficially these
events are mentioned in the *Confessions*. They constitute only
the shadowy background of the real history of his soul, which
for Augustine went on entirely in the inner sphere of responsible knowledge and spiritual decision. At that time, he began
to study Neo-Platonic philosophy, from which Ambrose also
was not far. He read the writings of Porphyry, and above all of
Plotinus, in Victorinus' Latin translation, and the knowledge he
encountered here released him from the intellectual blind alley
in which he had remained for so long a time. It brought him
all at once into the open air! Here finally the difficulties of his

conception of spirit and of God were really solved. God in his infinitude and perfection cannot be thought of at all as long as he is imagined materially, be it as a spiritual substance, as with Tertullian, or as a substance of light, as in the view of the Manicheans. The transcendent reality of the spiritual lies beyond all natural analogies. Spirit is not 'the abstract', but rather appears as the essence of all which is sensible and real, from which one has to proceed philosophically. In contradistinction to God, the world is not original, but derived, restricted, and virtually unreal. The problem of evil which distressed Augustine finds a corresponding solution. This too has no original, indeed, strictly speaking, no real substance at all. It exists only in the estrangement from the good and true. It is the destruction of sensible reality. Actually it appears only negatively in relation to real being as its perversion and deprivation. Neo–Platonism had changed these Platonic notions in an increasingly religious direction. God is the origin and goal of all that is true. He is the eternal One who reflects and 'reveals' Himself in many ways, but never Himself enters into this manifold existence, nor is He to be found in it. True philosophy therefore calls man to contemplation and conversion. It calls him to step outside to an intellectual transcendence of the multiplicity of the phenomenal world, to cognition and experience of God in His unity, beyond the limits of the finite. In adopting these ideas, Augustine certainly felt himself to be only at the beginning of his intellectual and philosophical journey; but his sceptical helplessness, his doubt-ridden absorption in the temporary and transitory, were now overcome. There is an attainable truth of God, the possession of which would make 'life precious and death gentle'. As formerly after reading the *Hortensius*, Augustine now without more ado understood this truth also in a Christian sense. Again he had recourse to the Bible, and what once had failed seemed now to succeed. The Bible spoke to his heart. Above all Paul confirmed the one great truth of pagan philosophy as the revealed truth of God. But he offered at the same time more than this. He not only testified to the transcendent superiority of the Absolute. By speaking also of Christ, and of God's active redemptive participation in history and, on the part of man, of the spiritual necessity to respond to this God in humility, repentance, and new dedication, he testified also to the personal gracious will of the merciful Creator.

Augustine was now confronted with a personal decision: he must change his life, and reform it to meet the new Christian demand. This seemed to be possible only by a determined break with all these previous ties which for so long a time had disgusted him, and which he considered basically vain and sordid. As long as the truth was still half-hidden, it was comparatively easy to evade the decision. Where could he hope to find the books, the helpers, and the time to go deeply into the new? Was it really necessary to make the break now, just at the moment when he had at last reached the point where he might at any moment obtain perhaps a governorship, or some other profitable and distinguished office, and perhaps make an advantageous marriage? We can see how the choice one way or the other had come to a crisis demanding a radical and ascetic decision. The striving for a career and human admiration, the desire to become rich, the sensuality which could not be held in check even for a short time, in fact, the whole of Augustine's manner of life contradicted with its empty activity both the Christian and the philosophical ideals. There was no third solution or middle course, which would allow him to do justice simultaneously to studies and to women, to outward advancement and to inner truth. Again and again this was considered by Augustine, and time and again rejected as half-hearted.

The development which ensued is described by him in detail, in a stylized form certainly, yet with an incomparable truth of psychological observation. We cannot reproduce the whole story in full; it is known to every reader of the *Confessions*. 'Thus with the baggage of the world I was sweetly burdened, as one in slumber, and my musings on thee were like the efforts of those who desire to awake, but who are still overpowered with drowsiness and fall back into deep slumber. And as no one wishes to sleep forever (for all men rightly count waking better)—yet a man will usually defer shaking off his drowsiness when there is a heavy lethargy in his limbs; and he is glad to sleep on even when his reason disapproves, and the hour for rising has struck—so was I assured that it was much better for me to give myself up to thy love than to go on yielding myself to my own lust. Thy love satisfied and vanquished me; my lust pleased and fettered me. I had no answer to thy calling to me, "Awake, thou that sleepest, and arise from the dead, and Christ shall give thee light" (Eph. v. 14). On all sides, thou didst show me that thy words are true, and I, convicted by the truth, had nothing at all to reply but the drawling and drowsy words: "Presently; see, presently. Leave me alone a little while." But "presently, presently", had no present; and my "leave me alone a little while" went on for a long while' (*Conf.* VIII, 5, 12; *LCC*, 7, 165). The difficulties did not exist any more in the intellectual realm, where they once had lain. The moral demand, also, appeared to be clear. God had 'encircled' Augustine from all sides, as he expressed it; yet the last, decisive change of will could not be forced—it was still lacking. Evidently, Augustine himself was now looking for a solution, but only an impulse from without, the definite example and model of a conversion, brought him the decision.

One day, an African compatriot, a high official named Ponticianus, visited him on some occasion Augustine had later forgotten. He found Paul's epistles lying on Augustine's card-table and showed his surprise at finding a Christian brother in a professor of rhetoric. He thereupon told him about Anthony, the first 'monk', whose biography, then translated into Latin, was at that time beginning to cause a stir in the West. It was still unknown to Augustine, who was impressed by the fact that such a renunciation of the world was possible not only in the remote past but even now in the present, 'in our time so to speak'. But Anthony did not remain an isolated case. The conversation turned to contemporary monks, and the guest said that he had recently been witness in Trèves when two of his

acquaintances found Anthony's 'life' in the cell of a monk, and
then without more ado had renounced their promising careers
in order to direct their heart from now on to heaven. (This
description perfectly matches Jerome and his friend Bonosus,
who had been converted in Trèves in the seventies of the fourth
century in just this way). Ponticianus, however, had returned
with tears in his eyes to the imperial palace, in order to drag out
his life in the usual secular way. This report shook Augustine.
He thought he saw his own fate before his eyes, and 'while the
man continued his narrative' it seemed to him as though he
himself 'was taken from behind his back', and unwillingly
forced to look himself in the face (*Conf.* VIII, 7, 16). When
Ponticianus had left, and only his friend Alypius stayed, he
burst out, highly excited, into furious self-accusations: 'What
did you hear?' he shouted at Alypius. 'The uninstructed start
up and take the kingdom of heaven by force, and we—with
all our learning but so little heart—see where we wallow in flesh
and blood!' (*Conf.* VIII, 8, 19; *LCC*, 7, 170). Augustine left the
room and dashed into the adjacent garden, of which the friends
enjoyed the use. Here, struggling step by step forward, he
fought the last 'frantic' battle 'between me and myself'. The
dreadful tension finally relaxed into a 'flood of tears': Augustine left the faithful Alypius alone and threw himself sobbing
under a fig-tree. 'Suddenly I heard the voice of a boy or a girl
—I know not which—coming from the neighbouring house,
chanting over and over again the same words, "Take up and
read! Take up and read!" (*tolle, lege; tolle, lege*).' Augustine
came to himself and began to think earnestly whether he had
ever heard anything like this, whether there was perhaps a
children's game with such a jingle; but this was not the case.
Thus he decided to take the words as a heavenly challenge. For
the third time Augustine had recourse to the Bible at a decisive
moment,—i.e. the copy of the Pauline letters left with Alypius.
He was resolved, according to Anthony's example, to accept the
first text he laid eyes upon as the ultimate order for his life. He
chanced—in the middle of a sentence—upon a passage in the

epistle to the Romans (xiii. 13 f.), which he read not aloud, but like Ambrose 'silently' for himself: '. . . not in rioting and drunkenness, not in chambering and wantonness, not in strife and envying, but put on the Lord Jesus Christ, and make no provision for the flesh to fulfil the lust thereof' (*Conf.* VIII, 12, 29; *LCC*, 7, 175 f.). This was the text which spoke to his condition. Augustine read no further, but simply gave the book without a word to Alypius, who read on at the marked place, and humbly referred to himself the following passage 'Him that is weak in faith receive'. He too was now ready to enter the new Christian way at the leading of his friend.

Now, everything was decided. The thunderstorm had passed, and radiant joy spread abroad. Both hurried to Monica, who jubilantly learned the good news. Augustine wished to avoid a public sensation. Since the vintage holiday was near at hand, he finished his teaching work. Then he pretended to have a 'chest-complaint'—it seems to have been a harmless bronchial catarrh—in order to resign from his office. Next a friend and colleague placed at his disposal a charming country estate, protected from the wind, the *rus Cassiciacum* (Casságo?) south of Lake Como, where he could spend the vacation with his mother, his son, some friends and students, and where he could breathe freely. After half a year, they returned to Milan, where together with Adeodatus, Augustine was baptized by Ambrose on Easter Eve of the year 387. Now Milan could offer nothing more. The little family decided to travel back to their native-land, together with a young fellow-countryman, who had also been converted, and to settle down there. The time of searching was over, a new period of life began.

What was the meaning to Augustine himself of this conversion, and what is its actual content and significance? The first answer is clearly laid down in Augustine's confession and report. It must neither be effaced nor softened down. Augustine was not converted from paganism to Christianity or from unbelief to faith, nor from philosophy to theology and from intellectual license to the authority of the church. Rather was he converted from worldliness to a new, a really Christian course of life. After a long and hard struggle, he renounced marriage and pleasure, money, glory, and the admiration of men. All this counted from now on as worthless, vain, and hollow. The breaking with his promising career and resignation from his former life were the essential signs of this change. As was frequently the case in those times, baptism was the seal of a decision already accomplished, and also outwardly marked the start of a new life. So far, Augustine's 'conversion' bears a practical character, and has an unequivocally ascetic meaning. Nevertheless, Augustine did not think of becoming a monk, and retreating as a hermit to the desert or cave. The life of the cloister under ecclesiastical supervision, as it had just been commenced at Milan, was also out of the question. He became a follower of Anthony only with regard to his absolute, total break with the former life. What Augustine actually desired was a quiet, 'philosophical' life with friends, outwardly frugal and withdrawn, dedicated exclusively to God and to the search for true knowledge. To that extent, it was to be also a life of intellectual work. Even in Cassiciacum Augustine began, as a matter of course, to engage in philosophical writing, after having until then—apart from that unimportant little tract—exclusively taught and worked by word of mouth. These first dialogues, composed according to the tradition of the schools, also describe the idyllic surroundings in which they were conducted and recorded. We are almost reminded of the garden discussions and 'Platonic' academies of the Renaissance. Monica took charge of the household, the men only occasionally doing a little gardening. Everyone had leisure for contemplation and private studies. The communal conversations occasionally began early in the morning, but usually only in the afternoon or toward evening, in bad weather in a bath-house, otherwise in the open air on the lawn in the shadow of a beautiful old tree. The proceedings were vivacious, at times even gay. Occasionally, Monica interjected a word, and was then admired by all for her 'wisdom' and religious understanding. Augustine of course took charge; he remained the guiding professor in the new milieu also. As before, they read and discussed the classical authors and poets, the beloved Virgil for choice; but essential philosophical problems had now become decisive, dealt with primarily in connection with Cicero. It was no accident that Augustine sought to direct his friends particularly to the *Hortensius*. The questions with which he had struggled so ardently himself occupied the central place: the problem was that of the possibility and certainty of knowledge of the truth, the problem of real happiness, of providence and God's world order, and of the immortality of the soul.

Coming from the *Confessions*, one is surprised at the academic and wholly unenthusiastic spirit of these early writings. It is remarkable what a secondary place the expressly Christian elements occupy, but, on closer examination, one realizes that they nevertheless always constitute the background and are not emphasized more strongly partly because the dialogues are composed on the classical model. The 'oracles' of the Bible are authoritative to all who are present. The words of 'our priest', namely Ambrose, are remembered, and Augustine is happy now to subscribe to the same 'philosophy' to the summit of which Monica had long ago climbed. The dialogues were interrupted by the chanting of hymns and common prayers. A welcome supplement to the dialogues are the *Soliloquies*, Augustine's 'monologues' with his soul, a peculiarly interesting early form of the later *Confessions*. Here the newly converted man, after a solemn prayer to God, undertakes a self-examination of the stage attained in his inner life. He confesses that certain temptations could still exert a dangerous power upon him, that his heart in particular still clung too much to certain who were dear to him. Yet he now lived ascetically; wealth and honours, matrimony and sensual enjoyments were no longer any serious enticement to him. In this early work comes the famous definition of his intellectual aim: 'God and the soul, I desire to know.' —Nothing more?—Absolutely nothing' (*Solil.* I, 2, 7).

At first sight, the sociological picture of the circle of friends

and scholars at Cassiciacum reminds one of the ideal life that
Jerome also longed for after his conversion, and later realized
in a more monastic form. But the new element lies in the intellectual aim of this ascetic community. To be sure, Scripture
study and common devotions, the main thing for Jerome alongside ascetic exercises, were also by no means neglected by
Augustine; but the philosophical search for the truth, the question about 'God and the soul,' has now become decisive. The
answer was sought and found in a truly 'maieutical' conversation. Augustine's dialogues were no lectures in dialogue form.
In this respect, they were something new and unique in
Christian literature. Philosophy, despised by the older Westerners and still suspect to Jerome, now flowed as a broad stream
into the church and into Christianity. Until that time, it had
remained an almost exclusively Greek interest in the West; in
Augustine's Latin dialogues it found for the first time a con-
spicuous recognition and acceptance. It was the Neo-Platonic
philosophy, amalgamated with older elements of the Aristotelian ontology and of the Stoic-Ciceronian academic tradition.
According to Augustine, the Platonists alone have reached the
climax of cognition of that truth which leads immediately to
the threshold of the Christian and Biblical revelation, and which
can be perfected in the Christian theology as the true philosophy. In this he is thinking primarily of the central position of
the conception of God, which he, as a Christian, always understood in the strictly theistic sense, and affirmed in his practical
and personal dedication. God, from whom everything proceeds, the knowledge and acceptance of God's thoughts and of
His eternal truth,—that is the real meaning and content of any
true life. The longing for religious fulfilment, aroused by Manicheism, found its intellectual clarification and perfection in the
similar striving of Neo-Platonism, as understood in a Christian
sense. The conceptions of divine light, of purification, and of
ascent have lost their half-mythological, hollow, materialistic
meaning and are elevated, in the spirit of Platonic dialectics,
completely into the sphere of the spirit. Augustine was no mystic

and no pantheist. He knew no immediate 'ecstatic' absorption in the divine being, yet his enthusiastic feeling of dedication to the knowledge of God, to the submission and elevation of man to Him remained unaltered, lively, and strong. It was as though this dedication were only purified by philosophical thinking, and gained further warmth, depth, and moral responsibility to the extent that it was permeated by Christian, and especially Pauline and Johannine, thoughts. The philosophical religion had become personal. It was no longer a matter of intellectual knowledge for its own sake, but of satisfaction of the inner longing of the heart for the living God, of dependence on Him in faith, hope, and love. On his path of exuberant longing, Augustine broke through beyond all things created to immediate life in God. The peace which was to be purchased by the overcoming of all worldly desires realized itself in a calm rest in God.

Yet this final religious goal also cannot be understood apart from the presuppositions of Neo-Platonic spiritualism. The traditional ascetic decision won a new and permanent significance and power in Augustine's life. From now on, asceticism changed the nature of its demand, as compared with the early Western view, and attained a deeper spiritual function. The meritorious or disciplinary meaning of the demand for individual ascetic acts diminished, and no longer interested Augustine for its own sake. Asceticism now meant the basic attitude of the life of devotion itself. It was the practical presupposition of the ascent toward truth and God, and so gained a positive meaning. As the overcoming of the 'world', with its sensuality and diversions, asceticism was, as it were, only the reverse side of spiritual contemplation and dedication to God. 'This was the whole matter,' the *Confessions* run, 'not to want what I wanted, but to want what thou didst want.' With this the 'doing without all sweet trifles' all at once became 'sweet' itself (*Conf.* IX, 1, 1). He who wishes to live entirely with God gladly renounces worldly desires. To be sure, he will use the good things of this world, but he must not wish to 'enjoy' them, that is to say, to love and desire them for their own sake. The older Augustine became, the greater the determination with which he emphasized that creation was not evil as such, even the material creation and the bodily nature of man. Rather as God's gifts were they good, and to be affirmed in their proper place. But his world-renouncing idealism sought to transcend and abandon this modest, provisional acceptance of their value as rapidly as possible. Setting aside all external acts of renunciation, Augustine remained an ascetic by nature and innermost volition. He always understood the Christian commandment of obedient love to God, and the total surrender of his own self as a demand to overcome the lower world and its sensuality altogether, and to rise to the spiritual realm of eternal and pure being. Here only did God encounter him in his full perfection.

This peculiarity stamped Augustine's entire theology and ethics, and imposed its idealistic philosophical character on his thinking even when he was interpreting the Scripture. This is particularly evident, for instance, in his aesthetics, especially in his theory of music (for the rhetorician thirsty for beauty had hardly any independent interest in the fine arts). The mathematical laws of harmony and beauty reflect the eternal order of the world of ideas, i.e. the thoughts of God. Everything depends on this, and the real goal therefore is not to experience 'phenomenal freedom', but on the contrary to leave the sensual appearance behind and to enjoy 'beauty itself at its source'. But Augustine also interpreted the highest values of friendship and love ascetically and theocentrically, in accordance with the hierarchical grading of the philosophical doctrine of goods. The final goal of all love is God. Love for one's neighbour is not co-ordinated with love to God, as originally in Christ's double commandment, but is only an emanation and effect of love to God, derived from it and bound to it. It is therefore 'true' and really desirable only when included in the movement of the soul to God and experienced as part of love to Him. This is the explanation of the convert's coolness with which Augustine, for instance, spoke of his pagan father, who was baptized only

shortly before his death, or the passionate intensity with which
he attempted to win over to the ascetic life his patron Romanianus, and Romanianus' son—and likewise the silent indifference
with which he ignored both after this attempt had failed. This
breach of human contact is the more striking, as Augustine by
nature possessed a strong need for fellowship, had many friends
at every period of his life, and was in his way almost a virtuoso
in friendship, as his letters prove. It is not really surprising in
view of his times, surroundings, and personal development that
he accounted the entire sphere of the erotic, in which he himself was at home for so long a time, merely as 'sensuality', not
prohibited within permitted limits, to be sure, but to be elimi-
nated from his life, and from the lives of all the fully converted.
Nevertheless the ascetic curtailment of life can be felt here too.

The question has often been put, how the Christian and Neo-
Platonic elements are really related to one another in his conversion, and how the influence of the two forces is to be differentiated. In his old age, Augustine himself retracted the exuberant
praise of Plato (and Cicero) found in his early works (*Retr.* I,
1, 4), and already in the *Confessions* (VII, 9, 13 ff.) he had
emphasized clearly enough, besides what he owes to the *Books
of the Platonists*, also what was missing there and was found to
be missing in comparison with revelation. The Platonists have
in truth known of God's transcendence, the dependence of the
soul upon His light, and even the glory of the Son existing in
the substance of the Father. Nevertheless they did not know of
the really redeeming event of Christ's incarnation, of His death
for us, or of the whole loving and active descent of God into
the world, and of His active mercy, which falls only to the lot
of the humble and poor, not to the proud and wise. They did
not know the way by which they could really have reached the
goal of their striving. It is not to be assumed that Augustine,
who had already found Christ's name missing in the *Hortensius*, and who let himself be led from Plotinus to Paul without
further ado, only discovered all this long after his conversion.
The question of Christian and Neo-Platonic elements is mean-

ingful only when we analyse the early and later writings of
Augustine from this point of view. As a biographical question
it is scarcely to be answered, and basically the question is probably wrongly formulated. The truth which Augustine believed
he had found philosophically was immediately understood by
him as a confirmation and recovery of the faith of his childhood,
which had never been lost completely. In so far as it was the
truth, it was for him identical with the revealed Biblical truth.
It thus actually led him back to the Bible and the Catholic church.
What Augustine experienced had been learned in a similar way,
though less decisively and consciously, by Marius Victorinus,
Simplicianus, and Ambrose before him. Neo-Platonism in other
ways too was the force which broke through the Judaistic
narrowness of the old Latin Christianity, overcame its legalistic
moralism and primitive rationalism with its teaching on the
Spirit and God, and opened the way from an Old Testament to
a New Testament Christianity. Augustine, who in his thinking
was more of a real philosopher than his predecessors, also surpassed them in his appropriation of this 'evangelical' element,
that which is genuinely Christian in Christianity. The imperfect
expression in his younger days of the purely Christian element,
and his criticism in old age of the Neo-Platonic element, do
nothing to alter the continuous movement of his life which
turned the Christian Neo-Platonist into the Biblical theologian,
who, however, never ceased even then to be a Platonist and a
philosopher. The loftiest testimonial to this are his *Confessions*,
which are the prayerful recording of his former life by Augustine himself, and form the ultimate interpretation of his life and
his conversion, as testimony to the undeserved guidance and
unfathomable grace that come from the almighty God.

Today, the *Confessions* are the best-known of Augustine's
writings, and it is understandable that they have always aroused
interest, particularly for their autobiographical material. They
were written in 397–398, more than a decade after the occurrences at Milan. It was the criticism of opponents who reproached Augustine for his Manichean past which made the

occasion for their composition. The structure of the work itself is surprising, and retains an element of the enigmatic, despite all the interpretations which have been attempted. Of thirteen books in all, nine deal with the course of Augustine's life until his departure from Italy, one with the mode of new life he had finally attained, and three offer a speculative interpretation of the account of creation at the beginning of the Bible. The main part of the book is powerful confession, a testimony to scrupulous self-examination, and to intense and acute self-criticism. At the same time there is no sign of torture or despair in this, because it is accompanied by the perpetual praise of God's mercy which in spite of all did not forsake his life, but precisely by the experience of sin and guilt brought him through hidden ways to the knowledge of salvation, and to the peace of forgiveness. He who confesses his sins, Augustine considers, must always accompany this confession with the praise of God. Only then is he 'pious' in a Christian sense, 'when it happens not in despair, but in appeal to God's mercy' (*Enarr. Ps.* xciv. 4). Therefore, a 'sublime peace' covers all. The impression this book leaves 'can be compared to the impression we get when after a dark, rainy day, the sun finally again prevails, and a pleasant sunbeam brightens the damp land' (Harnack). It is the ultimate truth which is to be acknowledged in a wholly personal manner, not even sparing the most intimate facts. Both the moving effect of this book, and the offence it again and again gives to more reserved modern feeling, consist precisely in this. Are such literary confessions, such self-revelations, really possible at all? The undeniable art and occasional artificiality of the highly developed form have increased this suspicion. Is not this still the old rhetorician, speaking with self-reflecting vanity? Can such an exaggerated feeling of sin be genuine, such a self-description and self-exposure be true at all? Augustine has anticipated this criticism. 'What is it to me . . . that men should hear my confessions. . . . People are curious to know the lives of others, but slow to correct their own. . . . And how can they tell when they hear what I say about myself whether I speak the truth, since no man knows what is in a man "save the spirit of man which is in him"' (I Cor. ii. 11) (*Conf* X, 3, 3; *LCC*, 7, 202)? By their very nature, such confessions have to be made before God, and this explains the almost voluminous character of the whole work. It is one single uninterrupted prayer, a laying out of reflections and reminiscences before Him who has created this whole life, and holds it in His hands from start to finish. Nevertheless, people shall hear this prayer, for its purpose is to thank God for the guidance of his own life, and in this way to praise Him and to glorify His name. In conformity with the language of the Latin Bible, the title of the work, *Confessiones*, has to be understood first of all as 'praises'; yet the praise and glorification of God here occur precisely in the 'confessions' which Augustine makes about his life, his sins, and the experiences of his faith.

This theme of the book is indicated from the very beginning. '"Great art thou, O Lord, and greatly to be praised (Ps. cxlv. 3); great is thy power, and infinite is thy wisdom" (Ps. cxlvii. 5). And man desires to praise thee, for he is a part of thy creation; he bears his mortality about with him, and carries the evidence of his sin and proof that thou dost resist the proud (I Peter v. 5). Still he desires to praise thee, this man who is only a small part of thy creation. Thou hast prompted him that he should delight to praise thee, for thou hast made us for thyself and restless is our heart until it comes to rest in thee' (*Conf*. I, 1, 1; *LCC*, 7, 31). The starting-point, purport, and goal of human existence is indicated by the mysterious way in which man is surrounded by a God who creates and sustains everything, and to whom man is personally allowed to turn after having once found him in this earthly life. It requires a special skill to describe how this human will, which seems to make itself independent and go its own way, free from God, must nevertheless again and again fit in with God's higher guidance and plans, encounter His call, and finally yield humbly to His unfathomable omnipotence. 'Man's confession is man's humility; God's mercy is God's majesty' (*in Joh.* 14, 5). A peculiar fascination of the narrative, which occurs nowhere else in Augustine, comes from the direct amalgamation of Biblical quotations, particularly of words from the Psalms, in his prayer. They flash up afresh, lively and bright, as never before in his usage. The strange Biblical illustrations and phrases deepen the classical eloquence, and attach to the clear and perspicuous rhetoric a mysterious, as it were exotic, charm. Much misunderstanding and dislike of the *Confessions* is due to the reading of translations. The text cannot be translated. The sentences, always clear, mostly concise, only occasionally of a more elaborate structure, have a firm and pure sound in the original language. In their 'Romanesque' beauty they have a well-formed and musical effect. In translation, on the other hand, they easily become inflated and stilted, their emotion is wearisome and at times almost boring and sentimental. One is tempted to forget that the author of the *Confessions* was an ancient thinker skilled in expression, and far from being a modern Pietist.

The *Confessions* were intended by Augustine as what they have been accounted throughout the centuries: a book of devotion. 'When they are read and heard, they stir up the heart . . .' (*Conf.* X, 3, 4). Countless Christians have recognized their own spiritual lives, and their own destinies before God, in the story of this life, and of that unique Augustinian ego. A mere biography could never have effected this. Herein the book proves its inner breadth and depth, and the peculiar combination of its personal and objective elements which constitute its theological uniqueness. With the *Confessions* there begins a new period in the history of human self-consciousness, of psychological understanding and anthropology. A relationship is established between man in his real nature and God, and so with an infinite being outside man himself. This means that the old, 'classical' uniformity of the conception of man has been abandoned. In the presence of God and of his real definition man becomes aware of his 'unreality' and hopeless disunity. The old definition of man as a rational being hampered only by some insignificant sensual 'passions' is transcended. Here are

exposed the strange limits of freedom in the decisive realm of
the will itself, the mysterious complexity of human nature to
the very frontier of the unconscious. In so far as in his life and
time man is encountered by God, and finds or loses his salvation, the whole area of history is seen as the decisive anthropological dimension. All this, of course, not proclaimed by
Augustine as a new teaching. He is surprisingly conservative in
all academic matters, and the new ideas appear as though spontaneously in the contemplation of his life and himself, and are
then developed, to his own philosophical amazement, in the
grand reflections on self-consciousness, memory, and the nature
of time. By the way in which the problem of time is seen as a
theological problem of God's creation the two main parts of the
book are linked together.

The biographical part of the *Confessions* ends with Monica's
death in Ostia, shortly before the proposed return to Africa.
The last great conversation between mother and son concludes
with anticipation of the joy to be found in the eternal blessedness of perfection, completely filled with the experience of God.
It is one of the high points of the whole work in which in a
wonderful manner the ultimate hope of the Christians permeates the Neo-Platonic vision of the One. Augustine himself
admits that he had not exactly used 'the very words' in his
report, but vouches once again for the full material accuracy of
his account. This accords with the circumstance that in this
passage, as almost everywhere in the *Confessions*, Christ is not
mentioned. Monica knew she had reached the goal of her life:
'There was indeed one thing for which I wished to tarry a little
in this life, and that was that I might see you a Catholic Christian before I died. My God hath answered this more than
abundantly, so that I see you now made his servant and spurn-
ing all earthly happiness. What more am I to do here?' (*Conf.*
IX, 10, 26; *LCC*, 7, 194).

When he arrived in Thagaste, Augustine tried to live as he
had done in Cassiciacum. With a circle of studious friends, he
made his home a refuge of the monastic and contemplative life.

They renounced all private property, and established themselves in permanent community. Augustine remained the intellectual leader of the circle: 'When the brethren saw that I had time they put different questions to me'. The answers were immediately written down, as had already been done in Cassiciacum, and were later worked up into a book (*Retr.* I, 25, 1). As previously, the problems were still mostly those of the philosophy of religion: on the nature of the soul and happiness, on the origin of evil, the knowledge of truth and suchlike questions. Augustine himself, however, now began to give his work a more definite direction, whereby it assumed a momentous significance for the church. After his repudiation of academic scepticism, he began to settle matters with the still extremely active Manichean sect. This task impelled Augustine to study the Bible more intensively, especially the Old Testament, which the Manicheans repudiated. Controversy with his former fellow-believers occupied Augustine for decades, and was occasionally not without embarrassment to him. On the whole, it did not benefit him personally. It was merely a problem which earlier he had touched upon lightly, but which was now to be treated thoroughly, and which remained important beyond its immediate occasion. The basic meaning and necessity of faith compared with fully conscious knowledge had to be clarified and justified. The catch-word of Manichean propaganda ran that it 'would be absurd to believe without reasonable grounds' (*Util. Cred.* 14, 31). The charge was that while the Catholics let themselves be intimidated and seduced by sheer authority, the Manicheans were able to convince all-comers on clear rational principles of the truth of their teaching. This was indeed a somewhat ludicrous pretension, and Augustine, who had experience of this very matter, did not miss his chance of tearing to pieces the theosophic nonsense of the Manichean speculation and explanation of the world. It was important to demonstrate that the demand for faith both prior to and along with perceptual knowledge was by no means absurd, but was rather entirely reasonable and unavoidable. It was therefore com-

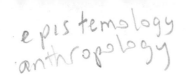

pletely in order, and was indeed necessary for salvation, that the Catholic church should above all demand faith from those turning toward Christianity. In consequence, authority precedes independent cognition.

In spite of the apologetic aim, it would be entirely wrong to see in these thoughts of Augustine an apologetic invention, devised in the interest of the church. With him they had already been formulated earlier in complete independence of any ecclesiastical purpose, and they cohered with his philosophical epistemology and anthropology. 'Faith' in this connection contained no specifically religious meaning. It denoted at first simply the acceptance of an opinion or piece of information, for the time being unverifiable, passed on by another and better informed person. Such a thing happens constantly, and quite rationally. If we were to maintain the standpoint of accepting only that which we ourselves had experienced and completely apprehended, no human life or community could exist. The result would be general and frightful chaos. Besides this, it is precisely true wisdom that is not available to any man from the beginning. He must first find it and come to know it, and this is only possible by joining those who already possess it, and by first listening trustfully to it. To be sure, everything depends on meeting with the right mediator of the truth, with Christ, who is God's Wisdom itself, and this takes place by the assistance of the church which testifies to Him on the ground of those Scriptures which themselves testify to Him. Both Scripture and church are endowed by God with such obvious privileges—Augustine is thinking here of the proof from prophecy and miracles, and of the Catholic universality and the apostolic succession—that it by no means runs counter to reason to put confidence in their leadership, and, for the time being, to 'believe' what the church authoritatively proclaims. It is perhaps possible in exceptional cases to see the truth without her mediation. There may be a stage of knowledge which renders sheer faith dispensable. In Augustine's early period such questions remained open, but most men would quite certainly never attain to the truth without authority, and to him who knows the truth it does no harm if he nevertheless joins the church, and acknowledges the sure way which she is willing to show to all, in keeping with her commission.

This whole way of thinking now underwent an essential deepening, so soon as Augustine dropped the initial and purely theoretical conception of faith, and, following the Bible, applied it no more to single truths, but to God who has revealed Christ as the truth. Faith thus received an existential character, and was joined essentially with love and hope. 'Faith' now means accepting with the will, and 'loving', as much as it does affirming. Only by this attitude can the living truth be experienced and 'known' at all, and it is known the more, the more intensively a man binds and dedicates himself to it. In order to know the truth, one must be open to the truth, and increase in purity and goodness, and not vice versa, as abstract intellectualism has at all times maintained. For this, Augustine time and again refers to Isaiah vii. 9 in his Latin Bible: 'Unless ye believe, ye shall not understand'. 'If thou art not able to understand, believe, that thou mayest understand'; to that extent, faith precedes knowledge (*Serm.* 118, 1). On the other hand, we must always already know something of an object, that is to say, we must have learned from the 'authority' of others, in order to be able to believe in it at all, and 'if we did not have rational souls, we could not believe' (*Ep.* 120, 3; *LPNF*, 6, 465). Faith and knowledge are continuously interwoven. One must therefore comprehend the Word of God in order to believe, and believe in order to comprehend. This does not mean that faith, as the Middle Ages tried to make it, is turned into an inferior form of knowledge. Augustine is not thinking of any kind of ability to know, but of an inner 'assent', which is the willingness and openness of dedication, without which experience of 'truth' is not possible at all. In contrast to an abstract epistemological theory, Augustine understands faith as an act of volition of the whole personality which, when it is a matter of a man's own being and his own 'truth', can never be detached from his

ethical powers and his personal attitude to God and the Good.
When in this context Augustine speaks of the church, it does
not imply that her authority is a substitute for the perception of
truth, but that she is the leader and way in which one comes to
the truth. She is at the same time the place at which truth has to
prove itself, and where it is to be exercised in love, because
God's truth leads us into fellowship, whereas in arrogant self-
sufficiency it perishes. 'Thy truth is neither mine nor His nor
anyone else's; but it belongs to all of us whom thou hast openly
called to have it in common; and thou hast warned us not to
hold on to it as our own special property, for if we do we lose
it. For if anyone arrogates to himself what thou hast bestowed
on all to enjoy, and if he desires something for his own that
belongs to all, he is forced away from what is common to all
to what is, indeed, his very own—that is, from truth to falsehood' (*Conf.* XII, 25, 34; *LCC*, 7, 290).

The new ascetic and theological writer swiftly attracted
attention in his home town. Despite his secluded life, people
increasingly turned to him in spiritual and at times even in
purely secular matters. Understandably, his friends felt such disturbances to be unwelcome; Augustine himself suffered under
the burden, but considered it his duty not to refuse advice whenever it was sought. Occasionally he had even to decide to travel
overland. Then he carefully avoided places in which the bishop's
see was vacant. As always, there was a certain shortage of really
competent men, i.e. theologically educated, and powerful in
preaching. Augustine could naturally be regarded as suiting the
episcopal office better than others, but he preferred independence. There might be, he wrote to a friend, churchmen who
succeed in sustaining inner peace amidst the storms of daily
work in the congregation, but to him it would be impossible.
'Believe me, I need complete detachment from the tumult of
transient things' (*Ep.* 10, 2). Only in this way did he think he
could remain faithful to the real truth. In the spring of 391,
Augustine stopped in the northern seaport of Hippo Rhegius,
where he hoped to win a friend for his ascetic community, and

went to divine worship there. He did not know that the local bishop Valerius, a Greek by birth, had for a long time been looking for an assistant who could help him with his Latin sermons. As he now again uttered his old lament, some men noticed Augustine in the congregation and dragged him, on a sudden impulse, to the front. The man was found! Augustine must be ordained priest, and henceforth take over the preaching. When they realized his consternation they presently added that they would surely make him bishop later. All reluctance, all desperate resistance was in vain. Valerius laid his hands upon Augustine, accommodated him in a house with a garden near the cathedral, and ordered him to begin his service at once. The only thing Augustine could secure was a leave of absence for a few months in which, as he said, he wished to strengthen himself for his new office with prayer 'and by the remedies of the Holy Scripture'. Augustine did not deny that he knew the Christian doctrines of salvation, and affirmed them personally without any reservation; but he did not know as yet 'how to communicate them to other people'. For this he expected, as at all turning-points of his life, advice and assistance from the Bible (*Ep.* 21, 3 f.). Then he began his new activity without fear, and worked out his first sermons and catechetical instruction. These found an immediate response. In the Africa of that day it was quite unusual for an ordinary priest to preach instead of the bishop, but soon he attended synods also, and arranged disputations with dissentients. Five years after his appointment, the ageing Valerius consecrated him joint-bishop—despite Augustine's misgivings this was then still possible—and when soon afterwards he died, Augustine became his successor as had been foreseen.

We must not doubt that the tears which Augustine tried vainly to suppress at his ordination really came from his heart. The surrender of his previous ideal life appeared to him as a sacrifice, and even as a punishment for his sins. He knew why he had been of a resolution never to return to the disturbances of a public office. 'Yet the Lord laughed at me and wanted to show me by reality itself what I really am' (*Ep.* 21, 2). 'A slave must not contradict his master' (*Serm.* 355, 2): Augustine submitted himself to his destiny without joy. The former possibility that he might do philosophical and theological work entirely according to his own plan and wishes, and free from any external obligation, was gone once for all. The countless duties of a bishop henceforth occupied him day in, day out. There was no more leave of absence. Augustine intended to be a conscientious bishop, and remained such for thirty-five years until his death. Hippo Rhegius, the modern Bône, which lies a little farther to the north, was no quiet country town, but the most populous city of the province of Numidia, second in importance only to Carthage. There were several churches, chapels of the martyrs, other church buildings, and pagan temples, a circus and a theatre. The schismatic Donatists were stronger than the Catholics, and moreover, there were other sects as well, while a considerable percentage of the population was still non-Christian. There were controversies and quarrels with all of these. The Catholic congregation itself was not undivided, and contained great contrasts, from the poor Berber or Punic-speaking inhabitants of the dock-side to the luxurious villas of the ruling class. For all of them, the bishop had to be available—he was indeed not only preacher and counsellor, but, in accordance with the system of the time, also judge, advocate, and representative of the people. The ecclesiastical interests dealt with here had little to do with the problems which had previously occupied Augustine. Quarrels, gossip, and sordid intrigues were an everyday occurrence. Augustine's consecration as bishop had almost fallen through because his opponents had spread abroad the rumour that he had provided a wife with a love-potion for adultery (in reality it was the usual gift of consecrated bread). In addition, there were the cares of the neighbourhood, and of the whole church. Soon from all sides they turned to Augustine for help. Countless times we find him travelling to councils and meetings in Carthage and other places. His correspondence went overseas into almost all the provinces of the empire. He was, however, already dead when the imperial invitation to the great Council of 431 summoned him to Ephesus.

We may be indignant when we see how much time and effort he had to spend in settling trivial quarrels, bringing to reason pugnacious theologians, or discussing all sorts of problems brought up from outside. It cannot be denied too that the permanent strain of his ecclesiastical duties had an effect upon his nature. In the course of the years, Augustine became less kind and versatile, dogmatically more rigid, ecclesiastically sterner and more 'Catholic'. But pressing duties and advancing years always change a man. All things considered, however, the ministry gave Augustine much more than it took. Indeed, only in his office and by his service to the church did he really become the man he was. Despite his great ability as an organizer, Augustine was by nature no pure theoretician, who takes up problems and solutions without a personal stimulus, and pursues them for their own sake. In spite of their dry academic form, his first attempts at a philosophical theology were already concerned with questions decisive for his personal development, for Augustine was trying to assure himself intellectually of his new way. The refutation of the Manicheans can be seen from the same point of view. Now he was finished with himself and his past. Should he spend the strength now released simply in spiritual service in untroubled peace, surrounded by a small circle of friends who readily followed him, and explore 'the truth'? This was obviously Augustine's own desire—the desire of a writer and philosopher who appreciates the value of intellectual activity, and therefore feels his need for a peaceful life to be fully justified, and defends it with ascetic and devotional arguments. But even before his election, the duties which came along unbidden drew him gently beyond the self-drawn circle, while his sudden appointment had the effect of a second life-changing conversion, which at first he did not want and hardly understood. The work of a bishop, the endless and difficult tasks in the service of the Catholic church, brought Augustine back to real life, and led his intellect increasingly to real and historically pressing questions which had to be decided in everyday life, and for this very reason had to be answered seriously. Augustine did not succumb to these things: he mastered them. And the unity of life and spirit which he had found for his personal existence thus appears even deeper and greater in the broad realm of the church, for which he must speak and teach.

At first sight, it seems almost impossible to imagine how Augustine could manage to remain uninterruptedly busy with intellectual problems amidst the current business of the ecclesiastical office. He wrote an extraordinarily large number of letters, sermons, essays, and some voluminous theological treatises. Most of his literary work was done while he was a bishop. Augustine himself was surprised when he realized at the end of his life that he had published 93 'works' or 232 'books' (there were in fact even more); and already his pupil and biographer Possidius gave it as his opinion that in all probability no one person could read them all. To be sure, Augustine was no modern scholar in his method of working, and also no historical polymath like Jerome. He conceived his ideas rapidly and independently, while their formulation caused no trouble at all to a trained speaker. The books (often several at the same time) were dictated directly to his amanuenses. Nevertheless Augustine loathed carelessness. He certainly did not extemporize his writings, but considered them carefully and subsequently revised them many times and emended the text. He made eager use himself of the church library of Hippo, which grew swiftly under his supervision, and even as an elderly bishop set about refreshing and improving his knowledge of Greek. Among Augustine's works there are of course some dry and rather flat pieces, but they are few. As a rule, one recognizes him at once by the vigour, directness, and relevance of his clear train of thought. Even when he must occasionally become more detailed and unfold material on a broader basis, one never gets lost. Augustine always knew why and to what end he was writing. His ideas at times digressed, but they never became detached; they always remain in the context, for they are

related to the great realm of truth, which as such is God's truth
and the truth of the Christian church. This was to him a personal help: 'When I am bowed down under my load, I am
equally lifted up by your love' (*Ep.* 101, 1; *FC*, 10, 144). Even
on the highest peaks of intellectual life, Augustine did not live
for himself alone, and the miserably depressing daily round
remained meaningful because it was the daily round of Christ's
body. This ultimate unity of his life-work is the secret of his
never tiring creative power.

He who wishes to know Augustine in this unity of his
spiritual activity must read his sermons. Particularly in the
original tongue they are still readable today, and grip the reader
not only as documents of church and cultural history, but also
immediately by their form and spiritual content. Like Ambrose,
Augustine preached regularly, and his sermons were similarly
in part written down as books; but the revision with respect
to style and subject was more intensive than with Ambrose.
So he began his episcopate with an exposition of the psalms
which originated partly from sermons actually delivered, partly
from exegetical notes. The famous work on the Gospel of John
originated later in a similar fashion. But we still have any
number of Augustine's sermons in their original form—as they
were written down in the church service, or as they were dictated subsequently by Augustine himself. Before the service
Augustine made no notes, but only prepared for his exposition
with prayer and meditation—*orator antequam dictor* (*de Doctr.*
IV, 15, 32). Depending on the occasion, time, and audience, the
sermons were entirely different. The speaker, Augustine thinks,
must not bring a ready-made idea along, but must continuously
have an eye to his hearers, and according to how well they
understand him, must either proceed or repeat in other words
what has already been said. The essential thing is that his sermon
reach the congregation, i.e. be heard with understanding, joy,
and obedience. In order not to tire it must not be too long—
after all, the hearers must stand whereas the bishop may sit!
Above all, it must be clear and really lead to the word of the

Bible. This last is the crucial point: even more important than popularity is the demand for substance and relevance, and from this point of view the whole ancient attitude toward speech underwent a basic revision. True, the sermon also is a rhetorical task, and Augustine seldom neglected to embellish it and make it more attractive by impressive antitheses, pleasantly constructed rhythms, and an occasional sparkling play on words or rhyme. Yet this cultivation of style becomes evil so soon as it becomes the main concern, and detracts attention from the content, on which everything depends. One might learn from Cyprian, Augustine thinks, 'how sound Christian teaching restrains the tongue from rhetorical excess, and places it under the discipline of a more dignified and moderate eloquence' (*de Doctr.* IV, 14, 31). Anyone who tries to see Augustine as only an artificial orator has not understood him, or has applied a wrong criterion. One must compare the old Augustine with the young, the preacher with the writer of letters, and compare him above all with his contemporaries. Then one realizes the extent of the self-training to which he has subjected himself, and one understands the power to rejuvenate language which he as well as others derived especially from his regular preaching. Augustine did not create the style of the Latin sermon, but he perfected it, and became the accepted model for future generations.

Besides, despite its short sentences, its direct intelligibility, and its closeness to life, the language Augustine uses in his sermons is by no means 'popular', and is not meant to be. When he rejected exaggerated purism he was thinking primarily of the Latin Bible, with its various linguistic oddities. With the word of the Bible he did not find fault. Moreover, the charm of his style lies in the very fact that the simplicity at which it aims is not based upon helplessness. The driest sentences Augustine composed still display something of the character of 'shot silk which, however folded, always glistens somewhere' (v.d. Meer). In content, too, what Augustine offered never sank below his level. He had the rare gift, arising

from inner freedom and sureness, of saying the deepest things
intelligibly, the complicated simply, and never being banal even
with what is simple. Undoubtedly the concise train of thought
in his sermons occasionally demands much of his hearers, and
must certainly have been above the heads of a part of the congregation. But they always led back to the spiritual possession
common to all, and appealed not in vain to the charity which
dwells in the congregation, and connects all its members. In his
handbook on *Christian Learning*, with which we will deal later,
Augustine himself expounded his teaching on homiletics. With
his charming little book *On the Instruction of Simple People* he
also composed the first book on catechetics. In spite of this he
confessed to being 'almost always' discontented with his own
achievements. 'I desire my hearers to understand everything as
I understand it; and I feel that my words are not achieving it.'
This is primarily due to the fact, as he explains in a mood of
philosophical reflection, that an intellectual perception flashes
up like lightning and is then complete, whereas its expression
in words and syllables always has to pass through a long and
laborious process. Yet the preacher may take solace in the knowledge that experience shows that the hearers often feel themselves edified even when he himself is distressed by a feeling of
failure (*Cat. Rud.* 2, 3; *ACW*, 2, 15).

Even as a priest Augustine personally maintained the ascetic
mode of life. On the estate assigned to him a cloister (*monasterium*) was immediately built. Some of his friends from Thagaste moved into it. The number of residents increased swiftly.
In part they travelled from afar, but the majority came from the
common people. The former pronouncedly 'intellectual' character of the community was thus changed. Admission was not
denied even to the illiterate, only they had then to be instructed
in reading and writing. Augustine had to emphasize more than
previously his own position as prior of the monastery, and firm
rules were issued. The rule composed by him is the oldest
Western monastic rule; even Benedict of Nursia knew it. When
Augustine was promoted to the bishopric, he had to entrust the

prior's office to another, and himself to move into the bishop's
palace. The crowd of visitors and guests he received, invited,
and often had to put up would have disturbed the monastic
peace too severely. Yet Augustine did not wish to give up his
ideal, so he now asked his clergy to live with him. All the clergy
of the town under his leadership founded a *vita communis*, and
everyone newly elected had henceforth to pledge himself also
to join it. Otherwise he would not be ordained. Such an order
had occasionally been attempted in Italy and Gaul even prior to
Augustine, but it is a question how far he knew anything about
these precursors. In any event, Augustine's 'clergy-house'
(*monasterium clericorum*) served as a model for the future. In
Africa this institution was at the same time a kind of nursery for
bishops. Priests called for service abroad rapidly made the new
order known, and in medieval times all cathedral and collegiate
chapters were based on Augustine's rule. In the priestly monastery, the manual work which Augustine highly esteemed in
general had to give way to the activity of the cure of souls, yet
the spirit of fellowship and of intimate association of all was not
to suffer in consequence. 'The first goal of your fellowship is
to live together in concord and to have one heart and soul in
God' (*Regula*, I, 1). Its model is the primitive community as
described in Acts (iv. 32). Intention is the decisive factor, not
ascetic achievement as such, the spirit and not the organization. The set order of the day, the hours for meals and prayers,
only mark out the framework. True charity does not treat all
and everything alike; rather it knows to take into account individual differences and needs. Only one demand was inflexible
for Augustine: there must be total poverty. Where this commandment was violated, he took ruthless measures. As a fixed
rule he himself gave away or sold every donation presented to
him; he would be ashamed, says he, to wear a better garb than
the rest of his brethren (*Serm.* 356, 13). 'We desire to live
according to the manner of the apostles' (*Regula*, I, 4).

The monastic community realizes what the Christian congregation should be: a fellowship of perfect love. In that way it

will serve as a model to the congregation; it is the outstanding
portion of the whole, as it were the hem of the Lord's garments
(*Enarr. Ps.* cxxxii. 9). Isolated disappointments occasioned no
change with regard to this. Augustine confessed that even
though he 'hardly found any men better than those who have
done well in the monasteries', it was also the case that many of
those who had 'broken into' the cloisters belonged to the worst
kind he has ever known (*Ep.* 78, 9). In principle, all monks in
the clergy-house should be willing to serve in the congregation.
The tension must be endured between the contemplative and
the active ideal of life, which Augustine himself had experienced so painfully. We must be Mary and Martha at the same
time, must love God and our neighbour equally. This last
tension will be resolved only in the life to come: 'It is love of
truth that prompts the search for holy leisure (*otium sanctum*),
while it is the compulsion of love that makes men undertake
a righteous activity in affairs. If this burden is not placed upon
us, we should use our freedom to discern and contemplate
truth; but if it is placed upon us it must be accepted because of
this compulsion of love. But even so, delight in truth is not to
be wholly abandoned, lest when that satisfaction is denied, the
compulsion in question may crush us' (*Civ. D.* XIX, 19; *LCL*,
VI, 205).

Philosophical activity in the strict sense now took a back
place in Augustine's writings. His work was directed towards
the understanding, exposition, and proclaiming of the Bible.
Criticism of the philosophers, their vanity and 'arrogance',
grew sharper. The positive significance of their assertions was
now seldom mentioned. But this impression might be deceptive. Augustine avoided direct reference to the works of the
philosophers; after having once found the full, unrestricted, and
infallible truth in the Bible, he did not need them any more.
Nevertheless, he did not cease even as a theologian from being
a philosopher. Augustine knew neither the medieval grading
nor the modern separation of theology and philosophy. To him
there is but one truth, which has shown itself to the pagan

philosophers imperfectly and to the Christians perfectly in Christ. If this Christian truth is to be understood, intellectually adopted, and confirmed, he has no hesitation in turning, consciously or unconsciously, back to the modes of thinking and logical laws, to the conceptions, expressions and traditions he had learned from Cicero, Aristotle, and the 'Platonists', which have there proved to be right. The most imposing outcome of this attitude is his *Fifteen Books on the Trinity*. He began them in 399 'as a young man' and did not conclude them until twenty years later 'as an old man' (*Ep.* 174). Even the external structure shows the concern of Augustine: after the first eight books have presented the Biblical teaching on the Trinity as such, its scientific, i.e. logical and metaphysical, justification and foundation follow in an even more voluminous second part. Without knowledge of the Neo-Platonic teaching on God, and of other findings of ancient philosophy, it cannot be understood.

In this attempt to treat the Trinity philosophically, Augustine had had a forerunner in the West. He was Marius Victorinus, the pagan philosopher who had become Christian, in whose translation Augustine came to know the writings of Plotinus. The starting-point for the philosophical interpretation of the dogma was Plotinus' teaching regarding the self-emanation of the deity, which had already led in his teaching to a kind of 'trinity', expressly differentiated from the further world of inferior spiritual realities. Nevertheless, it always remained difficult to prove from these Neo-Platonic presuppositions the 'unity' and 'equality' of the three divine entities, on which now everything depended theologically. At this point Victorinus still stood in a direct front against the Arians, whose power had since been crushed. In complete calm Augustine now brought the debate to a conclusion. The manner in which he assimilated and corrected the philosophical ideas has nothing to do with a merely external or forced accommodation to the needs of the situation. On the basis of an outline of the Christian teaching Augustine was trying once again independently to think over the correlations of the system, and to bring them

On
Trinity)

to a conclusion. In careful accomplishment of his design and in precise treatment of over-subtle conceptions, he may have fallen below the standard of his philosophical teachers. His researches, nevertheless, have their own proper importance, and under the pressure of his new concern were repeatedly advanced to new logical understanding. When in contrast to the classical and static definition of spirit and the divine perfection, as consisting in the conception of pure vision, Augustine, taking Victorinus further, began to stress the dynamic and volitional aspects of 'love' for the life of the Trinity, this was certainly also due to the special nature of the Christian and Biblical impulse.

Augustine approached the doctrine of the Trinity not by way of its historical origin—the sending of the 'Son of God' in the flesh, and the experience of the 'Spirit' in the primitive Christian congregation—he started off, as did the whole theology of the early church, 'philosophically' with the eternal being of the Godhead in itself. He was aware, more than were his predecessors, and above all more than the Greek theologians, that the mystery of the Deity transcends all imagination, and that any attempt to comprehend it conceptually of necessity therefore retains something of the symbolic. This gives him a certain broadmindedness and freedom compared with other attempts at comprehension. Yet, on the other hand, the new spiritual philosophy of the 'Platonists' permitted him in fact to overcome certain weaknesses of the older, materialistic picture-language, and to define things more appropriately than hitherto, yet at the same time not, as so often happens, to be satisfied with sheer assertion. According to Augustine, it belongs to the nature of the spiritual itself that it has a 'trinitarian' character, that it appears in a threefold form and is in itself such. This is observable already in the simple act of perception of the human self-consciousness, in that the self simultaneously experiences itself as the thought, as the thinking subject, and as the ego directing itself to itself; a phenomenon which Augustine described with a variety of expressions, and expounded very clearly. The trinity of our

The
Self
thought)

spiritual self refers back to the triune God who has created us, but we become God's image only if we find Him again in His Trinity and are able to love Him. God the Father, Son, and Holy Spirit are the prototype of all spiritual existence as personality, inasmuch as we have here too an indissoluble 'self-consciousness', 'self-knowledge', and 'self-assertion', the mutual relationship of lover and beloved through the third, which is love itself. A subordination or separation within the Trinity is now out of the question. The unity of God—an old theological concern particularly in the West—now appears with such emphasis that the divine 'Persons' really become mere elements within the one living being of the Deity, and are not to be isolated one from the other even in their external activity. At the same time, the personal character is also more clearly defined than previously. Augustine criticizes the traditional concept of the one divine substance, the bearer of the divine being and its 'attributes', to which the three 'Persons' of the Deity are then held in contradistinction. Carried to its logical conclusion this is a downright blasphemous anthropomorphism. As a person God has no attributes distinguishable from Himself, according to which one could think of Him like a human being, or on the basis of which one could standardize His 'Person', but His being is essentially His own personal being itself. God is not good because He possesses the attribute of goodness, but He is goodness itself in Person, with the consequence that all that is good can be called good only by Him and in Him.

We cannot here develop Augustine's teaching on the Trinity. He himself stated that his work was 'extremely difficult', and in his opinion 'understandable only by a few' (*Ep.* 169, 1). From now on it dominated the Western doctrine of the Trinity almost exclusively. Even Thomas did not really go beyond Augustine on this question. Even the later disputes with the East regarding the Spirit's relationship to the Son followed lines determined by Augustine. In other respects, the close connection of the divine Persons with each other inevitably resulted in complications in Christology. The divine and human natures of

Christ can be united only with difficulty, and the difficulty of proceeding from the intrinsically consistent doctrine of God to the basic dogma of the incarnation was much greater for Augustine than it had been for Ambrose, precisely because he tried to explain and 'understand' it philosophically. As we have seen, Augustine was aware that the decisive boundary between philosophy and revelation comes precisely here. The longer he was occupied with the problem the more he was concerned with the reality of the incarnate Christ, with the 'humility' of God, who wanted to redeem our pride by surrendering His divine abundance for our poverty, in order Himself to teach us the way of humility as the way to happiness.

The work on the Trinity occupies an exceptional position among Augustine's major works, in so far as it originated without a pressing cause and was written for the most part unpolemically. That is why its composition took up so much time: again and again other, more urgent, tasks intervened. The long quarrel with the Donatists was the most obstinate that occupied Augustine. The controversy with this typical 'sect' had repercussions upon his ecclesiastical thinking, and caused it to develop in a particular direction which was originally far from his thoughts. It is astonishing that in his early years the Donatists were entirely disregarded and unmentioned by Augustine, although they were found everywhere in Africa, and particularly in the interior were actually dominant. Outside Africa, however, they were of no importance and intellectually they were of no interest to him. Once he had entered the service of the church, no year elapsed in which Augustine did not write pamphlets or sermons against Donatism. For Augustine as a bishop, and even as a presbyter, there was no evading this problem—he had immediately to engage in the struggle and controversy. The Donatists were in a majority even in Hippo Rhegius. They possessed the finest basilica in the town, and influenced Augustine's congregation on all sides. Mixed marriages between Catholics and Donatists were not infrequent, conversions, rebaptisms, and petty irritations were everyday

occurrences. Once even a clergyman went over to them when
he had had a difference of opinion with Augustine, and was
naturally received with enthusiasm by the opposition. Actually
rebaptisms were prohibited by the state as sacrilege, and the
primacy of the Catholic church was protected by law in other
ways also, but in view of the actual balance of power the police
hesitated, and avoided as far as possible provoking the easily
aroused sectarians, who in any case complained on every occasion about earlier persecutions and the injustice done to them.
There was scarcely any difference this way or that in ritual and
doctrine, which at first glance made the unexampled animosity
with which the two churches opposed each other all the more
puzzling. Quite often it degenerated into bloody violence.

  The origin of this unhappy situation lay far back. After the
end of the last great persecution, at the beginning of the century, a bishop had been elected in Carthage who was unacceptable to the party of the uncompromising confessors, and it was
said that one of the ordaining bishops had himself shunned
martyrdom in the persecution. The schism having once started,
it swiftly spread, obviously owing to more general causes.
Accustomed as they were to persecution, resistance, and isolation, wide circles of African Christianity, which had all along
inclined to rigorism, were unable to adjust themselves so rapidly
to the changed situation. They mistrusted the new union with
the ruling classes, and after Constantine had rejected the Donatist
complaints, they presently resumed their old attitude of opposition. By contrast to the tolerant and allegedly lax Catholics,
the Donatists proclaimed themselves to be the sole 'pure' representatives of the true church of the saints, and they stiffened
themselves into an exclusive particularism. The animosity of
the Berber rural population against the Romanized society in
the towns joined with this, and the more the social differences
increased in the fourth century, the more easily did this hostility
at times also assume politically dangerous, revolutionary features.
Gangs of Donatist 'fighters' were actually formed, who sacked
the manors of rich landed proprietors, burned Catholic churches,

and forced the population willingly or unwillingly to support them. Yet along with this the Donatist congregations displayed real orthodox zeal and sacrificial devotion, which the Catholic congregations could no longer match. The different attempts of the government to suppress the sect by force achieved nothing, and only intensified the hatred against the ungodly, and an ominous readiness for 'martyrdom'.

Nothing could be effected against these people as a rule by theological argument. Indeed, since the days of the great Donatus who had given his name to the sect, outstanding literary defenders of its cause were not lacking in the Donatist camp. But what they put forward did not really touch the root of the passionate conflict, and shifted the controversy to secondary issues. It was not difficult for the Catholics to refute the Donatist contentions and complaints, convincing enough as such, and when they still did not achieve success they were the more disappointed and annoyed at the malevolence of the heretics. The claim, in opposition to the Catholic church which was 'spread throughout the whole world', to represent the sole true and holy Christian fellowship had something hopelessly stubborn about it, and the contention that the Donatist congregations consisted only of 'pure', real Christians, in contrast to the Catholic sinners, needed no refutation. Already before Augustine, the struggle had become focussed theologically on the problem of the sacraments in particular. The Donatists maintained, following Cyprian, that only the 'holy', i.e. persons free from serious sins, were able as priests to perform the sacramental consecrations, and administer efficacious sacraments. Since the Catholics had formerly violated this principle when ordaining the bishop of Carthage, and since that time had abandoned it completely, they were now no church, without baptism, without priesthood, and without the Holy Spirit. They were but a blasphemous society, which by the imitation of holy rites were even more defiled and worse than the pagans. Here, too, an originally quite serious concern had taken on a rather baroque appearance, and when logically pursued it could lead to nothing but impossible conclusions and contradictions. As a matter of fact, differences of opinion and schisms arose in the Donatist church also. But the Catholic contention that the sacraments possessed in themselves alone a sanctifying power if administered with correct outward form, also had its difficulties. The Donatists were not really concerned about a particular sacramental theory, but about concrete separation from the 'ungodly', and about resistance to the detested pressure of their 'persecutors'. It was precisely the favoured position of the Catholics and the corresponding detriment to the Donatists which made any reconciliation impossible.

At the time when Augustine began his activity, the earlier pressure upon the Donatists had declined considerably; only the exaggerated remembrance of former afflictions still poisoned the atmosphere. Not without reason, the Catholics on their part complained about excesses and encroachments of the sectarians, and so the prospects for a settlement were as slight as ever. It was essentially due to Augustine and his friend, the primate Aurelius of Carthage, that negotiations, theological activity and discussion were set in motion anew, in order to win back the schismatics. In contrast to the resigned attitude of many of his colleagues, the removal of a division both unfortunate and senseless was to Augustine a religious necessity. Why should it not be possible if both sides exercised good will? Is Christ really divided? (I Cor. i. 13). A church which acquiesces in schism ceases to be a church. Surprise has often been expressed at the determination with which Augustine embraced these convictions and acted accordingly the moment he assumed office. In view of his former, individualistic development he was the last man to be prepared for this. The new obligations and experiences which had of necessity come his way as presbyter were undoubtedly of the greatest importance in this, namely the preaching, pastoral advice, and work in the congregation of a confessionally mixed city, with all the unpleasantness with which it was attended. Yet this does not mean

that Augustine's ecclesiastical thinking was based upon purely
'practical' considerations. It had spiritual presuppositions which
reached further back, and which were essentially theological.
Where there is life, where the Spirit and God reign, there discord is overcome. To Augustine unity is the token of truth and
perfection—this is a conviction which went back to the Neo-
Platonic level of his thinking, and which the study of the Bible
had made concrete. Paul is above all decisive for the idea of
ecclesiastical unity. Christ has redeemed us for unity—this no
longer means for a mere unity of spirit, but for the unity and
fellowship of His body which is the church. Through Christ all
mankind was reconciled to God in the church and now partakes in his Spirit. In Christ, the 'new Adam', we find the way
back from enmity and dispersion to union with God, and remain henceforward in the fellowship of unity one with the
other worked by love. This love is the 'grace' of the New
Testament; it is peace and the Holy Spirit Himself. Outside this
'unity' there is no life 'in Christ', no justification of the sinner,
no sanctification and no salvation. This unity is no mere 'idea';
it is our new reality, the reality of service of the many members
in the church which cannot but be one by its very nature, as
Christ is one. Christ's church is the church for all in the whole
world; it cannot be a specialist or separatistic church like the
church of the Donatists. Upon this basis Augustine takes up
readily the old anti-Donatist argument of catholicity; not for
nothing does the Catholic church stand in firm connection and
communion with the church in Rome, with the ancient churches
in the East, and with the churches of the whole world—it is the
only universal church, and therefore the true church from which
nobody may exclude himself. Outside the catholic church no
one finds salvation. This argument, at first sight rather external
and brutal, now attains a deeper spiritual significance. The
majority is not right simply because it is the majority, but because in its midst the will to unity and fellowship becomes visible. 'Nobody will be so foolish, I think, as to maintain that
anyone whatever belongs to the unity of the church who does

not possess love' (*c. Crescon.* I, 34). The really evil and unchristian element in Donatism is the malignity of its inner attitude and disposition, the fact that it does not desire the unity
and fellowship of Christians at all, and in a spirit of hatred denies
it in favour of separation. It is perverse because it is opposed to
the basic Christian commandment of love. 'Love creates fellowship, fellowship loves unity, and unity preserves love' (*in Psalm
xxx. 2, 1*). By contrast, the Pharisaical affirmation of one's own
holiness and purity is completely untenable. The conventicle
ideal of the church is not feasible practically. Christ wanted the
wheat and tares to grow together until He Himself holds the
judgement (Matt. xiii. 24 ff.). We are not yet at the goal of our
pilgrimage through this age, but on the way. We must be satisfied with separation from evil people in volition and act; 'meanwhile, we can only await the final separation at the end of the
world faithfully, patiently, and bravely' (*Litt. Petil.* III, 4).

Augustine spared no pains in order to enter time and again
with endless patience into the particulars of what the Donatists
put forward. The matter of the election of the bishop of Carthage, decided three generations previously, was re-examined and
discussed anew. Augustine undertook laborious journeys in order
to provide himself with the complete record and documents.
He looked into all the theological misgivings item by item. He
sought to give to the Catholic teaching on the sacraments a
satisfying formulation by distinguishing more closely between
the validity, the legitimacy, and the efficacy of the sacraments.
Baptism can actually produce its full effect of blessing only when
it is received, or becomes alive, in the 'Catholic' community of
love, yet outside the true church it does not cease to be baptism.
Even there it is still the sign of attachment to the one Lord, as
it were the brandmark (*character*) with which each lamb of
Christ is branded. This claim of Christ's to ownership is valid
and indelible, and points at the same time back to the one flock
of the one Shepherd. Therefore there must be no 'rebaptism',
but also no persevering in separation. When the Donatists ask
about the moral uprightness of the administrator, they are

looking in the wrong direction. It is not the man, but the gift
of God, that counts. 'Is the servant of the evangelical word and
sacrament good? He becomes a companion of the Gospel! If,
however, he is evil, he nevertheless does not cease to be a
steward of the Gospel' (*Litt. Petil.* III, 67). The truth of God
uses many instruments, for of itself it is powerful and fruitful.

All these reasons appeared to Augustine convincing and irrefutable. And, indeed, they were far superior to the more or less
useless and obstinate objections which the Donatists brought
against them. But what was gained by that? The issue was, how
to bring them home to his opponents themselves, how to
initiate a discussion with them, and how really to obtain their
recognition at first intellectually, and then also in the practical
consequence of reunion. And here lay the greatest difficulties.
As always in such cases, it is the stronger party which is concerned about union and discussions of union. This very intellectual and moral superiority of the Catholic leaders took away
from the Donatists any inclination to negotiate, and made them
haughty and defensive. Negotiations and discussions, furthermore, were out of keeping with the intellectual tradition of a
church of martyrs and pietistic moralists. Augustine certainly
realized the awkwardness of the situation and did everything in
his power to overcome it. Immediately after he became bishop,
he sought an exchange of views with his Donatist colleague in
Hippo. Similar attempts were repeated at other places. The
opposition were allowed to choose the place, the circumstances,
and the witnesses for the disputation. Augustine was willing
even to withdraw, and to propose a less versatile partner to the
discussion, in case the Donatists feared his rhetorical training.
The practical regulations in case of union were also arranged as
generously as possible. Augustine was serious in desiring only
that the truth should prevail, and not that one party should
triumph over the other. In contrast to the evil tradition of the
struggle with heresy, he tried not to caricature and cheat the
dissentients; he really wanted to understand them. He was willing also frankly to admit the past errors of his church. He ad-

on anger –
interesting !!!

monished the members of his own congregation to patience, and checked his anger often when the opposition reacted rudely, dishonestly, or not at all. In fact, all was in vain. Augustine's sermons were heard by Donatists, to be sure, and again and again he was successful in converting individuals. But the great body, the leaders, the Donatist church as a whole, persevered in malignant opposition. Occasionally, when Augustine's kindness personally won over one or another authoritative figure for his plan, the possibility of discussion and of 'peace' seemed to be within reach. Then the opposition came to an understanding among themselves, retreated suddenly, and looked for excuses. In the end nobody appeared, and it came to nothing.

Taken as a whole, all Augustine's efforts for peace thus turned out fruitless. Whose fault was it? It has been pointed out that Augustine belonged intellectually and socially to a class, and accordingly also spoke a language, which was alien and hateful to the simple Donatists, especially those in the country. They would not, and could not, read or understand the writings of this 'Manichean' rhetorician educated abroad. They also scorned, it may be presumed, the cultivated townsman who associated with the wealthy, and seemingly did not know their sufferings. There is some truth in this. Even Augustine could not get away from his background, and despite all his personal renunciations remained a member of his society, a representative of literary education and cultured ideals from which the subject-masses of the late Roman empire had begun for some time to withdraw. He was a privileged citizen and spoke Latin exclusively. Yet Augustine took pains to achieve a popular style and be intelligible in his sermons and polemics, especially in dealing with the Donatists. His *Psalm Against the Donatist Party*, consisting of 300 verses, is a remarkable proof of this. 'I wished', he wrote, 'to bring the case of the Donatists to the knowledge of precisely the lower classes, and the uneducated and simple in general, and impress it upon them. For this purpose, I did not want to use any form of artistic poem, in order not to be compelled by the laws of metre to choose such words as are unusual among the

common people' (*Retr.* I, 19, 1). Augustine desired to speak
with complete plainness and clarity. So he threw completely
overboard all claims of literary culture, and composed a poem
which is certainly no 'poetry', though in its popular form it
nevertheless pointed to the future. The beginnings of the
stanzas are arranged consecutively according to the alphabet,
while a plain, singable refrain for the choir concludes them,
and all the lines have the same final sound -e (or -ae) and
so 'rhyme'. In place of the 'quantity', still rigidly observed
by Ambrose, we find, following the example of Punic (?)
poetry, the simple rhythm of the words. The melody, also,
which we do not know, was most likely adapted to the tunes
of Donatist hymns and chants. This primitive '*Psalm*' is sure
to have had its effect on the Latin-speaking population also.

The decisive difficulty in coming to terms with the schismatics was most likely not Augustine's education and social
position as such; it was due to the political position and tradition of his church which, in the opinion of the Donatists, had
been and still remained the 'church of the persecutors'. This
accusation was justified. Again and again, under Constantine,
and then above all under Constantius, the Donatists were punished, suppressed, and persecuted by the police, and even now
there were a number of regulations to their detriment, above
all the severe prohibition of rebaptism, which nevertheless continued to be performed. In this lay the decisive obstacle to any
Catholic attempt at winning them back, and likewise to a true
mission, which in conditions of freedom would have been
effective. Augustine was not blind to this endangering of his
'peace' work. With the candour which always distinguished
him, he tried to refute and invalidate the reproaches arising out
of this. First it is necessary to repudiate the Donatists' false pride
in martyrdom: sufferings and loss as such prove nothing of the
truth of a cause. Only true confession makes martyrs; for pagans,
criminals, and heretics are likewise persecuted. 'I have proved
countless times, both by debate and by writing, that they cannot
have the death of martyrs because they have not the life of

Christians, since it is not the pain but the purpose that makes a martyr' (*Ep.* 204, 4; *FC*, 8, 5). Besides this, the alleged martyrs permit themselves frauds, injustices, and abominations for which they are punished on good grounds, and with full right. Finally, however, there is actually a far-reaching freedom for the Donatists. They have their churches, congregations, and services—and it is not true that the Catholics thirst for their blood. Augustine prides himself that he is no extremist, that he repudiates denunciation to the police in certain cases, and had even pressed for a reduction of punishments already inflicted. This is honest, yet nevertheless somewhat naïve. Augustine did not think of disapproving the existing laws as such—it is only right that the heretics do not receive the same favours from the state as the servants of the truth. But he would nevertheless like to continue with and to succeed in discussion and conversion in complete freedom without interference; the last thing he wanted was to promote religious opportunism: but how could this be achieved in the given circumstances? We come here upon an ambiguity similar to that found in Ambrose and most of the fathers of this transitional period, who affirmed the right of freedom and the right of the state-church at the same time. Yet the development continued, and Augustine followed it.

Toward the end of the century, the situation of the Donatists again began to deteriorate. Their support of a rebellious governor caused them to fall into political disgrace. Above all, however, the notion of the Catholic empire, as framed by Theodosius, pressed by itself for an increasingly stricter realization. There were, of course, in the Catholic camp church leaders who welcomed this, and demanded a more rigorous enforcement of the laws against heretics. At the beginning of the year 405, the time came: the Emperor Honorius issued an edict which decreed the general repression of the Donatists by force. All their churches and properties were to be delivered to the Catholic bishops; their services were prohibited; those who broke the laws were threatened with confiscation and expulsion. Yet all this still could not break their resistance. Thus the state arranged a final official religious debate in 411. It is evident, and Augustine stressed this time and again, that at this council equality of rights and full freedom of discussion were actually granted to the Donatists. The Catholics did not let themselves be wearied by the desperate evasions and delaying actions of their adversaries: in negotiations which continued for days all their accusations and contentions were once more examined, discussed, and 'refuted'. Of course the result proclaimed by the imperial commissioner at the end was determined from the very beginning. The Donatists had come only because there was no other way out, and they refused to accept the decision. But now there was indulgence for them no longer. Imperial 'executores' took care of the enforcement of the 'Catholic peace', and took drastic measures against the obstinate dissentients. Catholic bishops who did not arrange the incorporation energetically enough were threatened in the same way, and were to be denounced. We hear of horrible scenes of suicidal resistance, of sanguinary measures, and of acts of revenge by the suppressed. Donatism was not dead, but vanished from public life. Entire congregations joined Catholicism in a body, sometimes with their clergy.

Augustine regretted the violence of these actions. Like Ambrose, he protested above all at the use by the government of capital punishment, which he considered to be wrong in all circumstances within the realm of the church, and in this he was successful. Even now he wished to win the reluctant by peaceful means, by preaching, by enlightenment, and by pastoral instruction. He made provision that the rights of those newly converted in the congregation were not curtailed, and disclaimed any military protection for his own person. Obviously, his endeavours had real success in some cases. Augustine's patient and friendly attitude succeeded in winning over, at any rate later, many former Donatists. Indeed, it was often only custom, innate prejudice, and lack of acquaintance with Catholic truth which had made these Christians resist reconciliation. Now, it appeared, they were actually thankful to have the opportunity to change their views, and in part accepted the new ideas gladly. It is shocking to see how it was exactly these personal successes which led Augustine to a revision in principle of his standpoint, the implications of which in world history he certainly could not then anticipate. 'Originally my opinion was, that no one should be coerced into the unity of Christ, that we must act only by words, fight only by arguments, and prevail by force of reason, lest we should have those whom we knew as avowed heretics feigning themselves to be Catholics. But this opinion of mine was overcome not by the words of those who controverted it, but by the conclusive instances to which they could point' (*Ep.* 93, 17; *LPNF*, I, 388). Such an 'instance', to which Augustine was referred by his colleagues, was first and foremost the changed situation in his own city, in which peace now finally reigned; and furthermore, the former dissidents were outspokenly happy regarding the changed circumstances. Was this not to be recognized and welcomed? The government actions were not in any case to be regarded as injustice, for the final negotiations in Carthage had proved with all clarity that the Donatist assertions were wrong, and that their resistance was unfounded, and explicable as merely due to stubborn ill-will, or simply factual ignorance. An energetic intervention was then imperative, after all. Thus Augustine came to his famous, or infamous, theological justification of force. Of course he considers it better if men voluntarily arrive at adoration and veneration of God in the right way; 'perfect love casts out fear' (I John iv. 18). Yet this does not mean that exercise of threats and force must in all cases be evil, or that it may not be actually indispensable in many cases. In conclusion, parents also force their children to obey, and teachers compel their pupils to work, for which they are grateful afterwards. 'You are also of opinion that no coercion is to be used with any man in order to his deliverance from the fatal consequence of error; and yet you see that, in examples which cannot be disputed, this is done by God(!), who loves us with more real regard for our profit than any other can.' Christ also himself exhorts us in the Parable of the Great Feast that we are to 'compel' everybody we can reach to enter his house (Luke xiv. 23 according to the contemporary, all too literal translation: *cogite intrare*, *Ep.* 93, 5; *LPNF*, I, 383).

Force is thus regarded as a short-cut only, and as a provisional means to the true goal of free and voluntary conversion, but this way must be employed in case of emergency. In the case of this schism, where things were clear as the day, proved and established, it would have been unjust to give way to the mani-festly malevolent obstinacy of the Donatist leaders, and simply to leave to ruin the poor misguided people, who neither knew the truth nor ever would come to know it in such a way. If we wish to understand Augustine's decision rightly, and contrast it with the medieval ideals of the Crusades and the Inquisition, we must not forget that the whole Donatist question was to him in no way a matter of conscience, or of a difference in faith to be taken seriously. It was plainly a matter of inveterate prejudice, of incitement of the people, and of the power of bad habit, for the overcoming of which the assistance of the police therefore seemed in order. It is quite wrong to explain Augustine's atti-tude in this question in terms of a particularly exaggerated hier-archical consciousness, or the 'domineering' instincts of a churchman. Rather is the contrary the case. Augustine did not decide by political instinct, but let himself be persuaded and de-termined by the favourable aspects of the situation. With the unconscious arrogance of a man of theoretical training he put all his confidence in the power and persuasion of his reason. After all his personal and literary endeavours had failed, he let himself be pushed, rather angrily, in just the opposite direction, and accepted the assistance of the secular power. He was sadly mistaken about the successes attained in this way. With the forced conversions of the Donatists the decline of the once proud African church began. Finally, at the Mohammedan invasion, it was the only church of the Mediterranean area which dis-appeared completely. It seems that the former Donatists wel-comed the Arabs as liberators, and, at any rate, the 'Catholic' heritage was not seriously defended by them.

He who wishes to become genuinely acquainted with Augustine's thought regarding the church, the world, and the state, must not stop at the anti-Donatist writings. The main work for these subjects is the ' *Twenty-four Books on the City of God*', *De Civitate Dei*, which is at the same time a kind of summary of the whole Augustinian theology itself. This is connected with the special intention of his *opus magnum*: it is the last great apology of the church against paganism, the final justification of her teaching and historical position at the end of time, and before the whole world. The whole material of traditional Christian polemic, collected through the centuries, is therefore expounded once more in a new and independent formulation. The repudiation of pagan religion and philosophy is combined with the positive exposition of the entire system of Christian doctrine and ethics. Yet this writing also originated in a specific cause; and this lends to it the particular manner, liveliness, and vivacity, in which the questions are posed. It took, however, twenty-two years to complete, proceeding from issue to issue according to a design drawn up at the beginning.

On August 28, 410, Alaric's troops had stormed and sacked Rome. This event had a shattering effect, far beyond its direct political importance. How had it come about that the capital of the ancient empire, the ruler of the world, the eternal city, had experienced such an overthrow? The world seemed to shake at its foundations, and the pagans knew the answer! In their eyes, the catastrophe was the recompense for abandoning the old guardian divinities and the traditional religion; the new Christian God of the empire had obviously proved impotent, and had failed. The Christians had no reply to this, for they had provoked precisely this criticism by their previous polemic. Since Constantine, and even during the later times of persecution, they had indefatigably propounded the view that the surrender of pagan superstition and the protection of true religion would renew and sustain the empire. Ambrose too had held to this, even though he temporarily developed other ideas under the stress of emergency (cf. p. 107). Theodosius had made the orthodox faith the foundation of his order for the empire on precisely these grounds. The embarrassment was now great. A serious moral set-back menaced the church. In this situation Augustine was urged from all sides to utter a word of aid, for he was regarded as the spokesman and theological adviser of all Latin Christianity.

The first hurriedly published books of his apology still reflect the acute danger of the religious and political situation. Augustine was concerned to show above all how ill-founded was the contention 'that human welfare must necessarily be promoted by adhering to the worship of the many gods venerated by the pagans' (*Retr.* II, 43). The old demons are simply unable to do this. It can be shown, at any rate, that they, whom people now seek to set in opposition to Christ, did not protect Rome in earlier years better than he is doing at present. For a direct refutation, more massive arguments are also not disdained by Augustine. So he points out in particular that only the asylum of the Christian sanctuaries had protected both pagans and Christians during the destruction of the city, and not the temples of the old gods. Nevertheless, it is clear from the very first that he does not really mean to base his main case on such obvious reasons, with which the pagans can be refuted at best by an external proof. Augustine has his eye also on the failure of his own fellow-believers, and takes up the whole problem on a deeper level. Why do so many who call themselves Christians face the new situation so helplessly, and think that their God should not have permitted all this? They have obviously no real understanding at all of their own faith, and therefore succumb to the deceptive logic of the pagans. In reality, one does not truly believe in God so long as one conceives of Him only as a means to provide the good things and happiness of this world, so that they may be enjoyed peacefully, and despairs of Him the moment external disaster occurs. One does not understand what life is so long as one expects its fulfilment in this age, and dares to demand this as a due claim upon God's government of the world. He only can participate in the meaning of life who is sincerely humble before

God, who accepts all that God sends, and who gladly and willingly continues on his pilgrimage because he believes in an all-perfecting eternity which will be just as much God's as are all the troubles of this present time.

The question is thus—in the context of an apology—that of the interpretation and foundation of the Christian faith itself, which has to distinguish itself from pagan idolatry not only by its object, but also by the manner of its devotion, and its inner relation to God and the world. But Augustine does not content himself with distinctions and postulates of principle. His theodicy is intended as pastoral guidance, and is to help the afflicted Christians. It plunges therefore into the whole perplexing misery which murder and rape, pillage and deportation have brought upon the individual, and the whole empire. And so he summons the whole art of his dialectics and rhetoric, in order not to evade any possible objection, and to give an answer to every question and doubt. He explains in detail that suffering is not mere suffering, but, depending on how one bears it, can be a curse or a blessing already in this life, in that it does indeed harden the ungodly, but it purifies and liberates the believer from his remaining inward burden. Furthermore, quite apart from all this, the seeming senselessness of this divine judgement, which befalls the wicked as well as the good, is rather in reality a religious necessity, to the end that God should be sought and found not for the sake of temporal welfare, but in truth, i.e. for His own sake. This statement also is divided further into regular cases and exceptions, and the exceptions also find an explanation, and have their apparently necessary place. Basically, all this is indeed not a matter of real 'proof', logical and conclusive. With relatively convincing proofs, Augustine appeals to the Christian conscience in the decision of faith to give up the empty scepticism, the instability, and the wretchedness of an unbelieving quarrel with God, and in the affirmation of God's will to find the way back to reality, truth, and the service of love. Toward the end of his work (*Civ. D.* XX, 2) he reverts once more to this whole range of questions. It is as if he wanted once again to secure the decisive

Faith [Test? of Life]

thoughts against any possible misunderstanding and reduction, by pointing out with extreme pungency that faith, and nothing but faith, is the power which alone can pass all the tests of life. It is hidden from us why God now holds back something good from the virtuous, and now spares a criminal from suffering. We do not know why this too is not valid without exception, and why at times even its reversal appears to be the rule. It is given to us to know only this much, that in principle it depends not upon the disposition in this world of so-called luck and misfortune, but upon that which will one day eternally separate us one from the other, before God's tribunal. Then, at dooms-day, all enigmas will indeed be solved—even down to this last mystery why it is necessary that God's justice should still in the present life so often, and indeed always, remain hidden. That it nevertheless exists and determines all events—this much is even today certain to Christian faith and this is sufficient.

The favourite term Augustine uses to designate the basic Christian attitude is 'humility' (*humilitas*). The defence of Christianity against paganism is therefore the same thing as a correct exposition of the meaning of humility against the demonic pride and haughtiness of men, their *superbia*. That is what this book is about. 'I know, of course,' writes Augustine in his preface, 'what ingenuity and force of arguments are needed to convince proud men of the power of humility.' Humility is powerful not of it-self, but by the grace of God which permits it to rise higher than all the trembling and vanishing heights of this world (*Civ. D.* I praef.; *FC*, 6, 19). Now it is the pride of the supposedly 'eternal' Rome, the pagan metropolis, which rises up against the peace of the 'City of God', which alone is in truth eternal. With reference to the old gods, and the departed Roman tradition, that same fundamental reversal of religion to make of it the servant of one's own greatness and glory, which already con-noted the very nature of paganism in the individual life, is applied once again as on a gigantically enlarged scale. Augustine views paganism in its final state as a political religion. The old idols are not believed in any more. They serve the pagan Roman spirit only as the self-confirmation of its own haughty desire, of its own past and its own glory. Augustine is by no means unaware of the greatness of Roman attainments. They would have been admirable if they had originated in a truly devout attitude and not in the dark desires of ambition. As it is, however, they are to be viewed in connection with the fertile ground of evil will, from which they derive. They then have to be 'reckoned as vices, rather than virtues' (*Civ. D.* XIX, 25), 'as splendid vices', *splendida vitia*, according to the later formula. One observes this, Augustine thinks, in the nature of their historical effect. Virgil's famous epigram on the calling of the people to rule, '*parcere subiectis et debellare superbos*' (to spare the vanquished, and to put down the mighty) denotes a violation of the glory of God, who alone gives grace to the humble and has the right to punish nations. This mentality is the ultimate reason why there is never peace in this world. It is the origin of all the wars and conquests, which have made Rome the terror of her neighbours for centuries, and finally the all-devouring world empire.

Along these lines Augustine, taking his cue from Sallust and other classical authors, ventures to give a thorough and terrible rehearsal of the whole of Roman history, beginning with the fratricide of Romulus up to the last abominations of the Republic. It is a single-minded attack upon the sacrosanct tradition, never before attempted in this manner, wherein he tears off the mask from the face of Roman hypocrisy. He is not concerned with historical objectivity, but with a perception of principle, if one may say so, and likewise with a new political ethos, for which he would prefer to win nobody more than the descendant of the old Scipios and Fabricii. In the true faith, says Augustine, their traditional virtues also would shine with a new and purer splendour.

Hence Augustine is not concerned with the rejection of the political interest as such, or of all political activity; against this he expressly guarded himself. 'Pride' is not a necessary by-product of power itself, 'but of the soul that is inordinately enamoured of its own power . . .' (*Civ. D.* XII, 8; Oates, II,

186). 'And in action it is not honour, or power in this life, which should be prized, since all things under the sun are vanity, but the task itself that is accomplished through that same honour and power, if rightly and helpfully performed; that is, if it contributes to the welfare of those who are set below us. This is according to God's law' (*Civ. D.* XIX, 19; *LCL*, VII, 203). A vast disillusionment, a cool detachment from any political 'mythos', and from any express political passion is voiced in these words. The empire was sick, and offered little cause for political enthusiasm. One cannot reproach Augustine for not having considered himself called to be a political reformer, for which he would have been utterly unsuitable. Augustine restricts himself to the essential, and to what is valid at all times. The subordination of all passing and temporal purposes, to which politics must not be more than a means, to the eternal, spiritual, and transcendent purpose of existence with God has in him perhaps still an ascetic, philosophical, Neo-Platonic sound. Yet the over-all outlook nevertheless remains Christian and Biblical. In place of the timeless hierarchy of gradations of value, the prevailing idea is of historical movement toward a goal, namely toward the judgement, and God's eternal realm of peace. It is a definite community which carries this movement through time, the eternal church, the citizenship of the City of God. Indeed, in striving for worldly peace these have a common task which must be accomplished in co-operation with the citizens of this world. Nevertheless, they have no common goal. The attitude and direction of men's hearts, i.e. hope, and future, and not present existence, determine men's nature, and give it its meaning. History, which moves onwards, and historical volition, have become decisive. With Augustine a new, Christian evaluation of time began, which was not previously known in antiquity. He stands at the beginning of a Western 'philosophy of history'.

From the very beginning there are two human 'states' or 'cities', two human communities in the world which are stamped by their attitude. 'Two cities (*civitates*) have been

formed by two loves: the earthly by the love of self, even to the
contempt of God; the heavenly by the love of God, even to
the contempt of self. The former, in a word, glories in itself, the
latter in the Lord' (*Civ. D.* XIV, 28; Oates, II, 274). Pride and
humility, 'faith and disbelief', in their coexistence and opposition constitute, as Goethe says, 'the real, sole, and deepest theme
of the history of the world and man'. Both attitudes are as old
as the history of the world. They found their origin in Adam's
fall, and ever since that time the development of 'citizenship
under God' or 'Jerusalem' runs down through the line of Abel
and the Old Testament '*Heilsgeschichte*' (the history of the saving acts of God) until Christ, and from Him again through the
church, to conclude only at the end of time in the eternal 'City
of God', 'where victory is truth, where dignity is holiness,
where peace is happiness, where life is eternity' (*Civ. D.* II, 29;
LCL, I, 263). Contrary to it, though interwoven with it in
many ways, there also takes its rise the state or citizenship of
the 'City of Earth', the selfish and proud who once in Babylon,
and now in Rome, gather around their great, demonic symbol.
By injustice and violence they strive for their own glory, and
for the earthly dominion and temporal peace which they can
neither maintain nor keep. They end in eternal damnation.
Despite all the conflict, God nevertheless remains the real and
only Lord of this double historical process, which he guides
according to his inscrutable counsel as he wills. One day the end
will come, in fact, when the number of predestined citizens of
God is reached, a number determined in order to substitute
exactly for the number of originally fallen angels. Yet the date
of this end is known to none, and Augustine expressly refuses
to ascertain and calculate it in advance on the basis either of
Biblical texts or of the philosophy of history. What matters to
him is the inner analysis of the meaning of history, for from
this is derived decision in favour of God's community and its
true, everlasting goal.

This view of the framework of '*Heilsgeschichte*' was not
created by Augustine himself. With many mythological details

he simply followed in this the Biblical, primitive Christian, apocalyptic view of history, which stretches from the creation and original fall until the end of the world, and the irruption of the kingdom of God, and which takes its centre and meaning from the Christ who calls 'all peoples' to conversion and renewal. Augustine was fully aware of the contrast to all ancient views of history, 'cyclical', aimless, and in his opinion totally comfortless. The classification, also, of the two states, cities, citizenship—the Latin denotes all this with one and the same word (*civitas*)—had already been developed prior to him by the Donatist Ticonius, from whom he adopted it. But only with Augustine did it attain to real historical vitality, because he not only relates the two *civitates*—according to his apologetical intention—to Rome, and to the (Old and New Testament) church, but from this point on attempts to trace them throughout the whole course of world history. On the basis of the Bible and the ancient historians, Augustine gives a detailed description of both 'cities', of their origin, development, and progress through earthly time, in order to conclude with the expectation of the resurrection, and the completion of time in eternity. This procedure alone makes the theologian into a historian and, we might say, into the first 'philosopher of history'. We must, however, beware of false modernizations when using this expression. It goes without saying that Augustine was no independent, and certainly no 'critical' historian. Moreover the criteria and interpretations he uses are not 'historical' in the modern sense. The development of the two 'cities' has nothing whatever to do with the modern, immanentist conception of evolution. God determines history, and what results from it is precisely the incomprehensibility of the concrete event as it is given at any moment, which we have to accept but which we cannot possibly explain. The faith which understands the goal of history renounces any prophecy immanent to the world. Therefore, Augustine intentionally leaves open any decision about the future of the Roman empire. He certainly repudiates the panic which the conquest of Rome immediately threatened to unchain. He demands that everyone fulfil his duty at his post. He hopes that everything may turn out well once again. Yet no greatness of this world is 'eternal', and it is for God to decree when Rome will perish. Even in retrospect, Augustine sees no essential connection between the decisions ordained by God in accordance with his secret counsel and the causal-genetic deductions and connections sought by the secular historian. The historical judgements which Augustine makes on events, persons, and the supposed necessities of former times, are mostly furnished by the Bible and given an exclusively theological evaluation.

Nevertheless, world history for Augustine is not constituted by sheer accidental facts and details. The tension between the two warring communities constantly gives a deeper meaning to the apparently isolated fact, and this religious meaning can be grasped and clearly described with the aid of the Bible. This is the particular and surprising achievement Augustine accomplishes with the aid of his symbolism. But this too is at first a general phenomenon. The whole of antiquity, especially in its last phases, gave reality an interpretation that is not exclusively causal in the modern sense of the word. It discovered everywhere in nature the 'spiritual' laws of analogy, harmony, and sympathy, which also determine human life. In a similar way it understood the words of the poets 'allegorically', as reflections and manifestations of general moral and philosophical truths. This alchemy of thought acquired in the Christian church a special significance from the beginning, because it was now applied to actual history. Christ had to be proved to be the fulfilment of the Old Covenant. For this purpose not only was reference made to individual prophecies which fitted Him, but there was a growing attempt to interpret the whole ancient 'Heilsgeschichte', with its real persons and events, in relationship to Him, and to understand them as exemplary 'types' of coming history. So, for instance, David is a type of Christ the king, or Isaac's sacrifice represents His death upon the cross. This old Biblical principle of exegesis is now extended by Augustine to world history as such. The antagonism of the two *civitates*, which in Adam were still comprised by a single human being, for the first time emerges 'typically' in the two brothers Cain and Abel. It continues in Israel's struggle with the Gentiles, assumes a visible form in the cities of Babylon and Jerusalem, and finds its last, demonic expression in the pagan Roman empire persecuting the church. On both sides it is primarily a matter not of simple identification with the single-mingled community of the ungodly, or of the righteous,—they are, indeed, intermingled and outwardly inseparable—but of a symbolical representation which nevertheless designates what the powers are in their historical reality. Just as in Augustine's symbolical teaching on the sacraments, so also here the object and the symbol cannot be separated. For that reason, the typological connections and structures which he creates with the aid of historical illustrations and 'signs' do not produce, like many medieval constructions of history, the impression of a game, but possess a power to elucidate real history. At all events, a great deal of the peculiar aesthetic charm which Augustine's conception of history still displays, with all its strange restriction to the categories of Biblical theology, is derived from the mysterious fascination of the historical parallels and correspondences pointing forward or backward, and from the magical reflection and iridescence of images and ideas which nevertheless retain their depth and meaning.

The *City of God* was the favourite book of the entire Middle Ages, being a work then read far more than the *Confessions*. But change of time brought also a change of understanding. Against the background of the controversies of state and church in the high Middle Ages the basic ideas of the book were instinctively given a political or clerical colouring. One discerned in them a devilish devaluation of the secular and a sanctification of the ecclesiastical, which meant by then papal, power. Such ecclesiastico-political interpretations were, of course, far from the thought of the historical Augustine— almost as far as the anti-hierarchical and spiritualizing reinter-

pretation of his thoughts which is also to be met in the late
Middle Ages. He supported the misunderstanding only in so far
as his work shows the demonic forces of the 'City of Satan'
manifest precisely in its political ambition, in the greed of states
for power and glory, whereas a corresponding demonic perversion of ecclesiastical ambition has not yet come under consideration. Therefore the 'City of God' readily assumed in the
eyes of posterity a Gregorian tendency. When speaking of
political and ecclesiastical problems, the real Augustine is not
yet thinking institutionally in medieval terms. In particular he
does not recognize the idea of a 'Christian state', but only recognizes individual Christians, rulers as well as subjects, who
then as persons in the state can serve justice and earthly peace,
while at heart they remain humble citizens of the heavenly city.

On the other hand, in Augustine the church certainly appears
as the city and citizenship of God which lasts through all time,
although by no means everyone who is outwardly counted as
in it belongs to it in reality. Yet in such connections Augustine
is not thinking of the visible ecclesiastical organization. In the
twenty-two books of the *City of God* it is scarcely mentioned.
Only in the anti-Donatist writings is it of great importance, as
is but natural. Otherwise it regularly recedes into the background so soon as the real religious meaning, the spiritual significance, and the true life of the church come under discussion.
The church is Christendom, the community of believers in
Christ in all the world, and in each single Catholic congregation, united in love by virtue of the power of the Holy Spirit.
This does not mean, of course, that Augustine was indifferent
to the external form of his church; rather is it a matter of course
to him. Like all theologians of the early church Augustine was
an episcopalian. He believed in the episcopal organization of the
church, which had its source in Christ and the apostles. All
bishops are equal in principle; they teach and administer their
own congregations, and every Christian is obliged to render
them obedience. Only if they 'err', or oppose the Holy Scripture itself, 'must we not agree with even the Catholic bishops'

(*Unit. Eccl.* 11, 28). This statement too is for Augustine a matter of course; he has not thought out the implications it might have if taken seriously. To him all canonical questions as such are basically uninteresting. The church lives through Christ, her Head, and all Christians are her members. The clergy are servants and, in the strict sense, priests, called to administer word and sacrament to the faithful, without their character as human beings having any decisive effect on their ministration. The whole congregation is the body of Christ, and experiences this particularly in the communal reception of His body and blood. 'If you yourself are Christ's body and His members, your mysterious nature appears on the Lord's table: you receive your own mystery.' The Holy Spirit makes the whole congregation into one bread. So 'then, be that which you see, and receive that which you are' (*Serm.* 272). Augustine is certainly very far from glorifying the church as a spiritual institution in its own right. She lives only so far as she continuously receives all things from her Head, by whom she is reconciled and united with God. The sinner is justified when believing in Christ, and receives also simultaneously with justification the Holy Spirit's renewing power of love. This event cannot be isolated. It happens only within the living fellowship of the Christian church, nevertheless the church does not save us, but Christ Himself through the church. We are 'nothing without Him, but in Him we are Christ Himself and ourselves' (*Psalm. Enarr.* xxx, 2, 3). The Head 'redeems His body', and the body then partakes in all blessings which the Head has won. Christ and His people cannot be separated; only as united with His body is He Himself the 'whole Christ'.

This work on the *City of God*, which was supposed to destroy the last bulwarks of paganism, ran parallel right from the beginning with a new controversy internal to the church, the repercussions of which can repeatedly be traced in the book itself. This is the so-called 'Pelagian controversy'. This quarrel occupied Augustine's thoughts more than all previous disputes, and he never came free from it until his death. He had taken it up on his own account, but during its course he recruited comrades everywhere, and then put them into action. In order to win the battle, he even became extremely active in the field of church politics, contrary to his usual way. Year by year his voluminous treatises were published, works which in attack and defence increasingly reached deeper levels of the problem, and envisaged ever more difficult and radical solutions—until finally death took his pen away from an unfinished work, the *opus imperfectum* against Julian. The controversy with the Pelagians was Augustine's real struggle for the doctrine of the church. The issue here was one of high theological hair-splitting problems, and of new answers which only became really pressing by this controversy. It was not an issue of traditional controversial views regarding old differences and ecclesiastical positions, as in the battle against the Manicheans or Donatists. With his teaching on the omnipotence and complete freedom of divine grace, of which the hereditary bondage of human will is the counterpart, Augustine sums up the whole of his theological endeavours and of the development of his life. He has to admit that at the beginning he was himself unable to formulate the truth in its full meaning and with complete consistency, and that his earlier writings, with which his adversaries now confronted him, left many things unclear and were more or less in need of correction. In spite of this, the basic theme of God's omnipotence and the sovereignty of his grace was firmly established from the outset. Already in his life confessions Augustine had testified to it unmistakably, and now he realized it as his sole task to establish the church's doctrine definitively in this sense. This led finally to the affirmation of complete divine predestination, that is to say, the foreknowledge of God, which as such must be at the same time a pre-determination and a predecision. On this the whole of Christianity depends. Only from this principle does it become incontestably certain that God alone is, and must ever remain, the goal as well as the only hopeful way for mankind, which is lost without Him, and that any strength and endeavour which tries to operate independently is necessarily perverted and directed against God. In consequence our own faith which effects salvation is also to be understood correctly only as God's gift and work. 'For in him and by him and to him are all things' (Rom. xi. 36). In the adoption of this Pauline confession, Augustine's philosophical theology and his conception of the Holy Scriptures converge. Apart from this belief there is for him no truth, and no true and real Christianity.

In the details also, Augustine developed his teaching on the basis of the Holy Scripture, and at the same time according to the logic of Platonic religious philosophy. This makes him theologically invincible; but at the same time pushes him far beyond the immediate data of the Bible, and also beyond Paul, and ties him down to positions difficult to defend. His opponents drove him further; in his own thinking he was not yet far enough ahead of them, and this explains many a weakness and rigour of the position he finally came to. Augustine did not wish to be an innovator; yet on the whole he had in fact no precursor in the claims for which he contended. Also he would hardly have found companions and successors had he not been, when the Pelagian controversy broke out, for a long time the spiritual master of the African church, the bishops of which stood behind him like one man. Despite his victory, Augustine, however, could not prevail in the long run without concessions, and just at this point his heritage has again and again caused difficulties and provoked new discussions. This is not only because this conflict really concerns an eternal opposition of factors, and faith and disbelief, pride and humility can in the Christian world also never come to a settlement. Nor is it due only to differences in practice, the complacency and readiness for compromise frequently blamed in the Catholic state-church, which he wanted to serve, and did serve. It is primarily a matter of the formal, logical insolubility of the problems, a systematic solution of which Augustine nevertheless tried to force by the methods of his time and school of thought. To this extent he was craving for something impossible of accomplishment, and the victories he obtained remain in their theological results Pyrrhic victories of logic, which never could end the war in which he was engaged. Nevertheless, the anti-Pelagian dogma marks a theological boundary which was reached once for all, behind which Latin Christianity, taking everything into account, could never fall back to the level of pre-Augustinian moralism and rationalism. It was now firmly established that in the realm of religion everything primarily depends always on God and not upon man. The conception of grace was from now on the central idea of Latin theology. Western Christianity saw itself henceforward basically as a religion of grace. While Augustine continued to build upon older foundations in his teaching on the church, the sacraments and God, he created something new here, and he marks a new epoch in the history of theology and of ideas.

Pelagius was an eminently moral and 'sanctified' personality. At the start of the controversy Augustine himself repeatedly attested this, and did not retract it even later, when the ambiguity and apparent deviousness of his opponent exasperated him. British by birth, no priest but a zealous ascetic, Pelagius found his intellectual field of action, like Rufinus, in Rome. Here he carried on propaganda for his monastic ideals, won disciples, and successfully preached against the laxity and immorality of Christian society. He also came forward as a theological writer, more independent and systematic than Rufinus, and tried to effect a combination of the older Western tradition and the ideas of the Greek, Origenist theology. There was, indeed, in Rome at the time the beginning of the renaissance of Origen's thought. A man quite orthodox, Pelagius argued against the Arians, yet his most determined opposition was directed against the Manicheans. Their dualistic fatalism infuriated the moralist. The problem was how to enforce against them the power and importance of the will, and to work out the free responsibility of man for his own actions. For this reason, Pelagius studied Augustine's anti-Manichean writings, and particularly his important work *On Free Will*, which had made the first attempt to unite the appeal to human freedom, inevitable in this connection, with the idea of grace. Pelagius too was far from regarding God's grace as of secondary importance or as unnecessary. As a skilled expositor of Paul he even stressed the doctrine that redemption comes about by faith *alone*, and by grace *alone*. But he considered this in relation to the liberation of man effected by baptism and forgiveness, and the freedom and self-determination of the will recovered 'by grace', in contrast to the bad 'habits' of pre-Christian humanity. While Augustine went further, and saw this liberated will itself as operative and determined by God's grace, Pelagius did not go beyond emphasizing the significance of man's free contribution as decisive for salvation. The systematic manner in which his practical activism was developed, and sought to combat the alleged perversity of any other doctrine of sin in the name of the liberated human nature, created good, was dangerous.

His criticism was originally directed not against Augustine, but against the understanding of Paul given by '*Ambrosiaster*', a writer unknown by his real name, whose commentaries then circulated under the name of 'Hilary'. It would be, he held, absurd to deduce from Rom. v. 12 a doctrine of the original sinful nature of all the descendants of Adam. The nature created good by God must remain unchangeable, and the assumption of a corporeal transference of guilt from generation to generation by procreation would, moreover, be Manichean and in contradiction to God's justice. Pelagius also spoke against Augustine's *Confessions*, which in Rome had become a fashionable book in the society of the 'religiously interested'. When objection was made to him from Augustine's prayer: 'Give what thou commandest—and command what thou wilt' (*Conf.* X, 31, 45), he passionately opposed such quietism. It was always his concern to show the lazy what human nature should and in fact could accomplish. The reference to God who 'creates from persons who do not will those who do' (*Op. Imperf.* III, 122) 'by helping him whom He commands, so that he can also do the good' (*Grat. et Lib. Arb.* 31), accordingly appeared as a complacent excuse.

Fleeing from the Visigoths in 410/411, Pelagius sought refuge in Africa. Probably intentionally, he avoided an encounter with Augustine. He feared a superior adversary, and, like so many moralists, was perhaps of the opinion that dogmatic controversies are in any case unproductive, and merely cause discord. From Africa he travelled on to Jerusalem, and soon gained a reputation and good friends in the East, where nobody took offence at his teaching. Meanwhile in Africa his pupil Caelestius, who was less cautious and also theologically more superficial, had one-sidedly and pointedly drawn out the consequences of the Pelagian teaching on freedom and when he applied in Carthage for the office of priest in 411, he was therefore solemnly rejected as a heretic, and excommunicated. The prime factor in most people's mind was that Caelestius did not accept the 'remission of sins' in infant baptism, and anti-Donatist Africa was, of course, particularly sensitive about any innovations in baptismal teaching. Yet for Augustine this condemnation bore a wider significance. Whoever asserted the 'innocence' of new-born babies, i.e. declared the natural, unredeemed man to be sound and free to do all good, was in his opinion denying the basic relationship in which all men stand 'since Adam', and rendered salvation by Christ superfluous. This meant opposing the idea of 'grace by which the ungodly is made righteous, and by which we are Christians at all' (*Retr.* II, 52). Augustine now sent his own disciple Orosius to the East with a letter of introduction to Jerome, in order to obtain a condemnation of Pelagius there. But these efforts failed completely. Pelagius tried to elude them, and maintained particularly that the teachings under discussion did not represent 'dogmas'. By reason of their whole way of thinking and tradition the Greeks were unable to see in the questions of anthropology and the doctrine of grace under consideration anything more than an obstinate quarrel about trivialities and commonplaces. They acquitted Pelagius. In Africa this decision produced indignation. With the active participation of Augustine, new synodal decrees were here issued, and in addition to this they constrained Pope Innocent I expressly to condemn the new heretics. When his successor, the Greek Zosimus, tried to revoke the decision, they renounced obedience to him, instigated the imperial government against the Pelagians, and finally coerced even the pope to endorse the condemnation and make it generally known (418).

Only when the cause of the Pelagians in church politics was lost did their most important spokesman, Julian, Bishop of Eclanum in Apulia, step into the foreground. Augustine considered that without him the Pelagian scaffolding would forever have remained without a master-builder. Julian was the only opponent Augustine encountered during his lifetime who was more or less his equal, and at times one has the impression that Augustine looked upon this indefatigable nuisance with a secret and reluctant sympathy. 'A self-assured young man' of good family, like Augustine a brilliant dialectician and stylist, yet more elegant, carelessly unconcerned and reckless in his polemic, Julian remained fundamentally a man of the world, fully content with himself and with the type of Christianity he had constructed, a rational and life-affirming Christianity. As the manifest enemy of grace, Pelagius was hardly understood by Augustine, and was in any case depicted one-sidedly. The picture of Julian, however, is clear and quite unmistakable. He was more than just a theological opponent of Augustine. In him a declining life-spirit tried for the last time to voice a cause for which there was no longer to be any place in the Augustinian-medieval church. As a theologian Julian spoke for the convictions of classical enlightenment. He was a popular philosopher in a Christian costume, the last defender of that Stoic 'dignity of man' which believed in God, yet did not fundamentally need his help, and which relied simply on one's own nature, even though this 'nature' is called 'creation'. The difficulties which Augustine came across in his self-examination never really worried Julian, because he did not know them. Thus the whole theological exposition of the terms grace, original sin, and the alleged perversion of man's being, itself appeared to him perverse, or at least utterly superfluous. Such things refute themselves by their own absurdity. Why should Adam's descendants have to suffer to all eternity for Adam's not too tragic guilt? How can sin in any way 'be hereditary' through procreation? And what kind of reason is it which for the future punishes the sinner with inevitable sinfulness? In what sense is it just to punish a sinner, if freedom for doing good has actually been lost? Like every 'enlightened' thinker, it was easy for Julian to proceed 'logically', and to disclose the obvious discrepancies and contradictions of his adversary. He did this with moral passion and with pleasure! The consistency of his system had but one defect, that it did not correspond with reality. But this was in Julian's opinion exactly the matter in question: whether Augustine had indeed arrived at the reality of man, or whether his whole teaching on sin and grace was based instead on one vast 'complex'. From his own presuppositions he simply could not understand how Augustine's conception of the totality of life recognizes the forlorn state of fallen mankind in the famous incident of stealing pears, a 'harmless' boyish prank reported in the *Confessions*, or indeed even in the helpless whimpering of the baby.

On one essential point Julian separated himself even from his own friends. Pelagius had naturally seen something wicked and dangerous in sensual and sexual desire. After all, he was a monk! Yet how can this be allowed if, on the other hand, the 'nature' of man is declared to be unchangeably good? Sexual lust, *concupiscentia*, does belong to human nature: without it the generation and continuance of mankind would not even be conceivable. Julian had been married, and refused to surround the sphere of the sexual with the tabu of the half-prohibited, the tempting, the blasphemous. The sensual urge as such is not evil; of course it has to be controlled, and must be rationally mastered, but in itself it is simply natural and therefore also good. He who teaches the reverse must be still in principle a Manichean, who denies the goodness of creation, consigns the corporeal to the devil, and so, of course, cannot take seriously the 'freedom' of man. There is no middle way here. One is either a Christian in Julian's sense, or a Manichean heretic. This accusation, advanced ever and anew, was for Augustine especially embarrassing, for it was not simply fabricated. There really was an obvious spiritual connection between Augustine's theology of grace and his former Manicheism. The arguments Julian introduced against him had earlier been used by himself against the Manicheans! Therein lay the extraordinary difficulty of his position, which constantly drove him to new and subtle distinctions. For Augustine also had no intention of giving up creation and freedom. Freedom was to him an ineradicable element of undefiled human 'nature'. By the Fall, however, the state of human nature had changed in such a way that now, in spite of its 'freedom', it is no longer able to liberate itself from its bondage to sin. Augustine realized that, regarding his terminology, he was in somewhat of an impasse with this conception of a bound freedom. The problem was to define grace in such a way that freedom was not abandoned, and, on the other hand, to define the freedom of the will in such a way that the all-embracing effect of grace was nevertheless neither reduced nor limited.

Seen as a whole, his teaching on *concupiscentia* caused Augustine the least trouble, despite difficulties in detail. Here he remained the ascetic he had always been. That sensual concupiscence had something to do with sin was for him beyond question. He spoke here out of experience, and had only to repeat the reminiscence of his own conversion-story. The involuntariness and uncontrollability of the sexual drive, and the shame connected with it, prove at least this much: that since the Fall the constitution and the psychological order of man are disturbed. Augustine developed the grotesque idea that in paradise Adam would have possessed, if he had not fallen, the faculty to procreate children without tumultuous desire by moving his organs in complete freedom and at will, like arms and legs. Yet this does not mean that the present predominance of sensual impulse has to be given a 'Manichean' explanation, by assuming an evil substance. Evil as such is for Augustine still a negative quantity, even though this nothingness expresses itself as a manifest power in perversion and confusion of nature and the will. On the other hand, it remains really difficult for him to explain how the transmission of original sin to all children of Adam could be conceived of. To be sure, they were all 'in' Adam when he ate the forbidden fruit, and in so far they participated in his sin. Yet the real abode of sin is the human spirit, by which Adam in disobedience and pride set God's government at naught. Augustine does not venture to maintain a generation of the soul analogous to physical generation, which Julian would have liked to chalk up as a new heresy. It is just because his teaching on original sin does not exhaust itself in the sensual connotation that it is so difficult for Augustine to define its nature. Sin was doubtless existent from the beginning. It adhered to man 'by contagion and not by decision' (*Op. Imperf.* IV, 98). Nevertheless it does not derive only from his sensual nature, but dwells precisely in the spiritual, willing ego, and determines him completely.

The decisive thing to be recognized, which mattered everything to Augustine, is that we are helpless when entirely dependent upon ourselves, and that God's grace must do no less than everything in order to save us. This does not mean that man does not possess any freedom of will at all, but only that this will is of itself always inclined to sin, and is never in a position to change its inclination. God's grace, therefore, cannot be moved by our good volition, but exactly the reverse: 'The human will does not achieve grace through freedom, but rather freedom through grace' (*Corr. et Grat.* 8, 17). When the human will redeemed by Christ finds its way back to faith, to hope, and to love, then it is truly set free. Here emerges a new and deeper concept of freedom. For Augustine freedom is no longer defined as the capability of arbitrary choice, but as the condition of determination by the good, and by God. Because He alone can be good, God is not therefore Himself unfree, but rather, on the contrary, free in an absolute sense. 'Our freedom consists in that we are subject to the truth' (*Lib. Arb.* II, 13, 37); the 'being a servant' of righteousness 'itself is the true freedom' (*Enchir.* 30). 'Thus only are we truly free, when God takes us in His fashioning hands, i.e. when He forms and creates us—not as men (for this He has already done), but to the end that we may become good men, and that is what His grace now does' (*Enchir.* 31). Consequently, there is something like an 'effected' freedom. The perfect freedom and humanity of man is just what is effected by God and yet remains freedom which man affirms, co-operates with and adopts in his own volition. 'Hence we will; but God works in us that we will. Thus we act, but God also works the action in us' (*Don. Pers.* 13, 33). The problem of co-ordinating grace and freedom—a novel problem not understood by Julian and also never considered by the entire Greek theology—is solved by Augustine in such a way that he no longer adjusts freedom and grace one to the other, but views them as a unity wherein grace is always the dominating element, and human will the subordinate element controlled by God. This by no means excludes, in fact it includes the notion that the liberated human will itself now actually do the good work, and to this extent also can earn 'merits'. It does not, however, have itself to thank for these merits. They are from God's grace living in the man, totally excluding all pride and 'glorying in one's works', and thereby making him entirely humble. 'When God crowns our merits', Augustine explains time and again, 'He crowns only His own gifts' (*Conf.* IX, 34), for grace alone creates merit, and before grace there is no human merit: 'What hast thou that thou didst not receive?' (I Cor. iv. 7).

But if this be so, how does it come about that this freedom of the redeemed does not fall to the lot of everyone, that so many are lost, and even that Christians who really have believed and lived in Christ's love can subsequently fall away and perish? To this there is only one answer: it is a matter for God alone, who certainly never in any circumstances wills what is evil, but can at His free discretion grant, refuse, or retract the divine grace without which none is able to do that which is

good. This is the ultimate proof that His grace really is nothing
other than grace, and that salvation 'is not of him that willeth,
nor of him that runneth, but of God that showeth mercy'
(Rom. ix. 16). 'For, just as the eye of the body, even when
completely sound, is unable to see unless aided by the brightness
of light, so also man, even when most fully justified, is unable
to lead a holy life, if he be not divinely assisted by eternal light
of righteousness' (*Nat. et Grat.* 26, 29; Oates, 1,540). In Augustine's usage predestination is the final testimony to God's glory,
and to the unconditioned sovereignty of His grace. Yet why has
God damned those not elected? 'Why except that He willed it?
As to why He willed it, "Who art thou, O man, that repliest
against God?" ' (*Ep.* 186, 23; *FC*, 12, 207). We must humbly
rest content with this answer already given by Paul (Rom. ix.
20)—and we must know at the same time that God remains
good and just in all things, even when we do not understand
him.

Augustine, however, would not acquiesce entirely in this last
ignoramus to which he confesses. Particularly in defending himself, time and again he tried to reach beyond it, and in some
way to make visible or show to be reasonable the incomprehensibility of God's decree. The question of God's righteousness
and of man's guilt is to find an answer at least to this extent,
that, not the predestination of the elect—for this is grace and
nothing else—but the rejection of the reprobate can still be
counted as 'merited'. For this purpose Augustine once again
refers to 'Adam' 'in whom' all have sinned in advance. For
Adam still really was 'free' for good or evil; only 'a penal corruption closely followed thereon, and out of (original) liberty
produced necessity (of evil)' (*Perf. Iust.* 4, 9; *LPNF*, 5, 161).
And because he voluntarily decided for disobedience and revolt,
he and his posterity were therefore justly damned by God.
Indeed, God is inexplicable in his mercy but not unjust in his
condemnation. For modern feeling it is, of course, extremely
unsatisfying to see how Augustine tries to solve the difficulties
of his theological interpretation of existence by throwing the

blame on 'Adam'. The vain fantasy of a 'freedom of choice', which with respect to present man he had rightly denied to Julian, now appears again for man in his original state. In order to remove moral and logical objections the myth which interprets Adam symbolically is rationalized in a way which must cause even greater offence. If we wish to follow the train of Augustine's thinking, it appears in fact more consistent to let Adam's fall also be determined by God's decision, and thus—as the theological formulation has it—to teach a 'supralapsarian' predestination. But is such a terrible consequence still tolerable to the religious mind? As we can see, Augustine, at any rate, could not or would not find it so.

There is no denying that on the whole predestination plays an essentially different role in Augustine's thought from that which it plays in the Biblical texts to which he refers. To be sure, with him also it ministers to God's glory as we have seen, yet the comforting and uplifting character it displays with Paul is here largely lost. Only with Augustine did the idea of predestination attain the gloomy inevitability which made it 'the horror of Christian thought in all ages' (Heinrich Barth). How does this come about? The answer leads us to the ultimate weakness of the Augustinian theology, a weakness which merely culminates in the doctrine of grace. In primitive Christianity likewise the salvation of man depended on God's election alone, and to this the impenitence and condemnation of the ungodly necessarily corresponded. Yet this election never took place in this connection in an abstract incomprehensibility, but always through Jesus Christ as God's incarnate Word. In the encounter with Christ human doubt has no room for play: there is opened an assured way in which faith may and must tread. 'He is righteousness to every one that believeth' (Rom. x. 4)—he is allowed to regard himself as of the elect, and from this view the theological speculations lose their relevance and justification. Now, of course, Augustine also wants to maintain the central position of the Saviour, and testifies to it with emphasis: 'This way has never been lacking to the human race . . . no one has ever been liberated, nor is being liberated, nor ever will be liberated, except by this way' (*Civ. D.* x, 32, 2; *FC*, 7, 184). But this Christ and His grace are in Augustine nevertheless not exclusively united to the proclaimed word. Christ as God's eternal truth attains to a much more general and almost timeless significance, and his actions become limitless. The theology of grace therefore largely follows its own theological and philosophical logic. It turns into an independent principle of thought which can no longer be clearly applied in the range of the particular and the individual. The question of a personal assurance of salvation remains explicitly unanswered in Augustine's theology.

From this standpoint it is no doubt theoretically possible to play off the idea of predestination against the concrete community and medium of salvation, i.e. against the church. If God's grace follows its own incomprehensible laws, then the church cannot possibly consist purely of the elect. In these circumstances, who can know whether he really belongs to their number? Augustine observed with sorrow the effect of his own teaching on grace: it threatened to entice men into false security, and this is exactly what it was intended not to do. Yet earnestly as he entertained such thoughts, in order to quench all spiritual pride, Augustine never turned them against the concept of the church as such, or against the certainty of ecclesiastical salvation itself. He wants her means of grace and her fellowship to be taken seriously and received in confident joy. To draw the opposite conclusion, along idealistic or sceptical lines, would no longer be Augustinian. The sole object of Augustine's teaching on grace is to rebuke the pride of man who is imprisoned by himself and who deceives himself. A piety developed by the sinner for himself, and thus not received in humility from God, is in his eyes pagan and demonic however Christian its appearance. For it rejects Christ and the Holy Spirit precisely at that point where one needs them the most: in one's own inner self, in the overcoming of egotism and the delusion of our ungodly self. The redeemed and therefore truly human man finds his centre and his 'freedom' no longer in himself, but as it were outside himself. The fountain of his life lies in God. His self-consciousness and self-confidence are replaced by confidence in God, who arouses faith, hope, and love. The 'idea of man' current in antiquity is thereby struck at the root, and religion likewise changes its meaning and idea. It no longer means the perfection of man, who inaugurates a relation with the higher powers for the sole purpose of securing or perfecting his own existence. It means rather that God, the Lord of the whole of reality, has become completely Lord of man also, and in a new sense. God is really present for man only when he permeates also the innermost man, i.e. his will, and when he becomes man's all in humble love.

The older Augustine grew, the more passionately and completely he devoted his life to his church and his congregation. This was the home of the revealed love of Christ and of mutual assistance. Here the Holy Spirit operated, and the truth of God was preached and lived for the whole world. Here he felt himself to be in the outer courts of his God. Augustine was concerned that the holiness and miraculous power of Christianity should remain no abstract thought but become visible, attractive and convincing in appearance. He welcomed the circumstance that now, when martyrdoms were an event of the past, monasticism supplied new saints. The emerging cult of saints and relics was ardently promoted by him. His teaching on grace offered the necessary theological justification for this. If it be God who works all grace and all miracles in His believers, then all the veneration one renders to them leads likewise back to God, and does not impair but rather augments his honour. Even more characteristic is Augustine's interest in concrete miracles, such as happen particularly at the tombs of the martyrs. It could be seen from them that the proofs of the Spirit, and of the power which once distinguished primitive Christianity had not been withdrawn from the contemporary church, and the Holy Spirit was still at work in it. Nothing more is to be seen of the cool reserve with which the young Christian philosopher once observed these phenomena. At that time Augustine had thought that 'since the Catholic church had been established and diffused throughout the whole world' miracles had become superfluous; God had stopped them 'lest the mind should always seek visible things, and the human race should grow cold by becoming accustomed to things which when they were novelties kindled its faith' (*Vera Rel.* 25, 47; *LCC*, 6, 248). Now he could report an abundance of miracles which were supposed to have happened in his lifetime alone, and in his own town, especially in the chapel with Stephen's relics. He concerned himself to list them authentically, he had these records read in the services, and he could not understand that such unheard of things were received so calmly by the congregation, and were so quickly forgotten. Augustine was of a surprising and almost sentimental naïvety and credulity. This great speculative thinker showed hardly a trace of criticism with regard to all historical questions. In this respect he put no impediment in the way of the Middle Ages, with their fondness for miracles.

If one reads the biography devoted by Possidius to Augustine, his revered teacher and example, the latter appears as the model of the faithful bishop and pastor, the man who paved the way for the monastic movement in Africa and contended as the faithful defender of the Catholic truth against heretics to right and left. Yet in the whole book there is no mention of a single theological question as such. It is instructive that Augustine could be seen and described like this at close quarters; but this picture of the man offers too little—not only in our opinion, but also in the opinion of Augustine himself. Augustine knew what he was. He did not wish to be merely a pious custodian of the orthodox tradition, but felt himself to be through and through a doctor of the church, pointing the way it must go. This was the highest responsibility he had to bear and meet. The remarkable monument of this intention is his *Retractationes*, i.e. 'revisions' of his earlier writings, which he had planned for a long time and began to dictate three years before his death, yet finishing only the revision of the 'books' properly so called,

not that of the letters and sermons. Augustine was aware of the
fact that his writings were read and heeded all over the world.
Yet how much there was that could be compiled from them,
which, though not exactly false, was nevertheless somewhat distorted and in need of correction. Even now as an old man,
Augustine did not consider himself infallible. But he knew he
'wrote by advancing in knowledge, and advanced by writing'
(*Ep.* 143, 2). He was concerned with stating publicly that 'even
I myself have not in all things followed myself' (*Don. Persev.*
21, 55) and since he could not now withdraw the books in
circulation, nothing else was left for him but to publish his
'corrections' in a new book. According to this, what he had
written could be 'read with benefit. Some things have to be
pardoned, or, if people will not pardon them, they should at
least not adhere obstinately to what is wrong in them' (*Retr.*
prol. 3).

These acts of self-accusation and—on the whole rarely—of
self-defence are, of course, an interesting source for studying the
'progress' of Augustine's principles and convictions. Some
corrections concern only external and small oversights, particularly in quotations which could be rectified without much
ado. The retraction goes deeper in relation to a number of statements, especially in the books of his youth, in which Augustine
had given too full scope to his rhetoric, and had used bombast
and pagan flourishes which had been better avoided. His judgement upon pagan mythology, literature, and education has
hardened. Augustine strives for a religious purism which previously was alien to him. Most instructive is his self-criticism in
actual dogmatic questions. It touches especially his teaching on
creation, and his eschatology. The Neo-Platonic contempt of
the corporeal, earthly, and visible contradicts, as Augustine now
realizes clearly, the historical and concrete thinking of the Bible.
The latter must be taken more strictly and more literally in its
utterances. In this short and thoroughly moderate book one can
detect no literary vanity, no evidence that Augustine has im-
modestly taken himself too seriously. Augustine is not con-

cerned with his fame after death, but with the church's truth,
i.e. with the correctness of the teaching for which he stood, and
with its protection against possible error and misinterpretation.
It depends really on this. He who does not see this objective
dogmatic striving of the old Augustine has not comprehended
the direction of his development.

The schoolmaster of former times had become the doctor of
the church. He was concerned with the organization of his
intellectual property, and with correct perception and the
accurate use of knowledge which, however, does not by itself
make a man 'wise'. He was concerned with the distinction of
the essential from the non-essential. Whoever hears Christ, the
one true teacher, and does not add anything of his 'own',
avoids the useless babble and superfluous talk against which the
Bible gives warning. Yet even though it sometimes becomes
extensive, and extremely circumstantial, the presentation of
what is requisite must not be regarded as mere babble—'by no
means!' (*Retr.* prol. 2). Already in Cassiciacum Augustine had
designed the plan of an encyclopedic work which was to deal,
after the pattern of Varro but in the spirit of Christianity, with
the seven traditional branches of 'Learning', the *artes liberales*
of medieval times. At that time he did not get beyond the
description of grammar and rhythm. As he complained, the
acceptance of his ecclesiastical office made further realization
impossible. Later, however, he took up the work again more
thoroughly. At the time when he began the *Retractationes*, his
new Christian teaching on education was completed. It is the
four books on *Christian Learning, De Doctrina Christiana.*

Until then the church had not possessed such a work. Its
basic significance reaches far beyond its detailed content, which
in part is only in rough draft, yet important even so. The problem of secular education and the schools had uninterruptedly
occupied the church since the end of the second century. It
could not be avoided, in so far as the Christians could not do
without higher education. The schools, and the whole educational tradition of the environment, however, were pagan and

in their classical curriculum could not be divorced from pagan
mythology and philosophy. The external Christianization of
the empire did not at first change anything here. We can see
this from the conflicts in which Jerome was involved, as well
as from his amateurish attempts to present Jerusalem as the
Christian Athens, and King David as the Christian Pindar or
Horace. With Augustine the situation had now changed. More
than any of his predecessors Augustine was at home in classical
education and culture, but he did not need to 'suppress' them
forcibly, because he had overcome them inwardly, in himself.
He thus ventured upon the project of a new education, determined throughout in the light of its goal, which should select
from the knowledge existing hitherto that which appeared useful, and be content to lay aside what it could use no longer. As
there is only one philosophy and one wisdom, that is the philosophy of Christ which has overcome and replaced all pagan
philosophies, so there is henceforward also only one true way of
knowing, and one 'Christian learning', which serves the Christian wisdom. This 'learning' is the knowledge of the Bible, and
most of all the art of correct interpretation of everything the
Bible says and the accurate proclamation of its truth. Augustine's work was published at first as a kind of manual 'for those
persons who interest themselves in the Holy Scripture', primarily therefore for the young clergy and preachers of the
Catholic church. It shows them what knowledge they must
obtain in order to do justice to their spiritual task. It indicates,
in traditional ways throughout, that the knowledge of grammar, rhetoric, etc., required up to then, including even the
knowledge of music, still remains necessary if one now wishes
to understand and to proclaim the Scripture alone, in place of
the classical authors. Subsequently, Augustine develops the
principles of interpretation (hermeneutics), and of preaching
(homiletics). Yet the knowledge he demands in this way is
nevertheless no mere professional knowledge for theologians
and churchmen. In his view it is the 'Christian' learning as such
on which everything depends for all, and beside which there is

nothing in the last resort essential. For the Bible is the book of truth; it is the whole and is sufficient for all.

The new element in this position is the methodological consistency with which perception of the Biblical truth is simply made the centre and basis of knowledge and of the spiritual life. In this Augustine operates like the first 'medieval' thinker, which in other respects he certainly never was. On the other hand, his unconditional acknowledgment of the Bible, and of its significance for the entire life of faith, is in itself by no means original. In this he is in complete accord with the entire early church. The Bible is God's book, inspired and dictated by His Spirit and deserves unlimited confidence. While bishops may err, one must 'in no manner doubt or dispute whether anything is true or false, once it is established that it is written there' (*Bapt.* 2; 3, 4). This verdict is valid in principle even with regard to the accessory data and statements contained in the Bible; it is not limited to the assertions 'significant for salvation'. Characteristically, however, this does not prevent Augustine—like so many believers in the Bible—from handling it in practice, if need be, with comparative freedom. Completely without prejudice he takes account of errors of translation or copyists' faults, and in certain cases even with later corruptions. He emphasizes that God, or His prophets and apostles, naturally had to accommodate themselves to the understanding of their hearers, and in case of obscure passages he referred to the clearer ones, or to the whole of Scripture, which indeed will always serve the true love of God and neighbour as taught by the church. Allegory also naturally plays its part, opening the possibility of turning to a higher or multiple meaning of the Scripture, and so reaching an acceptable result in every case. Augustine also took pains with the philological, archaeological, and chronological details—precisely for this purpose the exegete needs the different 'sciences', but on the whole he was no philologist like Jerome, and even disapproved of his labours on the original Hebrew text. Augustine looked for that which was theologically essential and decisive, and in doing so also time and again hit upon the correct content. 'Let us therefore hear the gospel, just as if we were listening to the Lord Himself present. . . . For the precious truth that sounded forth from the mouth of the Lord was both written for our sakes, and preserved for our sakes, and will be recited for the sake of our posterity, even until the end of the world. The Lord is above; but the Lord, the Truth, is also here' (*John tr*. XXX, 1; *LPNF*, 7, 186). So the horizon of the Scripture grew broader from within. It is for him who can hear the truth and who leaves idle curiosity aside. It is truly the book of books, containing everything, and furnishes answers to all the questions which really matter to us.

The notion of education centres around this, and the extent of significant knowledge is correspondingly reduced. This is done with full awareness of what this reduction to essentials means. One may say that in this also Augustine meets the need of his age. Late antiquity was the time of normative textbooks and standardized education: these generations were no longer carrying intellectually the superfluity of riches of a culture that had grown old. Now finally all its wisdom and knowledge was placed at men's disposal in a single book, and from this book one realizes again why a certain amount of knowledge and traditional education still remained indispensable. Christianity had intensified the impression of the sterility and 'scholastic' emptiness of the old grammatical and theoretical instruction. An ascetic withdrawal was now simultaneously justified and limited by Augustine. 'One thing is necessary', and but little is enough in order to do justice seriously to this one thing. The 'arts and sciences' are no longer there for their own sake; only as disciplines supplementary to the Bible do they have a right to exist. A 'knowledge for the sake of knowledge', which does not know and envisage any more of the ultimate goal of man, cannot serve truth, but ministers only to the ambition and vanity of scholars. 'Knowledge puffeth up, but charity edifieth' (I Cor. viii. 1). It is not accidental that this attitude of Augustine reminds us of the state of mind of the aged Plato; yet his concept of love leads him beyond the latter, and takes away the sullen undertone from his instruction. One need only remember too the new preaching of the church, which was so relevant to life, and for which there was no counterpart in the realm of secular education, in order to understand that the Augustinian ideal of education by no means remained fruitless; it lived and shaped life. To be sure, it is an ascetic ideal, carrying all the dangers that such a strictly limited plan also involves intellectually at all times. Augustine did not sense these dangers. In his youth, he had traversed in full freedom the whole range of intellectual experience, only in the end to find 'all the depth of the riches both of wisdom and knowledge' in Christ and His word. From this point he started with determination. He desires to preserve only the essential, and to avoid all the by-paths of intellectual play which turn it into a game. All détours are wrong ways. The result of an abundant life is made without more ado the basis and firm rule for all. Augustine did not ask whether such a thing is possible. To him the straight line between two points is unquestionably the 'shortest way'. He founded his instructions on the sole basis of theology, yet this foundation once again reveals the whole Augustine.

The love of man must not remain fixed upon this and that. It has its aim in the eternal and unchangeable things, i.e. in the last resort in God, and only secondarily in what can be loved for God's sake. By giving the command to 'love Him "with all thy heart, and with all thy soul and with all thy mind"' (Matt. xxii. 37), God has taken up our whole life and 'left no part of our life which could be empty and, as it were, give place to desire to enjoy any other thing. Whatever else comes to our attention to be loved is to be carried along to that place to which the whole torrent of our love rushes.' This applies also to love of our neighbour, and to the affirmation of the self; the love of God 'suffers no trickle to be led off from itself by whose diversion its own volume might be lessened' (de Doctr. I, 22, 21; FC, 4, 42). God remains the sole object of man's ultimate devotion. All love of the creature, which we may 'use' according

thoroughfare to God

to His will, is subject to this reservation. It is by the Christian
reservation of unconditioned obedience and joyful surrender
to the one Creator and Lord that we are withdrawn from the
dominion of 'this world', and have become 'free' as His redeemed. But, as always with Augustine, this is combined with
the reservation of the intellectual man, that is to say, the
Platonic pride which does not really acknowledge the lower
this-worldly existence as the object of its concern and love. The
spirit of man stems from God. God and his eternal truth are for
this reason the only truly worthy aim of his striving, inquiry,
and love. Augustine's love of God always displays something
of the impetuous pressure of a passionate lover, who feels as a
betrayal of his love any thought that leads away from the beloved object, or is not directly taken up and maintained for its
sake. It possesses nothing of the innocent security of children
as they play under the supervision of their mother, and are
therefore both completely with their play and entirely with
their mother. The ascetic feature of this piety is even more
strongly expressed in Augustine than it was in the Middle Ages
which he influenced so strongly, because, as already noted, he
neither tolerates nor knows any separation of theology and
philosophy, wisdom of God and the wisdom of this world. The
worldly things and sciences thus lose their relative independence
and intellectual autonomy. All things are only a thoroughfare
to life in God—and God is the real and immediate meaning of
life, and can nowhere be evaded or somehow edged away to
the periphery.

It is misleading to interpret Augustine's theology as a *com-
plexio oppositorum*, as a combination of mutually opposing elements. True, the Christian Augustine was a Platonist, because
the Platonist had become a Christian. But in his thought and
life, he was always concerned only for the exclusiveness and
completeness of his faith which he perhaps formulated most
precisely in his teaching on grace, but which he never lost sight
of and never denied. This theology of the unconditioned love
of God in its many-sidedness cannot be adopted and applied in

a new intellectual and historical environment, without undergoing change, in the course of which intellectual difficulties and tensions are bound to appear. But this characteristic it shares with all living intellectual systems, which never live or have their truth for themselves, but seek to touch living reality and are therefore never completely closed. In his historical setting Augustine can be understood only as an historical personality, and in what he wished to say and did say he is quite unmistakable.

The end of Augustine's life was passed under the shadow of the Vandal invasion, the horrors of which the aged bishop felt and experienced more deeply and painfully, as his biographer remarks, than most of his compatriots; 'for in much wisdom is much grief: and he that increaseth knowledge increaseth sorrow' (Eccl. i. 18). Whether he realized that this was the beginning of the decline of the Western empire nevertheless remains uncertain. Up to the last minute he sought to admonish and encourage the imperial officials and officers to carry out their duties energetically. He absolutely forbade the clergy to leave their congregations. Only when all had fled, would they be allowed to follow. He himself took care of the refugees who crowded besieged Hippo. He had the golden vessels of his church melted down in order to alleviate the misery, and continued 'incessantly, vigorously, and courageously' to preach the word of God. In the third month of the siege, Augustine, who was then 75 years old, contracted a fatal disease. He caused the penitential psalms of David to be pinned up on the wall in front of his bed. He accounted himself to be a penitent, and wept and prayed. Ten days before the end, he asked his friends not to visit him any more. They were to enter his room only when he needed in any case to receive the physician, or was taking food or medicine. Augustine wished to be alone, and remained so until the hour of death, when all hastened up in order to unite their prayers with his. He was fully conscious,—all the members of his body 'intact'—and retained until the end clear eyesight and good hearing. He had not made a will, because, as Possidius says, he, the poor man of God, possessed no property which he could have bequeathed. Yet 'he always ordered the church's library, with all the books, to be carefully preserved for posterity' (*Possid.* 31; *FC*, 15, 123). It was in large part made up of his own works. As a matter of fact, when the city was later taken and burned, his friends succeeded in saving the books. Whoever reads his writings, says Possidius, realizes that Aurelius Augustinus 'lived uprightly and wisely in the faith, hope, and charity of the Catholic Church', and will draw corresponding benefits therefrom. 'However, I think,' he adds, 'that greater profit was derived by those who were able to hear and see him speak when he was present in church, especially those who knew his life among men' (*Possid.* 31; *FC*, 15, 124). The personal fascination in Augustine's nature is no modern invention or discovery. He appears to have retained it even in extreme old age.

CHAPTER VII

BOETHIUS

THE century after Augustine's death was rich in theological writers, but poor in outstanding personalities. Though the intellectual impulses which Augustine had given to his time produced further effects, the spiritual level to which he had lifted every theological question could not be maintained. The external political and economic conditions were not conducive to the overcoming of a definite decadence, and furthered the decline. The Germanic mass migration pressed forward irresistibly. In the West it swept over almost all the provinces of the old empire, and the enormous efforts which had to be made in resistance and reconquest exhausted the over-taxed strength of the populace. Despite this, no permanent restoration and pacification was achieved. During this time monasticism spread widely in the church. Especially in Gaul, its thought became theologically productive. The radicalism of the Oriental ideal was here combined with the moralistic, rationalistic, and organizational tendencies of early Western Christianity. The ascetic conception lost the comprehensive and living significance it had attained with Augustine. Piety came into tension with his teaching on grace, and at the same time combined with the claims and expectations of a hope of salvation to be mediated by means strictly ecclesiastical. The 'semi-Pelagian' controversies were the expression of these unresolved tensions in the wake of the Augustinian theology. The difficulties which arose could not be solved within the circumscribed ambit in which the questions were raised, and were never really settled.

The transformation of the social order, as barbarians and Germans took over the old Mediterranean culture and social structure, meanwhile began to reach and influence the church too, but the changed situation was not yet realized as a task and a new opportunity for activity. It is true that here and there leading men adapted themselves skilfully to the new circumstances, but in general they still felt themselves to be Romans, citizens, and representatives of the empire, of its old judicial order and of its culture. While the Western imperial régime ceased to exist (476) and new, Germanic states sprang up everywhere, men still clung to the fiction of a continuing *orbis Romanus*, the Roman world and sovereignty. It was the churchmen who continued to look to the East, where the orthodox emperor reigned, who had to protect the church. The Germanic vassal peoples and their kings were not Catholic Christians, but adhered to the 'Arian' confession, and were for that reason also not accepted as real rulers. Even the theological literature of the fifth century still breathed the spirit and character of 'antiquity'.

The decadence of this period was by no means uniform and general. Under the rule of the Ostrogoth King Theodoric (493-526), Italy at least experienced once again a long period of peace and a revival which was also to the advantage of the church and of cultural life in general. To be sure, the military and political power lay exclusively in the hands of the king and his German followers; but Theodoric allowed the traditional order of civic life to exist, and indeed he enjoyed being considered a patron of the classical traditions. He did everything lying in his power to reconcile ancient society with his prudent and beneficent rule. The emperor had recognized him. The consuls for the year were now appointed as of old by consent between the two courts. The city of Rome in particular, with her senate, and her ancient practices, offices, and games, once again enjoyed a golden age.

Boethius, the man with whom we conclude the line of Latin church fathers, was at home in this world. Apart from Augustine, there is no other Christian teacher to whom the church of the Middle Ages went so consciously for instruction as

Boethius. He has been called both the last Roman and the first of the Schoolmen. Boethius was in fact both, for as a Roman he felt called upon to teach the true philosophy to the whole Latin-speaking world, and he did this in the 'scholastic' spirit of his time. Yet although he was a Christian, and even composed theological writings, he would hardly have allowed himself to be called a 'Father of the Church'. For this he stood too much apart from all ecclesiastical activity in the narrower sense, and not only externally. Boethius had his roots in the older humane, intellectual and religious traditions, and was faithful to them to a far greater degree than Augustine, the African Christian and 'philosopher'. In spite of his time and its manners, Boethius remained at heart a classic, the last Greek philosopher, and, just because he knew this, a Roman aristocrat and citizen.

All political turmoil and change could not interrupt the continuity of public life in the city of Rome. After the emperor had left the nominal capital of the empire, its old aristocratic character had even grown stronger, and the Byzantine caste-feeling and bureaucracy furthered this development. A small, exclusive circle of immensely rich landed families, privileged, and the bearers of very ancient names, still had in its hands the control of current business and bore the burden of a revered tradition and representation with solemn pride through the changed times. This noble Roman society no longer possessed serious political significance, yet to the mind of the inhabitants of the empire there was still a glamour and historical dignity about these consuls and senators which seemed incomparable and irreplaceable. Taken all in all these last Romans showed themselves not unworthy of their position and their high name. They not only willingly took over all the burdens of their position; they also cultivated higher education, particularly Greek, which otherwise had almost no home in the West, and they took care of educational institutions and libraries. We are largely indebted to them for the preservation to later times of the classical authors. Some also showed a keen interest in the church, for in the course of the fifth century the last families who had so long resisted became Christian without exception. Catholicism was from now on as much a matter of course as once the acceptance of pagan tradition had been, yet pride in the old tradition and the feeling of a duty to it was nevertheless preserved.

Boethius is the greatest representative of this late Roman society, and its strict, noble and somewhat inbred culture. He was born about 480. The *gens Anicia* to which he belonged had first begun to rise in the social scale under the later republic, and then, under the empire, had attained to extraordinary wealth and influence. Many consuls and two emperors belonged to it, and it was related by birth or marriage to all the leading families of the city. Boethius never experienced material want, or struggle for recognition or position. Once he listed among the annoying disadvantages, which can make a man's life a burden, low birth in the first place, and lack of a suitable fortune in the second (*Consol.* II, 4, 13). Fortuna had granted him both! His father, the elder Boethius, had been consul, and had held various municipal offices. If he is to be identified with a Boethius mentioned as a prefect in Alexandria, he would even have served the Eastern emperor directly at an earlier period; but this cannot be confirmed. The younger Boethius, Anicius Manlius Severinus Boethius junior, was still a child when his father died. He was received into the house of his relative Quintus Aurelius Memmius Symmachus, later his father-in-law, the great-grandson of that Symmachus who on one occasion had stepped forward in the name of the senate in favour of the subsidies for the pagan cult, and had been rejected by Ambrose (p. 105 f.). Symmachus was not only the guardian of the rich heir; he also became his mentor and friend, who introduced him to the world of higher education, literature, and philosophy, in which Boethius was later so much at home. Boethius dedicated various writings to him, and time and again confessed that he was indebted to this man for almost everything. Symmachus must have been an important personality. He wrote a (lost) Roman history in seven books, had a thorough knowledge of Greek, and was known in East and West as a brilliant speaker. He became prefect of the city, consul, and head of the senate. He was also honoured by Theodoric, although—perhaps indeed because—after Odoacer's overthrow he had come forward in the senate against the expulsion of the senators appointed by him. Yet Symmachus was reserved in his attitude to the new German lords. He was satisfied with his acknowledged position among his peers, and in occupying himself with philosophical and other studies. In this respect, too, Boethius became his pupil.

Boethius must have developed with amazing rapidity. He was, it is said, an indefatigable reader, a kind of infant prodigy 'whom industry had already in his boyhood changed into an adult, despite his youth' (*Ennod. Ep.* 7, 13). Delays and impediments did not exist for him. As the confidant of his father-in-law, with whom he agreed in all essential matters, he soon enjoyed the happiness of independent research which, as he expressed himself, was at the same time 'spiced by the sweet pleasant flavour of love' (*Hypoth. Syllog.* praef.). His marriage with Symmachus' daughter Rusticiana, who bore him at least two sons, was likewise happy. Even at the close of his life, when, at length overthrown and condemned, he tried to see through the vanity of all earthly good, he had to confess that he had never personally experienced the reputed disadvantages of marital life, and the trouble which wife and children may cause to a man (*Consol.* III, 7, 5). The outward course of his life also developed just as a man might wish. Soon from all sides fame and admiration were showered upon him. Boethius was esteemed a perfect speaker in Greek as well as Latin. He not only knew the works of literature, but was also completely familiar with the practical scientific disciplines which one 'ordinarily uses without real knowledge'—music, mathematics, and the technical arts; he had explored them, as Cassiodorus assures us, 'at the spring of science itself' (*Cassiod. Var.* I, 45). Boethius himself praised the beautiful library of his palace, adorned with mosaics and ivory (*Consol.* I, 5, 6) in which he used to work and philosophize in peace (*Consol.* I, 4, 3).

Yet one must not therefore imagine Boethius as an eccentric

recluse. He also entered with self-assurance and as a matter of course upon the usual career of the Roman aristocrat, for whom all doors were open. Before he was 30 years old, we find him already honoured with the most illustrious titles, which often 'remain denied to old men' (*Consol.* II, 4, 7). He was senator and patrician, and undoubtedly also held other high posts of honour. He was once commissioned by Theodoric to investigate certain payments, regarding which there had been loud complaints as to the weight of the coinage. Another time he successfully applied himself to secure a remission of taxes for the province of Campania, which had been afflicted by a bad harvest. In the year 507 the king asked him in the most flattering terms to procure a sun-and-water clock which the Burgundian king was to receive as a gift; and, as an expert in music, he was to find a singer and player of the zither for the Frankish king Clovis. (The letters are worded by Cassiodorus, Boethius' cousin, who was at that time Theodoric's right-hand man at court in all administrative questions.) In 510 Boethius was finally appointed consul, and without a colleague, the highest honour which traditionally could fall to the lot of a Roman. (The expenditure one had to make in this position for games, gifts and the like, was estimated a little later, in Justinian's time, at more than twenty hundredweight of gold.) Yet all these were functions which did not satisfy Boethius, and which he sought to perform more or less incidentally. He had long ago found his true lifework in the intellectual realm, i.e. 'in the complete study and treatment of all branches of philosophy', which meant to him the highest consolation and enjoyment of life (*Hypoth. Syllog.*, Migne, LXIV, 831 B). The methodical planning and steadfastness with which he pursued this aim, without ever letting himself be dissuaded or confused, is astounding, and typical of his scholarly character, and his firm, calm nature.

Boethius was conscious of the importance of his studies; they seemed to him imperative, an urgent, practical necessity. For he observed the disadvantage which Latin education still showed when compared with the Greek East, and felt that the gap was

then threatening to widen. The Latin world still lacked the
capability for a real, scholarly study of philosophy, such as
appeared to be the advantage of the Greeks. His literary work
was to answer to and correct this. As consul he emphasized that
this task of instructing the people was very appropriate to his
high office, and that he therefore wished to remain faithful to
it so far as his duties gave him time. The Roman statesman of
the time had a different calling from that of old. Even as the
man of time past subjected and made all states subservient to the
one city by military power, so there now remains 'nothing left
to do' but to further the moral life of the Roman common-
wealth, and for this purpose Greek wisdom and knowledge is
especially appropriate. It has indeed always been in accord with
the Roman nature to adopt and imitate the noble and worthy
traits possessed by other peoples (*in Categ. Arist.* II, praef.). The
traditional phrases on the *civitas Romana* as mistress of the world
must not be taken too seriously. Boethius knew very well what
was really becoming of the glory of Rome in the contemporary
world, and how insignificant had become the proud offices
which the city was able to confer (*Consol.* III, 3, 15). Yet Rome
should remain the capital of the world at least intellectually.
'We must see that we develop ourselves better and more effectively, not in the sphere where we cannot even distinguish ourselves from the brutes, but in the reflection of heavenly virtues
by noble action and speaking for eternal glory' (*in Isag.
Porphyr.* A. II, praef.). This is an unusual re-interpretation and
sublimation of the old Roman *virtus*, and sounds somewhat
doctrinaire. But Boethius thus did in fact grasp the last possibility which time 'had left' to the old custodians of Roman
greatness, and this decision was not without moral greatness
and genuine historical understanding. It is easy enough to mock
him. We still possess a spiteful epigram (*Carm.* II, 132) with
which the later Bishop Ennodius of Pavia, himself one of the
meanest flatterers and position-hunters of his century, tried to
take revenge on Boethius. The old military glory, he argues,
was forgotten today, the Roman pride was gone. Boethius had

substituted the distaff for the sword, and lived only for drinking and pleasure. But behind this aspersion merely stood the fact that Boethius had ignored, at first politely, and then coldly, the repeated begging letters of the unctuous poet, who wanted to be given a house in Milan. We may simply ignore this, as Boethius himself did.

When Boethius spoke of the wisdom of the Greeks which the Romans should learn and appropriate, he was thinking, in a word, of the latest, Neo-Platonic form of classical philosophy, the systematically arranged teaching of a comprehensive understanding of truth, encompassing God and the world. Yet he did not essay these heights without more ado. It was first necessary to give a *propaedeutic* introduction. This consisted of the disciplines of the 'Quadrivium', to which he was the first to give its name, that is to say, the fourfold method of education in the propaedeutic sciences: arithmetic, music, geometry, and astronomy. Only so could one arrive 'in the various branches of philosophy at the highest perfection' (*Inst. Arithm.* 1, 1). Accordingly, Boethius first dealt with arithmetic. The book is dedicated to Symmachus, and represents essentially an abbreviated Latin revision of the *Introduction to Mathematics* composed by the Greek mathematician Nicomachus of Gerasa in the second century A.D. Then follows a handbook of music, in reality rather an admonitory *Protrepticus* for these studies, and an introduction to the problems of acoustics and harmony. The rational relationship of music to numbers, the moral effect which was to be expected from such perceptions within an introductory *instrumentum philosophiae*, have but little in common with musical problems in the modern sense. This book also relied primarily on Nicomachus, but discusses other authors also, and, above all, regards the great Ptolemy as the decisive authority. We can trace the influence of Alexandrian Neo-Platonism and its tradition of learning. The geometrical and astronomical manuals—all but a few remains of the geometry —are lost.

The high-flown dedicatory epistle to the mathematics is in

marked contrast with the severe and nobly restrained style displayed by Boethius in his later writings, and shows him still to be an apprentice. He certainly did not win his lasting importance as a teacher of the *Quadrivium*, but as the great translator and interpreter of Greek philosophy, particularly of the logical writings of Aristotle. The *Dialectics* seems separated from the traditional context of grammar and rhetoric, and is already to be considered as the beginning of real philosophical education. In a famous preface to his commentary on the Aristotelian theory of judgement, Boethius expressed himself regarding the over-all plan of his work as he then envisaged it. Of course, he says, there has been up to the present no lack of excellent men who have taken pains to make known more intimately to the Latin-speaking world the things about which he is concerned, yet they did not preserve a satisfactory arrangement of the material, and did not present the philosophical disciplines step by step in the necessary sequence. This was now to be undertaken. Boethius wished to provide an *Organon* of the whole of philosophy in the Latin language, in which translations and explanations should mutually support one another. 'I wish', he says, 'to translate the whole work of Aristotle, so far as it is accessible to me',—a complete Aristotle was therefore even then no longer to be obtained without more ado,—'into the Roman idiom and conscientiously offer his complete utterances in the Latin tongue. Everything Aristotle ever wrote on the difficult art of logic, on the important realm of moral experience, and on the exact comprehension of natural objects, I shall translate in the correct order. Moreover, I shall make all this comprehensible by interpretative explanations. I should also like to translate all Plato's Dialogues, and likewise explain them, and thus present them in a Latin version. When this is accomplished, I will furthermore not shrink from proving that the Aristotelian and Platonic conceptions in every way harmonize, and do not, as is widely supposed, completely contradict each other. I will show, moreover, that they are in agreement with one another at the philosophically decisive points. This is the task

to which I will dedicate myself, so far as life and leisure for work
are vouchsafed to me. I know that this will be as useful as it is
laborious, and that it needs the assistance of those (powers)
which are ever alien to envy and jealousy' (*in Arist. de Interpret.
B. II praef.*).

This formalized summary bears, exceptionally for Boethius,
a character still pagan, but must not on that account be taken as
a concealed anti-Christian confession. Here is, indeed, a gigantic
task—a truly scholastic *Summa* of the whole of philosophy,
which can only be conceived as one, and which is to be erected
on the basis of the classical texts of the two greatest philosophers! The systematic goal, a complete harmonization of the
Aristotelian and Platonic systems, is not original; it accorded
with the systematic programme of the Neo-Platonic tradition.
In this Plato determined the ideological framework and structure, Aristotle is considered more as the teacher of logic, in the
narrower sense. (Yet this is an area for which Boethius had a
special liking, and to which he attributed again and again the
greatest scientific importance.) Here, however, the work was
actually to be done according to a uniformly designed outline
and presented in literary form. In view of the dimensions of
such a plan one may well ask whether it could be carried out
at all by a single individual; but if it could, then Boethius was
the right man to do it. His clear vision, and the sure energy of
his dedication to the task, once he had taken it up, show a certain grandeur. Boethius was untiring. Nobody, he suggests in
the passage quoted, who has once experienced the happiness of
work can ever give it up again, and 'whoever is discouraged
would have lost his courage already'. With the same imperturbability as the great theologians and dogmatists of his epoch,
the philosopher also believed in the objective reality and the
eternal meaning of the systematic perception of truth. And as
they built upon the revelation and tradition of the church, so
Boethius likewise confided in the 'invincible authority' of the
old teachers and masters—*veterum virorum inexpugnabilis auc-
toritas* (*Syllog. Categ. II praef.*).

It cannot be established for certain how far Boethius actually
came in the realization of his plan. Preserved are—after elimina-
tion of various false medieval writings of 'Boethius'—a commentary upon the teaching of categories, and two commentaries
on Aristotle's theory of judgement (*de Interpretatione*): a brief
one in two books for beginners, and a comprehensive and
scholarly one in six books for advanced readers who wish to
understand the problems in their whole complexity. The commentaries on the Aristotelian analytics, topics, and physics are
lost. On the other hand, the *Introduction* (*Isagoge*) to Porphyry
on the theory of judgement, indispensable in the opinion of
Boethius, is doubly preserved in two editions, of two and five
books respectively. In the older commentary, the earlier translation of Marius Victorinus is still taken as a basis; in the second,
more detailed commentary Boethius furnished his own, more
literal, translation. There was, moreover, a wordy commentary
on Cicero's *Topics* (the doctrine of arguments and proofs for
speakers) which has only come down in part and which itself
was intended to interpret Aristotle's *Topics*. Finally, Boethius
published five independent monographs on logical problems.
He was especially proud of his examination of hypothetical
judgements, a treatise in two volumes (*de Syllogismo Hypo-
thetico*), because this subject had not been treated by Aristotle,
nor by the Greeks at all adequately up to this time, and by the
Latins not at all. Otherwise his dependence on the Greek models
is mostly clear enough: Boethius frequently offered not much
more than Latin paraphrases of the writings of his predecessors.
Nevertheless, one must not just regard him as a mere plagiarist
and compiler. A derogatory judgement on his philosophical
independence and significance has definitely changed in his
favour in recent research, in the same way as the judgement
upon that medieval Scholasticism which depends upon him.
Boethius receives serious consideration in modern logic, partly
for his own sake.

At all events, the historical importance of what Boethius
created by his translations, commentaries, and his own

researches is indisputable. He did more than anyone to establish
the medieval reverence for Aristotle; and Aristotle remained
known to the Latin West only so far as he had translated him.
In their literary arrangement, also, his commentaries became
the model for the medieval commentaries on Aristotle, and
through the adoption of his translations Boethius created the
philosophical terminology of all the Middle Ages. In this way
he is also 'the father of our logical terminology' (Ernst Hoffmann). The famous *quinque voces* used so diligently by Scholasticism had its source in him. This is the *schema* of definitions:
genus, species, differentia, property and the added term accident. A basic theme of the entire medieval theology, the 'disputation on universals', concerning whether the universals possess more or less of real existence, took its rise from a passage in
his commentary upon Porphyry. This originated, in the final
analysis, in the combination of Platonic and Aristotelian elements of thought, i.e. in a Neo-Platonic dogma which through
the mediation of Boethius was determinative for the whole
Aristotelianism of the early and high Middle Ages.

Anyone comparing today the Aristotelianism of Boethius
with the genuine Aristotle has his eye immediately caught by
yet another difference in the whole style of thought of the two
men. The inner and free-ranging zest with which Aristotle
approached and so effectively developed his problems, has in
Boethius given place to quite a different kind of organization,
arrangement, and systematization, precise and often rather
pedantic in operation. Philosophy has become academic,
'Scholastic'. Characteristic is the value Boethius everywhere
attaches to an accurate and fixed terminology, in consequence
of which the meaning of a word once established can never
vary, or appear in a new light. He likewise considered it a
serious deficiency in a system if 'gaps' existed anywhere. He
was always pressing after completeness, and was tireless in
making references and pinning things down. Again and again
he expatiated on the appropriate arrangement of the material,
on the methodical development of the examination, and on the

correct form of instruction. To be sure, this corresponded to the general tendency of this late Roman period, but it also stood in an inner relationship to the specific concern of his whole enterprise. Boethius saw himself as the schoolmaster of the West. He wished to educate his fellow-countrymen at last to a scientifically based course of studies, and for that purpose it was imperative that everything be presented as unmistakably and precisely as possible, so that every serious student might immediately find his bearings and be sure of his way within the philosophical course. For this reason too translations must be so reliable that reference to the Greek originals could for the future be dispensed with. Boethius emphatically admonished his readers not to consider his elaborate expositions superfluous or of secondary importance. 'Since I have not shrunk, despite the immense labour, from writing such a voluminous work', the readers should be willing at least to read it at leisure, and not to pass judgement upon it prematurely (*in Aristot. De Interpret. B. VI praef.*). Boethius was concerned with superseding the usual rhetorical half-education. He knew that he would meet with resistance, and he anticipated personal criticism. But the high calling of his scholarship must not be dragged through the mire.

Boethius still gave the form of a dialogue to the first version of his commentary on Porphyry. The scene of the conversation, continued for two winter nights, is set in the solitude of a villa in the mountains, and is charmingly depicted. In his later works Boethius renounced such pleasant settings. Furthermore, the elegantly worded prefaces in which he sometimes says a little about his intentions are kept quite brief, and then as a rule pass over almost immediately into the scholarly presentation with a short 'But now to the subject-matter', or some such phrase. We can see with Boethius that he was a master of all the fine points of rhetoric; but they are not essential to him. Not only are 'moral questions more important than rhetorical skill' (*in Cicer. Top. I praef.*), but Boethius also did not wish to play to the gallery by misusing logical examination for the sake of rhetorical show-pieces, but above all to attain lucidity. 'If this

turned out well, then I have attained my purpose perfectly—
even if the form of my discourse perhaps seems to be very unpolished' (*Syllog. Categ.* I praef.). With Boethius this is not, as
so often, another rhetorical phrase. The style of his philosophical treatises is certainly chosen with care, and to that extent not
formless, yet at the same time it is also of an unsurpassable objective sobriety which has no place for aesthetic irrelevancies.
This is the more impressive, because Boethius, as we shall see,
was in reality also a rhetorician, and indeed a poet, and when he
wished could very well display his abilities in this area. In this,
however, the Platonist did not follow the example of the Platonic dialogues, which certainly were not even for Plato the
whole of his instruction. Even less has his manner anything
in common with the literary method of instruction used by
Cicero, whose philosophical essays he nevertheless knew and
esteemed, and in one case, as we saw, even commented upon.
Yet according to the preface it was only out of friendship for
the rhetorician Patricius who had commissioned it, and to whom
it also was dedicated, that he had undertaken this work,
primarily for the benefit of dialectics.

For the decade following his consulate hardly anything is
known about Boethius' life. The greater part of the works just
reviewed were probably written within this period. In retrospect it appeared to Boethius as a period of happiness, which
allowed him to proceed almost undisturbed upon the course
on which he had entered. Had it been granted to him to continue on it, the major work as he envisaged it might actually
have been completed. The change in his life was due to politics.
It was first to carry him to the highest peaks of fame and success,
only then to throw him down and ruin him in a sudden turn
which none had foreseen. All at once it became obvious how
artificial and uncertain were in reality the political assumptions
upon which Theodoric had built his whole régime, and upon
which also rested the fortunate peace which Rome and Italy
had until then enjoyed. In this connection ecclesiastical relations
also now attain a certain importance.

We have already mentioned that Roman society in the sixth
century had, like the whole empire, become Christian, indeed
Catholic Christian. Arianism was in Italy exclusively the religion of the caste of Gothic over-lords, and Theodoric himself
did not attach any great importance to the occasional oblitera-
tion through conversion or assimilation of the confessional distinction which was thereby established. On the other hand it
was not unwelcome to him that before the beginning of his
reign Catholic communion between West and East had also
been interrupted, and could not be restored for thirty-five
years. In 484 the doctrinal divergence on the Christological
question had led to the breach between Rome and Constantinople, in consequence of imperial church politics. The stubborn
maintenance by the pope of his condemnation of the Byzantine
Patriarch Acacius, who was then in charge, had converted the
so-called 'Acacian schism' between the two capitals also into a
question of prestige. So long as this quarrel was not settled, the
pope and the whole Catholic church of Italy had no interest in
returning to the direct dominion of the emperor, and adhered
with all the greater loyalty to their new Gothic over-lords. On
the other hand, those circles which were still interested in the
unity of the empire deplored this dissension on political grounds.
The majority of the senate, and Symmachus and Boethius too,
probably belonged to them. In the fourth century, the Anicians
had become Christians before other aristocratic Roman families,
and Boethius naturally wanted to be regarded as a good Catholic.
This does not, however, mean that he was bound to approve
papal actions in every respect. The intransigence of the Roman
see, which made it difficult even for the secret adherents of
orthodox doctrine in the East to remain in communion with it,
was perhaps the occasion of the first theological treatise Boethius
had written, probably in 512. It is dedicated to John, a deacon,
and in a thorough treatment discusses the Christological heresies
of Eutyches and Nestorius, i.e. the two extreme and equally
erroneous viewpoints on the question which was in dispute at
that time: namely, how the relationship of Christ's one Person

to His two natures, the divine and the human, was rightly to be understood. Boethius alludes only lightly in his introductory dedication to the current disputes, it is true, and he avoids dealing with the fierce controversies of church politics. He contents himself with rationally elucidating the complex logical problems which had arisen. Yet it seems that he wished in this way to make a contribution to peace, or at least to work for a theological reconciliation. This, at any rate, would fit in well with his political intentions as well as with his general intellectual attitude. As a matter of fact, his Christological researches did prepare the solution which was later to meet with general acceptance.

Some years later, the official peace between Rome and Constantinople was concluded (519). This was primarily to the credit of Justinian, the nephew of the reigning Emperor Justin, who obviously had not really understood the great political importance of the ecclesiastical union. Nevertheless, the theological tensions were not completely resolved. In the so-called 'theopaschite controversies' the contrasted points of view threatened to revive; only they now came to expression no longer only in a purely Christological form but as a question of the possibility of a Person within the Trinity being capable of suffering. This caused Boethius to take up from now on the Trinitarian problems too. He dealt with them in three smaller tracts, one of which is dedicated to Symmachus, the two others again to John. His restraint in the face of any public dispute, his exclusive concentration upon systematic questions as such, are even more strictly observed here than in previous treatises. The work *Why is the Trinity Only One God And Not Three Gods?* dedicated to Symmachus, carries this reserve so far that it expounds the questions in dispute with a terminology partly novel, and in such an over-subtle, seemingly contradictory, and intentionally complicated way that it discourages any unqualified reader immediately, and is intended to do so. This esoteric style gives the impression that Boethius did not intend in his writings to intervene in the actual discussion, and himself to bring about a decision. We must leave it open whether he was at all interested in the immediate effect of his tracts, or whether he was perhaps only stimulated to develop the systematic possibilities almost as a game for their own sake. On the point at issue, however, he actually took under his protection the threatened 'theopaschites', who had also appealed to the senate, against their adversaries in the Roman church. He thus found himself again in the camp of those who were interested in a settlement and in peace, not the least of whom was the Eastern emperor himself. The whole circle around Symmachus had always maintained a close, or in the political jargon of our day, 'cordial' relationship with the emperor's court.

The danger of the new situation could not possibly remain hidden from Theodoric. The restored peace of the church removed an essential guarantee of his own régime! Henceforth the Catholics again saw in the emperor their orthodox overlord, and the Goths therefore could again be regarded as a hostile army of occupation, heretics about whose dominion no one was concerned. It thus became more important for Theodoric to emphasize his good relations with the emperor, and, as a matter of fact, the latter also met his wishes to the extent that he recognized his son-in-law in due form as the successor to the royal throne, and on his part seemed to support the permanent existence of the Gothic dynasty. But simultaneously his diplomatic activity in ecclesiastical and patriotic circles of the West was increased. This resulted in a new honour for Boethius, probably proposed by the emperor, which represented something most unusual, and was welcomed by the whole pro-Byzantine aristocratic clique. For the year 522, Boethius' two sons, Flavius Symmachus and Flavius Boethius were jointly appointed consuls. Both were still boys so that the honour in reality fell more to their father. Soon afterwards, however, Boethius himself was appointed *magister officiorum* by Theodoric, i.e. supreme head of all court and government offices, and by this responsible position was brought into his immediate presence. This promotion of a Roman went beyond the framework of titular honours. It took on political significance, and in this was all the more extraordinary. For Boethius, however, it was the first step toward catastrophe.

Boethius would not have been an Italian had he not felt and enjoyed to the full the glory of the consulate of his two sons. Even during his last imprisonment he remembered this incomparable 'peak of happiness'. No misfortune of the days that followed, his 'philosophy' told him, is to be allowed to, or ever can obscure the light of that day 'when thou sawest thy two sons being both Consuls together carried from their house, the Senators accompanying them, and the people rejoicing with them; when, they sitting in the Senate in their chairs of state, thou making an oration in the King's praise deservedst the glory of wit and eloquence. When in public assembly, thou, standing betwixt thy two sons, didst satisfy with thy triumphant liberality the expectation of the multitudes gathered together' (*Consol.* II, 3, 8; *LCL*, 185). Boethius was perfectly equal to this situation. Entering upon his new office was something quite different. With this he left his former course of life, and entered upon a dangerous area. Until then Boethius had in every way kept away from real political life. He was hardly prepared for it, and in his whole nature was certainly not made to be a courtier. What had led him in spite of everything to this fatal step? Boethius later passionately protested that vulgar ambition had played only the remotest part. The acceptance of the office had appeared to him as his duty. In fact he may have been of the opinion that it was not open to him to decline the appointment at this moment. In Theodoric's court, influential forces were at work which did not approve of his policy of settlement. Feelings towards the Italian population had grown considerably more hostile: a general prohibition from carrying arms was issued for all non-Gothic subjects. Friction also occurred in church affairs. When Theodoric nevertheless now decided to call a representative of the old Roman tradition and of the idea of the Roman empire to an authoritative position, should Boethius have refused, even if he could? Actually, he had no choice. Boethius was much too much a Roman at the decisive moment to decline political responsibility, forgetting his name and tradition, and to retreat to the secure life of a wealthy private scholar, content with the mere semblance of a public reputation. Why, he asks, should government always be left only to the careerists and criminals, who then misuse it to the detriment of their fellow-citizens? Had not Plato rather taught him 'that commonwealths should be happy, if either the students of wisdom did govern them, or those which were appointed to govern them would give themselves to the study of wisdom' (*Consol.* I, 4, 5; *LCL*, 143-145). One dimly senses behind these declamations also a painful and personal motive for the disastrous decision: 'I desired to practise that by public administration which I had learnt of thee (philosophy) in private conference' (*Consol.* I, 4, 7; *LCL*, 145); 'I longed for the opportunity to perform deeds—why should my manhood turn grey and wither?' (*Consol.* II, 7, 1). Viewed like this, Boethius' fate attains a truly tragic character. It was precisely his sense of duty which united with his most secret desires, and thus enticed him to a step in which he deluded himself about the possibilities of his time no less than about his own capacity to prevail in it.

There is no doubt that Boethius at first fully possessed Theodoric's confidence, and also repeatedly enjoyed his support against his Gothic advisers. At any rate, in several cases, partly however in the earlier period, Boethius successfully prevailed over the 'covetousness' of the barbarians, as he called it. He was able to prevent the appointment of a certain Decoratus because he mistrusted the character of this parvenu. (After his downfall Decoratus, however, was immediately promoted *quaestor palatii*.) On the whole, the difficulties with which Boethius had to contend probably came from the very beginning more from the circles of his colleagues who had suddenly to accept as their chief this prominent Roman who had come from outside. His reserved and republican pride, his personal feeling of superiority, and his quite disturbing inclination to judge and decide all things from the point of view of moral principle certainly did not win him friends at the court. Furthermore, there was the difference of political conviction and tradition. Boethius was undoubtedly determined to serve the king with loyalty; yet the recognition of the Gothic régime was in his eyes itself always an act of resignation, a bitter necessity in view of the general political decline. There was nothing left but to resign himself to circumstances as they were, and to make the best of things for the sake of the empire and its culture. On the other hand, the other officials and advisers of Theodoric had quite another attitude. They had risen with him, admired his successes and his astute rule and perhaps even from the standpoint of Italian nationalism gave him preference over a Byzantine dominion. At all events, there was no sympathy with the ideals of restoration held by the Roman high aristocracy; all that was desired was accommodation with the new lords. So Cyprian the *referendarius*, one of the chief opponents of Boethius, had his children trained in the Gothic use of arms and made them learn the Gothic language. This whole clique must have felt itself provoked and neglected by the new course which the appointment of Boethius seemed to inaugurate, and accordingly hampered his activity.

However, this certainly would not have been enough to overthrow him, if a general reaction had not taken place at the same time. The policy of reconciliation towards the Eastern emperor had in reality already collapsed at the moment when Boethius assumed office. Byzantium was evidently playing a double game, even though it did not openly express itself against Theodoric. The Vandals in Africa suddenly threw themselves on the side of the emperor, and all Goths in that country were murdered or put to flight. The Franks invaded adjacent Burgundy, and only a remnant of that kingdom could be saved at the last minute by Theodoric's intervention. Also the question of succession had again become completely uncertain through the unexpected death of the heir to the throne. Moreover, there was the unfavourable shift in the ecclesiastical situation in Italy itself —the possibility of a Byzantine Catholic reconquest began to

appear. It is easy to understand that the elderly Theodoric followed the developments with anxiety, that his disposition grew
morose, and that he saw adversaries at work everywhere. 'The
King', wrote a later historian, 'held the Romans capable of evil
intentions . . . and believed false witnesses more than the Senators' (*Anon. Vales* XIV, 87). And although, as the Greek
Procopius assures us, he was in reality no tyrant, and was for
that reason respected by both Goths and Italians as a legitimate
ruler, he committed in this mood 'the first and last crime' of
his life. Boethius, whom 'malicious people' envied, was the
victim (*Bell. Goth.* I, 1, 34, 39).

In August of the year 523 Pope Hormisdas had died. Under
his pontificate the Acacian schism had been terminated; but he
personally always remained a faithful adherent to the Gothic
régime. So it must have been extremely unwelcome to Theodoric that the successor of Hormisdas was Pope John I, whose
election represented a clear victory of that group whose sym-
pathies were Greek and who looked to the imperial church. He
was possibly the same John to whom, when still a deacon,
Boethius had dedicated his theological monographs. The
Roman post which went at this occasion to Constantinople was
censored, and a letter of the senator Albinus detected which,
perhaps written in the name of the whole senate, produced suspicion. Besides a report of the election it perhaps contained still
further information about the ecclesiastical and political situation, and in the tone of traditional devotion and loyalty expressed all too openly a wide agreement with all imperial
wishes. The letter may have appeared to the senders as harmless
and correct. On the governmental officials, however, it made
the impression of high treason. The ambiguity lay in the odd
constitutional situation which on the one hand allowed the
empire to remain, and to be represented by the one emperor,
but which, on the other hand, had also subordinated the Roman
senate, proud of its nominal independence, to the Gothic
king. The confiscated papers were submitted to Boethius,
who checked them and then decided to let the whole matter

drop. He knew his colleagues in the senate, and shared or at least understood their attitude, and, on the other hand, he was doubtless afraid of arousing the misgivings of the barbarians if he specially called their attention to this correspondence not intended for their eyes. Yet this procedure was too bold. Happy to be able now to pull his rival to pieces, Cyprian went to the king on his own account. He represented the whole occurrence to him in the most dangerous light, and was believed. Albinus was at once summoned before the royal consistory. Boethius, who attended, could perhaps have still intervened and prevented the worst. But it seems that, offended in his pride, he made instead an unfortunate attempt to justify his behaviour up till then, and to treat the matter even now as a trifle. It is said that he explicitly declared that, if they found Albinus guilty, he would be, too! The whole senate would stand united with him in this matter; Cyprian's accusations were a slander! With this the case was immediately pushed to an extreme. The *referendarius*, who felt himself to be a dutiful official, and was by no means prepared to let himself be insulted as an informer, now had to assume the offensive. Further documents, forged as Boethius maintained, were adduced whereby he himself was charged with illegal actions on behalf of the senate, and with treasonable intent. And now decisions followed in rapid succession. Boethius was indicted, suspended from office, and then sentenced by a royal court to exile, to confiscation of his fortune, and to death. A last hope from the senate, which had to endorse the sentence, came to nothing. Threatened themselves, the senators approved it without objection, to the bitter grief of the fallen Boethius, who felt this failure to be perfidy and treachery. Nobody dared oppose the enraged king. However, the sentence was, as so often in such cases, not carried out for the time being. Boethius was merely interned in Pavia, so that a favourable turn of events was not yet impossible. Then some new deterioration of the situation seems to have taken place. In the autumn, perhaps in October of the following year, he was executed, most likely also in Pavia. Symmachus, too, was now put on trial, and he followed Albinus and Boethius to death. At last even Pope John fell into disgrace because he had not performed some action of church politics in Constantinople to Theodoric's satisfaction, and died in prison.

Thus Boethius' fall produced a sequence of dreadful measures which darkened the last years of the life of the great Gothic king. The good terms between Goths and Romans upon which the existence of his government had relied were broken. The subsequent restitution of the family fortune of Boethius' sons by Queen Amalaswintha, and the amnesty also for his widow, who under Totila had demolished statues of Theodoric, could not remove this impression. With Justinian's attack soon after Theodoric's death (526), the thirty years 'struggle for Rome' began, in which not only the rule of the Goths, but also the old tradition and culture of the country disappeared for ever. Henceforth, there was no ancient aristocracy, no Roman senate, no consuls, and no philosophy; the 'Dark' Ages were beginning. With such a background Boethius' fate automatically takes on an awesome and glorious light. Boethius felt himself to be a martyr of higher culture and reason, of justice and freedom, and of the upright attitude of the old Romans at the hand of barbarians, and so described himself to posterity. This view is at any rate more correct than the later legendary re-interpretation of his death as a martyrdom for Catholic orthodoxy. The confessional question played no role at all during his trial. On close examination, his case nevertheless appears in a more or less doubtful light, at any rate susceptible of more than one interpretation.

Apart from a few brief allusions, our picture of Boethius' fall comes exclusively from himself, and that only in an interpretative and rhetorically idealizing style appropriate to the special aims of his last work. The extensive and factual defence address to the king there mentioned has been lost. What we have is naturally an extremely one-sided account. In spite of all the complaints and protests which Boethius raises, and despite the similar position adopted by Procopius, we can hardly view his conviction as a miscarriage of justice. Naturally, it was a political trial, in which the question of guilt is always difficult to decide, yet the proceedings employed seem to have been correct, and we hear of no direct attempt to bring influence to bear. The unfavourable estimate, together with the atrocity legend of a sadistic form of execution, stems from a later time when, in the misery of the last struggles, the Gothic rule had long since forfeited all sympathy. At first public opinion seems to have fluctuated (*Consol.* I, 4, 44). It is interesting that during the trial Boethius was also accused of resorting to the '*sacrilegium*' (the adjuration of demons and witchcraft), for the purpose of obtaining office surreptitiously,—things which he himself was, of course, perfectly right in repudiating as unworthy of a philosopher. Philosophy itself, he thinks, is calumniated and accused in his person. It seems that his scholarly studies had a sinister and strange effect upon outsiders—in the eyes of the crowd Boethius was perhaps already something like 'the sorcerer' Virgil or Doctor Faustus. All this alone, however, was not decisive. The decisive thing was the suspicion of political conspiracy in which Boethius seemed to be involved with Albinus and probably some other senators. Boethius was accused of having 'hoped for Rome's liberty', and of wishing to protect the senate on his own. The manner in which he reacted to these double reproaches is quite characteristic. 'What freedom can still be expected, after all? If only it had still somehow been possible!' For then no plot would ever have been discovered through him (*Consol.* I, 4, 27). But he must not be charged with such political shortsightedness. On the other hand, the reproach that in his actions he had kept the senate's welfare in mind cannot in his opinion be esteemed as an accusation at all; it was his duty as a Roman to protect the senate. It is for Boethius still a far higher and holier institution than the whole governing power of the barbarian king. We do not know what real actions and intentions hid behind this general declamation; it can hardly be a matter only of his lax treatment of the Albinus affair. But that such an attitude and spirit in a leading official appeared as treason from the Gothic point of view is understandable. Perhaps Theodoric wanted to make a clear example by the execution of Albinus and Boethius. This was cruel, perhaps not completely just, and in any case an error politically, but the sentence should not be regarded as an act of sheer caprice and barbarity. Boethius was no politician, and for that reason at the decisive moment he was unable to take in hand the dangerous game into which he found himself and play it successfully to the end. In his opinion he was no traitor, and certainly never meant to be, when he indignantly took refuge in his clean conscience. But he had not served his king with that faithfulness and singlemindedness which the latter could expect from him, and to which he was otherwise accustomed from his vassals. Boethius failed through the inner contradiction between the confidential position he assumed and the ideals which he wanted to serve at the same time, and thus he was bound to perish. To himself his tragic fate appeared in a different and more basic light. Had he not in any case let himself be tempted, when the glory of executive action appeared to him higher than his philosophical calling? It had been a weakness to yield to that desire. Certainly it was the kind of weakness which 'can mislead just those who have elevated natures, when they are not led to the last stage of virtue and perfection' (*Consol.* II, 7, 2). This 'last step' Boethius reached only in imprisonment, and here he then established for posterity, as though a penitent, the ideal image of his true personality and his philosophical faith. It made him unforgettable, and it still lives on.

If we can imagine Boethius leaving the world without addressing this last word to it, he would indeed have occupied a secure place in all histories of philosophy and of doctrine. Humanly speaking, however, his name would not signify more than that of any commentator of late antiquity, or compiler of the Neo-Platonic school. He would be for us an able expert on Aristotle, who had occupied himself with certain logical and scholastic problems—and nothing more. We should never have known of what freedom of feeling and spirited expression this

man was at the same time capable, and what spiritual fire in
reality burned in his reserved inner self. The sole evidence for
this is his last work, *The Consolation of Philosophy*, *Philosophiae Consolatio*. This, too, is a philosophical writing, but at
the same time a work of art and a book of confessions which
can fairly claim a place beside the *Confessions* of Augustine.
Like the latter, it has been endlessly imitated but never equalled,
because in its spiritual and personal content it remains unique.
And even though the *Consolatio* does not equal the *Confessions*
in originality, it surpasses them in the refined elegance of its
artistic execution and in the bright clarity of its perfect composition. Boethius conceived this work in the painful situation
of a condemned man, and wrote it in a few months—not exactly in 'prison', as the medieval interpreters and illustrators
thought, but still without the luxury of his usual surroundings,
without his books and other resources, without friends and
converse, in complete solitude. When this is taken into consideration, his achievement almost borders on the miraculous.

Boethius began work on the *Consolatio* when the sentence on
him was already passed. To be sure, he still did not reckon, it
appears, with the worst; he did not know anything about the
indictments with which his father-in-law was probably already
then charged, and he perhaps still hoped for pardon. Yet there
is no mention of all this in his book. Instead of dwelling upon
tormenting surmise, Boethius resolutely turned his back on the
world which had betrayed him. In the presence of philosophical
truth he will account for his situation as it had now developed,
and speak about what remains to him imperishably and for ever.
The five books of the *Consolatio*, like Augustine's *Soliloquies*,
are a great monologue, or rather just as in that work the soul
holds a dialogue with 'reason', so here he holds one with philosophy herself, the teacher who had educated him in early youth,
and who was the only one who had kept faith with him. The
friendly 'muses' of former times can certainly share his pain,
but cannot help. In the introduction, Boethius describes his

mood of perplexity and loneliness, when a tall, strange figure suddenly enters his room. She carries books in the one hand, a royal sceptre in the other, and wears an odd home-spun gown. Boethius immediately recognizes her—she is Philosophy. Late antiquity had a predilection for such personifications, and Boethius also goes somewhat far in interpreting the allegorical details of her appearance; yet, all in all, his description retains something immediately clear and of gripping vivacity. With a glance of flaming anger the goddess banishes the 'muses', those vulgar 'whores of the theatre', from the bed of their pupil. Boethius is ill; he must not be weakened further by the sweet poison of melancholy excitement. But strict as her utterance sounds, Philosophy is not cruel. She, too, bends down as a Saviour over the suffering disciple, tries first only to soothe and strengthen him, and thus leads him slowly from his inner confusion once again to his senses. She awakens anew by her questions and answers his remembrance of the true good things of life, and finally guides him back into the realm of perfect freedom and understanding in which his soul finds repose. The dialogue is arranged according to these stages of the process of recognition. Formally, it stands of course in the Platonic tradition, but in some passages approaches the style of a philosophical hortatory writing, as the defence of the accused assumes the form of an address to the court, etc. . . . . Boethius evidently aimed at bringing into play the most varied literary forms one after another, and at producing with each a tiny piece of art. This is likewise true of the thirty-nine poems which enliven the discourse: there are at least eleven poetic metres which are not found elsewhere.

At the beginning Boethius still tries to justify despair over his fate, and in this way finds an opportunity to defend himself, and correspondingly to show the baseness of his opponents. But philosophy shows him how wrongly he acts in being enraged at the change of fortune, which had formerly spoiled him, and never was obliged to fidelity. Gradually by her questions he is brought to see the worthlessness and vanity of all external good things, wealth and luxury, glory and all success. The true possession consists only in the inner treasures of the spirit and of truth, and of true moral attachment to these values. A lover of philosophy ought not to complain, but rather be proud, of being allowed to suffer for his mistress and his love. Those who find satisfaction in the earthly strain after mere phantoms of happiness; they are like topers who in their intoxication have forgotten the way and are unable to find their true home. There is one sole highest good for which all strive unknowingly, a real power, beauty, goodness and perfection, which is sufficient in itself and alone can give satisfaction. This is the great One who unites and harmoniously sustains the variety of the universe and is called 'with a name familiar to everyone'—God (*Consol.* III, 12, 8). He, 'the Father of all things' is to be called upon in prayer according to the example of Plato (*Tim.* 27 c), if we wish to discover the highest happiness and good (*Consol.* III, 9, 32 f.). The popular philosophy of seeking consolation in resignation is now thrust into the background. Boethius feels freer and turns his gaze upward and forward. Now he partakes in the conversation on his own account, and correctly carries it further to the delight of his teacher. He perceives the uniform law of the world which animals, plants, and even minerals and crystals, follow in maintaining their being, and for which men also fundamentally yearn when they are striving for happiness. This law of ordered being does not tolerate any exception. 'Thus evil is nothing, for he cannot do it who can do anything' (*Consol.* III, 12, 29). The world is God's, and seen from the perspective of almighty God everything is necessarily set in its proper place. The world is the best and most perfect of all worlds.

What then was the misery which had befallen Boethius? How was the undeniable truth of the thought now grasped to be harmonized with the experience of the reality of injustice and disorder in the world? The answer to this question is given in the fourth book, with a detailed theodicy developed in the Platonic spirit. In reality the wicked are not happy but unhappy. Because of what they are doing they fall into nothingness, and

together with their good existence they lose their real existence.
The good man, however, preserves it and gains a richer and
more secure happiness the greater the determination with which
he sees through the vanity of all which at first tried to tempt and
distress him, and the more firmly he attaches himself to the true
and highest good, in which he is saved. God's indestructible
order secures that every man in the world draws upon himself
his reward or punishment, as he deserves. Everything depends
on having his eyes firmly fixed upon the eternal, divine reality.
It is this to which the old story of Orpheus is meant to testify:

> But you this feigned tale fulfil,
> Who think unto the day above
> To bring with speed your darksome mind,
> For if, your eye conquered, you move
> Backward to Pluto left behind,
> All the rich prey which thence you took,
> You lose while back to hell you look.
>
> (*Consol.* III, 12, 52 ff.; *LCL*, 297)

From this point the fifth book leads to a last and difficult problem. How is the leading principle of moral compensation com-
patible with God's omnipotence? Does not his 'providence'
annihilate man's freedom, on which all morality depends?
Here, too, the right solution consists in the correct way of seeing
things. We must be clear that God's Being exists in eternity,
i.e. not in the dimension of the transient, earthly time in which
our activity takes place. That which unfolds to us as past, present, and future, lies before his view as if it were eternally
present. For that reason the decisions of his 'providence' are not
really prior to our free actions, but can correspond to them
precisely at any given moment. It is therefore by no means
pointless to ask for Him, and to continue to strive with all our
strength for the good. This is the sum total of all the considerations which 'Philosophy' draws at the end: 'Neither do we in
vain put our hope in God or pray to Him; for if we do this well
and as we ought, we shall not lose our labour or be without
effect. Wherefore flee vices, embrace virtues, possess your minds

with worthy hopes, offer up humble prayers to your highest Prince. There is, if you will not dissemble, a great necessity of doing well imposed upon you, since you live in the sight of your Judge, who beholdeth all things' (*Consol.* V, 6, 46 ff.; *LCL*, 411). After Boethius, who evaded no difficulties, has followed his philosophical path to the end in strict consistency, he concludes the work with a direct appeal, moral and religious.

The *Consolatio* is anything but a naïve work. This is true of its content as well as of its form. Boethius consciously wrote it in his own defence, as an apology, and the picture of his personality which he portrays is therefore consciously stylized. We recognize this, for instance, from the manner in which he declares with a noble pride at the end of his political vindication that he must renounce any self-praise—it would violate too much the 'secret' of an upright mind (*Consol.* I, 4, 33). Then in the next paragraph he testifies expressly through the mouth of Philosophy that he has been too modest, and has not given his objective merits their due praise (*Consol.* I, 5, 7). Every detail in the structure of the writing and its arrangement of thought, too, is carefully considered. The *Consolatio* is a book for educated men; it is deliberately and consciously such. The refinement of its methods, its organization, its emphases, and its connections, the Greek quotations that are thrown in, and the countless reminiscences and echoes of older literature would even at the time be wholly clear only to the most learned reader. They make the book today an ideal field for the exercise of linguistic detection and of feeling for style. It is a typical book of late antiquity, in which originality is almost always expressed only as 'an originality of the synthesis of traditional elements' (Wolfgang Schmid). Yet while lesser spirits were bowed under the burden of the gigantic heritage, and with their artificial products appear only grotesque, pedantic, or ineffectual, Boethius remained inwardly one with the whole treasure of tradition, and freely and naturally works out its intellectual and literary possibilities as an artist and a master.

If we come from the reading of the scholarly commentaries

we are at first surprised how strongly the Platonic elements dominate the *Consolatio*: they are constantly expanding, and in the end control the field alone. Not only the ideas, however, but also the spirit and mood of the book are largely Platonic, or, more precisely, Neo-Platonic. In the sensitivity, rhetoric, and directness of his religious feeling Boethius surpasses Plato. A new and passionate accent gives to the whole dialogue an almost dramatic charm, because the psychic development of the questioner and the speculative unfolding of objective truth under the conversational guidance of 'Philosophy' again and again fall into line. In the same way the poetic insertions, the 'hymns' of the dialogue, are by no means artificial embellishments. By reflecting and purging the emotions, by first introducing the ideas, and then summarizing them and carrying them forward, the hymns are indispensable for the understanding of the intellectual movement in the framework of the whole. Boethius was indeed not 'original' even as a poet, but above all the custodian of a heritage. When we hear that in earlier days he once produced a '*carmen bucolicum*', an idyllic and perhaps also allegorical pastoral poem of the kind then popular, we need not particularly deplore the loss of these verses. But the poems of the *Consolatio* are undoubtedly more than skilled experiments in various types of poetry, although they are this too. Boethius reveals himself here as a true lyric poet of ideas. Indeed, apart from its beginnings in Seneca and others, he is perhaps the typical representative of this kind of poetry in its Latin late form. Since it corresponds to his whole nature, it is real poetry. This is true of the hymn to Orpheus already mentioned, and the great prayer in the third book. It is also true of the elegy in the first book, since Boethius sees order and beauty everywhere in nature, whereas harmony and justice are missing in man's world alone:

> O Thou that joinest with love
> All worldy things, look from Thy seat above
> On the earth's wretched state;
> We men, not the least work thou didst create,

> With fortune's blasts do shake;
> Thou careful ruler, these fierce tempests slake,
>   And for the earth provide
> Those laws by which Thou heaven in peace dost guide.
>
> (*Consol.* I, 5, 42 ff.; *LCL*, 159)

Who was the man who composed these prayers? In what sense was he a theologian as well as a philosopher? And was he a Christian at all? This is a question which is often asked, and which still finds no uniform answer. To it we must turn in conclusion.

It is surely a strange state of affairs that the same person whom the Middle Ages venerated as a 'Father of the Church' and a saint, in his last writing, composed in the presence of death, receives 'Philosophy' as his consoler, and nowhere mentions Christ the Saviour of the Christian. This cannot be set aside as a formal question, and explained simply from a traditional feeling for style, in that he wished to avoid speaking of Christ in a philosophical dialogue. In subject-matter also all reference to unequivocally Christian teachings and conceptions is missing. This is the more striking as the *Consolatio* is through and through a book of a religious, and indeed of a devotional, tone, and the 'Philosophy' who here speaks reveals herself as an outspokenly pious philosophy. By what she teaches she desires only to remind Boethius of the truth which he had all along known, believed, and stood for. There is actually no contradiction in the *Consolatio* of what he has written elsewhere, so far as we can judge. This rules out the possibility that we have to reckon with a surprising *volte-face*, which Boethius might have experienced during his last imprisonment, due either—even this view has strangely enough been held—to a subsequent 'conversion' to serious Christianity, or to a final abandonment of his former theological conviction in favour of a now consciously pagan philosophy. In reality Boethius never faltered in his belief in what he thought to be the truth.

At one time there was a common tendency simply to declare Boethius a pagan on account of his *Consolatio*, and to regard his theological treatises as medieval forgeries. Since they are, however, guaranteed by the explicit testimony of Cassiodorus, such a superficial solution of the problem is now out of the question. A formal paganism is impossible for this reason alone, that in the sixth century a non-Christian would never have been appointed to the highest offices of state. On the other hand, the theological writings do not yield as much for his personal faith as we might expect. We have already spoken of their inception and their strict dogmatic character. Boethius restricts himself to the formal exposition of certain Christological and Trinitarian problems, and proceeds according to the acknowledged rules and principles of logic in the same manner 'as is customary in mathematics and the other sciences' (*Opusc.* III praef.). These are indisputable for him. He does not seek, in the words of Anselm, to 'believe in order to understand' in the Augustinian sense, but vice versa seeks rather to penetrate faith with his rational understanding. Only so can he make it credible scientifically in its full, responsible meaning. This certainly does not exclude the fact that from the beginning Boethius acknowledges the 'Catholic faith' to be valid, including the condemnation of all heretics, and that for his part he also knows and cherishes Augustine's writings—especially his book on the Trinity. For his own examination of this topic he expresses the hope 'that the seeds of the writings of Saint Augustine' may have produced some fruit in it (*Opusc.* I praef.). The reserve which Boethius tried to maintain, as we have seen, toward all ecclesiastical party quarrels must not be interpreted as a secret scepticism. Yet just as he desires to know only one philosophy, and in this realm accordingly despises all quarrels of the schools, he probably acknowledged the teaching of the church as a given form of the truth, which only lacks to some extent strict philosophical perfection. He scarcely took note of the Biblical writings, and in any case never referred to them for the substantiation of his statements. He starts in his intellectual labours with the great philosophers, and here he finds spiritual exaltation and his real religion. How many philosophers after him have behaved in just the same way, and nevertheless have felt that they were good Christians! Boethius could do so all the more confidently, for he nowhere gave offence with his opinions, and found acceptance for his theological treatises even with the clergy, so far as they understood them. So far as we know, the *Consolatio* was also criticized by no one, and was for centuries read with joy by all Christians.

We here see how close Neo-Platonic philosophy and post-Augustinian Christianity had now come to one another in the West also. Christianity was no longer felt to be anti-philosophical, and Platonism pagan. There existed between the two a far-reaching community of religious temper and outlook. This also came to full expression in Boethius. All obvious 'pagan' elements of belief have disappeared from the *Consolatio*. The classical gods appear at most as poetical personifications. Strict monotheism is in absolute control, and in Boethius especially has a decidedly theistic colour: God hears prayer and as the Father rules the world. No less decisive is the ascetic feature of his thought. Personally Boethius was no ascetic, but the depreciating evaluation of earthly good things, in itself a stock feature of the whole ancient literature of consolation, assumed a deeper meaning in the light of Neo-Platonic religiosity, and reminds one of Augustine. The human spirit must not cleave to external things. It is really at home only with God, i.e. in the spiritual vision of God and his eternal perfection. From this point of view even the proud memories and political virtues of Rome lose their splendour. Measured by the ultimate, even they are vain and empty, the outflow of a senseless thirst for glory. Withdrawal from the political ideal of life is no less justified in principle, and goes even beyond that of Augustine's *Civitas Dei*. Suffering, however, gains in moral significance, and attains a positive value: 'I think that Fortune, when she is opposite, is more profitable to men than when she is favourable' (*Consol.* II, 8, 3; *LCL*, 221). However, the question is focussed remarkably in the innermost area of metaphysical questioning: the entire last book of the *Consolatio* deals with man's freedom in its relation to God's omnipotence. Boethius is here hardly dependent upon Augustine. At any rate, he still conceives the problem of freedom as a problem of the universal order, not of the inner experience of man himself, and in so far remains in the line of the traditional philosophical discussion. As a matter of fact, in this he only touches on the great theological theme of his century, that is, the question about predestination.

However, the decision regarding Boethius' Christianity cannot be made on the basis of such general contacts with the history of ideas—any more than by a mere demonstration of his church membership, and his dogmatic and theological literary work. The *Consolatio* itself directs us to ask the question about his faith in a more serious way; for surely in theme it is a book on man's eternal salvation, and even more, on his deliverance in the presence of a world that is hostile to him and outwardly destroys him. How does the oppressed human being win back his freedom in this extreme danger? The answer can only run: by philosophy, i.e. by the calm and reasonable consideration of that which proves itself eternally true and lasting beyond the confusion of the moment, the whole of the well-ordered world, the freedom of the moral self, and above both, sustaining and uniting everything, the omnipotence and kindness of the one God himself. Boethius begins his consideration with the cosmos. He realizes how ridiculous and insignificant are his petty earthly miseries, and likewise all the glory of monarchs and their seeming world-empires in reality, when measured by stellar space, and all human deeds, when measured by eternity. Yet this discovery only makes a man happy and free because the eternal order and justice exist and operate also in man's spirit. Only this is necessary, that he really recognize them, and resolutely follow their orders. Then he will see God himself, the 'true sun', who penetrates everything with his light (*Consol.* V, 2, 14). In this light he will ultimately perceive all existence as good, and everything which is real as rational. This perception renders the philosopher happy, reconciles him with his lot, and gives his moral self a lasting foundation in the truth and in God.

Such a teaching on salvation is not Christian. It has thrust aside everything which occasions the miseries of the Christian, the sufferings and historical struggles 'of this Age', the demonic power of evil, and the impossibility ever to overcome it by his own strength. For Boethius all these things do not possess ultimate importance. He certainly takes them into consideration, but merely in order to expose them in their nothingness, and to dissolve them theoretically by his philosophical examination —they are 'thought away'. For this reason all the elements which for the Christian establish salvation are lacking in Boethius. He does not need any help and revelation from outside, no historical change and renewal in time, least of all any real conversion of his human person. The gloomy 'physical' passions which at the beginning of his dialogue confused his mind and his moral attitude are precisely not his actual essential ego. And this ego can never really become lost to him—it can at most be forgotten, and go astray in 'inebriation'. Yet philosophy leads him back to himself, and thus man again attains existence in himself. Boethius believes in himself, in his reason, and in his moral freedom. The whole significance of what in his thinking corresponds to 'predestination' amounts to the protection of this freedom and the maintenance of the moral order which justly distributes rewards and punishments. By contrast, Augustine's teaching on predestination was the ultimate consequence of his doctrine of grace, and the expression of an 'absolute' ethical dependence of sinful man upon God, which is at the same time his happiness. Augustine became a Christian as a Neo-Platonist; Boethius as a Neo-Platonist and Christian theologian remained basically a pagan. That is why philosophical faith is here sufficient to itself. It is pious mediation and poetic reverence of the one divine principle rather than 'faith' in the strict sense, which expects everything from God's intervention and builds life on his firm promise. Boethius needs neither word nor Spirit nor mercy, neither church nor fellow-Christians in order to be what he is. It is therefore no accident but entirely appropriate that his last confession does not speak about Christ.

Boethius still enjoys a local cult in Pavia. It is, as it were, symbolic that his relics and those of Augustine are together here in the very same church, San Pietro in Cieldoro. The last two Latin church fathers of rank each in his own way brought to an intellectual conclusion an epoch of Western church history, and of all history. Yet in their conjunction the old tension still lives between the aspiration for virtue and humility, reason and faith, philosophy and theology, and between pagan and Christian antiquity. The Greek philosophy which, for Augustine, became the bridge for the understanding of Christianity as gospel in opposition to all moralism and rationalism in his church, conversely in Boethius led to the mistaking of Christianity for a higher form of pagan humanism and religion. Shortly after Boethius theological work was in abeyance for centuries. Gregory the Great (d. 604) and Isidore of Seville (d. 636) were only stragglers of the classical epoch, and lived spiritually in a changed world, educated no longer in an ancient but in a medieval fashion. When intellectual life revived in the Carolingian empire, pains were taken to comprehend the Golden Age of the church fathers as an inner unity. This in reality it had never been, and it did not conclude with a ready solution, but with an open question.

CHRONOLOGICAL TABLE

		197	Tertullian's *Apologeticum*
202	Emperor Septimius Severus forbids conversion to Christianity		
		248–249	Cyprian becomes Bishop of Carthage
250–251	Persecution of the Christians by Decius		
257–259	Persecution of the Christians by Valerian	258	Cyprian martyred
284–305	Diocletian		
		317	Lactantius called to Trèves
324	Constantine the Great sole ruler		
325	Council of Nicea		
353	Constantius wins the West		
364–375	Valentinian I (West)	374	Dec. 7, Ambrose, Bishop of Milan
375–383	Gratian (West)	381	Council of Aquileia
378	Victory of the Goths at Adrianople		
379–395	Theodosius the Great (West, 393 sole ruler)	382–385	Jerome in Rome
383–392	Valentinian II (West)	385–386	Church struggle in Milan
		387	Augustine baptized in Milan
390	Penance of Theodosius		
		391	Augustine ordained priest

395	Division of the Empire	395	Augustine Bishop of Hippo Regius
		397	April 4, death of Ambrose
410	Alaric conquers Rome		
		419-420	Death of Jerome
429	Vandals in Africa		
		430	August 28, death of Augustine
476	Odoacer deposes Romulus Augustulus		
493-526	Theodoric	510	Boethius Consul
484-519	Acacian schism		
		524	Death of Boethius

LIST OF ABBREVIATIONS

ACW   *Ancient Christian Writers*, ed. by J. Quasten, J. C. Plumpe, and W. J. Burghardt (Westminster, Md., London, 1946 ff.)

ANF   *The Ante-Nicene Fathers*, Edinburgh edition, rev. by A. C. Coxe (Buffalo, 1884–1886)

CC   *Corpus Christianorum, Series Latina* (Turnholti, 1953 ff.)

CSEL   *Corpus Scriptorum Ecclesiasticorum Latinorum*, ed. by the Wiener Akademie der Wissenschaften (1866 ff.)

FC   *The Fathers of the Church*, ed. by L. Schopp, G. Walsh, and R. J. Deferrari (New York, 1947 ff.)

LCC   *The Library of Christian Classics*, ed. by J. Baillie, J. T. McNeill, and H. P. Van Dusen (London, Philadelphia, 1953 ff.)

LCL   *The Loeb Classical Library* (London, Cambridge, Mass.)

LPNF   *A select Library of Nicene and Post-Nicene Fathers of the Christian Church*, first and second series, ed. by P. Schaff and H. Wace (Oxford, New York, 1886–1905)

ML   *Patrologia Cursus Completus, Series Latina*, ed. by J. P. Migne (Paris, 1844 ff.)

Oates   *Basic Writings of Saint Augustine*, with an introduction and notes by W. J. Oates (New York, 1948)

BIBLIOGRAPHY

Whenever the translations of quotations from individual church fathers have been taken from extant English editions, an abbreviation of the title has been added to the reference (cf. List of Abbreviations opposite). Otherwise the German translations of Professor von Campenhausen have been translated into English, with reference to the original sources. In many cases the second procedure has proved preferable, for the author's translation of quotations seemed to convey the thought of the particular church father more clearly. At the author's request, the translator has enlarged the following bibliographies for the use of English readers, and assumes the responsibility for this portion of the book as well as for the Index.

INTRODUCTION

A few general references to the literature may be appended here, as in *The Fathers of the Greek Church.*

Since 1866 the Wiener Akademie der Wissenschaften has been engaged in producing a critical edition of all the Latin Church Fathers in its *Corpus Scriptorum Ecclesiasticorum Latinorum (CSEL).* So far, 75 volumes have been published. Since 1953, the *Corpus Christianorum (Series Latina) (CC)* of St. Peter's Abbey in Steenbrugge (Belgium) has appeared beside it, making more rapid progress. Besides these, the comprehensive collection of J. P. Migne, *Patrologia Cursus Completus, Series Latina (ML)* (Paris, 1844 ff.), extending to the time of Innocent III, still has to be used. It is now being completed with critical supplementary volumes (*Supplementum,* 1958 ff.) by A. Hamman.

E. Dekkers and E. Gaar, *Clavis Patrum Latinorum* (Sacris Erudiri III, Steenbrugge, 1957²), provide a survey of the whole material (with titles, catalogue of the best editions, and critical supplements added). A large selection of English translations is found in *The Ante-Nicene Fathers (ANF)* (Edinburgh edition, rev. by A. C. Coxe, Buffalo, 1884–86); P. Schaff and H. Wace, *A select Library of Nicene and Post-Nicene Fathers of the Christian Church (LPNF),* first and second series (Oxford, New York, 1886–1905); J. Quasten, J. C.

Plumpe, and W. J. Burghardt, *Ancient Christian Writers* (*ACW*) (Westminster, Md., London, 1946 ff.); L. Schopp, G. Walsh, and R. J. Deferrari, *The Fathers of the Church* (*FC*) (New York, 1947 ff.); *The Library of Christian Classics* (*LCC*), ed. by J. Baillie, J. T. McNeill, and H. P. Van Dusen (London, Philadelphia, 1953 ff.); some translations in *The Loeb Classical Library* (*LCL*) (London and Cambridge, Mass.).

The most substantial history of the literature of the ancient church is that of O. Bardenhewer, *Geschichte der altkirchlichen Literatur* (Freiburg, 1913²–1932), in five volumes. In the *Handbuch der klassischen Altertumswissenschaft*, newly edited by W. Otto, the Latin Christian literature has been treated by G. Krüger (III³, Munich, 1922; IV, 1-2, Munich, 1914–20). Concise but excellent information is given in the summary presentation *Leben, Schriften und Lehre der Kirchenväter* (with further references to literature) of B. Altaner, *Patrologie* (Freiburg, 1960⁶; English tr., *Patrology*, by H. C. Graef, Edinburgh, London, New York, 1960). Available in English are particularly: J. Quasten, *Patrology I-III* (Westminster, Md., 1951, 1953, 1960); and E. J. Goodspeed, *A History of Early Christian Literature* (Chicago, 1942).

The following standard general histories of the ancient church should be mentioned: K. Müller, *Kirchengeschichte I, 1* (Tübingen, 1941³, in association with H. v. Campenhausen); H. Lietzmann, *Geschichte der alten Kirche I-IV* (Berlin, 1953²/³; English tr., *A History of the Early Church I-IV*, by B. L. Wolff, London, New York, 1937–51, 1953²); and the first four volumes of the collective work *Histoire de l'Église* (Paris, 1934 ff.), edited by A. Fliche and V. Martin (Vol 1: J. Lebreton and J. Zeiller, *The History of the Primitive Church*, tr. by E. C. Messenger, London, New York, 1942–47); and its continuation: J. R. Palanque, G. Bardy, and P. de Labriolle, *The Church in the Christian Empire*, tr. by E. C. Messenger, London, New York, 1949–52. Another translation from the French into English: L. Duchesne, *Histoire ancienne de l'Église I-III* (Paris, 1906–11²⁻⁵; English tr., *The Early History of the Christian Church I-III*, by C. Jenkins *et al.*, London, New York, 1908–24). In English: B. J. Kidd, *A History of the Church to A.D. 461* (Oxford, New York, 1922); and the *Cambridge Ancient History*, vols. 11 and 12, ed. by S. A. Cook *et al.* (Cambridge, 1936–39). A short but very good introduction to the history of the ancient church (with select readings) is to be found in R. H. Bainton, *Early Christianity* (Princeton, 1960).

The most important accounts of the history of doctrine in the early church in the German language are: A. v. Harnack, *Lehrbuch der Dogmengeschichte I-III* (Tübingen, 1932[5]; 1909-10[4]; tr. by N. Buchanan *et al.*, *History of Dogma*, 7 vols., London, 1894-99); R. Seeberg, *Lehrbuch der Dogmengeschichte I-II* (Darmstadt, 1953[4]; English tr., *Text-book of the History of Doctrines*, by C. E. Hay, Philadelphia, 1905). F. Loofs, *Leitfaden zum Studium der Dogmengeschichte I-II*, ed. by K. Aland (Halle, 1959[6]); the Roman Catholic *Handbuch der Dogmengeschichte*, edited by M. Schmaus, P. Geiselmann and H. Rahner, has been appearing since 1951 in thematic rather than chronological order. Translated from the French into English is: J. Tixeront, *Histoire des dogmes* (Paris, 1930[11]; *History of Dogmas*, tr. by H. L. B., 3 vols., St. Louis, 1923 ff.). English works are: A. C. McGiffert, *A History of Christian Thought* (2 vols., New York, London, 1932-33); J. F. Bethune-Baker, *An Introduction to the Early History of Christian Doctrine* (London-Cambridge, Mass., 1933[5]); D. L. Neve, *A History of Christian Thought* (Philadelphia, 1946); and J. N. D. Kelly, *Early Christian Doctrines* (London, New York, 1958); cf. also Ch. N. Cochrane, *Christianity and Classical Culture* (Oxford, New York, 1940).

When quoting the writings of the fathers, I have frequently made tacit use of older translations. I beg my predecessors not to consider this a plagiarism. In other instances too it would have been possible in innumerable passages to name older authors whom I have followed consciously or unconsciously. I prefer, however, to take my stand with Cervantes, who in the prologue of his *Ingenious Gentleman Don Quixote de la Mancha* expressly renounces marginal citations, footnotes, and other noble things of this kind 'partly because I do not consider myself clever and learned enough, and partly because I am too lazy to hunt up in other authors what I can perfectly well say without them'.

Ch. I—TERTULLIAN

The critical edition of Tertullian's works in the *CSEL* is not yet entirely completed; the most recent and complete edition was published in *CC* (Turnholti, 1954). There are in addition the numerous editions of individual books, among which the edition of *De Anima* by J. H. Waszink, with its detailed commentary, should be especially mentioned (Amsterdam, 1947), as well as C. Becker's Latin-German edition of the *Apologeticum* (Munich, 1961[2]). Many of his works are found in English translations in *FC*, *ACW*, *ANF*, *LCC*, and in individual editions. Besides these, the excerpts and interpretations of A. Neander in his *Einleitung* to the writings of *Antignostikus* (*Geist des Tertullianus*, 1849[2]; tr., *Antignostikus, the Spirit of Tertullian*, by J. E. Ryland, London, 1851) are still helpful and worth reading.

A real biography of Tertullian, such as that once attempted for instance by E. Noeldechen (1890), can hardly be written. We know of him and of his history practically solely from his works, which are not sufficient for this task. Newer general presentations come from P. Monceaux (in the first volume of his *Histoire littéraire de l'Afrique chrétienne*, Paris, 1901), A. d'Alès (*La Théologie de Tertullien*, Paris, 1905), R. E. Roberts (*The Theology of Tertullian*, London, 1924), and others. A brilliant characterization is given by K. Holl, *Tertullian als Schriftsteller* (Berlin, 1897, *Gesammelte Aufsätze III* (Tübingen, 1928–1932), 1 ff.). For Tertullian's literary style particularly compare—besides various special examinations—E. Norden, *Die antike Kunstprosa II* (Leipzig, 1959[3]), 606 ff., 943 f., as well as the profound study of his setting by H. Koch in Pauly, *Realencyclopädie V, A* (Stuttgart, 1934), 822 ff. Important aspects are treated, among others, by J. Lortz, *Tertullian als Apologet I-II* (Münster, 1927–28); A. Labhardt, *Tertullien et la philosophie* (*Mus. Helv.* 7 (1950), 159 ff.); J. Morgan, *The Importance of Tertullian in the Development of Christian Dogma* (London, 1928); C. de L. Shortt, *The Influence of Philosophy on the Mind of Tertullian* (London, 1933); H. Karpp, *Schrift und Geist bei Tertullian* (Gütersloh, 1955); on the penitential question, see H. v. Campenhausen, *Kirchliches Amt und geistliche Vollmacht in den ersten drei Jahrhunderten* (Tübingen, 1953), 243 ff.

Ch. II—CYPRIAN

The abundant and, to some extent, also complicated transmission of the letters and writings of Cyprian makes a critical edition very difficult. The edition of Hartel in *CSEL* (1868–71), out of date and from the beginning deficient, is today still not yet entirely superseded. There is no lack of translations into modern languages, for instance into English in *ANF*, *ACW*, *FC*, *LCC*, and in *Patristic Studies* of the Catholic University of America.

Among over-all presentations of Cyprian should be mentioned: E. W. Benson, *Cyprian, his Life, his Time, his Work* (London, New York, 1897); P. Monceaux, *Saint Cyprien, évêque de Carthage* (Paris,

1914²); J. Ludwig, *Der hl. Märtyrerbischof Cyprian von Karthago* (München, 1951); especially the chapters dealing with Cyprian in H. Achelis, *Das Christentum in den ersten drei Jahrhunderten II* (Leipzig, 1912) 387 ff.; and H. Lietzmann, *Geschichte der alten Kirche II* (Berlin, 1953²), 229 ff., 261 ff. (tr. *The Founding of the Church Universal* [*A History of the Early Church*, vol. II, London–New York, 1938], 298 ff.). The best expert on Cyprian's writings, which he treated time and again in his essays, was H. Koch: especially in his *Cyprianische Untersuchungen* (Bonn, 1926), and *Cathedra Petri: Neue Untersuchungen über die Anfänge der Primatslehre* (Giessen, 1930). On Cyprian's conception of the church and its ministry, see H. v. Campenhausen, *Kirchliches Amt und geistliche Vollmacht in den ersten drei Jahrhunderten* (Tübingen, 1953), 292 ff.

Cн. III—LACTANTIUS

A critical collective edition of the prose works of Lactantius was, in his day, produced by S. Brandt in *CSEL* (1890–97). Some special editions of particular works are now to be added to it, especially that by J. Moreau (with commentary) of *De Mortibus Persecutorum* (Paris, 1954), by H. Kraft and A. Wlosok of *De Ira Dei* (Darmstadt, 1957), and by M. C. FitzPatrick of *De Ave Phoenice* (Philadelphia, 1933, with an English translation). The *Epitome* is translated by E. H. Blakeney (London, 1950), the *Death of the Persecutors*, by D. Dalrymple (Edinburgh, 1782), selections of the *Institutes*, by T. W. Radius (Grand Rapids, Mich., 1951) and in *ANF*.

The standard biography was written by R. Pichon, *Lactance* (Paris, 1901). In addition, see P. Monceaux, *Histoire littéraire de l'Afrique chrétienne III* (Paris, 1905), 287-371. Useful recent examinations of the biography of Lactantius are to be found, among others, in: S. Prete, *Der geschichtliche Hintergrund zu den Werken des Laktanz*, in *Gymnasium 63* (1956), 365-382; J. Stevenson, *The Life and Literary Activity of Lactantius*, in *Studia Patristica I, Texte und Untersuchungen*, 63 (1957), 661-677; J. Moreau and H. Kraft in the introductions of their editions, mentioned above; A. Wlosok, *Lactantius und die philosophische Gnosis* (Heidelberg, 1960).

Cн. IV—AMBROSE

The edition of Ambrose's writings in *CSEL* is now approaching its conclusion. A selection of English translations is available in *FC*,

LPNF, and the *Patristic Studies* of the Catholic University of America. The best edition of the Latin hymns is found in W. Bulst, *Hymni Latini Antiquissimi LXXV, Psalmi III* (Heidelberg, 1956).

The best German biography, by Th. Förster, *Ambrosius, Bischof von Mailand* (Halle, 1884), is today out of date. The most comprehensive account was written by F. Homes Dudden, *The Life and Times of St. Ambrose I-II* (Oxford, 1935); cf. also P. de Labriolle, *Saint Ambroise* (Paris, 1908²; English tr., *The Life and Times of St. Ambrose*, by H. Wilson, St. Louis–London, 1928). For his ecclesiastical politics mention should be made of H. v. Campenhausen, *Ambrosius von Mailand als Kirchenpolitiker* (Berlin–Leipzig, 1929), and J. R. Palanque, *Saint Ambroise et l'Empire romain* (Paris, 1933); for his dogmatic views L. Herrmann, *Ambrosius von Mailand als Trinitätstheologe* (*Zeitschrift für Kirchengeschichte*, 69 (1958), 198-218).

Ch. V—JEROME

The most fascinating part of Jerome's literary work, the letters, are critically edited by I. Hilberg in *CSEL*, 54-56 (1910–18) and more recently by J. Labourt in the *Collection des Universités de France* (Paris, 1949 ff., with French tr.). Since the *CSEL* edition is making only slow progress, Jerome is still generally quoted from Migne (*ML*, 22-30). A selection in English is provided by *FC, LPNF, LCL, LCC*, and individual editions.

· The German biography by G. Grützmacher, *Hieronymus I-III* (Leipzig, 1901–08), is obsolete since F. Cavallera's book, *Saint Jérôme I-II* (Louvain–Paris, 1922). This work has remained basic for all later accounts. For particular topics, mention should be made of P. Monceaux, *Saint Jérôme—sa jeunesse* (Paris, 1932; English tr., *St. Jerome, the Early Years*, by F. T. Sheed, London, 1933); W. Süss, *Der hl. Hieronymus und die Formen seiner Polemik* (*Giessener Beiträge zur deutschen Philologie*, 60 (1938), Hepding-Festschrift), 212-238; M. Villain, *Rufin d'Aquilée: La Querelle autour d'Origène* (*Recherches de Science religieuse*, 27 (1937), 5-37, 165-195); the collection of essays by F. X. Murphy, *A Monument to S. Jerome* (New York, 1952), with contributions by G. Bardy, L. Hartmann, J. R. Palanque and others; and the relevant essays by A. Vaccari, *Scritti di Erudizione e di Filologia II* (Rome, 1958). For Jerome's relationship to the Greeks, see P. Courcelle, *Les Lettres grecques en Occident* (Paris, 1948), 37-115; for his dependence upon classical Latin writers, see H. Hagendahl, *Latin Fathers and the Classics* (Göteborg, 1958), 89-328.

Ch. VI—AUGUSTINE

Augustine's works were completely edited by the Maurists (Paris, 1679–1700) and have been reprinted repeatedly, as in Migne (*ML*, Paris, 1841 f.) and now also in a new Latin-French edition (Paris, 1949 ff.), partly also already in *CC*. So far *CSEL* has edited little more than one half of the writings and is already superseded by many new special editions of particular books. These are as innumerable as the translations. In larger collections they can be found particularly in *ACW*, *FC*, *LPNF*, *LCL*, *LCC*, and the *Patristic Studies* of the Catholic University of America.

Whereas Possidius believed (chap. 18, see p. 219) that hardly any scholar could read all the works of Augustine, this is even more true of the literature on Augustine, which is boundless in every respect. It is continuously brought together in the periodical *Augustiniana* (Louvain, 1951 ff.) and the *Revue des Études Augustiniennes* (Paris, 1955 ff.). In addition we shall mention here only the papers and transactions of the Paris Augustine Congress of 1954 (*Augustinus Magister I-III*, Congrès International Augustinien, Paris, 1954, 3 vols.) and the report on *Die Augustinliteratur seit dem Jubiläum von 1954*, by R. Lorenz in *Theologische Rundschau*, 25 (1959), 1–75. An excellent and comprehensive bibliography of the literature on Augustine has been recently provided by C. Andresen in *Zum Augustin-Gespräch der Gegenwart* (*Wege der Forschung V*, Darmstadt, 1962). I have not myself been able every time to indicate where I have followed other authors (and sometimes also their translations). In what follows, I single out—more or less at random—some works as particularly important or easily accessible, and completely leave aside the systematic-theological examinations.

No comprehensive biography has been written since LeNain de Tillemont's *Mémoires pour servir à l'histoire ecclésiastique XIII* (Paris, 1702). The literature on Augustine's conversion is particularly abundant. I mention: J. Nörregaard, *Augustins Bekehrung* (Tübingen, 1923); R. Guardini, *Die Bekehrung des hl. Aurelius Augustinus* (Freiburg, 1959³; English tr., *The Conversion of Augustine*, by E. Briefs, London, Glasgow, Westminster, Md., 1960); P. Courcelle, *Recherches sur les Confessions de saint Augustin* (Paris, 1950); J. O'Meara, *The Young Augustine* (London, 1954). F. van der Meer, *Augustine de Zielzorger* (Utrecht, 1947; English tr., *Augustine the Bishop*, by B. Battershaw and G. R. Lamb, London–New York, 1961), gives a superb description of Augustine as a bishop. A. v. Harnack in his

Lehrbuch der Dogmengeschichte II, 2 (Tübingen, 1932⁵), 59-236 (English tr., *History of Dogma*, by N. Buchanan *et al.* (London, 1894–99), vol. V, p. 3-13, 61-240) provides an interpretation of his personality which is still readable and, despite its modernizations, in many aspects congenial. There is a valuable collection of essays on his thought and personality in *A Monument to St. Augustine* (London, 1930). In his excellent sketch, *S. Augustin et l'augustinisme* (Paris, 1955; English tr., *St. Augustine and his Influence through the Ages*, by P. Hepburne-Scott, New York, 1957) H. I. Marrou also touches upon the history of Augustinianism (though the consideration of the Reformation and Protestantism is inadequate). K. Holl's essay on *Augustins innere Entwicklung* (Berlin, Leipzig, 1922, reprinted in *Gesammelte Aufsätze III*, Tübingen, 1928) presents a magnificent study of a deep-seated hostility to Augustine. Regarding Augustine's monasticism see A. Zumkeller, *Das Mönchtum des hl. Augustinus* (Würzburg, 1950); for his teaching on the Trinity: E. Benz, *Marius Victorinus und die Entwicklung der abendländischen Willensmetaphysik* (Stuttgart, 1932); on the *Civitas Dei*, W. Kamlah, *Christentum und Geschichtlichkeit* (Stuttgart, 1951²), F. G. Maier, *Augustin und das antike Rom* (Stuttgart, 1955), J. O'Meara, *Charter of Christendom, the Significance of the City of God* (New York, 1961); for his teaching on grace: H. Barth, *Die Freiheit der Entscheidung im Denken Augustins* (Basel, 1935), and J. Burnaby, *Amor Dei, A Study of the Religion of St. Augustine* (London, 1947², 226 ff.); on Augustine's education and position in his time, see the great work of H. I. Marrou, *Saint Augustin et la fin de la culture antique* (Paris, 1958³) with his appended 'Retractatio' of 1949, and R. Lorenz, *Die Wissenschaftslehre Augustins* (*Zeitschrift für Kirchengeschichte*, 67 [*1955–56*], 29-60, 213-251).

Ch. VII—BOETHIUS

The learned philosophical writings of Boethius have still substantially to be used from the reprint of an old edition in Migne (*ML*, 64). The *Commentary on Cicero's Topics* was published by J. C. Orelli and I. G. Baier in *Ciceronis Opera V, 1* (Zürich, 1933), those writings on the *Quadrivium* which have been preserved were published by G. Friedlein (Leipzig, 1867), the *Porphyry Commentaries*, by S. Brandt in *CSEL*, 48 (1906). The theological *Opuscula* are best found in H. F. Stewart and E. K. Rand (Cambridge, 1936³), together with the text of the *Consolatio*, the last edition of which was excellently produced by L. Bieler in *CC* (*Series Latina*, 94, 1957). The *Consolatio* has been repeatedly translated into English; a translation of the theological *Tractates* (by H. F. Stewart and E. K. Rand) is found in their 1936 edition. The introduction (by F. Klinger) of the German translation of the *Consolatio* (by K. Büchner, Leipzig, Dietrich'sche Verlags-buchhandlung, no date) is worth reading. L. Cooper has produced *A Concordance of Boethius* (Cambridge, Mass., 1928).

The literature on Boethius deals for the most part with particular historical, philological and philosophical questions. The best survey of his life and work is that of M. Cappuyns, article *Boèce* in the *Dictionnaire de l'Histoire et de Géographie Ecclésiastique IX* (Paris, 1937), 348-380. For the biographical and historical connections, see particularly J. Sundwall, *Abhandlungen zur Geschichte des ausgehenden Römertums* (Helsingfors, 1919), and E. Stein, *Histoire du Bas-Empire II* (Paris, 1949), 107 ff.; also H. M. Barrett, *Boethius, Some Aspects of his Times and Work* (Cambridge, 1940); for the literary questions, P. Courcelle, *Les Lettres grecques en Occident* (Paris, 1948), 257-312; K. Dürr, *The Propositional Logic of Boethius* (Amsterdam, 1951); and for the theological writings, V. Schurr, *Die Trinitätslehre des Boethius im Lichte der 'skytischen Kontroversen'* (Paderborn, 1935). As to Boethius' classification within the history of ideas, see also E. Hoffmann, *Pädagogischer Humanismus* (Zürich, Stuttgart, 1955), 117 ff.

INDEX OF PROPER NAMES

326